TOKENS

Culture, Connections, Communities

Edited for the

ROYAL NUMISMATIC SOCIETY SPECIAL PUBLICATIONS

by

CLARE ROWAN

TOKENS
Culture, Connections, Communities

EDITED BY

ANTONINO CRISÀ, MAIRI GKIKAKI
and CLARE ROWAN

ROYAL NUMISMATIC SOCIETY
SPECIAL PUBLICATION NO. 57

LONDON

2019

Royal Numismatic Society
Special Publication No. 57

ISBN 0 901405 35 3

Typeset by New Leaf Design, Malton, Yorkshire
Printed in Malta by
Gutenberg Press Ltd, Tarxien, Malta

CONTENTS

INTRODUCTION

Antonino Crisà, Mairi Gkikaki, Clare Rowan

Scope of the volume

This volume arises from the three day international conference *Tokens: Culture, Connections, Communities*, held at the University of Warwick from 8–10 June 2017. The event represented a significant milestone for the *Token Communities in the Ancient Mediterranean* research project, funded by the European Research Council (ERC) under the European Union's Horizon 2020 research and innovation programme under grant agreement no. 678042. The conference brought together 24 international speakers from different countries (Australia, France, Germany, Greece, Italy, United Kingdom and the USA) and professional categories (museum curators, archaeologists, historians, anthropologists, numismatists and material culture specialists). Since 'tokens' are deceptively simple objects whose boundaries remain difficult to define, the conference focused on an interdisciplinary approach to these objects in order to develop a better understanding of these artefacts and their ubiquitous presence in cultures across time.

The volume contains 15 of the contributions offered by speakers at this event. While the conference had a thematic format to encourage scholarly exchange, the chronological presentation of papers here will allow readers to trace the development of tokens over time. We wish to thank all the participants and attendees at the original conference: your comments and insight during the event have contributed to a better understanding of this category of material. We also wish to acknowledge the funding of the European Research Council once more, without which the event and this volume could never have occurred, as well as the Royal Numismatic Society, particularly Andrew Burnett, Roger Bland and Kris Lockyear for their support during the publication process, as well as the anonymous reviewers of each contribution.

This work is the first ever multi-regional, multi-period, interdisciplinary volume on tokens. It emerges from a scholarly tradition that has been mainly focused on the publication of catalogues. The first such catalogue known to the editors (of ancient Roman lead tokens) was produced by the Italian antiquarian Francesco Ficoroni in 1740 as part of a broader publication of ancient lead objects, *I piombi antichi*.[1] Further catalogues of material have been produced since and tokens have continued to appear in excavation reports and as sporadic finds.[2] This volume seeks to build on this scholarship by adopting a comparative approach to these objects in order to better understand their characteristics and roles in society. Although the case studies presented here can only be selective we hope the contributions will serve to further study in this field.

Defining tokens

As Schmandt-Besserat has argued, tokens in prehistoric, preliterate societies contributed to the creation of writing and abstract number. These early tokens appeared in conjunction with the birth of agriculture (civilisation), and with it the need to store, protect, and redistribute communal resources. The tasks of collecting, recording, retrieving, calculating, and communicating needed a formal administration that was enabled by tokens.

Accounting and administration go hand in hand, and we find tokens once more in classical Athens, where they were employed in the selection procedures of democracy. Athens has a particular place in the history of these objects. Tokens here were principally a democratic device used in the process of distributing offices; they enabled the participation of citizens in running the affairs of the city. The use of tokens can be related to the increasing democratisation of the constitution during the course of the fifth century BC. *Symbolon* (σύμβολον), the ancient Greek word for token, derives from the verb *symballein* (συμβάλλειν), which means 'to bring closer' and signifies an object that has to be brought closer to another in order to acquire its full significance.[3] The earliest tokens found in Athens (dated to the fifth century BC) are little puzzle-like pieces cut along an irregular line so that any given half could join only its original mate and no other. Parts of a word were written on the

[1] Ficoroni (1740).
[2] Postolacca (1868); Svoronos (1900); Rostovtzeff (1903); Ingholt, Seyrig, Starcky and Caquot (1955); Crosby (1964); Simonetta and Riva (1981); Mitchiner (1988–2007); Bateson (1991); Hvidberg Hansen and Ploug (1993); Overbeck (2001); Benassi, Giordiani and Poggi (2003).
[3] Gauthier (1972), 62–75.

tokens so that, when the two pieces came together, a full word was revealed – by being brought together the two tokens created meaning.[4]

The names of demes and tribes immortalised on the puzzle-style tokens reveal a desire to prevent vote buying and indicate a balance between the power of demes (the geographic entities of the state) and the influence exercised by the ten tribes in sortition procedures (**Maurer**). The year 403 BC, which saw the reinstitution of democracy, the reconciliation agreement (amnesty) and the compilation of a formal code of primary laws (*nomoi*) is not only significant for the constitutional history of the polis, but can be regarded as a turning point concerning the use of tokens in governmental procedures.[5] Not only in terms of conception but also in terms of materiality, the *symbola* changed radically around this time. Reforms in the operation procedures of the Boule, the Assembly and the Law courts, as well as the transformation of thought on financial affairs and currency, resulted in the earliest monetiform tokens. **Sheedy,** in this volume, argues that Athenian juror tokens were inspired by contemporary bronze coinage. Possible connections to inflation of the fourth century BC are yet to be explored.[6]

Symbolon refers not only to the form and function of the object, but also to the design it carried (called in numismatics the type). The design of tokens is a sign and a prearranged signal. In this context it is worth mentioning the Greek word *synthēma* (σύνθημα), which refers to a code that functions as a passport or password: the words *symbolon* and *synthēma* are more or less synonymous. Similarly, one of the Latin words for token, *tessera*, could also refer to a watchword written on a tablet, and the Latin word has appeared in the modern world in association with computer password software.[7]

Symbola are first mentioned in ancient Greek texts in narratives of hospitality and transaction, where they served as forms of identification.[8] As well as *someone*, tokens might represent *something*, as discussed by **Schmandt-Besserat** in this volume for prehistory.[9] In ancient Greek texts tokens also enable procedures for concluding agreements or contracts and facilitate practices of authorisation or admission.[10] At the peak of the Athenian Empire the members of the Delian League (an alliance of city-states led by Athens) were compelled by *symbola*, issued by Athens as the leading city, to contribute taxes to the joint treasury.[11] In Athens of the fourth century BC tokens stamped with inscriptions function as credentials, official passports guaranteeing safe passage or favoured treatment. Similarly in the Roman world *tesserae hospitales* were made for mutual agreement and contract and were exchanged between a host and their guest.[12]

Tessera (pl. *tesserae*) derives from the ancient Greek word *tessares* (τέσσαρες = four) and is used to refer to a whole category of objects in Latin: square or cubic pawns, dice, or tablets with inscribed texts.[13] These are all square objects that can be convincingly connected to the number four; whether *tessera* also referred to the circular lead tokens discussed by **Rowan** is debatable. These circular objects were labelled *tesserae* by Ficoroni, but they may never have been known by this name in antiquity.[14] Although the word *tessera* may have at times indicated a Roman token, other words might have been used as well. For example *missilia* (something that is thrown) and *tesserae* are both used within a single section of text describing the

[4] Agora Museum inv. nos. MC 820–22, found in a pit filled with 'rubbish' behind the Stoa of Attalos and dated to 450–25 BC: Thompson (1951), 51–52, pl. 25c; Lang (1959), 80–89; Staveley (1972), 70–72. See also *Inscriptiones Graecae* (*IG*) I², 916 = *SEG* 38,50 = 36,232, previously housed at the National Archeological Museum in Athens but now lost. According to Hermann (1987), 62–69 the words LEO and POL on these tokens could be personal names, making these particular tokens objects exchanged between friends or *xenoi*, but Thompson (1951), Lang (1959) and Staveley (1972) read names of tribes, demes and public offices and think that these tokens were used in the allotment of offices.

[5] Lang (1959).

[6] Gallo (1987).

[7] https://archive.org/details/tucows_369506_Tessera_Password_Generator (accessed 07/06/2019).

[8] Euripides, *Ion*, 1386.

[9] See also MacGinnis, Monroe, Wicke and Matney (2014).

[10] Homer, *Hymn to Hermes*, 21–22.128–36; Herodotus, *Histories*, 5.92.16, 6.86.28–35; Euripides, *Medea*, 613.

[11] *Inscriptiones Graecae* I², 34, lines 11–16.

[12] Daremberg and Saglio (1877–1919), vol. 3, s.v. '*hospitium*', 298, figs. 3908–09, and vol. 5, s.v. '*tessera hospitalis*', 135.

[13] Justin, *Epitome Historiarum Trogi Pompeii*, III, 5,10.

[14] Rostovtzeff (1897), 463.

emperor Domitian's gifts to his subjects.[15] These might have been different words that referred to the same type of object, or the different words might have referred to different types of tokens. The multiple words for tokens no doubt reflected their multiple uses, also witnessed in their multiple shapes and materials across the Roman Empire. The existence in English of only a single word – token – for this category of material can make its discussion dauntingly large, and often demands the use of another word to provide further information (e.g. communion token, locker token, love token).

Indeed, when examining the category 'tokens' we are confronted with the paradox that it is almost impossible to have a single definition of the word. Tokens have served a variety of functions and their roles in human society have evolved over thousands of years. A pluralism of terminology is thus not surprising. In English 'token' signifies something that is a tangible representation of a fact, quality, feeling, or value. To this effect, a token may be a voucher that can be exchanged for goods or services in a pre-arranged way, sometimes given as a gift or as part of a promotion (*Oxford English Dictionary*). As well as this concrete meaning, the word also possesses a metaphorical one: it can describe things or actions that are small and unimportant but that are meant to show particular intentions or feelings (*Collins Dictionary*). These may or may not be sincere, but are manifested with tokens. The concrete and metaphorical aspects of tokens are evident throughout this volume, from the armour tokens discussed by **Schäfer** to the emotional meanings explored by **Millmore** or **Mondello**. The *Collins Dictionary* also notes that a token might be a coin-like object, made of metal or plastic, that can be used instead of money for special purposes (e.g. to make a call from a public phone).

The complexity of tokens is also reflected in other languages. The French term 'jeton' derives from the verb 'jeter', having the dual meaning 'to throw' and 'to add up accounts'. Jetons were counters used on a board for accounting before going on to fulfil representational and prestigious functions in the royal court as coin-like medals (**Valin**). The French term has entered the English-speaking world as jetton – a token used as a gambling chip or to operate slot machines. Equally, jeton entered Italian as 'gettone' in the late sixteenth century to indicate a token used for accounts and then in gambling. The word is still used and was very popular until the late 1990s, when metal 'gettoni' were used for public telephones. According to the German Dictionary *Duden*, 'die Marke', the German term for token, is an abbreviated form for a great spectrum of terms – Erkennungsmarke, Dienstmarke, Garderobenmarke, Lebensmittelmarke, Briefmarke – all of which reflect the multiple roles played by tokens. In modern day financial affairs 'Marke' means the design a company choses for its products. This design or logo is singular and copyright protected – it also is a visible representation of something, in this case an organisation.

It is thus clear that, like the tokens themselves, the language we use to describe these objects and their functions is multifarious. The diversity of terminology observed in European languages reflects the transformations and multiple roles played by tokens across cultures. Nevertheless, there are some intrinsic features of tokens that have persisted over time: their *cryptic* nature, their role as *credentials* and in *information storage,* and their *singularity*.

Tokens have a *cryptic character*. Particularly in Classical Athens, where the state was faced with the problem of how best to ensure the legitimate use of official tokens, the images placed on tokens are characterised by an extraordinary heterogeneity, which would have served to prevent fraud. The same concern with security and protection against fraud or misuse can be found in the use of cryptography in modern day alternative cryptocurrencies. Furthermore, tokens have diachronically functioned as *credentials*. In the prehistoric period tokens enabled members of the community to claim their portion of the harvest (**Schmandt-Besserat**), while tokens in the Roman city of Palmyra, for instance, appear to have served as tickets to grant entrance to particular feasts or events (**Makrypodi**). Short-term circulation and one-off exchange (*singularity*, discussed further below) guaranteed that tokens would

[15] Suetonius, *Domitian*, 4.5.

not fall into the wrong hands. Favoured treatment was granted to the bearers of tokens, as highlighted in multiple contributions within the volume.

Tokens also frequently serve as devices for storing and recording an important bulk of information regarding human relationships, emotions, transactions, agreements, and obligations. Tokens were meant to motivate relationships between issuers and recipients: this is the case in the Holme Cultram Abbey tokens discussed by **Rennicks**, as well the promises and emotions discussed by **Millmore**. Tokens kept a register of goods amassed or funds raised on the one hand and the beneficiaries involved on the other. In this memory capacity tokens overlap with official governmental money (which is also, essentially, a medium of memory), and it is thus no surprise that there are strong interactions between the two forms of media.[16]

Money, coinage, and tokens

The boundaries between 'coin', 'money' and 'token' are fluid: tokens can function as coins, or have currency-like functions, and money itself can be token. The movement between coin, money and token is evident in many of the contributions in this volume. Tokens might be pressed into service as money, and money itself might be transformed into a token, as with the silver shilling transformed into a sailor's love token (**Millmore**). If there is not sufficient information it can be difficult to classify a particular artefact as a token, a coin, or a token coin.[17]

A clear case of tokens operating as coinage can be found in early modern Britain: seventeenth century trade tokens, for example, declare their purpose 'for necessary change'. These tokens clearly functioned as small denominations in a monetary system, their value recognised by a particular local community. They appeared in a vacuum of officially supplied small change; we find a similar situation and similar tokens in colonial Australia, where penny and half penny tokens bore the names of merchants and even the names of token makers or die engravers.[18] The scale of seventeenth century tokens in Britain is evident in the fact that over 12,700 different types of token have been catalogued for the period 1644–72; there was even a problem of token counterfeiting (**Burnett**).[19]

The 'Big Problem of Small Change' has been a recurring issue since the adoption of coinage. Indeed, the need to provide small change has resulted in some absurdly small monetary media (e.g. the *hemitartemorion* in ancient Greek city states, a silver coin weighing ca. 0.10g with a diameter of ca. 5mm), while the cost of producing small change often outweighs the value of the money produced, meaning governmental authorities have little incentive to issue such pieces (in the US today, for example, it costs 1.5 cents to make a single one cent coin). The Roman government ceased to strike small change for some fifty years (ca. 82–46 BC) and it is evident that locally created imitations, older coinages and 'pseudo-currencies' filled the void; in the later Roman Empire small change was often the prerogative of individual cities rather than the Roman government, and wealthy citizens might sponsor or pay for small change as a public good.[20] The prestige associated with this last activity (coins funded in this way often carried a reference to the benefactor) is also seen on the tokens presented by **Burnett**: here it is wealthy individuals in a community (although not the wealthiest) who sponsored tokens, which carried their names and often their occupation. The potential role of tokens in creating hierarchy and prestige is further discussed below.

But although the tokens of early modern Britain provide a tantalisingly clear example for scholars, Mitchiner and Skinner have warned against using tokens of the seventeenth century as a model to understand tokens from earlier eras; they argued that tokens in England in the medieval period, on the contrary, should be understood more as a 'chit-for-service' than an

[16] Hart (2000); Hart (2005); Rowan (2017).

[17] Kroll and Mitchell (1980), 94, n. 11 and Sheedy (2015), 215 for an example from antiquity.

[18] A representative sample of these objects can be found in the National Museum of Victoria (https://collections.museum victoria.com.au/search?query=token; accessed 07/06/2019).

[19] Sargent and Velde (2002), 267–71.

[20] Crawford (1982); Hollander (2007), 25; Stannard and Frey-Kupper (2008); Rowan (2018), 11, 13.

item with a set monetary relationship with official currency.[21] This is the type of function the tokens of Holme Cultram Abbey served, which do indeed appear to be earlier in date: 1300–1490 (**Rennicks**). Tokens representing particular goods such as bread likely functioned as credit given out by the abbey for goods and services; these enabled the abbey to defer payment. We might envisage similar situations in other cultures and time periods. In the Roman world, for instance, lead tokens are regularly found in bathhouses, and may have, similarly to the abbey, been used within a small closed economy as a chit for service to gain access to bathing complexes and/or the services within (the purchase of food and wine, massage, etc); the various workers within the bath complex may then have had their pay tallied up by the number of tokens they possessed.[22]

In these scenarios tokens operate as a media of accounting to enable the redistribution of goods and services within an economy. This should come as no surprise; tokens developed in response to the rise of agriculture, resulting in the ability to plan and distribute a settlement's wealth (**Schmandt-Besserat**). Modern cryptocurrencies like Bitcoin also use tokens to facilitate a distributed ledger, that is, a system to keep track of exchanges.[23] Tokens can operate in a similar manner to money (facilitating the distribution of goods and efficient account keeping) without ever taking on all the roles of money: that is, without becoming general-purpose money. The use of particular accounting systems, and particular numbers and values, is one method by which a community is formed and maintained. The specific *number* of tokens given during exchanges between the king and his officials in France, for instance, is a number significant to a particular cultural group (**Valin**). Tokens, having assisted in the creation of the concept of abstract number, continued to form media of account that constructed and then cemented particular social groupings.[24]

Many of the tokens presented in this volume possess a materiality (shape, material, imagery) that closely resembles (but does not exactly reproduce) contemporary official government coinages. Why should this be? Tokens are known in other forms: eighteenth and nineteenth century 'pee' tokens from Siam (modern Thailand), used in gambling houses, were made of porcelain and could come in a variety of shapes that were chosen because they were considered lucky or auspicious.[25] These were very different in material to the official currency of the time. But large numbers of tokens do imitate the shape of contemporary coinage, and often their designs (**Crisà**, **Küter**, **Wilding**). Indeed, even the modern blockchain has adopted some of the features of coinage: the term is 'Bit*coin*', for example, and the visual representation of this media is of a gold coloured circular coin-like object engraved with a design. For those who cannot understand how the blockchain works, the image of a 'coin' communicates that the cryptocurrency is a currency, and provides a point of reference for understanding.[26] Indeed, for an object to function as a currency it is commonly recognised that those using the medium need to accept that it has value, whether this value is imposed above from a government or authority, or created from below amongst local users in the market.[27] Perhaps token makers adopted many of the characteristics of coins to ensure that their products might be more readily accepted, and the function of these objects clearly communicated. Even so, the influence of official governmental money (largely coinage in the examples discussed in this volume), on the mentality and ideologies of the groups creating and using tokens is evident. One wonders whether some tokens might be commenting upon or parodying existing monetary and value systems; the recent Tulip mania coin, for instance, satirises the recent explosion of cryptocurrencies with a reference to the tulip mania of the seventeenth century, when the price of bulbs skyrocketed only to collapse.[28]

[21] Mitchiner and Skinner (1983), 30.
[22] Pedroni (1997), 209.
[23] On the parallels between prehistoric tokens and modern cryptocurrencies see: Wilding et al. (2017).
[24] Dodd (2014), 289–302 on the role of accounting in society and Schmandt-Besserat (2010) on the role of tokens.
[25] As an example, see ANS 1937.179.24477 (http://numismatics.org/collection/1937.179.24477; accessed 07/06/2019), shaped as a butterfly. See also van Dongen (n.d).
[26] Golumbia (2015), 121.
[27] Hart (1986).
[28] http://tulipmania.co/ and https://thetulip.auction/ (accessed 07/06/2019).

The playful scenes on some tokens like those presented by **Küter** may perhaps be similarly tongue in cheek.[29]

And yet there are also some clear differences to official all-purpose money. Often the design of a token is slightly different from official currency (**Wilding**), or made from a different metal, like the lead tokens discussed by **Rowan** or the clay piece found in a necropolis in Sicily (**Crisà**). As mentioned above, tokens also regularly possess *singularity*, a term used here with reference to uniqueness, and hence status and hierarchy (**Maurer**). The very first tokens in fact are singular: each represented *one* object (e.g. 'one corn'), they were counted 'one', 'one', 'one' (this was before the development of abstract number), and were used once before being thrown away (**Schmandt-Besserat**).[30] Tokens, in contrast to general purpose money, continued to have a singular aspect to their use: they may only be used in exchange for one particular good (e.g. for a particular piece and size of military armour, **Schäfer**) or within one particular sphere (e.g. a particular abbey's holdings, **Rennicks**). As mentioned above, in ancient Athens tokens may represent particular pieces of armour, but also particular individuals.[31] The foundling tokens, left by parents alongside their children deposited at the London Foundling hospital, were also singular and offer an interesting parallel. Since abandoned children would be renamed, mothers were asked to leave a token so that the child might be identified if necessary; these objects were placed in a sealed envelope that was only opened if a claim were made.[32] The single use of tokens seen in prehistory continues in the present day: the electronic tokens used in pin and chip credit card transactions, for example, are unique to each transaction. This singularity, as **Maurer** notes, leads to hierarchy. For example, the use of tokens to mediate charity in the medieval period meant that *who* gained access to charity was controlled, as were the number and type of goods (e.g. specific quantities of bread, meat, charcoal).[33] In this way tokens might act very differently to money broadly conceived, which can be used in multiple contexts, reused, and can be exchanged for a variety of goods and services.

The functions of money continue to elude precise definition despite studies of the media since Aristotle. Moreover the adjective token plays a large part in the discourse surrounding money (for instance, much of our physical modern money is a token, since the specific media we handle, coins and paper notes, has no intrinsic value in and of itself). Consequently the relationship of the artefacts discussed within this volume with money more generally cannot be definitively assessed here.[34] While it might be tempting to see many of the tokens presented here as Polanyi's special purpose money – currency issued for a specific function and/or sphere of exchange – it is increasingly accepted that no money, in fact, can be described as general purpose in the true sense of the phrase (money that can be used to purchase anything).[35] Indeed, perhaps the study of tokens can help us better elucidate money.

Tokens and human society

Comparing the diverse case studies presented here a salient absence among the discussions are the rituals that involved the handling of tokens. Details of the practices involved largely escape us, but they must have contributed to the formation and maintenance of different types of community. Find spots, the materiality of the artefacts, and method of manufacture enable only tentative reconstructions of the procedures of token issuing, distribution, collection, and deposition. The find of an important hoard in a 'house' in the Athenian Agora and the dolphin countermark placed on almost all the tokens within it (**Gkikaki**) point to such practices, but the context of the countermarking can only be guessed at (a timestamp, sign of the issuer, stamp of validation?).

[29] See also the thoughts on 'playfulness' emerging in the cryptocurrency world by Maurer in Tooker (2014), 29.
[30] Schmandt-Besserat (2010).
[31] Kroll and Mitchel (1980).
[32] https://foundlingmuseum.org.uk/collection/whats-on-display/the-tokens/ (accessed 07/06/2019).
[33] Courtenay (1972).
[34] Similarly defining or discussing money is complicated by the fact that many discussions of semantics use money as a metaphor. See Maurer (2006), 16.
[35] Dodd (2014), 286.

Zelizer has proposed to see money as a *process* through which different kinds of human interactions are actively created and valued.[36] We might study tokens in a similar lens. Money and culture, as Dodd notes, are mutually constitutive, with money acting as a tool of calculation, a material form, and a means of creating and sustaining hierarchy and rank.[37] **Maurer**'s exploration of the somewhat paradoxical situation in which a cryptocurrency aimed at 'true' democracy nonetheless results in hierarchy is of relevance here. The way tokens can reinforce rank is also evident in the discussion of French royal tokens by **Valin**: the annual exchange of tokens between the king and his high officials ceremonially reinforced their relative status and relationship, further cemented by the use of a complex 'aristocratic language' that could only be understood by individuals of a particular cultural background and class. The cryptic designs on the Roman lead tokens explored by **Rowan** might similarly be understood as a visual language that enforced the cohesion of a particular group, who alone understood the full significance of the imagery portrayed. Indeed, **Maurer**'s conclusion that tokens, more so than coins, are about status, is also evident in **Burnett**'s analysis of token issuers in Britain in the seventeenth century: while these were not the wealthiest individuals in their communities, they were certainly better off than others, and the imagery on the tokens would only have served to further reputation and prestige. So too **Gkikaki**'s exploration of the use of tokens in Roman Athens suggests that they were used by members of the elite to further enhance their prestige and reputation.

Tokens can enable particular types of community by incentivising particular human activity. In Athens participation in the democracy was mediated by tokens, which were used to control access and reward participation (**Makrypodi** and **Sheedy**). The use of tokens as an incentive for particular human action can also be found elsewhere: the 'jetons de presence' of French academies or the 'méreaux' of French religious orders, for example. In the latter case a chaplain received a token that might be redeemed for money for attending church services.[38] This particular use of tokens continues in the modern day: 'Christ coins', for example, are 'used to financially reward people who read the Bible, post/view content and interact with the community' on a relevant online platform, while 'Sweatcoin' rewards users for physical activity.[39]

Hart observed that money is a media of *memory* that remembers our interactions with others.[40] Tokens, just like coins, can also trace movements across time and space and carry the memory of social interactions. In this context **Millmore**'s discussion of eighteenth century sailor's tokens is of particular interest: here a piece of physical money (a coin) was converted into a token that acted as a memento of the 1797 Spithead mutiny. This particular token, which, as **Millmore** notes, 'communicated and made manifest a community's system of beliefs', reminds us more broadly of love tokens (and convict love tokens), coins converted into objects embodying a deep human connection and a series of emotions. Here the act of engraving coins with personal and meaningful messages was an important process; it imbued the object with an ideological and emotional import that was not present in the circulating currency.[41] An earlier parallel can be found in Christian graffiti on the contorniate pieces of late antiquity – here too the act of engraving imbued the objects with a meaningful message that must have contributed to and reflected Christian identity. Similar to the love tokens of the more modern era, these pieces show a mix of hands from the professional to the more amateur (**Mondello**).

Concluding remarks

While scholarship has focused on how monetary media influences human interactions and society, there has also recently been a movement to explore how particular human

[36] Zelizer (2011), 303–43; Zelizer (2012), Dodd (2014), 294.
[37] Dodd (2014), 296.
[38] Mitchiner and Skinner (1983), 30.
[39] https://christcoins.io/ (accessed 07/06/2019). The sweatcoin app is currently available for download on the i-Tunes store.
[40] Meadows and Williams (2001); Hart (2005).
[41] Platt (2006), 247: the author draws a similar comparison between engraved seals and coinage.

relationships and communities reshape exchange media to mark social distinctions and different groups. Tokens are an ideal media to further this approach: how and why a particular society, community, or 'circuit' (to use Zelizer's terminology) creates new money or media of exchange, and how these media in turn 'take on particular connections and understandings, practices, information, obligations, rights, symbols, and idioms'.[42] If a community produccs a token in its own image, so to speak, what do these products, the tokens themselves, reveal about those involved and their ideals, beliefs and practices?

The presentation of material here may seem unwieldy at first glance – after all, what connection could there be between Neolithic tokens, mutiny tokens, French royal tokens and Bitcoin? But there is something inexplicably profound that unites these contributions across time and space. Tokens expressed values and beliefs shared by a community and at the same time enabled the achievement of a community's goals. Tokens antedate the invention of writing, are as old as accounting itself, and yet as a media remain remarkably fresh since they continue to respond successfully to the human need for societal life.

The creation and maintenance of networks is an integral part of a token's function. If tokens came about at the very moment when hunters settled into farmers, and from the beginning served as credentials and memory banks, then they almost immediately evolved into dynamic regulators of networks. These networks of participant farmers, citizens, beneficiaries, merchants, rebels, artisans, courtiers, and nowadays servers and high-speed processors, form an integral part of how we conceptualise tokens as they keep track of registers, distributions, emotions, transactions, and relationships. This is a system based on trust, mutual agreement, and consensus. The system is decentralised (there are multiple actors) and constantly subject to independent authentications. Based on the very essence of communal life, and especially on the principle of collectivity, with individual participants acting as part of a wider whole, tokens will continue to exist and regulate economic and political life. This is possible due to tokens' unique ability to keep a balance between participation and hierarchy, individual reward and the secrecy of personal data. Two and a half thousand years after the birth of democracy token systems have made an emphatic return in a new, digital form. Further developments in the media are undoubtedly yet to come.

Bibliography

Bateson 1991: D. J. Bateson, 'Roman *spintriae* in the Hunter Coin Cabinet', in Martini and Vismara (eds.) (1991), vol. 2, 385–97.

Benassi, Giordiani and Poggi 2003: F. Benassi, N. Giordiani and C. Poggi, 'Una tessera numerale con scena erotica da un contesto funerario di *Mutina*', *NAC* 22 (2003), 249–73.

Courtenay 1972: W. J. Courtenay, 'Token coinage and the administration of poor relief during the Late Middle Ages', *The Journal of Interdisciplinary History* 3 (1972), 275–95.

Crawford 1982: M. H. Crawford, 'Unofficial imitations and small change under the Roman Republic', *AIIN* 29 (1982), 139–63.

Crosby 1964: M. Crosby, 'Lead and clay tokens. Part II', in Lang and Crosby (1964), 69–146.

Daremberg and Saglio 1877–1919: C. V. Daremberg and E. Saglio, *Dictionaire des Antiquites Grecques et Romaines* (Paris, 1877–1919).

Dodd 2014: N. Dodd, *The Social Life of Money* (Princeton, 2014).

Ficoroni 1740: F. Ficoroni, *I piombi antichi* (Rome, 1740).

Gallo 1987: L. Gallo, 'Salari e inflazione: Atene tra V e IV sec. a.C.', *Annali della Scuola Normale Superiore di Pisa* 17 (1987), 19–63.

Gauthier 1972: P. Gauthier, *Symbola: les étrangers et la justice dans les cités grecques* (Nancy, 1972).

Golumbia 2015: D. Golumbia, 'Bitcoin as politics: distributed right-wing extremism', in Lovink, Tkacz and de Vries (eds.) (2015), 118–31.

Hart 1986: K. Hart, 'Heads or tails? Two sides of a coin', *Man* 21 (1986), 637–56.

Hart 2000: K. Hart, *The Memory Bank: Money in an Unequal World* (London, 2000).

Hart 2005: K. Hart, 'Notes towards an anthropology of money', *Kritikos* 2 (2005) (http://intertheory.org/hart.htm; accessed 07/06/2019).

Hermann 1987: G. Hermann, *Ritualised Friendship and the Greek City* (Cambridge, 1987).

Hollander 2007: D. B. Hollander, *Money in the Late Roman Republic* (Leiden, 2007).

[42] Zelizer (2011), 337.

Hvidberg Hansen and Ploug (eds.) 1993: F. O. Hvidberg Hansen and G. Ploug (eds.), *Katalog Palmyra Samlingen NY Carlsberg Glyptotek* (Copenhagen, 1993).
Ingholt, Seyrig, Starcky and Caquot 1955: H. Ingholt, H. Seyrig, J. Starcky and A. Caquot, *Recueil des tessères de Palmyre* (Paris, 1955).
Kroll and Mitchel 1980: J. H. Kroll and F. W. Mitchel, 'Clay tokens stamped with the names of Athenian military commanders', *Hesperia* 49 (1980), 86–96.
Lang 1959: M. Lang, 'Allotment by tokens', *Historia* 8 (1959), 80–89.
Lang and Crosby 1964: M. Lang and M. Crosby, *The Athenian Agora X: Weights, Measures and Tokens* (Princeton, 1964).
Lovink, Tkacz and de Vries (eds.) 2015: G. Lovink, N. Tkacz and P. de Vries (eds.), *Moneylab Reader: An Intervention in Digital Economy* (Amsterdam, 2015).
MacGinnis, Monroe, Wicke and Matney 2014: J. MacGinnis, M. W. Monroe, D. Wicke and T. Matney, 'Artefacts of cognition: the use of clay tokens in a Neo-Assyrian provincial administration', *Cambridge Archaeological Journal* 24 (2014), 289–306.
Martini and Vismara (eds.) 1991: R. Martini and N. Vismara (eds.), *Ermanno Arslan. Studia dicata* (2 vols.) (Milan, 1991).
Maurer 2006: B. Maurer, 'The anthropology of money', *Annual Review of Anthropology* 35 (2006), 15–36.
Meadows and Williams 2001: A. Meadows and J. Williams, '*Moneta* and the monuments: coinage and politics in Republican Rome', *JRS* 91 (2001), 27–49.
Mitchiner 1988–2007: M. Mitchiner, *Jetons, Medalets and Tokens* (4 vols) (London, 1988–2007).
Mitchiner and Skinner 1983: M. Mitchiner and A. Skinner, 'English Tokens, c. 1200 to 1425', *BNJ* 53 (1983), 29–67.
Morley and Renfrew 2010: I. Morley and C. Renfrew, *The Archaeology of Measurement* (Cambridge, 2010).
Overbeck 2001: M. Overbeck, *Tessere plumbee romane, Civiche raccolte numismatiche. Römische Bleimarken im Civiche raccolte numismatiche zu Mailand* (Milan, 2001).
Pedroni 1997: L. Pedroni, 'Tessere plumbee dalle terme di *Fregellae*', *BdN* 28–29 (1997), 203–10.
Platt 2006: V. Platt, 'Making an impression: replication and the ontology of the Graeco-Roman seal stone', *Art History* 29 (2006), 233–57.
Postolacca 1868: A. Postolacca, 'Piombi inediti del Nazionale Museo Numismatico di Atene', *Annali dell'instituto di corrispondenza archeologica* 40 (1868), 268–316.
Pritchard 2015: D. Pritchard, *Public Spending and Democracy* (Austin, 2015).
Regling 1934: K. Regling, s.v. '*tessera*', *Pauly-Wissowa's Real-Enzyklopädie* (Stuttgart, 1934), vol. 9.2, 851–54.
Roselli 2009: D. K. Roselli, '*Theorika* in fifth century Athens', *GRBS* 49 (2009), 5–30.
Rostovtzeff 1897: M. Rostovtzeff, 'Étude sur les plombs antiques', *RN* 1 (1897), 462–93.
Rostovtzeff 1903: M. Rostovtzeff, *Tesserarum urbis Romae et suburbi plumbearum sylloge* (St. Petersburg, 1903).
Rowan 2017: C. Rowan, *Token characteristics: some preliminary thoughts* (16 June 2017) (https://blogs.warwick.ac.uk/numismatics/entry/token_characteristics_some/; accessed 07/06/2019).
Rowan 2018: C. Rowan, *49 BC – AD 14. Using Coins as Sources* (Cambridge, 2018).
Ruschenbusch 1979: E. Ruschenbusch, 'Die Einführung des Theorikon', *ZPE* 36 (1979), 303–08.
Sargent and Velde 2002: T. J. Sargent and F. R. Velde, *The Big Problem of Small Change* (Princeton, 2002).
Schmandt-Besserat 2010: D. Schmandt-Besserat, 'The token system of the ancient Near East: its role in counting, writing, the economy and cognition', in Morley and Renfrew (eds.) (2010), 27–34.
Sheedy 2015: K. Sheedy, 'The emergency coinage of Timotheus', in Wartenberg and Amandry (eds.) (2015), 203–23.
Simonetta and Riva 1981: B. Simonetta and R. Riva, *Le tessere erotiche romane (spintriae): quando e a che scopo sono state coniate* (Lugano, 1981).
Stannard and Frey-Kupper 2008: C. Stannard and S. Frey-Kupper, '«Pseudomints» and small change in Italy and Sicily in the Late Republic', *AJN* 20 (2008): 351–404.
Staveley 1972: E. S. Staveley, *Greek and Roman Voting and Elections* (London, 1972).
Svoronos 1900: I. N. Svoronos, 'Κατάλογος των Μολύβδινων Συμβόλων του Εθνικού Νομισματικού Μουσείου', *JIAN* 3 (1900), 322–43.
Thompson 1951: H. A. Thompson, 'Excavations in the Athenian Agora: 1950', *Hesperia* 20 (1951), 45–60.
Tooker 2014: L. Tooker, 'Conversation with.... Bill Maurer', *Exchanges: the Warwick Research Journal* 2 (2014), 20–34.
van Dongen (n.d.): Paul L. F. van Dongen, *Playthings in Porcelain: Siamese Pee in the National Museum of Ethnography* (Leiden, n.d.).
Wartenberg and Amandry (eds.) 2015: U. Wartenberg and M. Amandry (eds.), *KAIROS. Contributions in Numismatics in Honor of Basil Demetriadi* (New York, 2015).
Wilding et al. 2017: D. Wilding, C. Rowan, B. Maurer and D. Schmandt-Besserat, 'Tokens, writing and (ac) counting: a conversation with Denise Schmandt-Besserat and Bill Maurer', *Exchanges: the Warwick Research Journal* 5 (2017), 1–14.
Zelizer 2011: V. A. Zelizer, *Economic Lives. How Culture Shapes the Economy* (Princeton, 2011).
Zelizer 2012: V. A. Zelizer, 'How I became a relational economic sociologist and what does that mean?', *Politics and Society* 40 (2012), 145–74.

THE INVENTION OF TOKENS

Denise Schmandt-Besserat

Introduction

It seems appropriate for a volume dedicated to 'tokens' to investigate the genesis of the earliest presently known archaeological tokens. In my paper I show how the chronology, the geographic distribution, and the duration of tokens were linked to the cultivation of cereals. Moreover, the sizeable quantities of foods tokens administered, and the large sized silos built by early farming communities to amass reserves, provide evidence that tokens were created to manage an early redistribution economy.

In 1992 I published an analysis and catalogue of 8,000 Near Eastern clay tokens dated ca. 9000–3100 BC.[1] Since then the idea that, after an existence of 6,000 years, tokens morphed into writing has been widely circulated.[2] However, what prompted the need for tokens in the first place has yet to be further elucidated. What was the impetus for creating a new counting technology at the dawn of the Neolithic?

In this paper I analyse the early assemblages of Near Eastern clay tokens. I highlight five remarkable facts: 1. The appearance of tokens coincides with the cultivation of cereals. 2. The geographic distribution of tokens corresponds with the areas where the cultivation of cereals was practiced. 3. The duration of the use of tokens concurs with the rural agrarian economy that preceded the creation of cities. 4. Large silos for communal storage occur at the same time as tokens. 5. According to their corresponding signs on the first Uruk tablets, tokens referred to measures of goods. These five facts allow me to conclude that, from their incipience, the tokens were linked to the management of goods. The need for counting arose when the survival of the early farming communities depended on an economy of redistribution.

It should be acknowledged that the cultivation of cereals is to be understood in the broad sense of domestication of plants or agriculture. Cereals always represented the staple food of the ancient Near East, but they were not the only food crops. It is likely that legumes such as lentils, peas, chick-peas, horse beans, and vetches were also cultivated.[3] Cereals are, however, the easiest to detect in excavation because, once roasted, their capacity to germinate is destroyed and the grains become practically indestructible.

The appearance of tokens coincided with the cultivation of cereals (fig. 1)

At the site of Mureybet (Syria) the earliest levels (I, II and IIIa) held the remains of hunters and gatherers. The following level, IIIb, dated 9000–8700 BC, produced the earliest evidence for agriculture[4] as well as the first specimens of tokens.[5] The small token assemblage of Mureybet consisted of two discs.[6] The cultivation of cereals was signalled in several ways. First, by a quantum jump in the quantity of cereal pollen in the soil compared to that of the preceding strata. Because cereal pollen is heavy, it does not travel far from the plants that generated them. The pollen deposits of Mureybet, therefore, point to the presence of cereal fields near the settlement.[7] Second, carbonised grains of barleycorns, and especially einkorn (*triticum-boeticum*), became numerous in level IIIb, whereas they were scarce in the earlier levels.[8] Third, the analysis of organic deposits on the surface of flint sickle blades denote cereal residues in level IIIb, but reed cutting in the previous levels.[9]

The first piece of evidence and the timing of the appearance of tokens show that the new technology of counting coincided with the cultivation of cereals.

[1] Schmandt-Besserat (1992), vol. 1; http://sites.utexas.edu/dsb (accessed 17/05/2019).
[2] Harford (2017).
[3] Scott (2017), 44.
[4] Cauvin (1978), 74.
[5] Schmandt-Besserat (1996), 102.
[6] Schmandt-Besserat (1992), vol. 2, 362.
[7] Cauvin (1997), 82–86.
[8] Cauvin (1997), 83.
[9] Cauvin (1997), 83.

Fig. 1: Plain tokens from Tepe Gawra (Iraq). Photo by author.

Tokens were adopted wherever cereals were cultivated

In the ninth millennium BC, the domestication of cereals and the technology of counting with tokens spread jointly over the breadth and width of the Fertile Crescent, where they were adopted by myriads of cultures, which had their own traditions, customs and dialects.[10] For instance, the sites of Tell Aswad (Syria), situated along the Mediterranean shores, and Tepe Asiab, located further away beyond the Euphrates and Tigris rivers in north-western Iran, had dissimilar settlement patterns and tool industries but shared cereal cultivation and the same clay tokens in identical shapes (table 1).[11]

Table 1: Scheme showing counting objects at Tell Aswad and Tepe Asiab.

Object/typology	*Tell Aswad (Syria)*[12]	*Tepe Asiab (Iran)*[13]
Animals		1
Cones	65	6
Cylinders	3	73
Discs	5	5
Ovoids		4
Rectangles	1	1
Spheres	245	101
Tetrahedra		1
Triangles		1
Vessels	7	

[10] Nesbitt (2002), 124; Bellwood (2005), 59; Lafont, Tenu, Johannès and Clancier (2017), 26–27.
[11] Tell Aswad: De Contenson (1995), 226. Tepe Asiab: Braidwood, Howe and Reed (1961), 2008.
[12] Schmandt-Besserat (1992), vol. 2, 366–70.
[13] Schmandt-Besserat (1992), vol. 2, 103–10.

The second piece of evidence, namely the widespread association of cereal cultivation and tokens over the entire Near East, indicates that the technology of counting was adopted wherever cereals were grown.

Tokens remained unchanged as long as the Near East had a rural agrarian economy

From 9000 to 3500 BC, tokens represented mostly products of the farm, such as measures of cereals, oil and small cattle. These tokens were 'plain' – that is to say they had a smooth surface, devoid of markings, and were modelled in a dozen simple geometric shapes, including cones, spheres, discs, ovoids and cylinders.[14] What is remarkable about 'plain tokens' is that they remained the same during their 5,500-year lifespan. Whereas coexistent cultural artefacts, such as pottery, never ceased to evolve, plain tokens continued to be modelled from the same material, in the same shapes and sizes. For example, in 9000 BC Mureybet (Syria) and Tell Asiab (Iran) yielded plain tokens before pottery ever appeared. Plain tokens were numerous during the Jarmo Culture of 6000 BC, when pottery was crude and barely fired. One thousand years later, the same tokens were also present in the Halaf Culture (ca. 5000 BC), when pottery was at its finest, perfectly fired and decorated with harmonious complex compositions. Again, one thousand years later (ca. 4000 BC) the same smooth faced cones, spheres and discs were still used in the Ubaid Culture, when pottery was overfired and sloppily decorated. Contrary to all other contemporaneous Neolithic artefacts, which were in constant flux, plain tokens remained for five and a half millennia persistently and obstinately identical.

Finally, tokens changed in the urban centres of the fourth millennium BC.[15] The new 'complex tokens' referred to goods manufactured in urban workshops, such as textiles and garments. Their shapes multiplied to 16 types, including bi-conoids, paraboloids or rhomboids and bore markings in the form of series of lines and dots. At this time, the Mesopotamian metropolis of Uruk (Eanna Level IV–VI) produced a collection of 812 tokens, which included as many as 16 types and 241 subtypes. The 783 tokens excavated in the Elamite city of Susa (levels 17–18), consisted of 16 types and 190 subtypes.

Compared to the plain tokens, complex tokens had a short duration. Within two or three centuries (ca. 3200 BC) (Uruk IVa and Susa 17) writing was invented. Entries and expenditures of merchandise were then recorded on clay tablets, and no longer with tokens.

The third piece of evidence, namely the fact that tokens were used continuously throughout the Near East for over 5,500 years, certainly attests to their usefulness in farming communities. Their collapse when trade, commerce and industry started to play a role in the economy shows that the counting technology was only suited for the administration of a simple agrarian market.

Tokens coincided with the creation of food reserves

A new type of rectilinear building appeared among the round houses of level IIIb of Mureybet and in the contemporaneous site of Cheikh Hassan (Syria).[16] These rectangular or square structures were small, they had no door at floor level and their inside was divided into cubicles. The rectangular building of Cheikh Hassan was built of rammed earth reinforced with sticks laid horizontally into the mud. The walls of the square building of Mureybet were made of a single row of loaf-shaped pieces of soft chalk, set in mortar. This latter structure measured 3.5 x 3.5m and was internally divided into four cells paved with flagstones.[17] Each cell measured 1.5 x 1.5m, which made them unsuitable for habitation. The multiple exiguous cells therefore suggest that the first rectilinear architecture, devoid of doors, was designed for the storage of goods.[18] The structures were silos or granaries, meant

[14] Schmandt-Besserat (1992), vol. 1, 35–48.
[15] Schmandt-Besserat (1992), vol. 1, 49–92.
[16] Cauvin (1997), 64, 40.
[17] Van Loon (1968), 271; Akkermans and Schwartz (2003), 52.
[18] Cauvin (1978), 42; Simmons (2007), 97.

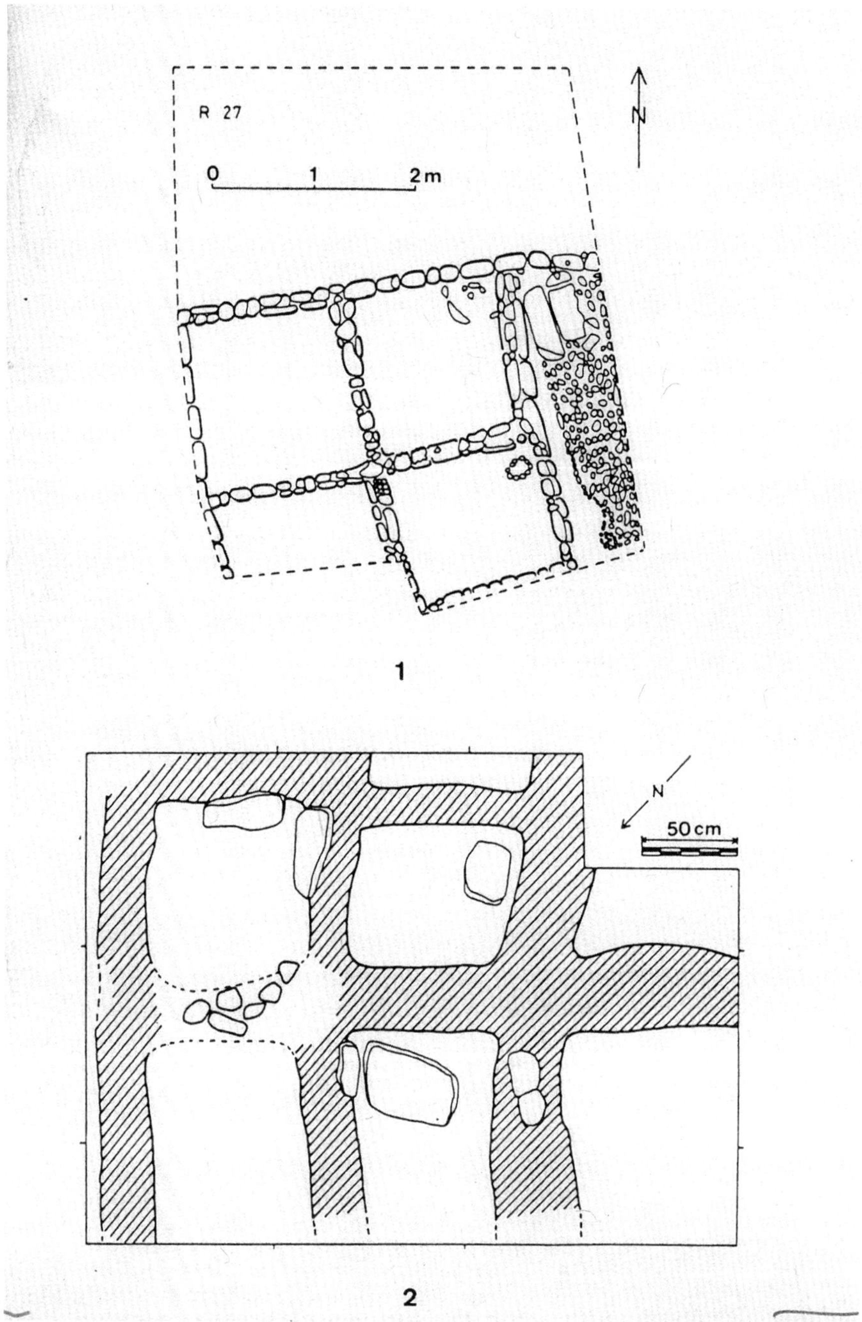

Fig. 2: Plans of silos in Mureybet IIIb (Syria) (no. 1) and Cheikh Hassan (Syria) (no. 2) (Cauvin (1997), 67).

to be filled through an opening high in the wall or from the roof (fig. 2). Furthermore, the size and number of cells in the silos were visibly intended to store goods in quantities disproportionate to the needs of an individual household. Instead, they seem to indicate a communal storage facility.

The fifth piece of evidence, that is the architectural context of the tokens, documents the existence of silos large enough to store communal resources. The simultaneous introduction of public food reserves and of a technology for counting suggests the objective was to control collective goods. Such an administration prefigures the redistribution economy that presided over the brilliant fourth millennium Mesopotamian civilisation.

Tokens administered large quantities of cereals

Tokens morphed into writing when quantities of goods were communicated by signs made by impressing tokens onto a clay tablet. Tokens in the shapes of spheres, discs and cones were replaced by two-dimensional circular and wedge-shaped impressed signs, which perpetuated their meaning. Today the value of early pictographs and their token antecedents can be retrieved by tracing the evolution of cuneiform signs backwards through the centuries. This is the case for the cuneiform signs indicating measures of cereals, which can be traced back to their three-dimensional cone, sphere and disc token antecedents. Consequently, these tokens are considered as having represented the following values:[19]

an isosceles cone = a small measure (perhaps equivalent to one peck?)
a small sphere = a large measure of grain (one bushel?)
a large cone = a very large measure of grain (one bag? = 3 bushels)
a large sphere = larger measure of grain (one cauldron? = 36 bushels)
a flat disc = an even larger measure of grain (one load? = 40 bushels).

Accordingly, the token collections of Tell Aswad and Tepe Asiab can be tentatively computed (table 2).

Table 2: Scheme showing tokens and their values at Tell Aswad and Tepe Asiab.

Site	*Tokens*	*Value*
Tell Aswad (Syria)	54 isosceles cones	54 pecks
	1 large cone	1 bag (3 bushels)
	240 spheres	240 bushels
	2 flat discs	2 loads (80 bushels)
Tepe Asiab (Iraq)	1 isosceles cone	1 peck
	96 spheres	96 bushels
	1 flat disc	1 load (40 bushels)

It is significant that most tokens represented substantial quantities of cereals. For instance, the spheres, which were most frequently used, denoted a large measure of grain. It is striking that the earliest tokens recovered at Mureybet were two discs, equivalent to very large quantities of grain. This suggests a considerable cereal production, probably unimaginable for a single household, but rather that of a communal enterprise.

The fourth piece of evidence, the meaning of the cones, spheres and discs, makes it evident that the volume of goods ordered by the tokens denotes a public rather than a private administration. In sum, the excavations of early farming communities provide multiple pieces of evidence associating the creation of a counting device (tokens) with the domestication of cereals, as well as the management of public food reserves. These facts can be interpreted as follows.

Sharing food in the Neolithic Period

When cereal agriculture spread in the Fertile Crescent, people became increasingly sedentary, and by doing so, they became vulnerable to famine during the harsh Near Eastern winter months or the unpredictable lean years.[20] The early farmers had the wisdom to join forces to amass the amount of food necessary for every individual in the group, the strong and the weak, to survive dire times.[21]

The farmers were not the first to altruistically partake of food communally. Already thousands of years earlier, Palaeolithic hunters broke rank with the other primates by dividing their game catches between the members of their band.[22] In both instances, sharing resources increased the chances of survival of the group.

[19] Schmandt-Besserat (1996), 81.
[20] Blumler (2002), 101.
[21] Cappers, Bottema, van der Plicht, Streuman and Woldring (2002), 4–5.
[22] Binmore (2001), 156; Hayden (2014), 36.

The practices of sharing, however, were very different. During the Palaeolithic, the distribution of meat took place as the hunter came back to camp. It was an immediate and direct operation because tradition assigned a specific morsel to each individual according to his or her kinship rank. But during the Neolithic, the lengthy and complex process of accumulating, protecting and redistributing communal reserves fairly necessitated formal management. And, as communities grew and resources multiplied, the administration required the mastery of counting and accounting.[23]

Palaeolithic hunters had no need for counting to redistribute meat one piece at a time. But computing the cereal reserves of farming communities went far beyond subitising, the minimal innate numerical capacities humans are born with.[24] The invention of tokens brought a structure to expand the needed cognitive skills.[25] By just moving and removing the counters in one-to-one correspondence, individuals could learn to perform the simplest form of adding and subtracting. Throughout the centuries, a continuous cross-fertilisation took place between the redistribution economy's increasing complexity and the development of administration. The tokens were used to perform more complex tasks such as collecting, organising, recording, storing, retrieving, communicating, calculating or controlling data. For example, with the help of tokens, a leader could compute the yields of the forthcoming harvest, request contributions in correspondence with the estimated surplus and control the actual delivery of the goods. Once the collected grain was stored in communal granaries and the quantity of the reserves calculated, a leader could allocate amounts for: a) seeds; b) a reserve for subsistence in dire times; c) ritual offerings to the gods; d) the preparation of festivals.[26]

There was no hiatus between the Neolithic and the Early Bronze Age accounting procedures in the ancient Near East. From 9000 to 2700 BC, tokens and written tablets formed a straight trajectory: both served exclusively to register the same goods in similar quantities and both acted in tandem with the same system of seals. It is well established that tablets recorded the movement of goods in the Early Bronze Age Mesopotamian redistribution economy. It should be recognised that tokens had exactly the same function in prehistory. They enabled control of the collection of communal goods at the harvest and administered their redistribution for the good of the community and the pleasure of the gods. Tokens should be recognised as the cornerstone of the Near Eastern redistribution economy, at its genesis and during its first 6,000 years.

Conclusion

In this paper I have presented data indicating that tokens and counting were related to the most seminal event of the Neolithic period: the cultivation of cereals. I have further discussed the evidence suggesting that, following the fundamental, universal and immemorial altruistic human tradition of sharing food, tokens were created to administer communal reserves of agricultural goods.[27] I conclude that these tokens became the centrepiece of the agricultural redistribution economy of the ancient Near East, which can be credited with two major achievements. First, this economy successfully kept people and their culture alive over the course of some 6,000 years of food uncertainty, hardship and adversity. Second, the cognitive skills created by handling data in the abstract brought humans onto a path that ultimately led to writing and civilisation.

[23] Frangipane (2010), 81.
[24] Lakoff and Nunez (2000), 52–53.
[25] Stewart (2008), 12–13.
[26] Schmandt-Besserat (2001), 399–400.
[27] Wilson (2014), 22–23.

Bibliography

Akkermans and Schwartz 2003: P. M. M. G. Akkermans and G. M. Schwartz, *The Archaeology of Syria* (Cambridge, 2003).

Bellwood 2005: P. Bellwood, *First Farmers* (London, 2005).

Binmore 2001: K. Binmore, 'How and why did fairness norms evolve?', in Runciman (ed.) (2001), 149–70.

Blumler 2002: M. A. Blumler, 'Changing paradigms, wild cereal ecology, and agricultural origins', in Cappers and Bottema (eds.) (2002), 95–111.

Bolger and Maguire (eds.) 2010: D. Bolger and L. C. Maguire (eds.), *The Development of Pre-State Communities in the Ancient Near East* (Oxford, 2010).

Braidwood, Howe and Reed 1961: R. J. Braidwood, B. Howe and C. A. Reed, 'The Iranian Prehistoric project', *Science* 133 (1961), no. 3469, 2008–10.

Cappers and Bottema 2002: R. T. J. Cappers and S. Bottema (eds.), *The Dawn of Farming in the Near East* (Berlin, 2002).

Cappers, Bottema, van der Plicht, Streuman and Woldring 2002: R. T. J. Cappers, S. Bottema, H. van der Plicht, H.J. Streuman and H. Woldring, 'Modelling the emergence of farming: implications of the vegetation development in the Near East during the Pleistocene-Holocene transition', in Cappers and Bottema (eds.) (2002), 3–14.

Cauvin 1978: J. Cauvin, *Les premiers villages de Syrie-Palestine du IXème au VIIème millénaire avant J.C.* (Lyon, 1978).

Cauvin 1997: J. Cauvin, *Naissance des Divinités. Naissance de l'Agriculture* (Paris, 1997).

De Contenson 1995: H. de Contenson, *Aswad et Ghoraifé. Sites Néolithiques en Damascène (Syrie) aux IX* éme *et VIII* ème *millénaires avant l'ère Chrétienne* (Beyrouth, 1995).

Dietler and Hayden (eds.) 2001: M. Dietler and B. Hayden (eds.), *Feasts: Archaeological and Ethnographic Perspectives on Food, Politics and Power* (Washington, 2001).

Frangipane 2010: M. Frangipane, 'Different models of power structuring at the rise of hierarchical societies in the Near East: primary economy versus luxury and defense management', in Bolger and Maguire (eds.) (2010), 79–86.

Harford 2017: T. Harford, 12 June 2017, 'How the world's first accountants counted on cuneiform', *BBC News. World Service* (12 June 2017) (https://www.bbc.co.uk/news/business-39870485) (accessed: 17/05/2019).

Hayden 2014: B. Hayden, *The Power of Feasts from Prehistory to Present* (Cambridge, 2014).

Lafont, Tenu, Johannès and Clancier 2017: B. Lafont, A. Tenu, F. Johannès and P. Clancier, *La Mésopotamie* (Paris, 2017).

Lakoff and Nunez 2000: G. Lakoff and R. E. Nunez, *Where Mathematics Comes From* (New York, 2000).

Nesbitt 2002: M. Nesbitt, 'When and where did domesticated cereals first occur in southwest Asia?', in Cappers and Bottema (eds.) (2002), 113–32.

Runciman (ed.) 2001: W. G. Runciman (ed.), *The Origin of Human Social Institutions* (Oxford, 2001).

Schmandt-Besserat 1992: D. Schmandt-Besserat, *Before Writing. From Counting to Cuneiform. A Catalogue of Near Eastern Tokens* (2 vols.) (Austin, 1992).

Schmandt-Besserat 1996: D. Schmandt-Besserat, *How Writing Came About* (Austin, 1996).

Schmandt-Besserat 2001: D. Schmandt-Besserat, 'Feasting in the Ancient Near East', in Dietler and Hayden (eds.) (2001), 391–403.

Scott 2017: J. C. Scott, *Against the Grain* (New Haven, 2017).

Simmons 2007: A. H. Simmons, *The Neolithic Revolution in the Near East* (Tucson, 2007).

Stewart 2008: I. Stewart, *Taming the Infinite, The Story of Mathematics* (London, 2008).

Van Loon 1968: M. Van Loon, 'The Oriental Institute excavations at Mureybit, Syria: preliminary report on the 1965 campaign', *Journal of Near Eastern Studies* 27 (1968), 265–90.

Wilson 2014: E. O. Wilson, *The Meaning of Human Existence* (London, 2014).

SOME NOTES ON ATHENIAN BRONZE TOKENS AND BRONZE COINAGE IN THE FIFTH AND FOURTH CENTURIES BC[1]

KENNETH A. SHEEDY

The history of token use in ancient Greek communities has yet to be written. The evidence we have is overwhelmingly from Athens; we tend to be wary about the bias towards Athens in the surviving literature and inscriptions, and in the archaeological record generally, but it seems clear that the Athenians were more interested in tokens than anyone else.[2] In this short study I wish to make some comments on the manufacture of Athenian dikastic tokens, which come into production at the end of the fifth century BC. In particular, I want to focus on the use of foreign bronze coins as flans to make the tokens. I also wish to discuss something of the relationship between these tokens and the earliest issues of Athenian bronze coinage. It has been argued by scholars such as Kroll in his important study of the excavation finds from the Athenian Agora that the Athenians were relatively late in adopting bronze coinage (perhaps not until the 330s BC).[3] Nonetheless, there is evidence which I now propose to examine that the Athenian mint in fact began striking both bronze coins and bronze tokens at about the same time, towards the end of the fifth century BC. The record of bronze coins found in the Athenian Agora itself proves to be important in the discussion of these questions.

The common Greek term for a token was *symbolon*. Margaret Crosby noted that the words in both Greek and English 'could be used in a variety of ways, both concrete and abstract'.[4] In origin (cf. Plato, *Symposium*, 191D, 193A), a *symbolon* was a two-part object by which the possession of one half served to determine the identity of the bearer, and this concept of determining identity is present in the function of the tokens given to the members of an Athenian law court.[5] In her 1964 publication of the lead and clay tokens from the Athenian Agora, Crosby found that the 'exact use of a particular token is often impossible to determine' (in good part because they themselves carry little information).[6]

It was then reasonable to look to the tokens produced by the Romans for guidance, for here we have better evidence for context and use; Crosby saw that they were employed in 'various distributions, to be exchanged later for money or a present', as a means of admission to theatres or the baths, and also, 'as small change used by individual small merchants or shops'.[7] It then seems reasonable to conclude that Athenian tokens probably had 'a similar variety of uses'.[8] The role of Athenian tokens as a form of petty currency, however, has been challenged, notably by J. H. Kroll.[9] This appears to be an important distinction, for the unofficial use of tokens as money in Roman, Byzantine and medieval societies is well attested.[10] William Bubelis concluded that the close relationship between medieval tokens and contemporary coinages could be contrasted with the absence of any relationship between the early tokens of Athens and Athenian coinage.[11] Medieval coinage provided the archetype for contemporary tokens – supplying elements of design and iconography – but this source of inspiration, according to Bubelis, is not evident in Athenian tokens until the Hellenistic period when Athenian coins and lead tokens start to share certain images.[12] Nonetheless, the matter is still under review. The 'emergency coinage' authorised and issued by Timotheus in order to pay his

[1] I wish to thank Dr. Clare Rowan for her kind invitation to speak at the *Tokens: Culture, Connections, Communities* conference (June 2017) and for her hospitality during this event. I have benefitted from discussion, very generous commentary and valuable criticism of my drafts from Professors J. H. Kroll and J. Melville Jones, and I thank them both. Similarly, I thank the anonymous reviewers. The short comings of this paper are very much my own. The following abbreviations are used: *IGCH* = M. Thompson, O. Mørkholm and C.M. Kraay, *Inventory of Greek Coin Hoards* (New York, 1973).

[2] Very little is known of non-Athenian tokens. It will undoubtedly be one of the great achievements of Dr. Rowan's *Token Communities in the Ancient Mediterranean* project to bring this material together.

[3] Kroll (1993), 24–48.

[4] Crosby (1964), 77.

[5] Crosby (1964), 77.

[6] Crosby (1964), 77.

[7] Crosby (1964), 76.

[8] Crosby (1964), 77.

[9] Kroll (1976); Kroll (1993), 25 and n. 7; Kroll (2015).

[10] See a recent study, for example, of the lead token money in the kingdom of Jerusalem: Kool (2013), noting the bibliography for Roman and Byzantine token use on p. 293 and n. 5.

[11] Bubelis (2011), 182.

[12] Bubelis (2011), 192.

troops in 364–342 BC while on campaign in Northern Greece was arguably an issue of military tokens and not an official coinage.[13]

It is not my intention in this paper to engage directly with the question of a possible monetary use for Athenian Greek tokens. I can see no means of deciding this question at the moment. Here I propose to step back somewhat and re-examine the objects themselves. Or rather to re-examine the so-called larger Athenian bronze tokens that have been discussed by Boegehold in terms of the operating equipment of the law courts.[14] The more problematic, and very scarce, smaller bronze tokens (11 examples have been found in the Athenian Agora; most measure 6–8mm and weigh 0.2–0.8g), once described as *kollyboi*, have been re-examined by Kroll; the function of these small objects, however, remains a mystery.[15] On the subject of this problematic term we should note that Kroll agreed that the *kollybos* was the well-known value equivalent of an eighth of a silver obol, but has argued that it was not a minted coin (state or private).[16] Instead, like a mina or talent, he believes that it was a notional unit, and as a weight and a value in silver the term *kollybos* may go back to a time before Athens struck coins.[17]

Perhaps the most famous discussion of an officially sanctioned token (σύμβολον δημοσίᾳ) is to be found in Aristotle's *Athenaion Politeia* 65, 2. We are told that the token was presented to a juror when he entered the court; this was later exchanged for payment in coinage.[18] It seems probable on current evidence that the earliest Athenian use of bronze tokens occurred in the operation of its law courts.[19] The surviving bronze *symbola* from the Athenian Agora (some 58) have been catalogued by Boegehold.[20] He identified 40 as dikastic tokens which he divided into Series A–F; this system does not reflect a chronological order.[21] Each token has a letter or image on one or both sides; these letters are predominantly in the Attic-Ionia script of the fourth century BC suggesting that their production was largely confined to this period.[22] An example of Series A was found in the famous fourth century BC 'Ballot Deposit' (containing items, such as bronze balls, which all served as instruments of allotment) under the north end of the Stoa of Attalos.[23] There are no reported contexts for any of these tokens earlier than the fourth century. Nonetheless, Boegehold suggests that as Philochoros testified that the Athenian *bouleutai* began to be allotted to their seating in 410/9 BC it is likely that the dikastic tokens were first used by the Athenians at this time.[24]

Athenian bronze tokens and bronze coins were produced by the same means – a blank was struck using dies to produce the images and inscriptions; they were not cast.[25] The instruments for production and the work processes were essentially the same. The mint workers carefully weighed the metal for the coins (there was more precision for precious metals issues) and adopted standard modules for each denomination. A similar practice was extended to the tokens. The flans for bronze coinage were typically produced by the mint using moulds or rods.[26] The Athenian bronze *symbola* Series A (for which Boegehold provides more information) is represented by 13 finds at the Agora; on average they have a flan of 18–20mm and weigh around 4–5.5g.[27] Less commonly, in producing bronze coinage the mint might simply overstrike coins either produced by the mint itself or struck at other mints. Svoronos was apparently the first to note that some Athenian bronze tokens are made

[13] Kroll (1993), 39, cat. nos. 35—36 listing eight examples found in the Athenian Agora. Now see Sheedy (2015) and Sheedy, Gore and Ponting (2015).
[14] Boegehold (1960); Boegehold (1995).
[15] Kroll (2015).
[16] Kroll (2015), 112–15.
[17] Kroll (2015), 114.
[18] Boegehold (1960) for a discussion of this passage.
[19] Boegehold (1995), 71.
[20] Boegehold (1995), 67–76.
[21] Boegehold (1995), 72 n. 17.
[22] Boegehold (1995), 67.
[23] Boegehold (1995), 68–69.
[24] Boegehold (1995), 71, 155–56, cat. no. 73.
[25] It was thus possible for Boegehold to identify some of the dies used to strike the tokens (see, for example, Boegehold (1995), 73, series C, cat. nos. T14, T17).
[26] Camp and Kroll (2001).
[27] Boegehold (1995), 72–73.

Fig. 1: Bronze dikast's token, early fourth century BC (inv. B1564) (Athens, Agora) (Boegehold (1995), 73, T5) (photo by C. Mauzy) (courtesy of the Agora Excavations, American School of Classical Studies at Athens).

Fig. 2: Bronze dikast's token, early fourth century BC (inv. B1133) (Athens, Agora) (Boegehold (1995), 73, cat. T6) (photo by C. Mauzy) (courtesy of the Agora Excavations, American School of Classical Studies at Athens).

from overstruck foreign coins.[28] Two examples in Boegehold's Series A, T5–6 (figs. 1–2), showing an obverse type of the helmeted head of Athena to left and a letter (Sampi) on the reverse, were overstruck on Syracusan bronze *litrae*.[29] Two other Attic tokens (not found in the Agora excavations) from the same series are similarly overstruck suggesting that a good number in this series were produced through overstriking.[30]

The Syracusan bronze coins over which Athenian tokens T5–6 were struck, curiously also showing the helmeted head of Athena on the obverse (like the tokens) and a hippocamp and ethnic on the reverse, came into production during the reign of Dionysius I (432–367 BC).[31] The common date for the beginning of this coinage at the very end of the fifth century BC, however, is not certain; the evidence of excavations at Motya suggests a date after the destruction of the city in 397 BC.[32] The weights range from 4–11g and they may be seen as bronze *litrae* or obols; Boehringer is quoted as suggesting that there were earlier emissions of 4–5g (matching the Athenian bronze tokens) and later heavier issues, weighing 7–8g.[33] The two main bronze types struck under Dionysius I, both with the obverse Athena head type, are present in the Agora: the dolphin and scallop shell reverse, and the hippocamp reverse.[34] These coins (dated by Kroll to ca. 410–400 BC) fit in, interestingly, with a group of Sicilian bronzes from Akragas and Gela and combined they are among the very earliest foreign bronzes in the Agora.[35] On this evidence we can see that the earliest known bronze tokens of the Athenians came into production at the same time as bronze coins from foreign

[28] Svoronos (1898), 50–52 (overstrikes noted in cat. nos. 48–71).
[29] Boegehold (1995), 73.
[30] Boegehold (1995), 73, cat. no. T5; Svoronos (1923—1926), pl. 101.24.
[31] Morcom (1998), 290–91.
[32] Morcom (1998), 291.
[33] Boegehold (1995), 72 n. 18.
[34] Kroll (1993), 172, cat. nos. 425 (dolphin and scallop shell), 426 (hippocamp).
[35] Kroll (1993), 171–72, cat. nos. 421 (Akragas), 422 (Gela).

mints were appearing in the Athenian Agora. The Athenian mint seized on the availability of foreign bronzes to facilitate the manufacture of tokens.

The presence of significant quantities of foreign bronze coins in the main markets of Greece, attested by the excavation of sites such as Olynthus, Corinth, as well as the Athenian Agora, indicates that they were widely accepted as petty currency.[36] The reception in mainland Greece of the Syracusan bronzes minted by Dionysius I, one of the earliest examples of a mass bronze coinage and one of the first to circulate widely, has yet to be explored. The introduction of bronze coinage into the Greek world, breaking the link between the intrinsic metal value of a coin and its nominal value, occurred in the second half of the fifth century BC.[37] It seems the use of a fiduciary currency was pioneered by states in Sicily and South Italy in the decade 450–440 BC.[38] The reasons for the production of bronze coins need to be studied on a case by case, and probably regional, basis, but the decision can certainly be linked to a growing monetarisation of exchange and market practices, and with demands governing the production of fractional silver coinage. It should also be associated with a greater complexity in the administration of public finances (notably regarding military activities).

During the fifth century BC the Athenians coined vast quantities of silver. But they resisted minting bronze coinage in the name of the citizen body until ca. 330 BC.[39] Kroll has suggested that after two earlier emergency issues the populace could hardly have had any confidence in bronze coins – in contrast to the 'long standing national pride in local silver'.[40] These earlier issues he identified as the plated coins probably struck in Athens in 406/5 BC, as the Peloponnesian War came to an end, and the bronze coins of Timotheus struck in northern Greece during 364–42 BC to finance attempts to recapture Amphipolis; both were described as 'relatively high-value fiduciary coinages'.[41] In discussing theories that the Athenian mint did in fact began minting bronze coinage at an earlier date, though not in the name of the Athenians, I would like to place stress on the quantities of these coins found in the Athenian Agora.

Bronze coins with the obverse type showing the head of a nymph Salamis and a reverse with the shield and sword of Ajax, together with the inscription ΣΑ–ΛΑ, are attributed to the community on the island of Salamis known from inscriptions as the '*demos* of the Athenians on Salamis'.[42] There have been various attempts to explain why Salamis would mint a bronze coinage, once dated to the fourth century BC. Taylor has proposed that the coins were in fact minted at Athens.[43] It seems evident that Salamis was not an independent state, and that these issues cannot be seen as a declaration of their sovereignty; Salamis was part of the territory of the Athenians.[44] It is also unclear why this very small community would see a need to mint its own bronze coins. Kroll, who rejected Taylor's attribution of these bronzes, has suggested that 'as none was being supplied by Athens, the cleruchy government was left to produce its own'.[45] Kroll has now demonstrated that the production of this coinage began in the decade 430–420 BC; the evidence comes from a grave, a child's burial in the Kerameikos (Heilige Strasse 12), which the excavator has tentatively associated with other burials related to the great plague that broke out in Athens in 430 and 429 BC.[46] As Kroll has noted, this dating makes it the earliest bronze coinage in Aegean Greece.[47] This is perhaps another reason why it is unlikely that the mint was Salamis.

[36] Kroll (1993).
[37] Price (1968).
[38] After a certain neglect of the 'origins' topic we now have the proceedings of a conference signalling the advent of new research: Grandjean and Moustaka (2013). On the early use of bronze coinage in Sicily and South Italy see Brousseau (2013).
[39] Kroll (1993), 24–27.
[40] Kroll (1993), 26.
[41] Kroll (1993), 26–27.
[42] Taylor (1997), 173–74, 188–95. See Kroll (1993), 216; Kroll (2013).
[43] Taylor (1997), 192–95.
[44] Taylor (1997). I thank Prof. Kroll for pointing out that Hansen (2004), 637–39, reviews the evidence for the community on Salamis and challenges some of the conclusions in Taylor (1997).
[45] Kroll (1993), 216.
[46] Kroll (2013).
[47] Kroll (2013), 112.

At least 55 'Salamis coins' were found at the Athenian Agora; this is a large number, especially when one considers their date.[48] Kroll made a distinction between the earlier large module coins which are more common (42 coins) and later, less common varieties still of the fourth century.[49] He noted that the earlier coins were recovered from some ten different locations.[50] This number of coins matches the 54 bronzes of Corinth (Pegasos/trident) found at the Agora for the years from the late fifth to the third century BC.[51] In the catalogue of coins from the Pnyx excavation, Davidson and Thompson list a further eight examples, and this number surpasses the Eleusis bronzes (6) and any individual Athenian bronzes, with the exception of the Athena/double headed owl varieties (9), found at the site.[52] This output, which on current evidence was the dominant bronze coinage circulating in the Agora from the late fifth to the mid-fourth centuries, seems far too large for an apparent cleruchy mint. I think it likely that it is the product of the mint at Athens, as was suggested by Taylor.[53]

Taylor based her suggested attribution on an analogy with the bronze coinage minted with the inscription ΕΛΕΥΣΙ.[54] The completion of this inscription is debated but Nollé has proposed that these coins were minted in the name either of (Demeter) Eleusinia or the Eleusinian goddesses, Demeter and her daughter Kore.[55] Kroll was the first to demonstrate that these 'festival' issues were produced by the mint in Athens (though he also argued that their production was the responsibility of individual festival officials, so that it stands outside the usual administrative structure controlling the issue of Athenian coinage).[56] Again, the evidence from finds in the Agora is suggestive; some 77 coins of the Triptolemos/ ΕΛΕΥΣΙ piglet variety from the period 350s – mid-330s BC were recovered, making it the dominant bronze coinage in the Agora during the third quarter of the fourth century.[57]

If we can accept that the Athenian mint struck both the Salamis and Eleusis issues then the decision to avoid directly naming the Athenian state, and at the same time not to employ the traditional coin types of its silver issues, speaks for an idiosyncratic but very deliberate policy towards bronze coinage. It appears that the Athenians wished to establish a separate identity for the bronzes, but an identity that was localised and in part almost anonymous. Is it possible that these early bronze issues were treated as if they were tokens and thus not appropriate for the normal marks of Athenian coinage?

The beginning of bronze token production in Athens to facilitate the operation of the law courts has been dated to ca. 410 BC (see above). If the Salamis coinage was struck by the mint in Athens, then we can see that the production of bronze tokens began shortly after the issue of the earliest bronze coins. The fifth to fourth century Salamis bronzes typically have a diameter of 16–18mm and weigh 3.3–3.5g.[58] The later Eleusis bronzes (beginning in the 350s) which also measure 16–17mm typically weigh 3.5–4.5g.[59] In contrast, the earliest bronze coin (*chalkous* Æ3) to carry the name of the Athenians, introduced in the decade 340–330 BC, has an average diameter of 13–15mm and an average weight of 2–4g; as Kroll demonstrated, these soon declined to 10–13mm and 1–2g.[60] The Athenian bronze law court *symbola* of Boegehold's Series A have a flan of 18–20mm and weigh around 4–5.5g.[61] They are thus very similar to the modules of the Salamis and Eleusis coinages, but are distinct from the later coins minted in the name of the Athenians. As noted above, the mint officials were prepared to recycle foreign bronze coin as flans for the tokens (just as they might

[48] Kroll (1993), 214–16, cat. nos. 640–41.
[49] Kroll (1993), 214–16. For the earlier large module coins see: Kroll (1993), cat. no. 640; less common varieties are reported in cat. nos. 641—42.
[50] Kroll (1993), 214–15.
[51] Kroll (1993), 221–22, cat. no. 667.
[52] Davidson and Thompson (1943), 14 (Athens) and 19 (Salamis).
[53] Taylor (1997), 192–95.
[54] Taylor (1997), 192–95.
[55] Nollé (2014). I owe this reference to Prof. Kroll.
[56] Kroll (1993), 27–30. On Eleusinian magistrates controlling production see Kroll (2013), 113, n. 23. See also Nollé (2014).
[57] Kroll (1993), 40, cat. no. 38.
[58] Kroll (1993), 214–15.
[59] Kroll (1993), 40.
[60] Kroll (1993), 37; Kroll (2015), 114.
[61] Boegehold (1995), 72–73.

overstrike coins). How convenient that the overstruck Syracusan coins of Dionysius I should have had exactly the weight and module size as Athenian dikastic tokens.

I believe that Athenian bronze tokens and bronze coins were part of the same policy in the last years of the fifth century BC to improve the operation of state bodies. Both offered significant advantages and savings as an efficient means of dealing with transactional costs (especially when stocks of silver were short). At the moment, however, we need a better understanding of the chronology of early Athenian bronze coin production before a proper understanding of the relationship between tokens and petty currency is possible.

I wish to conclude with some observations on two examples of context. The first is literary and is well known, while the second is archaeological and has only recently come to light. In the *Frogs*, produced in 405 BC, Aristophanes, through the chorus ('the Blessed Mystics'), bemoans the shunning of good men (*kaloi k'agathoi*) in public life just as the good old silver currency and new gold is now being shunned in favour of base men and base currency – the 'cunning bronzes', the *ponera chalkia*.[62]

> τοῖς δὲ χαλκοῖς καὶ ξένοις καὶ πυρρίαις
> καὶ πονηροῖς κἀκ πονηρῶν εἰς ἅπαντα χρώμεθα
> ὑστάτοις ἀφιγμένοισιν, οἷσιν ἡ πόλις πρὸ τοῦ
> οὐδὲ φαρμακοῖσιν εἰκῇ ῥᾳδίως ἐχρήσατ' ἄν.

> 'Indeed, the Athenians now use the bronze ones for every purpose, foreigners, red-heads, villains from evil stock, recent arrivals whom the city in the past would not have used even in the most random way as scapegoats' (translation by Melville Jones).

In trying to sort out the identity of these cunning bronzes, commentators have dwelt on the 'redheads' (plated silver), largely ignoring the complaint against the *xenoi* – the foreigners, who were among the recent arrivals that the city would not have used in the past.[63] The Sicilian bronzes found in the Agora would seem to fit this reference nicely, and their use in the production of bronze tokens might also be included in the complaint against the Athenian state's unprecedented use of these 'villains'.

My second example comes from the excavations on the Koile road leading from Athens which were conducted by Dr Dakoura-Vogiatzoglou in 2000.[64] The road passes through the double Agora of the deme of Koile, and at the NE edge of the Agora an oval basin (0.41m wide and 0.46m deep), carved into the bedrock, was discovered under a destruction layer. Inside this basin, at a depth of 8–27cm, in a homogenous layer of soil (yellowish clay compressed with small stones), were 44 coins and tokens, a copper bead, a lead ring, iron slag, a large quantity of lead joins, lumps of lead and scrap iron rivets. The mix of coins is interesting: four small Athenian silver denominations (including a *Wappenmünzen* obol) and eleven bronzes minted in Athens (or at least within Attica), including two examples of the Salamis issues (nymph / Ajax shield) and one from the Eleusis series (Triptolemos in chariot / piglet) and from abroad, at least four bronzes from Myrina, Megara and from the mint of Antigonas Gonatas. This deposit also included one bronze jury token (fig. 3; helmeted Athena / letter Π), which dates to the fourth century BC, and 20 lead tokens.[65] The excavators believe the rock-carved basin was used to collect water or other liquids. In a forthcoming publication Dakoura-Vogiatzoglou and Apostolou will present this material and propose that the material within this basin was deliberately assembled and should be regarded as a hoard from the second century BC.

If this is correct it is a unique example of a hoard containing coins, a dikast's bronze token and lead tokens (cf. *IGCH* 157 from the Agora, which contained armour tokens along with silver and bronze coins).[66] It is a perplexing find. It might be argued that the contents of the basin were somehow lost to their original owners (dropped in the dirt?) in the Agora

[62] Melville Jones (1993—2007), vol I, cat. no. 86 = Aristophanes, *Frogs* 730–33.
[63] A good deal has been written about this passage. See, for example, Kroll (1976), and Figueira (1998), 497–504, for an account of the most recent discussion.
[64] Dakoura-Vogiatzoglou and Apostolou (forthcoming). I thank Dr. O. Dakoura-Vogiatzoglou and Dr. E. Apostolou, who have most generously made available the text and illustrations of their forthcoming article.
[65] Boegehold (1993), 73, series C.
[66] Kroll (1977).

Fig. 3: Bronze dikast's token, early fourth century BC (Athens, Koile) (photo by E. Stefanidou) (courtesy of Dr O. Dakoura-Vogiatzoglou).

and then eventually washed into the basin; the excavators, however, believe that it was deliberately assembled. Whatever the case, does this find offer an insight into the composition of circulating petty currency in an Attic market?

Bibliography

Ashton and Hunter (eds.) 1998: R. Ashton and S. Hunter (eds.), *Studies in Greek Numismatics in Memory of Martin Jessop Price* (London, 1998).

Boegehold 1960: A. L. Boegehold, 'Aristotle's *Athenaion Politeia* 65, 2: The «Official Token»', *Hesperia* 29 (1960), 393–401.

Boegehold 1995: A. L. Boegehold, *The Lawcourts at Athens. The Athenian Agora* (vol. 28) (Princeton, 1995).

Brousseau 2013: L. Brousseau, 'La naissance de la monnaie de bronze en Grande Grèce et en Sicile', in Grandjean and Moustaka (eds.) (2013), 81–96.

Bubelis 2011: W. Bubelis, 'Tokens and imitation in Ancient Athens', *Marburger Beiträge zu antiken Handels-, Sozial- und Wirtsschaftsgeschichte* 28 (2011), 171–95.

Camp and Kroll 2001: J. M. Camp and J. H. Kroll, 'The Agora mint and Athenian bronze coinage', *Hesperia* 70 (2001), 127–62.

Crosby 1964: M. Crosby, 'Lead and clay tokens. Part II', in Lang and Crosby (1964), 69–146.

Dakoura-Vogiatzoglou and Apostolou forthcoming: O. Dakoura-Vogiatzoglou and E. Apostolou, 'A small numismatic group from the ancient road of Koile', in Sheedy and Davis (eds.) (forthcoming).

Davidson and Thompson 1943: G. R. Davidson and D. Burr Thompson, *Small Objects from the Pnyx: I, Hesperia Supplement* 7 (Princeton, 1943).

Figueira 1998: T. Figueira, *The Power of Money. Coinage and Politics in the Athenian Empire* (Philadelphia, 1998).

Grandjean and Moustaka (eds.) 2013: C. Grandjean and A. Moustaka (eds.), *Aux origins de la monnaie fiduciaire. Traditions métallurgiques et innovations numismatiques* (Bordeaux, 2013).

Hansen 2004: M. H. Hansen, 'Salamis', in Hansen and Nielsen (eds.) (2004), 637–39.

Hansen and Nielsen (eds.) 2004: M. A. Hansen and T. H. Nielsen (eds.), *An Inventory of Archaic and Greek Poleis. An Investigation Conducted by The Copenhagen Polis Centre for the Danish National Research Foundation* (Oxford, 2004).

Kool 2013: R. Kool, 'Lead token money in the Kingdom of Jerusalem', *NC* 173 (2013), 293–339.

Kraay and Jenkins (eds.) 1968: C. M. Kraay and G. K. Jenkins (eds.), *Essays in Greek Coinage Presented to Stanley Robinson* (Oxford, 1968).

Kroll 1976: J. N. Kroll, 'Aristophanes' πονηρὰ χαλκία: a reply', *GRBS* 17 (1976), 339–41.

Kroll 1977: J. N. Kroll, 'Some Athenian armor tokens', *Hesperia* 46 (1977), 141–46.

Kroll 1993: J. N. Kroll, *The Greek Coins. The Athenian Agora* (vol. 26) (Princeton, 1993).

Kroll 2013: J. N. Kroll, 'Salamis again', in Grandjean and Moustaka (eds.) (2013), 109–15.

Kroll 2015: J. N. Kroll, 'Small bronze tokens from the Athenian Agora', in Wartenberg and Amandry (eds.) (2015), 107–16.

Lang and Crosby 1964: M. Lang and M. Crosby, *The Athenian Agora X: Weights, Measures and Tokens* (Princeton, 1964).

Melville Jones 1993–2007: J. R. Melville Jones, *Testimonia Numaria* (vol. 1, Texts and Translations) (vol. 2, Addenda and Commentary) (London, 1993–2007).

Morcom 1998: J. Morcom, 'Syracusan bronze coinage in the fifth and early fourth centuries BC', in Ashton and Hunter (eds.) (1998), 287–91.

Nollé 2014: J. Nollé, '«Panegyris coinages» – Eine moderne Geisterprägung', *Chiron* 44 (2014), 285–324.

Price 1968: M. J. Price, 'Early Greek coinage', in Kraay and Jenkins (eds.) (1968), 90–104.

Sheedy 2015: K. A. Sheedy, 'The emergency coinage of Timotheus (364-362 BC)', in Wartenberg and Amandry (eds.) (2015), 203–24.

Sheedy and Davis (eds.) forthcoming: K. A. Sheedy and G. Davis (eds.), *Metals, Mines and Money*.

Sheedy, Gore and Ponting 2015: K. A. Sheedy, D. B. Gore, and M. Ponting, 'The bronze issues of the Athenian general Timotheus: evaluating the evidence of Polyaenus's Stratagemata', *AJN* 27 (2015), 9–28.

Svoronos 1898: J. N. Svoronos, 'Περί των εισιτηρίων των αρχαίων', *JIAN* 1 (1898), 37–120.

Svoronos 1923–1926: J. N. Svoronos, *Les Monnaies d'Athènes* (completed by B. Pick) (Munich, 1923–1926).

Taylor 1997: M. C. Taylor, *Salamis and the Salaminioi. The History of an Unofficial Athenian Demos* (Amsterdam, 1997).

Wartenberg and Amandry (eds.) 2015: U. Wartenberg and M. Amandry (eds.), ΚΑΙΡΟΣ: *Contributions to Numismatics in Honor of Basil Demetriadi* (New York, 2015).

TOKENS INSIDE AND OUTSIDE EXCAVATION CONTEXTS: SEEKING THE ORIGIN.

EXAMPLES OF CLAY TOKENS FROM THE COLLECTIONS OF THE ATHENS NUMISMATIC MUSEUM

STAMATOULA MAKRYPODI

Introduction

This contribution presents important new material to the research community, supplemented by additional information that can be added from the current state of research. A study of the clay tokens of the Numismatic Museum is presented along with known counterparts from excavations or with known provenance. Information on the origin of the clay tokens that were not recovered through excavations is based on the Numismatic Museum's archive and the information accompanying these objects in the museum.[1] This study is the result of personal observations during the process of recording the museum's clay tokens as part of the preparation of my doctoral dissertation.

The large number of known tokens and the lack of information concerning their provenance explain why their study is usually limited to their iconography. Most scholars attempt to date tokens based on their iconographic and typological features, and these same features are used to discuss their possible function and to draw other conclusions. However, in my opinion, the study of tokens requires a multidimensional approach that includes available excavation data, the parallel study of ancient written sources, as well as additional information coming from the official archives of museums.

Despite the fact that the Numismatic Museum has several clay tokens in its collections, the publication of this material is extremely limited and no full corpus yet exists. The few known publications are simply catalogues of the material without further information. The earliest presentation of the clay tokens from the collections of the Numismatic Museum and other Athenian private collections was published in 1905 by Svoronos, who was then the museum's director.[2] A second discussion of clay tokens was presented in the *Archaiologikon Deltion* (1930–31).[3] This second publication included descriptions and photographs of clay tokens that formed part of a larger collection of these objects acquired by the Numismatic Museum between 1929 and 1931. A third publication was recently written by the author discussing clay tokens (*tesserae*) in the museum, which were attributed for the first time to Palmyra in Syria.[4] These last were acquired by the Numismatic Museum in 2005, as part of a larger group of objects given by the collector Adonis Kyrou.

Even though iconography is not a factor of minor value concerning the study of the tokens, I suggest that knowledge of the excavation context provides us with the most comprehensive 'tool' to interpret these objects. What is more, beginning with iconography, we will show the correlations between the tokens in the Numismatic Museum's collection, tokens coming from excavations, and lastly tokens whose provenance is unknown. In doing so, I explore whether it is possible to attribute a possible origin to artefacts whose contextual provenance is otherwise lost forever.

I begin with a case that proves that excavation material can invalidate theories developed for objects removed from their context. Bone or ivory counters were well known among archaeologists from the early days of the discipline. Several theories were formulated in the late nineteenth and early twentieth century concerning their use, presenting them as amphitheatre, circus and theatre

[1] I would like to thank Clare Rowan for her kind invitation to participate in this conference, and for providing the ideal forum for me to discuss this material in its appropriate context. Special thanks are owed to J. H. Kroll for his comments and enthusiastic encouragement. I also thank Mairi Gkikaki for her warm hospitality in Warwick, Katerina Panagopoulou, Ioannis Voskos and especially Katerina Dimitriadi, who gave their time for a critical reading of the English text. Finally, I warmly thank the President and members of the Local Council of Monuments in Attica, whose unanimous positive opinion allowed the study of this important material, despite the Numismatic Museum's partially negative recommendation. I also heartily thank all those who boosted my morale in this endeavor. The study and the publication of the clay tokens is carried out on the basis of the Decision of the Directorate of Prehistoric and Classical Antiquities of the Hellenic Ministry of Culture and Sports with Reference Number **ΥΠΟΠΑΙΘ/ΓΔΑΠΚ/ΔΙΠΚΑ/ΤΕΕΑΕΙ** 64960/38294/3142/357/ 24/3/2015 and **ΥΠΟΠΑΙΘ/ΓΔΑΠΚ/ΔΙΠΚΑ/ΤΕΕΑΕΙ** 67382/40047/3212/375/ 24 /3/2015.

[2] Svoronos (1905).

[3] Konstantopoulos (1930–1931), 32, 36.

[4] Makrypodi (2016).

tickets. They were scattered in various museums and private collections. On one side, they were decorated with a variety of representations, including heads of gods, portraits of Roman emperors and scenes from Alexandria. On the reverse, they carried legends naming the image on the obverse as well as a numeral in both Greek and Latin. Their actual function was revealed by the discovery of a child's burial in 1903 dated between the first and second century AD in Kerch (Russia). A complete series of bone tokens bearing numbers from 1 to 15 was discovered near the head of the dead child. Since these tokens were found together as a set in a box created specifically for them, they were interpreted as gaming pieces. Further finds from other excavations where these counters were combined with dice and game tables confirmed this hypothesis.[5]

During my study of the Numismatic Museum's clay tokens, the question of provenance was a recurring problem. Three case studies from the Numismatic Museum's collections are presented below. These studies demonstrate that a combination of literature review and on the spot archival research can lead to fruitful discoveries.

The clay tokens from Palmyra

As previously mentioned, part of the material was attributed to Palmyra (cat. nos. 1–3, figs. 1–3). A Near Eastern provenance seems to me extremely possible based both on the legends in Aramaic script and the style of the representations. Systematic research amongst the related literature has led me to infer Palmyra as the locus of their origin. Indeed, a secure date between the first and third century AD can be given since Palmyra exclusively produced such *tesserae* during this period. In Makrypodi (2016) six *tesserae* were identified with certainty, and others are presented that are more poorly preserved and so cannot be securely identified. Figures 1–3 illustrate three of the six identified *tesserae*.

Clay tokens from the Pnyx?

A second case study is formed by the clay token initially published by Ioannis Svoronos in 1905, decorated with the head of a bearded man facing right. He has short hair and wears a wreath (cat. no. 4, fig. 4). According to Svoronos, the token was given to the Numismatic Museum in exchange for something else.[6] Svoronos noted that the token was found in Athens.

A second token carrying an identical image was acquired by the Numismatic Museum in 2005 (cat. no. 5, fig. 5). It is made of reddish clay. My examination of both specimens indicates that they must have been made from the same type of clay, since the colour and the composition appear the same for both tokens. A specific analysis of the clay has not been performed, but the similarity between the two objects is remarkable. Both specimens were produced by the same stamp.

Fig. 1: Clay *tessera* (Ø 26mm, 12h) (cat. no. 1).

Fig. 2: Clay *tessera* (16 x 16mm, 12h) (cat. no. 2).

Fig. 3: Clay *tessera* (13 x 12mm, 3h) (cat. no. 3).

[5] Rostowzew (1905), 110–24. Unfortunately, Rostovtzeff gave no further information concerning the excavation.

[6] Even though nowadays the practice of exchanging antiquities between a state museum and private collectors would seem out of the question, this used to be a common practice.

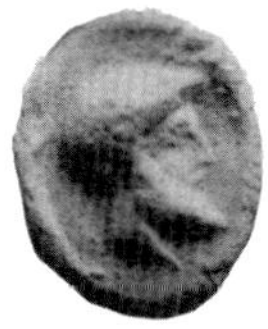

Fig. 4: Clay token (16 x 20mm) (cat. no. 4)

Fig. 5: Clay token (Ø 15 x 18mm) (cat. no. 5)

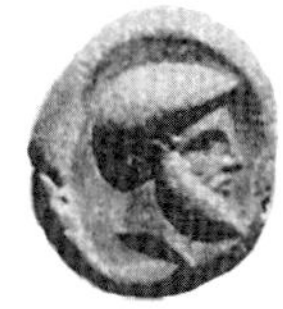

Fig. 6: Clay token (Ø 18mm) (cat. no. 6).

A third token (cat. no. 6, fig. 6) was uncovered during an excavation in the area of Pnyx. The excavation was conducted by the American School of Classical Studies at Athens between 1931 and 1937, and the finds published in 1943.[7] Once again, the publication records that the token was made of reddish clay. The publication further records that the token bears the impression of an oval stamp with the head of a bearded man facing right wearing a peaked cap, which bears horizontal striations. Although the description is different from Svoronos' description of a male head with short hair and a wreath, the resemblance between the two specimens is indisputable. The clay token from the Pnyx and the two tokens from the Numismatic Museum were produced from the same stamp. The dimensions of the stamp perfectly fit those that Svoronos provided for the first token, as well as the second token acquired by the Numismatic Museum in 2005.

The stratigraphic level where the third token was discovered is related to the Third Period of the Assembly Place (400–330 BC).[8] It is almost certain that this object was stamped with the same oval stamp used for the aforementioned objects kept in the Numismatic Museum. Therefore, all three tokens are related to the Pnyx.

Athenian clay tokens

The third case is more complicated, but more interesting. It is related to a large group of clay tokens that were acquired by the museum between 1929 and 1931. They were published by Konstantinos Konstantopoulos in *Archaiologikon Deltion* 1930–31.[9] According to this publication, they are identified as entrance tickets for the theatre or the assembly, based on the dominant interpretation put forward by Svoronos.

The published catalogue included only 12 clay tokens, reported to have been sold to the Numismatic Museum by a private individual, Ioannis Lerakis. According to the publication, these tokens had the same origin as many other similar tokens that were accessioned at the Numismatic Museum in the period between 1929 and 1930, which originated from the same places and were handed in by the same person. The northwest slope of the Hill of the Muses, southeast of the Pnyx, and southwest of the Acropolis, were recorded as their places of origin. The identification of their provenance as the Hill of the Muses was based on the statement of the person handing the tokens in. Apparently, these specific tokens were finds coming from an illegal surface survey.

Among the tokens published in 1930–31 are the following types, also listed at the end of this paper (see table 1):

- Herm right, bush with three branches in the field r. / Sampi in double lines (cat. no. 7, fig. 7 and cat. no. 8)
- Herm right / Upsilon (cat. no. 13, fig. 8)
- Human head right bearing little wings / Sigma (or Mu) (cat. no. 20, fig. 9)
- Human head right bearing little wings / Phi (cat. no. 23, fig. 10)[10]

[7] Davidson and Burr Thompson (1943), 104–08, table XII.

[8] Hansen (1989), 143–53; Rotroff and Camp (1996), 263–94 with a thorough discussion of the deposits and their dating.

[9] Konstantopoulos (1930–1931), 32, fig. 3, 36, fig. 9.

[10] It remains uncertain which of the tokens from this series in the Numismatic Museum and acquired between 1929–31 (cat. nos. 21–24) are those published by Konstantopoulos (1930–1931), 36 cat. no. 6, fig. 9, sixth seen from above. The identification with my cat. no. 23 is only tentative.

- Dove right / Omicron in double lines (cat. no. 28, fig. 11)
- Tripod / Sampi in double lines (cat. no. 33, fig. 12)
- Horse right / Rho retrograde in double lines (cat. no. 37 fig. 13).

Among the tokens published in 1905 by Svoronos there are two that deserve particular attention. The first bears a representation of a dove on one side and the letter upsilon in double lines on the other side (cat. no. 29) and the second has a young man riding a deer on one side and Artemis driving a deer chariot on the other (cat. no. 52). Svoronos gives Athens as the provenance for both of these tokens.

Following the 1930–31 publication, further work on the clay tokens introduced during this period took place within the museum. A large number of clay tokens were catalogued and categorised. The results were impressive. It appears that not just 12, but 62 clay tokens were sold or offered to the museum in the period between 1929 and 1932. According to the information found in the archive, these clay tokens were all handed in by the same person, Ioannis Lerakis. Their provenance was once again declared to be the Hill of the Muses. Many tokens among these bear the types of the tokens published in 1905 and 1930–1931. We will focus mainly on those bearing letters of the Greek alphabet, since it is more likely for these to be a connected series with a common provenance or a common use in antiquity.

Research in the Numismatic Museum collections yielded many new types and several new letter-combinations (table 1). The new varieties are catalogued at the end of the paper and are briefly mentioned here:

- Head of Apollo right / Sphinx right (cat. no. 41, fig. 15 and cat. nos. 42–48)
- Rose / Pi in double lines (cat. no. 50, fig. 16)
- Wreath / Beta in double lines (cat. no. 58, fig. 18)
- Wreath / Retrograde Gamma or Pi (cat. no. 62, fig. 19).

What is more significant is that more specimens of known varieties were identified:

- three of 'Young man riding a deer / Artemis driving deer chariot' (cat. no. 53, fig. 17, and cat. nos. 54–55)
- one of 'Dove / Upsilon in double lines' (cat. no. 30, fig. 20)
- three of 'Human head right bearing little wings / Phi' (cat. nos. 21–22, 24)
- four of 'Herm right / Sampi in double lines' (cat. nos. 9–12)
- one of 'Herm right / Upsilon in double lines' (cat. no. 14).

New type and letter combinations were also uncovered, combining a known iconographic type with a different letter. These are:

- Dove / Zeta in double lines (cat. no. 32, fig. 21)
- Human head right bearing little wings / Chi (cat. no. 25, fig. 22 and cat. no. 26)
- Herm right / Xi in double lines (cat. nos. 17–18 and cat. no. 19, fig. 23)
- Horse right with a bird on its back / Rho retrograde in double lines (cat. no. 38, fig. 24).

Cat. no. 38 (fig. 24), recovered in this second phase of the investigation, enabled a better reading of the 'horse right' type: it is possible to identify a bird on the back of the horse, a significant detail of the design which was never mentioned by Konstantopoulos because cat. no. 37 (fig. 13), the specimen presented in the 1930–1931 publication, was struck off-flan. Similarly, cat. no. 14 (fig. 23), also uncovered in the second phase of the investigation, revealed a *kerykeion* in the left field, which was not visible on the known specimen published by Konstantopoulos, cat. no. 13. A further specimen of 'Head of Apollo / Sphinx' was also identified, donated by Michael Vlastos in 1928 (cat. no. 40). Another token acquired by the Numismatic Museum in 1929 was added to our research catalogue, a specimen of the 'Young man riding a deer / Artemis driving a deer chariot' variety that was already published by Svoronos in 1905 (see above). The specimen is denoted as 'Tsamados' gift' (cat. no. 56).[11]

[11] The information derives from the records associated with the objects in the place of safekeeping of the Numismatic Museum: 'Δῶρον Τσαμαδοῦ'.

Fig. 7: Clay token (Ø 17mm, 1h) (cat. no. 7).

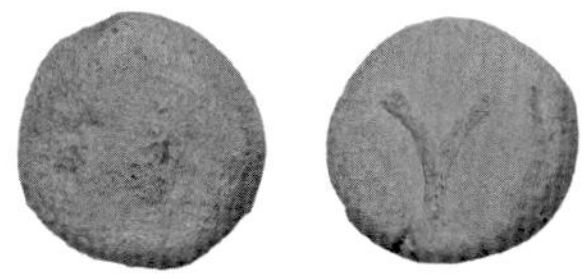
Fig. 8: Clay token (Ø 17mm, 6h) (cat. no. 13).

Fig. 9: Clay token (Ø 12mm, 1h or 4h) (cat. no. 20).

Fig. 10: Clay token (15 x 13mm, 9h) (cat. no. 23).

Fig. 11: Clay token (Ø 17mm, 6h or 12h) (cat. no. 28).

Fig. 12: Clay token (Ø 16mm, 9h) (cat. no. 33).

Fig. 13: Clay token (Ø 17mm, 7h) (cat. no. 37).

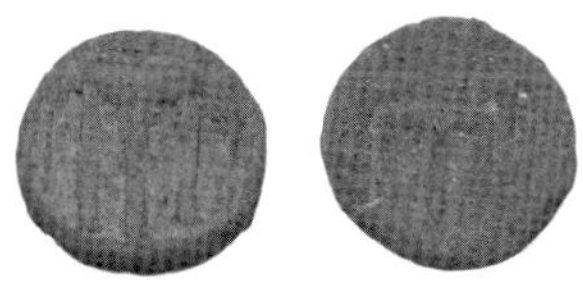
Fig. 14: Clay token (Ø 17mm, 2h) (cat. no. 36).

Fig. 15: Clay token (Ø 16mm, 3h) (cat. no. 41).

Fig. 16: Clay token (Ø 17mm, 7h) (cat. no. 50).

Fig. 17: Clay token (Ø 18mm, 1h) (cat. no. 53).

Fig. 18: Clay token (Ø 17mm, 9h) (cat. no. 58).

Fig. 19: Clay token (Ø 17mm, 9h) (cat. no. 62).

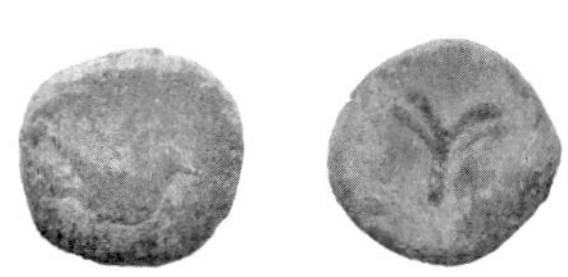
Fig. 20: Clay token (Ø 15mm, 2h) (cat. no. 30).

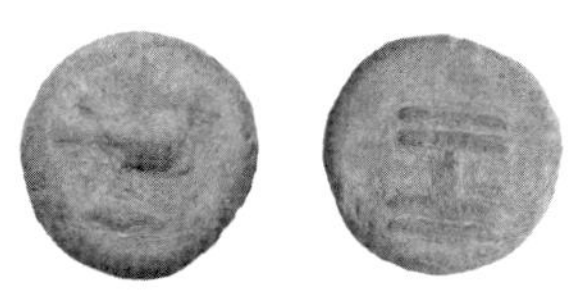
Fig. 21: Clay token (Ø 17mm, 11h) (cat. no. 32).

Fig. 22: Clay token (Ø 14mm, 10h) (cat. no. 25).

Fig. 23: Clay token (Ø 18mm, 11h) (cat. no. 19).

Fig. 24: Clay token (Ø 18mm, 2h) (cat. no. 38).

Further research on the collections brought to light yet another group of clay tokens. They were handed in to the Numismatic Museum in 2005 by Adonis Kyrou, as was the case with the Palmyrene *tesserae*. Among these many specimens bear a remarkable resemblance to those already in the museum in terms of types and the colour and quality of the clay. The origin of these tokens remains unknown. Their provenance was not declared when they were given to the Numismatic Museum. The '2005 lot' adds two more specimens of the 'Herm / Upsilon' variety (cat. nos. 15–16), one more specimen of the 'Human head right bearing little wings / Chi' (cat. no. 27), one more specimen of the variety 'Dove / Upsilon' (cat. no. 31), two more specimens of 'Tripod / Sampi in double lines' (cat. nos. 35–36), one more specimen of 'Head of Apollo right / Sphinx right' (cat. no. 49), one more specimen of 'Rose / Pi in double lines' (cat. no. 51), one more of 'Young man riding a deer right / Artemis driving deer chariot right' (cat. no. 57), and three more of 'Wreath / Beta' (cat. nos. 59–61). A new and unique Horse / Letter combination also appears with the letter Xi (cat. no. 39, fig. 25). A better-preserved specimen of the 'Tripod / Sampi' type was also contained in the '2005 lot', with the tripod much clearer than on other specimens (cat. no. 36, fig. 14).

Fig. 25: Clay token (Ø 15mm, 12h) (cat. no. 39).

We thus now have a total of 56 tokens distributed over nine types. Each type or image is combined with several different letters. The letter combinations and the number of specimens of each type is given below.

- **Herm and:** Sampi in double lines (6 specimens), Xi in double lines (3 specimens), Upsilon in double lines (4 specimens).
- **Human head right bearing little wings and**: Phi (4 specimens), Chi (3 specimens), Sigma (1 specimen).
- **Tripod and:** Sampi in double lines (4 specimens).
- **A horse with a bird on its back and:** retrograde Rho (2 specimens), Xi (1 specimen).
- **Dove and:** Omicron in double lines (1 specimen), Zeta in double lines (1 specimen), Upsilon in double lines (3 specimens).
- **Head of Apollo and:** Sphinx (10 specimens).
- **Rose and:** Pi in double lines (2 specimens).
- **Young man riding a deer and:** Artemis riding a deer chariot (6 specimens).
- **Wreath and:** Beta (4 specimens), Gamma or Pi (1 specimen).

Provenances and Finds

Of the 56 clay tokens gathered here, it is desirable: 1) to attribute their origin to a specific area or to a broader region; 2) to associate these tokens with secure excavation data in order to achieve a better interpretation of their use and purpose.

In first case discussed above, the tokens' style and iconography point to Palmyra beyond any doubt. I have as yet been unable to associate them with a specific locus or excavation. Obviously, the discovery of most of these tokens is the outcome of illegal excavations and the illicit trade of antiquities. Judging by their broad chronological range it is possible to classify them as a group gradually collected together as occasional finds. Portable objects like tokens could be found anywhere. The circumstances under which they were transferred to Greece remain unknown.

According to researchers, these *tesserae* were associated with ritual meals that took place in Palmyra during religious ceremonies.[12] These objects and the inscriptions they bear provide us with valuable insight into society and the organization of the state, the role of the *thiasoi* (θίασοι), religious habits, the role of the four tribes of the city of Palmyra, and the role of large families or certain social groups in religious ceremonies and events.[13]

[12] Ingholt, Seyrig, Starcky and Caquot (1955), iv.

[13] Al-As'ad, Briquel-Chatonnet and Yon (2005), 1; Smith (2013), 16; Raja (2015), 179–80, 182–84.

The data concerning the second case is more encouraging. One of the specimens in the museum is said to have been found in Athens and another specimen excavated on the Pnyx, where the Assembly of the Athenian citizens took place. It is worth recalling at this point the theory connecting tokens with the functions of the Athenian democracy.[14] As it is common to find tokens with identical stamp impressions in the same excavation, it cannot be excluded that all three objects come from the Pnyx or from the surrounding area. In any case, it appears that the tokens were issued at the same time and presumably also for the same purpose. Most indications lead to the conclusion that these clay objects were produced in Athens.

The third example offers more data. The majority of the tokens come from the northwest slope of the Hill of the Muses. The repetition of the same types and the similarity of the clay suggest that the two groups (that of 1905 and 1929–1932 and that of 2005) may be classified as a single ensemble. That so many specimens come from the northwest slope of the Hill of the Muses suggests that they might all originate from this location.

However, the conditions under which these tokens were found are not the same as if they had come from official excavations. The tokens were probably occasional finds coming from illegal surface surveys. The bulk of the material was given to the museum between 1929 and 1932, which coincides with the preparation and commencement of the excavations of the American School of Classical Studies at the adjacent Athenian Agora. During the same period, Greek and American archaeologists excavated on the hill of the Pnyx, near the Hill of the Muses, as well as on the Hill of the Nymphs and the Hill of the Muses itself.[15] The fact that the Numismatic Museum acquired these tokens approximately at the same time might not have been unconnected with the general archaeological activity in the area. Paradoxically, the official excavation reports of this period do not record any tokens among the finds.

Clay tokens have been found in the Athenian Agora.[16] They usually bear representations on only one side. Only ten of these tokens have a letter or letters on the other side. Most Agora examples were found in and around public buildings alongside public objects. Their find contexts suggest, albeit not conclusively, that they were used by the Athenian government. Most of these clay tokens date from the fourth and the first half of the third centuries BC.[17] According to Crosby, clay tokens bearing letters may have been used at law courts in a similar way to the bronze and lead tokens.[18] She suggests that all the clay tokens known from more than one example may have been tokens that the citizens were given in order to participate in the Assembly or the Council. They would exchange these tokens for the money due them. It cannot be excluded that they were theatre tickets, even though those found in the excavations of the Agora do not fall into this category.[19]

There is only a limited similarity between the types of the clay tokens of the Numismatic Museum and the clay tokens of the Athenian Agora. A retrograde Rho type appears on a clay token found in the northwest area of the Agora from a fourth century BC context. In this case the other side of the token depicts a cock and it has been identified as a token used in the law courts (a dikastic *symbolon*).[20] An Upsilon appears on a clay token found in a Roman context in the Great Drain southeast of the Tholos, with a woman's head on the other side.[21] The same woman's head is observed on clay tokens of the Numismatic Museum, here combined with the letter Psi on the other side.[22]

An additional unifying factor of the clay tokens of the Numismatic Museum is the type and colour of the clay. It is a reddish clay, sometimes orange, at other times darker. The clay

[14] On the use of tokens in Athens see Crosby (1964), 77–78 with previous bibliography and reference to written sources of antiquity.
[15] Kourouniotis' excavations: Kourouniotis (1910).
[16] Crosby (1964), 124–30, pl. 31–32.
[17] Crosby (1964), 125.
[18] Crosby (1964), 125, n. 9.
[19] Crosby (1964), 125–26.
[20] Crosby (1964), 126, cat. no. C4, pl. 31.
[21] Crosby (1964), 126, cat. no. C5A, pl. 31.
[22] Svoronos (1905), 325, no. 5, pl. IX.6; Crosby (1964), 127.

tokens found in the Athenian Agora seem to have the same clay colour in several cases.[23] Traces of red glaze are observed on two clay tokens of the Numismatic Museum (cat. no. 23, fig. 10 and cat. no. 28, fig. 11), another common feature found on the clay tokens of the Athenian Agora.[24] As was previously mentioned, the similarities between the material of these tokens are based on personal observation and references in bibliography rather than scientific or specialist analysis.

Functions of the clay letter tokens

Clay tokens bearing letters of the Greek alphabet on one side is without a doubt the most important group examined in this paper. What is impressive and at the same time odd is the fact that the number of published Athenian clay tokens bearing such letters is overly small. This is true for tokens published among the finds both from the Athenian Agora and the Pnyx. The new pieces published here more than triples the total specimens known. Another issue that raises questions is that clay tokens coming from the excavations of the Athenian Agora and the Pnyx are individual finds, whereas the group presented in this paper seems to have a certain coherence and homogeneity, even though they lack an excavation context. Moreover, their thorough study in comparison to the previously published tokens could lead to the compilation of series, the identification of common dies, and shared iconographic types with tokens from clay or another material. This prospect was not possible in the past. However, this will be the topic of a future detailed paper.

These tokens are related to the workings of the Athenian government.[25] Specifically those that bear the letters of the Greek alphabet are thought to be used either as entrance tickets for citizens to attend religious festivals such as the Greater Dionysia, for citizens' attendance at the law courts or at the Assembly, or to later collect the money due to them from the state for their participation. Another use attributed to the tokens pertains to the free distribution of goods.[26]

According to Professor J. H. Kroll (via personal communication) the double lines of the letters may indicate the doubling of letters, as one finds in some Greek alphabetic-numeral sequences. This idea was already suggested by Svoronos on the otherwise out-dated plan of the seating sections of the Dionysos Theatre.[27] We now possess a large number of types, with single or double letters combined with a variety of representations on the other side. The total number is more than 25, the number of seats in the law courts. If the theory these tokens represented seating is correct, then the number of combinations leads to the conclusion that these clay tokens were intended for a larger body, presumably the Assembly.[28] A future study may supplement Table 1 and complete this series of clay tokens, leading to more conclusions concerning their use.

Conclusion

One may therefore conclude that, even if we associate tokens from museum collections with their counterparts from specific excavation contexts or from identified places of origin, the exact provenance of the former may not be easily specified. The tokens may have been found anywhere, away from their original production locus or from the site in which they were used. Even so, considering the above restrictions, a comparative study between museum tokens and tokens of known origin may still be argued to be beneficial in multiple ways.

With the methodology introduced by the present paper, groups of similar tokens or tokens with identical provenances may be unified. Secondly, certain groups may be assigned to their

[23] Crosby (1964), 125–26, cat. nos. C3–5, pl. 31.

[24] Crosby (1964), 125, cat. no. C1 pl. 31.

[25] Svoronos (1898) and (1900) believed that all these tokens were used for governmental purposes. See also Pickard-Cambridge (1953), 272–75; Boegehold (1960), 393–401; Guarducci (1969), 453–54; Kroll and Mitchel (1980); Kroll (2015), 114–15.

[26] Crosby (1964), 77, with bibliography concerning the *theorikon*, the *ekklesiastikon*, the *dikastikon*, the *bouleutikon* and the *sitonikon*.

[27] Svoronos (1898), 44–45, pl. A. Cf. the double-lettered bronze tokens in Svoronos (1923–1926), pl. 101, nos. 40–41.

[28] I would like to thank Professor Kroll for his interest in the subject of my presentation and for his utterly significant observation, as well as his permission for me to include it in this text.

place or places of origin, and, third, new examples may be added to the known specimens. Sometimes the new examples may give new information on fragmentary iconographic representations, as we have shown above. Fourth, tokens may be classified into series if we assume that examples with the same 'obverses' but with different 'reverses' may have formed part of a systematic production pattern in the same way as coins. One might thus initiate a valuable inventory of tokens, which might serve as a prerequisite for their subsequent linking with excavation finds.

Last but not least, bringing forth the significance of such small finds might increase the excavator's awareness of these objects, resulting in more careful collection and study. It may also possibly allow us to identify tokens that still appear in trade illegally. The specimens from the Numismatic Museum in Athens may thus be taken to constitute a case study which not only illustrates the difficulties in contextualising this material, but also highlights the potential benefits that may spring from engaging in this detailed but promising endeavour.

Catalogue[29]

Hexagonal shaped token.

Side a[30]: Frontal bust of priest.
Side b: Two human figures. Possibly a banquet scene. On the left, the impression of a private stamp can be distinguished. An inscription is in the exergue.

1. NM[31] 214/2005 (fig. 1) (Ø 26mm, 12h). Makrypodi (2016), fig. 1.

Square shaped token.

Side a: Bust of a deity flanked by stars.
Side b: A wreath.

2. NM 229/2005 (fig. 2) (16 x 16mm, 12h). Makrypodi (2016), fig. 2.

Rectangular shaped token.

Side a: Two human figures either side of an altar. Scene of incense offering.
Side b: Two gods reclining on a couch. Scene of a sacred marriage. An inscription is in the exergue.

3. NM 235/2005 (fig. 3) (13 x 12mm, 3h). Makrypodi (2016), fig. 3.

Oval shaped token. Uniface.

Bearded head right.

4. NM without inv. no. (fig. 4) (16 x 20mm). Provenance: Athens. Svoronos (1905), 329, no. 24, pl. IX, 24.
5. NM 231/2005 (fig. 5) (15 x 18mm).
6. PNT[32] 134 (fig. 6) (18mm). Provenance: Pnyx. Davidson and Thompson (1943), 107–08, fig. 48.14.

Circle shaped token.

Side a: Herm right, bush with three branches in the field r., *kerykeion* in the field l.
Side b: Sampi in double lines.[33]

7. NM 1929/36 (Π67) (fig. 7) (Ø 17mm, 1h). Konstantopoulos (1930–1931), 32, cat. no. γ, fig. 3, the third seen from above (this specimen).
8. NM 1929/35 (Π66) (Ø 17mm, 4h). Konstantopoulos (1930–1931), 36, cat. no. 4, fig. 9, the fourth seen from above (this specimen).
9. NM 1929/12 (Π43) (Ø 17mm, 4h).
10. NM 1932/KE' /8 (Π27) (Ø 19mm, 5h).
11. NM 1932/KE'/7 (Π26) (Ø 17mm, 4h).
12. NM H4/1931 (Π16) (Ø 18mm, 12h).

[29] All the tokens catalogued were previously unpublished, unless otherwise specified.
[30] We consider it more appropriate to use the terms side a and side b instead obverse and reverse, usually used to describe coins, because the way these particular objects are made differs from that of coins.
[31] The NM inventory numbers refer to the Numismatic Museum.
[32] The PNT inventory number refers to the American School of Classical Studies excavations.
[33] On the Sampi and its function: Boegehold (1960), 398–99; Boegehold (1995), 69–70.

Circle shaped token.

Side a: Herm right, bush with three branches in the field r., *kerykeion* in the field l.
Side b: Upsilon.

13. NM H6/1931 (Π18) (fig. 8) (Ø 17mm, 6h). Konstantopoulos (1930–1931), 36, cat. no. 5, fig. 9, the fifth seen from above (this specimen).
14. NM 1932/KE/5 (Π24) (Ø 18mm, 2h).
15. NM 221/2005 (Ø 17mm, 3h).
16. NM 234/2005 (Ø 18mm, 1h).

Circle shaped token.

Side a: Herm right, bush with three branches in the field r., *kerykeion* in the field l.
Side b: Xi in double lines.

17. NM 1929/13 (Π44) (Ø 18mm, 12h).
18. NM 1929/14 (Π45) (Ø 17mm, 11h).
19. NM 1929/15 (Π46) (fig. 23) (Ø 18mm, 11h).

Circle shaped token.

Side a: Human head right bearing little wings.
Side b: Sigma (or Mu).[34]

20. NM 1930/KH (Lerakis 1929 B') (Π11) (fig. 9) (Ø 15mm, 1h or 4h). Konstantopoulos (1930–1931), 32, cat. no. δ fig. 3, the fourth seen from above.

Circle shaped token.

Side a: Human head right bearing little wings.
Side b: Phi.

21. NM 1929/22 (Π53) (Ø 14mm, 11h).
22. NM 1929/21 (Π52) (Ø 14mm, 12h).
23. NM H7/1931 (Π19) (fig. 10) (13 x 15mm, 9h).
24. NM 1929 (Lerakis)/H5 (Π8) (12 x 15mm, 3h). Cf. Konstantopoulos (1930–1931), 36, cat. no. 6 fig. 9, sixth seen from above. None of the above specimens matches the one published by Konstantopoulos. A tentative identification would be with cat. no. 23.

Circle shaped token.

Side a: Human head right bearing little wings.
Side b: Chi.

25. NM 1929/23 (Π54) (fig. 22) (Ø 14mm, 10h).
26. NM 1929/24 (Π55) (Ø 14mm, 2h).
27. NM 243/2005 (Ø 15mm, 12h).

Circle shaped token.

Side a: Dove right.
Side b: Omicron in double lines.

28. NM H3/1931 (Π15) (fig. 11) (Ø 17mm, 6h or 12h). Konstantopoulos (1930–1931), 36, cat. no. 3 fig. 9, the third seen from above (this specimen).

Circle shaped token.

Side a: Dove right.
Side b: Upsilon in double lines.

29. NM 8146 (Ø 18mm).[35] Museum exchange, allegedly found in Athens. Svoronos (1905), 325, cat. no. 3 pl. IX, 3 (this specimen).
30. NM 1929 (Lerakis)/H5 (Π7) (fig. 20) (Ø 15mm, 2h).
31. NM 247/2005 (Ø 16mm, 11h).

[34] Cf. the discussion in Boegehold (1960), 396.
[35] Die axis is not indicated in the publication of Svoronos.

Circle shaped token.

Side a: Dove right.
Side b: Zeta in double lines.

32. NM 1929/34 (Π65) (fig. 21) (Ø 17mm, 11h).

Circle shaped token.

Side a: Tripod.
Side b: Sampi in double lines.

33. NM H1/1931 (Π13) (fig. 12) (Ø 16mm, 9h). Konstantopoulos (1930–1931), 36, cat. no. 7, fig. 9, the seventh seen from above (this specimen).
34. NM 1932/KE'/6 (Π25) (Ø 16mm, 4h).
35. NM 241/2005 (Ø 15mm, 1h).
36. NM 286/2005 (fig. 14) (Ø 17mm, 2h).

Circle shaped token.

Side a: Horse right, with a bird on its back.
Side b: Rho retrograde in double lines.

37. NM H2/1931 (Π14) (fig. 13) (Ø 17mm, 7h). Konstantopoulos (1930–1931), 36, cat. no. 1, fig. 9, the first seen from above (this specimen).
38. NM 1929/33 (Π64) (fig. 24) (Ø 18mm, 2h).

Circle shaped token.

Side a: Horse right.
Side b: Xi.

39. NM 268/2005 (fig. 25) (Ø 15mm, 12h).

Circle shaped token.

Side a: Head of Apollo right.
Side b: Sphinx right.

40. NM 1928/H5 (Vlasto's donation) (Π5) (Ø 15mm, 12h).
41. NM 1929/3 (Π32) (fig. 15) (Ø 16mm, 3h).
42. NM 1929/6 (Π37) (Ø 16mm, 4h).
43. NM 1929/7 (Π38) (Ø 16mm, 2h).
44. NM 1929/4 (Π35) (Ø 17mm, 3h).
45. NM 1929/5 (Π36) (Ø 15mm, 4h).
46. NM1929/8 (Π39) (Ø 15mm, 4h).
47. NM1929/9 (Π40) (Ø 14mm, 8h).
48. NM 1932/KE'/2 (Π21) (Ø 18mm, 11h).
49. NM 254/2005 (Ø 16mm, 4h).

Circle shaped token.

Side a: Rose.
Side b: Pi in double lines.

50. NM 1929/39 (Π70) (fig. 16) (Ø 17mm, 7h).
51. NM 222/2005 (Ø 17mm, 9h).

Circle shaped token.

Side a: Young man riding a deer right.
Side b: Artemis driving deer chariot right.

52. NM Athens 8143 (Ø 20mm.)[36] Provenance: S. Lafazani. Svoronos (1905), 330, cat. no. 31, pl. X.1.
53. NM 1929 (Lerakis)/ Π5 (Π6) (fig. 17) (Ø 18mm, 1h).
54. NM 1932/KE'/1 (Π20) (Ø 17mm, 7h).
55. NM 1929/1 (Π32) (Ø 17mm, 9h).
56. NM 1929/40 (Π71) (Ø 16mm, 1h). Provenance: Tsamado's donation.
57. NM 248/2005 (Ø 17mm, 1h).

[36] Die axis is not indicated in the publication of Svoronos.

Circle shaped token.

Side a: Wreath.
Side b: Beta in double lines.

58. NM 1929/31 (Π62) (fig. 18) (Ø 17mm, 9h).
59. NM 215/2005 (Ø 17mm, 2h).
60. NM 226/2005 (Ø 19mm, 7h).
61. NM 242/2005 (Ø 17mm, 7h).

Circle shaped token.

Side a: Wreath.
Side b: Gamma or Pi.

62. NM 1929/32 (Π63) (fig. 19) (Ø 17mm, 9h).

Table 1: A summary of clay tokens in the Numismatic Museum of Athens.

Side a / Side b	**Svoronos 1905**	**1928–1929**	***Arch. Deltion* 1930–1931**	**1929–1932**	**2005**	**Total**
HERM/ SAMPI in double lines			2	4		6
HERM/ Ξ in double lines				3		3
HERM / Y			1	1	2	4
HUMAN HEAD / Φ			1	3		4
HUMAN HEAD / Σ			1			1
HUMAN HEAD / X				2	1	3
TRIPOD / SAMPI in double lines			1	1	2	4
HORSE / P retrograde in double lines			1	1		2
HORSE / Ξ					1	1
DOVE / O in double lines			1			1
DOVE / Y in double lines	1			1	1	3
DOVE / Z in double lines				1		1
APOLLO / SPHINX		1		8	1	10
ROSE / Π				1	1	2
YOUNG MAN / ARTEMIS	1	1		3	1	6
WREATH / B				1	3	4
WREATH/ Γ or Π				1		1

Bibliography

Al-As'ad, Briquel-Chatonnet and Yon 2005: K. Al-As'ad, Fr. Briquel-Chatonnet, and J.-B. Yon, 'The sacred banquets at Palmyra and the function of the *tesserae*: Reflections on the tokens found in the Arşu temple', in Cussini (ed.) (2005), 1–10.

Ando and Rüpke (eds.) 2015: C. Ando and J. Rüpke (eds.), *Public and Private in Ancient Mediterranean Law and Religion* (Berlin, 2015).

Boegehold 1960: A. Boegehold, 'Aristotle's *Athenaion Politeia*, 65.2: The «Official Token»', *Hesperia* 29 (1960), 393–402.

Boegehold 1995: A. Boegehold, *The Athenian Agora XXVIII: The Lawcourts at Athens: Sites, Buildings, Equipment, Procedure and Testimonia* (Princeton, 1995).

Crosby 1964: M. Crosby, 'Lead and clay tokens. Part II', in Lang and Crosby (1964), 69–146.

Cussini (ed.) 2005: E. Cussini (ed.), *A Journey to Palmyra. Collected Essays to Remember Delbert R. Hillers. Culture & History of the Ancient Near East 22* (Leiden, 2005).

Davidson and Burr Thompson 1943: G. R. Davidson and D. Burr Thompson, *Small Objects from the Pnyx: I, Hesperia Supplement* 7 (Princeton, 1943).

Guarducci 1969: M. Guarducci, *Epigrafia Greca II* (Rome, 1969).

Hansen 1989: M. H. Hansen, *The Athenian Ecclesia II. A Collection of Articles, 1983-1989* (Copenhagen ,1989).

Ingholt, Seyrig, Starcky and Caquot 1955: H. Ingholt, H., Seyrig, J. Starcky, and A. Caquot, *Recueil des tessères de Palmyre* (Paris, 1955).

Konstantopoulos 1930–1931: K. M. Konstantopoulos, 'Προσκτήματα του Εθνικού Νομισματικού Μουσείου', ΑΔ 13 (1930–31), 30–37.

Kourouniotis 1910: K. Kourouniotis, 'Ανασκαφή Πνυκός', *Praktika* 65 (1910), 127–36.

Kroll 2015: J. H. Kroll, 'Small bronze tokens from the Athenian Agora: *symbola* or *kollyboi*?', in Wartenberg and Amandry (eds.) (2015), 107–16.

Kroll and Mitchel 1980: J. H. Kroll and F. W. Mitchel, 'Clay tokens with the names of Athenian military commanders', *Hesperia* 49 (1980), 86–96.

Lang and Crosby 1964: M. Lang and M. Crosby, *The Athenian Agora X: Weights, Measures and Tokens* (Princeton, 1964).

Makrypodi 2016: S. Makrypodi, 'The tokens (*tesserae*) of Palmyra. New data from the collections of the Numismatic Museum (Note 1)', *Archaeology and Arts*, 13 June 2016 (http://www.archaeology.wiki/blog/2016/06/13/tokens-tesserae-palmyra/) (accessed 26/07/2018).

Pickard-Cambridge 1953: A. Pickard-Cambridge, *The Dramatic Festivals of Athens* (Oxford, 1953).

Raja 2015: R. Raja, 'Staging "private" religion in Roman "public" Palmyra. The role of the religious dining tickets (banqueting *tesserae*)', in Rüpke and Ando (eds.) (2015), 165–86.

Rostowzew 1905: M. Rostowzew, 'Interprétation des tessères en os avec figures, chiffres et légendes', *RA* 5 (1905), 110–24.

Rotroff and Camp 1996: S. I. Rotroff and J. Mc K. Camp, 'The date of the third period of the Pnyx', *Hesperia* 65 (1996), 263–94.

Smith 2013: A. Smith, *Roman Palmyra. Identity, Community & State Formation* (Oxford, 2013).

Svoronos 1898: I. N. Svoronos, 'Περί των Εισιτηρίων των Αρχαίων Μέρος Α΄: Εισιτήρια χαλκά του Λυκούργειου Διονυσιακού Θεάτρου και της Κλεισθενείου Εκκλησίας του Δήμου', *JIAN* 1 (1898), 37–120.

Svoronos 1900: I. N. Svoronos, 'Κατάλογος των Μολύβδινων Συμβόλων του Εθνικού Νομισματικού Μουσείου Μέρος Α΄: Ενεπίγραφα', *JIAN* 3 (1900), 322–43.

Svoronos 1905: I. N. Svoronos, 'Αρχαία πήλινα σύμβολα και εκμαγεια νομισμάτων και δακτυλιολίθων (Εισιτήρια Θεάτρων και Χαρώνεια Νομίσματα)', *JIAN* 8 (1905), 323–38.

Svoronos 1923–1926: I. N. Svoronos, *Les Monnaies d'Athénes. Trésor de la Numismatique Grecque Ancienne* (Munich, 1923–26).

Wartenberg and Amandry (eds.) 2015: U. Wartenberg and M. Amandry (eds.), ΚΑΙΡΟΣ. Contributions to Numismatics in *Honor of Basil Demetriadi* (New York, 2015).

THE ARMOUR TOKENS FROM THE ATHENIAN AGORA

MARTIN SCHÄFER

Introduction

The subject of this study is a group of Hellenistic tokens from the political centre of ancient Athens, the ancient Agora, which mostly depict defensive armour and which therefore differ greatly from the usual depictions on Athenian tokens.[1] Nine lead tokens (cat. nos. I.a–I.i, figs. 1–9) were found in 1971 in a well in the northwest corner of the Athenian Agora (figs. 10–11), opposite the Royal Stoa within the intersection of the Panathenaic Way and the West Road, only three metres north of a small square sanctuary, the so-called Crossroads Enclosure (fig. 12).[2] They were published by J.H. Kroll only a few years after their discovery.[3] Depicted on one side of the tokens is a symbol – a helmet, greave, corselet, shield (decorated with an Alpha) or the figure of Nike – and on the other side is a letter – A, Γ or Δ (I.a–I.i, figs. 1–9). The diameter of the tokens, whose fields are all deeply sunk because they were restruck,[4] varies between 18 and 23mm, their thickness from around 2 to 4mm. Before taking a closer look at the tokens themselves, as well as similar examples and their iconography, it is necessary to recall briefly the context of their discovery and discuss the distribution of weapons to Athenian citizens for the period in question, the third century.

The Crossroads Well and its contents

The well contained rich finds that mostly date from the Classical to the Hellenistic periods. The excavator T. Leslie Shear Jr. believed, on the basis of the striking differences in content, that the finds from these periods were probably 'dumps from two distinct sources': a small sanctuary, the so-called Crossroads Enclosure, lying almost three metres south of the well (figs. 11–12),[5] and a public office, the exact location of which is unknown.[6] Unearthed beneath an upper level dating to the Byzantine period, the lower strata of the well shaft date from the late fifth to the early second centuries BC. Most of the material from the lower fill of the well consisted of vases and other dedications similar to those found in the Crossroads Enclosure.[7] These finds could be interpreted as

Fig. 1: Cat. no. I.a. AM, IL 1575, Pb token (Ø 19mm) (photo by K.-V. von Eickstedt).

Fig. 2: Cat. no. I.b. AM, IL 1574, Pb token (Ø 20mm) (photo by K.-V. von Eickstedt).

[1] For the permission to study unpublished tokens in the Numismatic Museum I am very grateful to its director G. Kakavas and to Y. Nikolaou, V. Stephanaki and A. Nikolakopoulou. I am indebted also to the Ephoreia of Antiquities of the City of Athens, Prof. J. Mck. Camp and especially to S. Dumont for the permission and assistance to study published and unpublished material from the Agora excavations. I am most grateful also to M. Gkikaki, E. Vikela and K. Papoutsis for helpful remarks and other support. Additional abbreviations: AM = Athens, Agora Museum; NM = Athens, Numismatic Museum; *ARV*^{2} = J.D. Beazley, *Attic Red-figure Vase-painters*^{2} (3 vols.) (Oxford, 1963); *IDélos* = *Inscriptions de Délos; IG = Inscriptiones Graecae;* IGCH = *Inventory of Greek Coin Hoards; SEG = Supplementum Epigraphicum Graecum*. For an overview of the tokens from Athens see Postolacca (1868); Engel (1884); Svoronos (1900). All images of tokens reproduced at 2:1.

[2] For the 'Crossroads Well' (Agora Deposit J 5:1) and its contents see Shear (1973a), 130–34, fig. 1, pl. 25a, 26a, 27f, 27h, 28a–o, 36a–d, 39a–g, 165–68, pl. 36a–d, 176–79, pl. 39a–g. See also Kroll (1977a), 84; Monaco (2004), 28–32; Camp (2010), 86; Di Cesare (2014c), 978–79, fig. 591.

[3] Kroll (1977b).

[4] Kroll (1977b), 141.

[5] For the Crossroads Enclosure see Shear (1973a), 126–30, 134, fig. 1, pl. 25–27e; Shear (1973b), 360–69, figs. 1–2, pl. 65–67; Camp (2010), 84–86, figs. 51–53; Di Cesare (2014c), and Rotroff and Lynch (forthcoming), who are preparing the final publication of the complex of discovery.

[6] See Shear (1973a), 131; Monaco (2004), 29.

[7] See Shear (1973a), 131.

Fig. 3: Cat. no. I.c. AM, IL 1573, Pb token (Ø 23mm) (photo by K.-V. von Eickstedt).

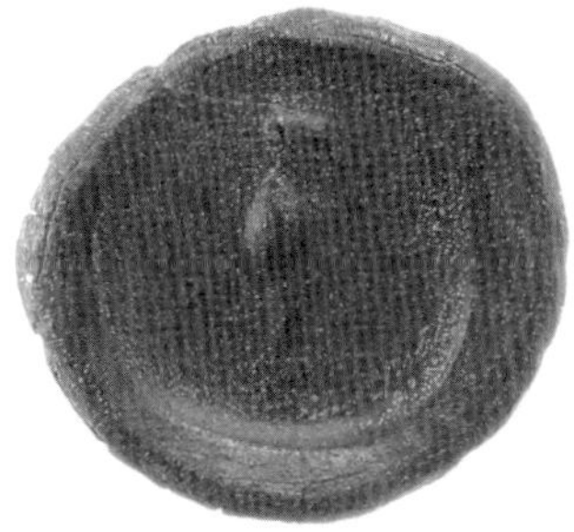

Fig. 4: Cat. no. I.d. AM, IL 1572, Pb token (Ø 21mm) (photo by K.-V. von Eickstedt).

Fig. 5: Cat. no. I.e. AM, IL 1576, Pb token (Ø 21mm) (photo by K.-V. von Eickstedt).

Fig. 6: Cat. no. I.f. AM, IL 1577, Pb token (Ø 18mm) (photo by K.-V. von Eickstedt).

Fig. 7: Cat. no. I.g. AM, IL 1579, Pb token (Ø 20mm) (photo by K.-V. von Eickstedt).

Fig. 8: Cat. no. I.h. AM, IL 1578, Pb token (Ø 22mm) (photo by K.-V. von Eickstedt).

dedications from this very sanctuary, which according to similar finds from within the enclosure itself was in use from the fifth until the end of the fourth century.[8] They suggest that the divinity or divinities venerated there were female.[9] These objects were found in the lower strata of the shaft; the pottery in the upper part, dating to the third and early second century, seems not to be connected with dedicatory practices according to the excavator.[10]

Also found in the same well were 30 clay tokens from the fourth century naming Pheidon of Thria as the hipparch on Lemnos, which was by this time an Athenian cleruchy governed by this official.[11] Pheidon is known from a literary source, Mnesimachos (mentioned in Athenaeus, *Deipnosophistae* 9.402f), as the official responsible for the training of cavalry recruits in mounting and dismounting at a location called 'the Herms', which was in the northwest corner of the ancient Agora, in the immediate environs of the well, and which had

[8] Shear (1973a), 128; Shear (1973b), 364, 366–67, 369. However, the precise end of use still needs clarification: see Shear (1973a), 134.

[9] Shear (1973a), 134; Camp (2010), 85; see also Shear (1973b), 369; Di Cesare (2014c), 978–79. However, according to Rotroff and Lynch (forthcoming), there are also other possibilities regarding the final interpretation of the determination of the complex.

[10] Shear (1973a), 133–34.

[11] For the clay tokens see Shear (1973a), 178–79, pl. 39b and f–g; Kroll and Mitchel (1980), 89–91, pl. 14; *SEG* 30.114 (2); Camp (2010), 108, fig. 70. For the Athenian cleruchy on Lemnos see Clinton (2014). For the hipparch on Lemnos see Bugh (1988), 209–18; Spence (1993), 316–18.

Fig. 9: Cat. no. I.i. AM, IL 1580, Pb token (Ø 20mm) (photo by K.-V. von Eickstedt).

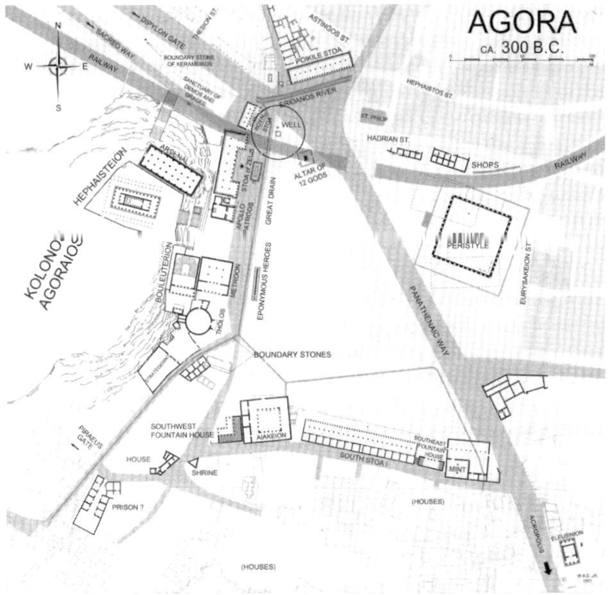

Fig. 10: Plan of the ancient Agora, Athens, ca. 300 BC. Crossroads Enclosure and Well in the centre of the circle (courtesy of the Agora Excavations, American School of Classical Studies at Athens; reproduction after Camp (2010), 20, fig. 4).

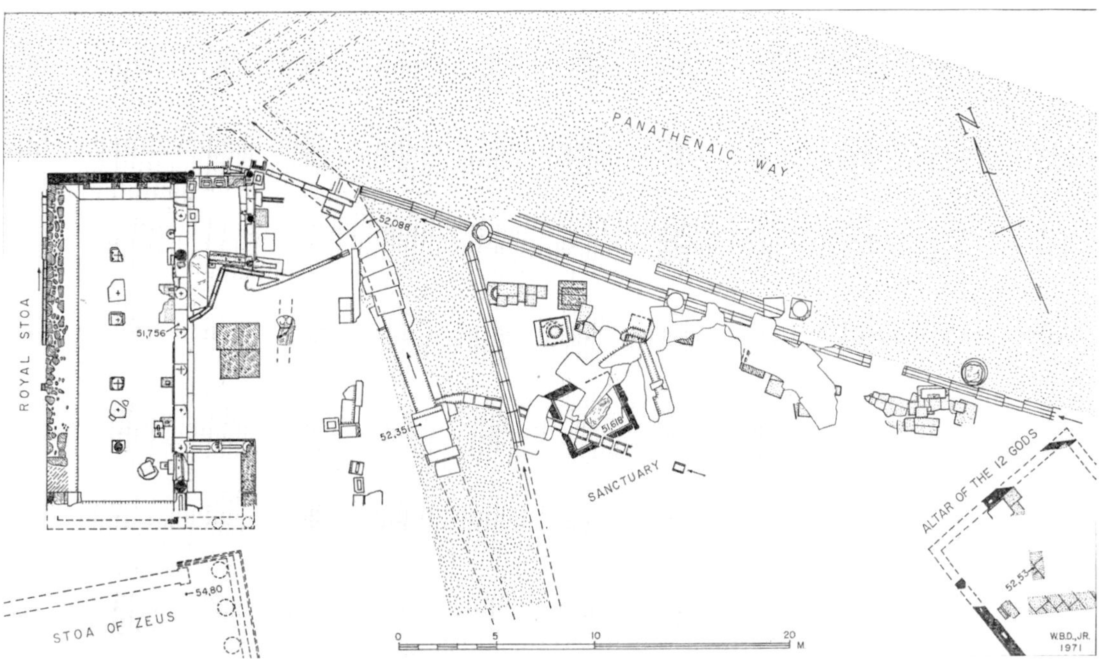

Fig. 11: Plan of the northwest corner of the ancient Agora, Athens, with Crossroads Sanctuary and Well. Reproduction after Shear (1973a), 123, fig. 1.

special links with the cavalry.[12] These tokens have been interpreted as 'credentials', that is to say a kind of official passport which were used by 'persons sent out from Athens to the commanders', such as 'official couriers on state business and private individuals' guarantee-

[12] For 'the Herms' see Di Cesare (2014a), 945–49; Di Cesare (2015), 63–64. For the connection of this area with the Athenian cavalry see Schäfer (forthcoming).

Fig. 12: Crossroads Enclosure with Crossroads Well in front, ancient Agora, Athens (today's view from the North) (photo by author).

ing 'a safe passage…or favoured treatment'.[13] Bugh proposes their use also by 'replacement *hippeis*…for their journey to Lemnos' as part of a suggested system of rotation of the cavalrymen, who were sent to the island.[14]

In addition to these tokens, 111 inscribed lead tablets came to light.[15] On one side they bear the name of the owner of a cavalry horse in the genitive case and on the other side the same name is given with additional information about the horse: its colour, the designation of a symbol with which the horse was branded (such as an axe, eagle, serpent, caduceus, Nike etc. or the word ἄσημος (*asēmos*), 'unmarked'),[16] and finally the price, indicated by the word τίμημα (*timēma*) and the sum of money, in hundreds of *drachmae*, i.e. 100–1,200,[17] or in *minae*. In two cases from the third century a πρόδρομος (*prodromos*) is mentioned, a

[13] Kroll and Mitchel (1980), 95–96.
[14] Bugh (1988), 215–16.
[15] Shear (1973a), 176–79, pl. 39a; Kroll (1977a); see also Bugh (1988), 57–58.
[16] Braun (1970), 251–67; Kroll (1977a), 86–88; see also Blaineau (2015), 129–30.
[17] Braun (1970), 267.

mounted scout or mounted aide of a cavalry officer.[18] Twenty-six of the tablets are from deeper in the well with pottery from the second half of the fourth century, while the greater number, 85 pieces, were thrown in the well together with the armour tokens at a later time, as indicated by pottery of the third century and some coins of Antigonos Gonatas. According to Shear this was 'about the middle of the third century', or, according to Kroll, in the 'middle or third quarter of the third century'.[19] These lead tablets have been interpreted by Braun, who published more than 550 similar specimens found in a well at the Dipylon Gate at Kerameikos,[20] and also by Kroll, as archive records relating to the annual evaluation of cavalry horses (called *timēsis*), which is mentioned in inscriptions of the first half of the third century BC.[21] In this way, i.e. by recording the actual value of the mount annually, the fair reimbursement of a state loan called *katastasis*, which was provided for the acquisition of a horse for each new recruit, could be guaranteed in case of its loss in action.[22]

Also thrown in the well was a bronze spear butt, belonging to the same level as ten of the lead tablets already mentioned and seven clay sealings of Pheidon. According to the inscription on the spear butt it was dedicated to the Dioscuri from the spoils of war taken from the Lesbians, probably as a result of the Athenian campaign in 428/27 BC.[23] However its connection with the cavalry, suggested by some scholars,[24] is no more than hypothetical, since it was dedicated by the *Athenaioi* and not by members of the cavalry or its officers.[25]

Remarkably, the remains of an early Hellenistic gilded bronze equestrian statue were also found in the well, deposited together with pottery at about 200 or slightly earlier. The statue is hypothetically linked with the Macedonian rulers Antigonos Monophthalmos or Demetrios Poliorketes.[26] Besides the above-mentioned finds other lead tablets of a private character from the fourth century were also discovered, mostly curse tablets, indicating that the well probably contained dumps from more than two sources.[27]

The two sets of lead tokens

This observed concentration of finds related to the cavalry led Kroll to consider it very likely that the lead tokens, like the other two categories of military archive material mentioned above, were connected with the Athenian cavalry. They probably came from its headquarters, the so-called Hipparcheion,[28] which is generally believed to be located not far from the well in the northwest corner of the ancient Agora (fig. 10).[29] Unfortunately, the exact location of the Hipparcheion is not yet known, but – bearing in mind that, unlike the Stoa of the Herms, it is mentioned only once to date in the epigraphic material[30] – it is not impossible that it may

[18] Braun (1970), 234, 239, no. 565; Shear (1973a), 177; Kroll (1977a), 85, 125–27, no. 62, fig. 8, pl. 37. For the *prodromoi* see also Bugh (1988), 222–24; Spence (1993), 134, 150, 151, 274; Camp (1996), 256–57.

[19] Shear (1973a), 177–78; Kroll (1977a), 84–85; Camp (1996), 256; cf. also Bugh (1988), 189.

[20] Braun (1970), 198–269.

[21] Braun (1970), 267–69; Shear (1973a), 177; Kroll (1977a), 85–86, 97–100; Bugh (1988), 57–58, 189.

[22] Bugh (1988), 53, 56–58.

[23] AM, B 1373: Camp (1978); *IG* I^3 521bis; *SEG* 58.56; Baitinger (2011), 15–16, fig. 6. Camp (1978), 195 mentions that the level is dated 'to the middle of the fourth century or earlier', which does not seem to correspond with the chronological assignment given by Shear (n. 19 above).

[24] e.g. Di Cesare (2014b), 959–60, fig. 576b; Di Cesare (2015), 74.

[25] See also Camp (1978), 194–95.

[26] Shear (1973a), 165–68, pl. 36; Batino (2001), 64–65, fig. 6; Gawlinski (2014), 155–56, fig. 94.

[27] See Jordan (1985), 209, table 1, 210, n. 6 and table 2; Jordan (2000); *SEG* 50.276. Jordan (2000), 91 dates the tablets merely to the fourth century BC.

[28] Kroll (1977a), 84; Kroll (1977b), 145; Monaco (2004), 29–30; Aldrete, Bartell and Aldrete (2013), 76–77; Di Cesare (2014c), 979 (with caution); see also Jarva (1995), 130.

[29] Habicht (1961), 138; Shear (1973a), 179; Bugh (1988), 64; Camp (1996), 259. For the possible locations of the Hipparcheion see Monaco (2004), 31–32, who proposes to locate it northwest of the Crossroads Well or in its vicinity. Its localisation immediately west of the northern part of the Stoa of Zeus was proposed by Thompson (see e.g. Wycherley (1978), 46, n. 48; Habicht (1982), 93, n. 73) and recently by Di Cesare (2014d), 989, figs. 598–600 a–e; Di Cesare (2015), 71–74, fig. 104, no. 4, figs. 105, 122–25; see also Longo (2014a), 875. For the Hipparcheion in general see Bugh (1988), 219–20 Appendix C; Monaco (2004), 19–20, 30–34; Di Cesare (2014a), 947–48; Di Cesare (2014b), 959–60; Di Cesare (2014c), 979; Di Cesare (2014d), 989.

[30] Pointed out by Monaco (2004), 19–20. *IG* II^2 895 = *IG* II^3 1, 5, no. 1281b; *SEG* 21.436 (187/86 BC); see also Di Cesare (2014b), 959, fig. 575.

have been situated within the Stoa of the Herms, which also has not been located with certainty yet.[31]

Kroll believes that the tokens were the means by which the state distributed state-owned armour to the citizens in arms serving in the cavalry of Hellenistic Athens. It was expected that the men of the cavalry, as in the Classical period, would purchase their weapons and other equipment; only the acquisition of their mount was supported financially by means of the *katastasis*, the government loan already mentioned.[32] In addition to this, they received a wage, called *misthos*, and a grain allowance, called *sitos*.[33] However, on an inscription it is recorded that the hipparch of 220/19 BC, Theophrastos, paid for the feeding of the mounts of the cavalrymen and – by means of a financial donation of ten *minae* given to the officers – the improvement of their armour.[34]

While the majority of the symbols represent – as we have seen – a corresponding piece of armour (helmet, shield, greaves, corselet), the Nike (I.i, fig. 9), according to Kroll, would have represented 'a military standard' or most likely a weapon which was difficult to display iconographically, such as a sword or spear, which are the only pieces of equipment of a panoply that are missing from the repertoire of symbols. The letters A, Γ or Δ on the reverse could – according to Kroll – represent the size of the certain piece of armour. Tokens representing pieces of armour for which the exact size is important, namely the corselet, helmet and greaves, are found with Γ or Δ on the reverse, and only the shield, which was supposed to be a standard size, is linked on both tokens with an Alpha. The letter Alpha inside the shield (I.g, I.h, figs. 7–8) has been interpreted as indicating 'A[θηναίοι], 'A[θηναίος] or 'A[θήνη], i.e. *Athenaioi* (Athenians) or *Athenaios* (Athenian) or *Athene* (the goddess Athena).[35] Already in the Classical period there were Alpha *episemata* (shield devices in form of an Alpha) on depictions of Attic vases. For example, a Nolan amphora (ca. 440–435 BC), a work by the Phiale Painter (fig. 13), shows a young man or ephebe wearing a himation and holding a helmet, and opposite him a woman holding his shield with an Alpha blazon.[36]

A second, smaller set of related tokens was found in a closed context in the southwest corner of the ancient Agora, mixed in with 92 bronze and two silver coins from the late fourth and the early third centuries, together with pottery and other finds. The coins provide a date for the deposit in the second quarter of the third century or slightly later.[37] Three of the four tokens, all originally 17–18.5mm in diameter with badly worn reliefs, illustrate respectively a corselet (II.a, fig. 14), a shield with an Alpha blazon surrounded by dots (II.b, fig. 15) and – absent in the set of tokens from the well – a strung bow (II.c, fig. 16). The fourth was badly preserved and is now lost (II.d). If the latter depicted a helmet, according to Kroll the four tokens would have represented a complete panoply, which a citizen, who must have hidden the tokens and coins, had at his disposal to exchange for the armour itself should he be called to active duty. However, one may ask how a bow would fit with the shield, since Greek archers usually had no shield.[38] The absence of a token with Nike should also be noted. Bubelis interprets this find as a 'hoard of official armoury tokens, mixed with coins' and suggests the tokens possibly were used as 'fiduciary coinage', i.e. as money, by an Athenian. This interpretation is not convincing, not least because these lead tokens are made from a different, much inferior metal than coins.[39]

[31] For the Stoa of the Herms see: Di Cesare (2014a), 947, 949–52; Di Cesare (2014b), 956–59; Di Cesare (2015), 51, 59–70.
[32] Kroll (1977b), 145–46. See discussion above.
[33] For *sitos* see Kroll (1977a), 97 with n. 36; Bugh (1988), 53, 59, 60, 184, 191, 205. For *misthos* see: Bugh (1988), 193, 215.
[34] *IG* II^2 1303; *SEG* 25.157; Kroll (1977b), 146; Couvenhes (2007), 536. See also Bugh (1988), 192–93, 230, no. 32.
[35] Kroll (1977b), 143; Couvenhes (2007), 530; esp. Cromey (2001), 95–96; cf. also Anderson (1970), 19–20; Chase (1979), 31; van Wees (2005), 54. According to Cromey (2001), 95–96 the appearance of the Alpha *episema* in Attic vase painting seems to be documented only within the period ca. 510–440/30 BC.
[36] Warsaw, National Museum 142338: *ARV*^{2} 1016, no. 29; Cromey (2001), 95, pl. 28, 1.
[37] Agora deposit 18:8, Section Ξ – Ξ: Kroll (1977b), 144; see also Kroll (1974), 202; Thompson (1942), 223–24; IGCH 24, no. 157; see also Bubelis (2010), 185 with n. 45 (mentioned falsely as being of bronze).
[38] Cretan archers could exceptionally be armed with shields, as attested for the army of Antiochus the Great: Snodgrass (1999), 124. For archers in Athens, who were recruited from Athenian citizens at least from the fifth until the early fourth century BC, see Trundle (2010), 147–52, 158–59. For Hellenistic Athens see Snodgrass (1999), 126.
[39] Bubelis (2010), 185; see also note 37 above.

Fig. 13: Nolan amphora, Warsaw, National Museum 142338 Reproduction after Cromey (2001), pl. 28, 1.

Fig. 14: Cat. no. II.a. AM, IL 831, Pb token (Ø 18mm) (photo by K.-V. von Eickstedt).

Fig. 15: Cat. no. II.b. AM, IL 832, Pb token (Ø 17mm) (photo by K.-V. von Eickstedt).

Fig. 16: Cat. no. II.c. AM, IL 830, Pb token (Ø 18.5mm) (photo by K.-V. von Eickstedt).

The storage of arms by the Athenian state

Indeed, it is known from literary sources that the Athenian state possessed storage facilities for arms, albeit without referring specifically to an armoury for the cavalry. In the early fourth century BC the banker Pasion gave 1,000 shields to the Athenians, and in the second half of the century Lycurgus, elected as arms commissioner, seems to have brought a lot of weapons to the Acropolis, amongst them 50,000 missiles.[40] A large amount of infantry armour was donated by Demetrios Poliorketes to the Athenians as bounty from the spoils of war after his victory at Salamis on Cyprus in 306 BC, consisting of 1,200 hoplite panoplies,

[40] Pasion: Demosthenes, *In Stephanum I*, 45.85; Couvenhes (2007), 529. Lycurgus: Plutarch, *Moralia* 852C.

obviously intended to be used by the Athenian army, which was an ally in Antigonos Monophtalmos' on-going war against Cassander.[41]

But where were such quantities of weapons stored? In addition to storage facilities for weapons on the Acropolis, such as the Parthenon and the Chalkotheke (as is indicated by several inscriptions of the fourth century),[42] there was a building on the edge of the north-west corner of the Athenian Agora in the Hellenistic period which could be interpreted as a state arsenal. It is the large building north of the Hephaisteion and only about 70 metres away from the well (see fig. 10). On account of its typological shape and size and its vicinity to administrative buildings of the city and to the quarter of the metalworkers, the structure, which probably dates to the middle of the first half of the third century, is interpreted as an arsenal.[43]

Which soldiers were equipped by the armour and weapons stored in the state arsenals is a matter of debate, since, as is well known, until the late Classical period regular hoplites had to acquire their armour at their own expense. This became important during the third century BC, when 'military service was no longer compulsory' but voluntary.[44] In the Classical period Athens had a cavalry of 1,000 horsemen,[45] but this number decreased around 300 BC, which is connected with the general decay of the strength and importance of mounted troops in the armies of the Greek East in the third century.[46] During the early and middle Hellenistic periods the city maintained a citizen cavalry. In the beginning of the third century BC this consisted of 200 men and in 282/81 BC it was reorganised and increased to 300 men.[47] The mounted troops were reduced again to 200 after the Chremonidean War of 267–261 BC, a number that remained stable at least during the following decades.[48] In addition to the cavalry in the third century BC the Athenian army had both citizen soldiers and mercenaries serving in the infantry.[49]

The iconography of the lead tokens

A closer look at the symbols depicted on the lead tokens, without considering the other two categories of finds from the well which are definitely related to the cavalry (i.e. the clay tokens of Pheidon and the lead tablets), suggests that a direct reference to the cavalry cannot be derived from the lead tokens themselves. The reason is that the armour depicted was not used exclusively by cavalrymen, but also by hoplites and other infantry units. Therefore, it is necessary to take a closer look at the individual pieces of armour that are depicted on tokens, and the iconographic evidence for their use by the cavalry. Some of the tokens were found in different contexts during the American excavations in the ancient Agora and are published by Crosby, or are later finds. Others are stored in the Numismatic Museum and were published in 1868 – with only a few illustrated – by its director Achilleas Postolakas.[50] The latter examples lack information regarding their original provenance and therefore their chronological setting. However, keeping in mind that the armour tokens from Athens with

[41] Plutarch, *Life of Demetrius* 17.1; Couvenhes (2007), 528.
[42] Couvenhes (2007), 526–27.
[43] Kroll (1977b), 145; Pounder (1983); Camp (2010), 42, fig. 18, no. 2; Longo (2014b); Couvenhes (2007), 528–29.
[44] Kroll (1977b), 144, who speaks of a 'volunteer citizen cavalry'. However, the cavalry service was not fully voluntary according to Bugh (1988), 185–86; cf. Pritchard (2018), 443–44. For the Athenian cavalry in the early and middle Hellenistic periods in general see Bugh (1988), 184–97; Habicht (1997), 138; Oliver (2007), 173–75.
[45] For the Athenian cavalry in the Classical period see Bugh (1988), 39–183; Spence (1993), 9–17, and *passim*; Spence (2010); Blaineau (2015), esp. 203–17; Pritchard (2018).
[46] See Sekunda (2007), 347; Serrati (2013), 188.
[47] Apparently in response to the invasion of the Gauls in 279 BC the Athenian cavalry force sent to Thermopylai was raised to 500 men according to Pausanias 10.20.5 (see Bugh (1988), 188, 190), possibly consisting of additional mercenary cavalry troops (see below n. 48).
[48] Kroll (1977a), 95–97; Bugh (1988), 190–91. However, apparently there were additional mounted troops, mercenaries called *Tarantinoi*, from at least the second decade of the third century onwards: see Camp (1996), 254, 257–58.
[49] Oliver (2007), 176–77, 189.
[50] Postolacca (1868), 293 nos. 544–50; 294, nos. 584–96; 296, nos. 622–23, 635–44; 300–01, nos. 742–47, pl. LII (only 545, 586, 589, 622, 640, 743, 747 are illustrated); Crosby (1964), 88–89, L 26–27, pl. 19; 102, L 166–69, pl. 25; 104, L 184–86, 189, 191–92, pl. 26; 107, L 222–23, pl. 27; 108, L 227–29, pl. 27. Unpublished armour tokens from the Agora (see also III.c) and in the Numismatic Museum will be presented in a future study by the author.

Fig. 17: Cat. no. III.a. AM, IL 946, Pb token (Ø 15mm) (photo by K.-V. von Eickstedt).

Fig. 18: Cat. no. IV.a. NM, 7909, Pb token (Ø 14mm) (photo by author).

Fig. 19: Cat. no. IV.b. NM 7928, Pb token (Ø 14mm) (courtesy of the Numismatic Museum, Athens).

a known provenance all come from the ancient Agora, it is highly probable that the pieces in the Numismatic Museum are originally from the same area. Interestingly, only a very small minority of the tokens (not listed in the catalogue) have letters (again Α, Γ, Δ) on their reverse like the ones from the well (see e.g. I.b, I.c, I.f, I.i, figs. 2, 3, 6, 9), whilst the others uniface.

Greaves, depicted on four tokens from the ancient Agora (I.d, I.e, I.f, III.a, figs. 4–6, 17) and also on some specimens in the Numismatic Museum (like IV.a, fig. 18),[51] are always shown as a single piece (which indicates the pair). From the Archaic period onwards, at least on some occasions greaves belong to the armour of mounted warriors, as is shown by the iconographic evidence. In contrast to the Archaic and Classical period,[52] greaves are seldom worn by horsemen in Hellenistic art,[53] and then mostly in peripheral regions of the Greek world.

A helmet of Attic type is depicted only on one token from the Agora (I.a, fig. 1). It bears a low crest and a visor, which is shallowly pointed. On the lower part of the bowl there is a row of curving leaves. Some tokens in the Numismatic Museum show similar helmets, but with important differences: they have a more spherical form above the front of the visor, which is quite shallow, are without leaf decor and have bigger cheek pieces, as the example presented here (IV.b, fig. 19). The visor of this helmet starts on the left in a volute-like small circle and splits into two parts, from which their peaked ends on the right are visible.

With the great variety of the Attic helmets, especially in the Hellenistic period, it is difficult to find a parallel for a spherical helmet body (calotte) of the same height. Some basic features are paralleled for example, on a helmet from Melos in Berlin, which has been dated recently to the second half of the third century (fig. 20).[54] A closer look, however, shows it is quite different, for instance it has a lower, not fully spherical, calotte. However, a helmet depicted on a banquet relief from Kos from around 100 BC (fig. 21)[55] is more similar in shape to the example on the token in the Numismatic Museum (IV.b, fig. 19).

In general the helmet of Attic type, known from the Archaic period, but especially popular from the Classical period,[56] is well suited for use by cavalrymen, because it does not restrict the field of view in the way, for instance, a Chalkidian helmet would. In the scene depicting a competition on a Panathenaic amphora in Berlin from the beginning of the fourth century, horsemen with Attic helmets are shown throwing spears at a shield (fig. 22).[57] Attic helmets

[51] Postolacca (1868), 296, nos. 622–23, pl. LII (only no. 622 is depicted); Engel (1884), 21, no. 217, pl. 6.
[52] Jarva (1995), 130, n. 866; Schild-Xenidou (2008), 191, 243–44, cat. no. 10, pl. 4.
[53] cf. Sekunda (2007), 345.
[54] Berlin, Antikensammlung SMB, Fr. 1010: Picón and Hemingway (2016), 186–87, no. 105 with figs. [A. Schwarzmaier]; see also Dintsis (1986), 121–23, 277–78, no. 217, pl. 55, 5–6; Grüßinger, Kästner and Scholl (2012), 524, cat. no. 5.54 with fig. [U. Peltz]; Bottini, Egg, von Hase, Plug, Schaaff, Schauer and Waurick (1988), 170, 443–45, no. 52, fig. K 52a–g, Beil. 1, no. 24, esp. fig. K 52a, K 52f. [G. Waurick].
[55] Kos, Archaeological Museum inv. no. 235: Dintsis (1986), 106, 110, 274, no. 210, pl. 48,1, Beil. 8, 311.
[56] Egg and Waurick (1990), 21; Schäfer (1997), 71–89. For the Hellenistic period see: Dintsis (1986), 105–33; Bottini, Egg, von Hase, Plug, Schaaff, Schauer and Waurick (1988), 169–77 [G. Waurick].
[57] Berlin, Antikensammlung SMB, V.I. 3980: Beazley (1986), 89, pl. 100, 2; Valavanis (1990), 357, fig. 26; Eschbach (2001), 86–90, pl. 26, 1–2; 27, 3.

Fig. 21: Helmet from banquet relief, Kos, Archaeological Museum 235 Reproduction after Dintsis (1986), Beil. 3, no. 311.

Fig. 20: Berlin, Antikensammlung, Fr. 1010, Bronze helmet (courtesy of the Antikensammlung, Staatliche Museen zu Berlin – Preussischer Kulturbesitz, Photo by Uwe Peltz).

Fig. 22: Panathenaic Amphora, Side B, Berlin, Antikensammlung, V.I. 3980 (courtesy of the Antikensammlung, Staatliche Museen zu Berlin – Preussischer Kulturbesitz, photo by Photowerkstatt der Staatlichen Museen Berlin, DDR).

belonged of course also to the standard equipment of late Classical and early Hellenistic hoplites.[58]

Other types of helmets are depicted on tokens from the Agora and in the Numismatic Museum, like that which belongs to Dintsis' category of the *pilos-konos* helmet (IV.c, fig. 23).[59] For the Classical period there are attestations of further types of helmets used by cavalrymen, such as the *pilos* and the Boeotian helmet.[60]

An *aspis* (round shield) with an Alpha blazon is shown on two tokens from the well (I.g, I.h, figs. 7–8), which come from the same die, and on three others from the ancient Agora (II.b, fig. 15),[61] one of which is quite small (III.b, fig. 24, only 12mm diameter) without dots around the edge, i.e. without a riveted rim. Others like that from the Numismatic Museum (IV.d, fig. 25) depict shields without an Alpha blazon.[62]

In the Athenian iconography of the Classical period cavalrymen are not usually depicted with shields.[63] Shields were introduced possibly to the cavalry around 280 BC.[64] In the Hellenistic period a round shield was in use, which was smaller than that used in the fifth and fourth centuries, with a diameter ranging from 66 to 100cm, which allowed the infantryman and cavalryman greater agility in action.[65] There were two main types of cavalry shields: that used by Macedonian horsemen with a medial spine,[66] and the other with a bronze umbo or boss.[67] Both of these shield types are absent from the tokens.

In the fourth century BC the use of the *aspis* declined and after the Gauls invaded Greece in the early third century many cities introduced a new troop type. These troops carried a large oblong shield similar to the Celtic shield (θυρεός), and these so-called *thureophoroi* replaced the hoplites.[68] There is evidence that this type of shield was used also by mounted troops.[69] Indeed, there are some tokens with depictions of this form of shield from the ancient Agora (III.c, fig. 26), and also in the Numismatic Museum (IV.e, fig. 27). However, the greater size of the latter shield and the coarser stylistic workmanship suggests a later date for this specimen, in or – more likely – after the third century.

Fig. 23: Cat. no. IV.c. NM 7930, Pb token (Ø 11mm) (courtesy of the Numismatic Museum, Athens).

Fig. 24: Cat. no. III.b. AM, IL 322, Pb token (Ø 12mm) (photo by K.-V. von Eickstedt).

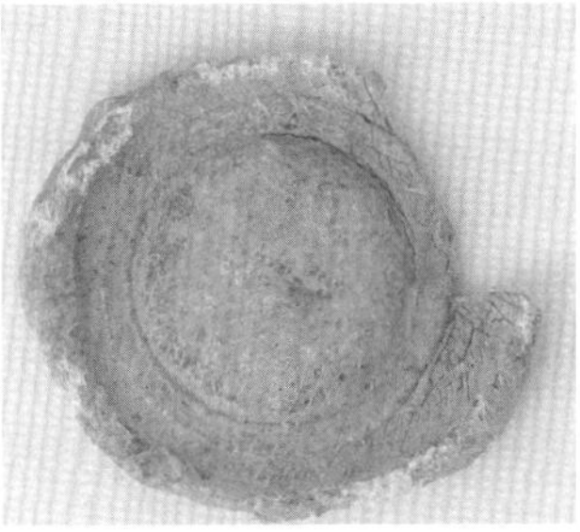

Fig. 25: Cat. no. IV.d. NM 7873, Pb token (Ø 20mm) (courtesy of the Numismatic Museum, Athens).

[58] See e.g. Bentz (1998), 68, 178, no. 4.105, pl. 131.

[59] Dintsis (1986), 67–73, Beil. 3. The specific type of helmet shown on IV.c seems to appear on coins mainly in the late fourth and the third century BC (Dintsis (1986), 233–40, nos. 94, 96–103, 106–07, 109–12, pl. 29, 2, 4–15). For tokens with differing helmets see Crosby (1964), 104, L 189–92, pl. 26.

[60] Aristophanes, *Lysistrata*, 561–62. Gawlinski (2014), 46–48, fig. 28.

[61] AM, IL 2016 (unpublished).

[62] AM, IL 1154: Crosby (1964), 89, L 27a. Cf. also Postolacca (1868), p. 294, nos. 584–85, 587–88, 589–91, pl. LII (only no. 589 depicted); Svoronos (1900), 330, no. 135, pl. 18, 20, with Alpha blazon.

[63] See also Schäfer (1997), 36. For a possible exception see: Brenne (1992), 162–64, fig. 1, pl. 39,1.

[64] Sekunda (2013a), 1388; see also Snodgrass (1999), 120, 122. Serrati (2013), 189 supposes that the Macedonian cavalry introduced it in the middle of the third century BC.

[65] Berlin, Antikensammlung SMB, Y 1767: Grüßinger, Kästner and Scholl (2012), 524, cat. no. 5.55 with fig. [U. Peltz]. See also Sekunda (2007), 345. For the size and weight of the pre-Hellenistic *aspis* see Bardunias and Ray (2016), 30.

[66] e.g. the Macedonian riders on the Monument of Aemilius Paulus at Delphi (see Taylor (2016), 564, fig. 1, no. 9, 567, fig. 5, no. 22, 567, fig. 7, no. 26, 570).

[67] For the two different kinds of shield used by cavalrymen see Sekunda (2013b), 69. For other Hellenistic depictions of horsemen with round shields see: Sekunda (2013b), 70–71, fig. 4.3; Taylor (2016), 573, fig. 10.

[68] Sekunda (2007), 339–43; Bardunias and Ray (2016), 35; cf. also Snodgrass (1999), 123.

[69] Sekunda (2007), 345–46.

Fig. 26: Cat. no. III.c. AM, IL 2012, Pb token (Ø 17 mm) (photo by K.-V. von Eickstedt).

Fig. 27: Cat. no. IV.e. NM 7882b, Pb token (Ø 20mm) (courtesy of the Numismatic Museum, Athens).

Fig. 28: Cat. no. III.d. AM, IL 903, Pb token (Ø 16mm) (photo by K.-V. von Eickstedt).

The corselet, represented on numerous tokens from both the ancient Agora (I.b, I.c, figs. 2–3) and the Numismatic Museum, shows in general a short breast piece, under which are attached two rows of *pteryges* or leather flaps; obviously, this is a leather or rather a linen corselet (λίνεος) of the 'Laschenpanzer' type.[70] The breast piece of the corselets on the two tokens from the Crossroads Well shows four horizontal bands, conspicuously absent on other tokens from the Agora (e.g. III.d, fig. 28).[71] On all three of the tokens presented here the side of the breast piece is covered by vertical shoulder flaps; at the neck there seem to be poles from the frame on which the corselet was positioned.[72] Another token from the Agora (III.e, fig. 29) shows the armour perhaps in three quarter profile, the contours of the upper part may indicate a different cuirass type.

Fig. 29: Cat. no. III.e. AM, IL 988, Pb token (Ø 16mm) (photo by K.-V. von Eickstedt).

The use of corselets by Athenian cavalrymen is attested in the Classical period, for example on the Parthenon frieze.[73] The form of corselet shown on the tokens from the well is known from sculptures of riders, like the two bronze statues from the late third or early second century from Kalymnos (fig. 30).[74] But hoplites also wore this type of corselet, depicted for instance on a grave relief from Rhodes from the second century.[75] A linen corselet of a panoply belonging to a horseman is listed in a Delian catalogue of sacred objects from a little after 166 BC, (in fact the list contained older dedications, possibly from Demetrios Poliorketes), which according to Jarva could have been the shoulder piece type.[76]

A bow, more specifically a reflex bow of the S-bow type (in antiquity called the Scythian bow), is depicted on several tokens from the ancient Agora (e.g. II.c, fig. 16) and in the Numismatic Museum.[77] According to Aristotle in Athens weapon training for the ephebes included archery.[78] But it is unlikely that there were mounted archers, the so-called

[70] See Jarva (1995), 33–46 (in particular, 40–44, type IV); Laube (2006), 19–20; cf. Siedentopf (1968), 77–78. For Hellenistic bronze cuirasses and corselets see: Snodgrass (1999), 122–23; Graells i Fabregat (2018).

[71] Crosby (1964), 108, L 227c–e, L 228, pl. 27.

[72] Kroll (1977b), 141–42.

[73] Brommer (1977), 85, pl. 131 (British Museum, south frieze, slab XIII, figure no. 36); see also Schäfer (1997), 36–37. The use of the corselet by Macedonian cavalrymen is attested at about the same time in Thucydides, *Historiae*, 2.100.6: Snodgrass (1999), 115.

[74] Ephorate of Underwater Antiquities, Athens, BE 2009/28, BE 2006/1 (fig. 30): Koutsouflakis and Simosi (2015), 75–78, figs. 5.3–4.

[75] Rhodes, Museum inv. no. 1154: Stampolides (1992), 160, no. II 15, fig. 21; Laube (2006), 48, pl. 18,2.

[76] *IDélos* 1403; *SEG* 37.692; Jarva (1995), 41 with n. 248, 130.

[77] Postolacca (1868), 293, nos. 545–49, pl. 52 (only no. 545 is depicted); Crosby (1964), 102, L 166 a–c, L 167a–b, L 169, pl. 25; Ober and Hedrick (1993), 67–68, fig. 7.5 [D. Buitron-Oliver and J. McK. Camp II]. For this type of bow see Tölle-Kastenbein (1980), 14, fig. 3, 17–20.

[78] Aristotle, *Constitution of the Athenians*, 42.3. Also attested for the third century BC, see Pélékidis (1962), 170. For the Athenian *ephebeia* in the Hellenistic period see Kennell (2006), x.

Fig. 30: Bronze statue of a rider from Kalymnos, Ephorate of Underwater Antiquities, Athens, BE 2006.1. Reproduction after Koutsouflakis and Simosi (2015), 77, fig. 5.4.

hippotoxotai, which are attested for Athens only until the first half of the fourth century.[79] Of particular interest is a token in the Numismatic Museum (IV.f, fig. 31), which shows a bow and the letters ΔH, possibly indicating property of the *demos* (state).[80] Noteworthy here is a lead token found on the foot of the Pnyx, which depicts a quiver with strap, perhaps from the third century.[81] This and another token of unknown find location with quiver and inscription AΘE[82] could have served the same purpose as the other armour tokens.

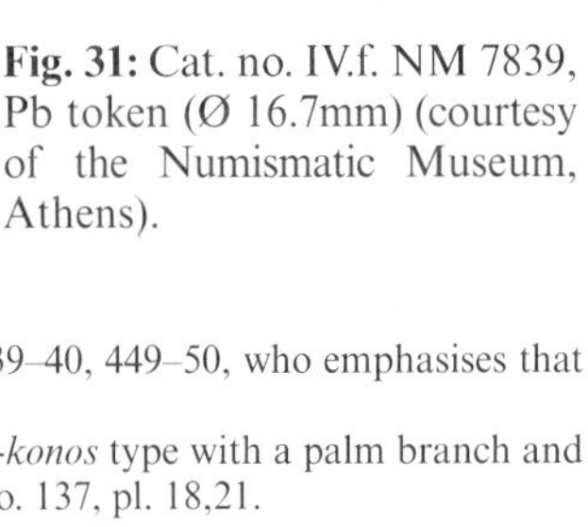

Fig. 31: Cat. no. IV.f. NM 7839, Pb token (Ø 16.7mm) (courtesy of the Numismatic Museum, Athens).

Finally, we examine the figure of Nike standing left, depicted on two tokens from the ancient Agora and several listed by Postolakas.[83] One token from the Crossroads Well (I.i, fig. 9) depicts the figure of the goddess, clad in a chiton,

[79] Bugh (1988), 222; Spence (1993), 58; Spence (2010), 112 with n. 6; Pritchard (2018), 439–40, 449–50, who emphasises that they did not belong to the wealthy classes.

[80] cf. Postolacca (1868), 305; Lang (1964), 52–53, DM 44–51. See also the helmet of *pilos-konos* type with a palm branch and the same letters on another token in the NM (inv. no. unknown): Svoronos (1900), 330, no. 137, pl. 18,21.

[81] Crosby (1964), 107, L 216, pl. 27.

[82] Svoronos (1900), 326, no. 87, pl. 18,7; see Crosby (1964), 107, L 216.

[83] For those which are not mentioned in this text see: Postolacca (1868), 280, nos. 236–39.

Fig. 32: Cat. no. III.f. AM, IL 944, Pb token (Ø 15.5mm) (photo by K.-V. von Eickstedt).

Fig. 33: Cat. no. IV.g. NM 7539, Pb token (Ø 17mm) (photo by author).

with her right hand raised holding an object which is difficult to identify. According to Kroll it is definitely not one of her usual attributes such as a wreath, garland or palm branch, but could be a trophy;[84] another possibility is the interpretation as a *xoanon*-like figure (as stated on the relevant record card from the Agora archive) – or a small cult statue. The left hand is lowered and not holding an object. A standing Nike of a slightly different type is shown on a smaller token (III.f, fig. 32) from the ancient Agora, also holding an object in her right hand, which is outstretched. According to Crosby this is probably a wreath.[85] A very similar figure of the goddess holding an object, presumably a wreath, is shown on a token in the Numismatic Museum.[86] The details of the figure reveal the mastery of the die's artist (IV.g, fig. 33).

The figure type of Nike holding wreath in her right hand and a stylis in her left was introduced to coinage on gold staters of Alexander the Great (fig. 34)[87] and was continuously used from that point onwards on Hellenistic coins; some scholars suggest that this figure on Alexander's coins was a copy of a monument in Athens,[88] perhaps a statue of the goddess on the Acropolis dedicated by Alexander the Great on the occasion of a victory against the Illyrians in 336/35 BC.[89] Indeed, a precursor of this type of Nike can be found on Panathenaic prize amphoras of the archon Pythodelos from 336/35 BC,[90] indicating that the object in the right hand of Nike on the two tokens (III.f, IV.g, figs. 32–33) could be a wreath, as suggested already by Postolakas.[91] The figural type of the Nike on these tokens is not derived from the iconography of coins, because the wing on the left is minimised and only a small upper part above the right shoulder is visible. The image must be derived from another iconographic prototype, maybe a statue dedication on the Acropolis.

The interpretation of the Nike remains elusive. Kroll's interpretation, that it represents a piece of armour which 'does not lend itself to depiction in the small field of a token', such as a spear or a sword rather than a military standard, is not satisfying, because the skilled artists producing the dies for the tokens surely would not have had any difficulty in rendering such objects of military equipment. Instead of a single piece of armour it is possible that the Nike could represent a whole set of armour.

[84] Kroll (1977b), 143, no. 9.
[85] Crosby (1964), 96, L 93.
[86] Postolacca (1868), 280, no. 235 with interpretation as wreath.
[87] Mørkholm (1991), 42–44, 243, no. 7, pl. 1; Price (1991), 29, 109–11, nos. 185–200, pl. 2; Grote (1992), 890, nos. 594–95, pl. 598, 902; Stampolidis, Tsangari and Tassoulas (2017), 213, no. 141 with fig. [D. Tsangari].
[88] See Jenkins (1990), 122.
[89] See Tiverios (2001), 51 with n. 144.
[90] Tiverios (2001), 50–51, pl. 19,1; see also Mørkholm (1991), 43–44.
[91] See note 86 above. A wreath is shown by another token formerly in the collection of the Archaeological Society at Athens: Engel (1884), 15, no. 130, pl. 4.

Fig. 34: Gold stater of Alexander the Great, Athens, Alpha Bank Collection 2144. Reproduction after Stampolidis, Tsangari and Tassoulas (2017), 213, no. 141.

Conclusions

As we have seen there are different dies with the same type of armour (for instance the corselet), indicating different sets of tokens, perhaps from different years or periods. This is perhaps confirmed by the smaller diameter (11–12mm) of some of the tokens and a correspondingly smaller depiction of the piece of armour than the tokens from the Crossroads Well and elsewhere of equivalent size (18–23mm).

From the iconography of the armour tokens from the well it is obvious that the armour depicted is not related necessarily to the cavalry. The tokens could well have been destined for soldiers of the infantry or hoplites, as suggested by Couvenhes.[92] The depictions on the other tokens from the Agora Museum and the Numismatic Museum lead to the same conclusion. When one also considers the relatively small value of this military equipment in comparison to that of a horse, this possibility becomes all the more obvious. According to an inscription from the island of Keos from the early third century BC, the price for a bow was seven *drachmae*, a bronze helmet about six *drachmae*, a bronze cuirass significantly more than ten *drachmae* and a metal-faced hoplite shield 20 *drachmae*,[93] whereas a war horse – as we have seen – was valued at a minimum of 100 to 1,200 *drachmae*. This means that for a wealthy citizen joining the cavalry the expenditure for his armour would only be a small percentage of that required for the mount and other related expenses.[94] Indeed, according to Xenophon the Athenian cavalrymen of the fourth century BC seem to have had to take care of their armour and weapons themselves.[95] Therefore, the tokens could have been used in third century BC Athens above all by the less wealthy citizens, enrolled as hoplites or serving

[92] Couvenhes (2007), 531; a similar opinion was expressed earlier by D. Buitron Oliver and J. McK. Camp II in Ober and Hedrick (1993), 107, figs. 16.12–18.
[93] *IG* XII 5, no. 647; Jarva (1995), 151. For the cost of armour in the Classical period see van Wees (2005), 52–53 with n. 14, 55, 62.
[94] See Pritchard (2018), 444–47.
[95] Xenophon, *On the Cavalry Commander* 1.23; Pritchard (2018), 447.

in other infantry units like archers, to show their entitlement to particular pieces of armour from the state arsenal.[96]

Interestingly, with the exception of the bow and the quiver, the tokens represent only defensive, and not offensive, equipment. If the tokens are not to be associated with the armour of cavalrymen, then their provenance from the Hipparcheion is unlikely, and a different provenance, such as the Arsenal or the *Strategeion*, should be considered.

Catalogue of tokens[97]

I: Athens, ancient Agora, Crossroads Well (Agora deposit J 5:1)

I.a Fig. 1
AM, IL 1575 (Ø 19mm).
Attic helmet to right / Γ.
References: Kroll (1977b), 141, no. 1, pl. 40, 1.

I.b Fig. 2
AM, IL 1574 (Ø 20mm).
Corselet with protruding pole at the neck / A.
References: Kroll (1977b), 141, no. 2, pl. 40, 2; Aldrete, Bartell and Aldrete (2013), 203 no. M-42 (1).

I.c Fig. 3
AM, IL 1573 (Ø 23mm).
Corselet with protruding pole at the neck (same die as I.b) / Γ.
References: Kroll (1977b), 141–42, no. 3, pl. 40, 3; Aldrete, Bartell and Aldrete (2013), 203 no. M-43 (1).

I.d Fig. 4
AM, IL 1572 (Ø 21mm).
Greave to right / A.
References: Kroll (1977b), 142, no. 4, pl. 40, 4.

I.e Fig. 5
AM, IL 1576 (Ø 21mm).
Greave to right (same die as I.d) / Γ.
Reference: Kroll (1977b), 142, no. 5, pl. 40, 5.

I.f Fig. 6
AM, IL 1577 (Ø 18mm).
Greave to right (same die as I.d) / Δ.
Reference: Kroll (1977b), 142, no. 6, pl. 40, 6.

I.g Fig. 7
AM, IL 1579 (Ø 20mm).
Round shield with A blazon / A.
References: Kroll (1977b), 142, no. 7, pl. 40, 7.

I.h Fig. 8
AM, IL 1578. (Ø * 22mm).
Round shield with A blazon (same die as I.g) / A.
References: Kroll (1977b), 142, no. 8, pl. 40, 8.

[96] cf. Couvenhes (2007), 531.
[97] The measures of the author are marked with *. If available, the find place is indicated. The description is presented as obverse/reverse. A blank reverse is indicated by –.

I.i Fig. 9
AM, IL 1580 (Ø 20mm).
Nike standing left, holding an object in her right hand / A.
References: Kroll (1977b), 143, no. 9, pl. 40, 9.

II. Athens, ancient Agora, southwest corner (Agora deposit 18:8, section Ξ – Ξ)
II.a Fig. 14
AM, IL 831 (Ø 18mm).
Corselet (surface badly worn) / –.
References: Crosby (1964), 108, L 227b; Kroll (1977b), 144.

II.b Fig. 15
AM, IL 832 (Ø 17mm).
Shield with a very worn A blazon / –. Small piece of the token separated.
References: Crosby (1964), 89, L 27b; Kroll (1977b), 144.

II.c Fig. 16
AM, IL 830 (Ø 18.5mm).
Bow / –.
References: Crosby (1964), 102, L 168, pl. 25; Kroll (1977b), 144.

II.d
AM, without inv. no., now lost (Ø 15mm).
Obverse: either shield (Crosby) or Attic helmet (Kroll).
References: unpublished, see Crosby (1964), 89, L 27b; Kroll (1977b), 144.

III. Tokens from elsewhere in the Agora
III.a Fig. 17
AM, IL 946 (Ø 15mm).
Agora, Great Drain South, disturbed late Hellenistic context.
Greave / –.
References: Crosby (1964), 104, L 184, pl. 26.

III.b Fig. 24
AM, IL 322 (Ø 12mm).
Agora, section P #.
Shield with A blazon / –.
References: Crosby (1964), 88–89, L 26, pl. 19.

III.c Fig. 26
AM, IL 2012 (Ø 17mm).
Agora, J/12-2/5, west side of Room B.
Oblong shield in round (?) field / –.
References: unpublished.

III.d Fig. 28
AM, IL 903 (Ø 16mm).
Great Drain South, disturbed late Hellenistic context (C 19).
Corselet in deep round field / –.
References: Crosby (1964), 108, L 227a, pl. 27.

III.e Fig. 29
AM, IL 988 (Ø 16mm).
Great Drain South, late Hellenistic context, deposit C 18:14.
Corselet (heavily worn) in round field / –.
Crosby (1964), 108, L 229, pl. 27.

III.f Fig. 32
AM, IL 944 (Ø * 15.5mm).
Great Drain South, disturbed late Hellenistic context.
Nike standing left, head lowered / –.
References: Crosby (1964), 96, L 93, pl. 22; Ober and Hedrick (1993), 67–68, fig. 7.6 [D. Buitron-Oliver and J. McK. Camp II].

IV. Tokens in the Numismatic Museum in Athens
IV.a Fig. 18
NM 7909 (Ø * 14mm).
Greave in round field / –.
References: Postolacca (1868), 296, no. 622, pl. 52.

IV.b Fig. 19
NM 7928 (Ø * 14mm).
Helmet of Attic type with low crest in a nearly round field / –.
References: Postolacca (1868), 296, no. 641.

IV.c Fig. 23
NM 7930 (Ø * 11mm).
Pilos-konos helmet with cheek pieces in round field / –.
References: Postolacca (1868), 296, no. 643.

IV.d Fig. 25
NM 7873 (Ø * 20mm).
Shield with distinct rim in deep round field (obviously restruck) / –.
References: Postolacca (1868), 294, no. 586, pl. 52.

IV.e Fig. 27
NM 7882b (Ø * 20mm).
Oblong shield in deep round field / –.
References: Postolacca (1868), 294, no. 596.

IV.f Fig. 31
NM 7839 (Ø * 16.7mm).
Bow, above the slightly oblique bowstring the letters ΔH / –.
References: Postolacca (1868), 293, no. 550; Svoronos (1900), 327, no. 101, pl. 18, 44.

IV.g Fig. 33
NM 7539 (Ø * 17mm).
Found 1860 in Athens in a pit inside a house.
Token of oval shape. Nike standing left (corroded) in a round field / –.
References: Postolacca (1868), 280, no. 235, pl. 52.

Bibliography

Aldrete, Bartell and Aldrete 2013: G. S. Aldrete, S. Bartell and A. Aldrete, *Reconstructing Ancient Linen Body Armor: Unravelling the Linothorax Mystery* (Baltimore, 2013).

Anderson 1970: J. K. Anderson, *Military Theory and Practice in the Age of Xenophon* (Berkeley and Los Angeles, 1970).

Bagnall, Brodersen, Champion, Erskine, Huebner (eds.) 2013: R. S. Bagnall, K. Brodersen, C.B. Champion, A. Erskine, S.R. Huebner (eds.), *The Encyclopedia of Ancient History* (3 vols.) (Chichester and Malden, 2013).

Baitinger 2011: H. Baitinger, *Waffenweihungen in griechischen Heiligtümern* (Monographien des RGZM 94) (Mainz, 2011).

Bardunias and Ray 2016: P. M. Bardunias and F. E. Ray, Jr., *Hoplites at War. A Comprehensive Analysis of Heavy Infantry Combat in the Greek World, 750-100 BCE* (Jefferson, NC, 2016).

Batino 2001: S. Batino, 'Il *Leokorion*. Appunti per la storia di un angolo dell'Agora', *ASAA* 89 (2001), 55–82.

Beazley 1986: J. D. Beazley, *The Development of Attic Black-Figure*[2] (Sather Classical Lectures 24) (Berkeley, Los Angeles and London, 1986).

Bentz 1998: M. Bentz, *Panathenäische Preisamphoren. Eine athenische Vasengattung und ihre Funktion vom 6.-4. Jahrhundert v. Chr.* (Antike Kunst Beiheft 18) (Basel, 1998).
Bentz and Eschbach (eds.) 2001: M. Bentz and N. Eschbach (eds.), *Panathenaïka. Symposion zu den Panathenäischen Preisamphoren, Rauischholzhausen 25.11.-29.11.1998* (Mainz, 2001).
Blaineau 2015: A. Blaineau, *Le Cheval de guerre en Grèce ancienne* (Rennes, 2015).
Bottini, Egg, von Hase, Pflug, Schaaff, Schauer and Waurick 1988: A. Bottini, M. Egg, F.-W. von Hase, H. Pflug, U. Schaaff, P. Schauer, and G. Waurick, *Antike Helme. Sammlung Lipperheide und andere Bestände des Antikenmuseums Berlin* (RGZM Monographien 14) (Mainz, 1988).
Braun 1970: K. Braun, 'Der Dipylon-Brunnen B₁. Die Funde', *MDAI(A)* 85 (1970), 129–269.
Brenne 1992: S. Brenne, '«Porträts» auf Ostraka', *MDAI(A)* 107 (1992), 161–85.
Brommer 1977: F. Brommer, *Der Parthenonfries* (Mainz, 1977).
Bubelis 2010: W. Bubelis, 'Tokens and imitation in Ancient Athens', *Marburger Beiträge zur antiken Handels-, Wirtschafts- und Sozialgeschichte* 28 (2010), 171–95.
Bugh 1988: G. R. Bugh, *The Horsemen of Athens* (Princeton, 1988).
Camp 1978: J. McK. Camp II, 'A spear butt from the Lesbians', *Hesperia* 47 (1978), 192–95.
Camp 1996: J. McK. Camp II, 'Excavations in the Athenian Agora: 1994 and 1995', *Hesperia* 65 (1996), 231–61.
Camp 2010: J. McK. Camp II, *The Athenian Agora. Site Guide*[5] (Princeton, 2010).
Campbell and Tritle (eds.) 2013: B. Campbell and L. A. Tritle (eds.), *The Oxford Handbook of Warfare in the Classical World* (Oxford and New York, 2013).
Chase 1979: G. H. Chase, *The Shield Devices of the Greeks in Art and Literature* (1902, Reprint Chicago, 1979).
Clinton 2014: K. Clinton, 'The Athenian Cleruchy on Lemnos', in Matthaiou and Pitt (eds.) 2014, 327–37.
Couvenhes 2007: J.-C. Couvenhes, 'La fourniture d'armes aux citoyens athéniens du IVe au IIIe siècle avant J.-C.', in Sauzeau and van Compernolle (eds.) 2007, 521–40.
Cromey 2001: R. D. Cromey, 'Athena's Panathenaic *episema* and democracy's return in 403', in Bentz and Eschbach (eds.) 2001, 91–100.
Crosby 1964: M. Crosby, 'Lead and clay tokens. Part II', in Lang and Crosby (1964), 69–146.
Daehner and Lapatin (eds.) 2015: J. M. Daehner and K. Lapatin (eds.), *Power and Pathos: Bronze Sculpture of the Hellenistic World* (Florence, 2015).
Di Cesare 2014a: R. Di Cesare, 'Le Erme', 'La Stoa Nord-Occidentale (Poikile o delle Erme)', in Greco (ed.) 2014, 945–52.
Di Cesare 2014b: R. Di Cesare, 'La Stoa Poikile', 'La Stoa dell'Erme', 'L'*Hipparcheion*', in Greco (ed.) 2014, 953–60.
Di Cesare 2014c: R. Di Cesare, 'L'*abaton* all'incrocio ('Crossroads Enclosure') e il pozzo', in Greco (ed.) 2014, 978–79.
Di Cesare 2014d: R. Di Cesare, 'Le strutture alle spalle della Stoa Basileios e della Stoa di Zeus', in Greco (ed.) 987–91.
Di Cesare 2015: R. Di Cesare, *La città di Cecrope. Ricerche sulla politica edilizia cimoniana ad Atene* (Studi di Archeologia e di Topografia di Atene e dell'Attica 11) (Athens and Paestum, 2015).
Dintsis 1986: P. Dintsis, *Hellenistische Helme* (Archaeologica 43) (2 vols.) (Rome, 1986).
Egg and Waurick 1990: M. Egg and G. Waurick, *Antike Helme, Katalog zur Ausstellung, Speyer 26. Mai – 10. Juni 1990* (Mainz, 1990).
Engel 1884: A. Engel, 'Choix de tessères grecques en plomb tirées des collections Athéniennes', *BCH* 8 (1884), 1–21.
Eschbach 2001: N. Eschbach, 'Rotfigurig – Schwarzfigurig. Panathenäische Preisamphoren und Vasenmaler des späten 5. und des frühen 4. Jhs. v. Chr.', in Bentz and Eschbach (eds.) 2001, 83–90.
Gawlinski 2014: L. Gawlinski, *The Athenian Agora. Museum Guide*[5] (Princeton, 2014).
Graells i Fabregat 2018: R. Graells i Fabregat, *Corazas helenísticas decoradas. 'ΟΠΛΑ ΚΑΛÀ, Los 'Siris Bronzes' y su contexto* (Studia Archaeologica 223) (Rome, 2018).
Greco (ed.) 2014: E. Greco (ed.), *Topografia di Atene. Sviluppo urbano e monumenti dalle origini al III secolo d.C. Vol. 3: Quartieri a nord e a nord-est dell'Acropoli e Agora del Ceramico. Vol. 2: Agora del Ceramico* (Studi di Archeologia e di Topografia di Atene e dell'Attica 1) (Athens and Paestum, 2014).
Grote 1992: U. Grote, 'Nike, C. Hellenistische Zeit', *Lexicon Iconographicum Mythologiae Classicae* VI 1–2 (Zurich and Munich, 1992), 881–95, 902–04.
Grüßinger, Kästner and Scholl (eds.) 2012: R. Grüßinger, V. Kästner and A. Scholl (eds.), *Pergamon. Panorama der antiken Metropole, Begleitbuch zur Ausstellung* (Berlin and Petersberg, 2012).
Habicht 1961: Ch. Habicht, 'Neue Inschriften aus dem Kerameikos', *MDAI(A)* 76 (1961), 127–48.
Habicht 1982: Ch. Habicht (1982), *Studien zur Geschichte Athens in hellenistischer Zeit* (Hypomnemata 73) (Göttingen, 1982).
Habicht 1997: Ch. Habicht, *Athens from Alexander to Antony* (Cambridge, MA, and London, 1997).
Jarva 1995: E. Jarva, *Archaiologia on Archaic Greek Body Armour* (Studia Archaeologica Septentrionalia 3) (Rovaniemi, 1995).
Jenkins 1990: G. K. Jenkins, *Ancient Greek Coins*[2] (London, 1990).
Jordan 1985: D. R. Jordan, '*Dexifiones* from a well near the southwest corner of the Athenian Agora', *Hesperia* 54 (1985), 205–55.
Jordan 2000: D. R. Jordan, 'A personal letter found in the Athenian Agora', *Hesperia* 69 (2000), 91–103.

Kennell 2006: N. M. Kennell, *Ephebeia: A Register of Greek Cities with Citizen Training Systems in the Hellenistic and Roman Periods* (Nikephoros Beihefte 12) (Hildesheim, 2006).
Koutsouflakis and Simosi 2015: G. Koutsouflakis and A. Simosi, 'Hellenistic bronze sculptures from the Aegean Sea: recent discoveries (1994–2009)', in Daehner and Lapatin (eds.) 2015, 72–81.
Kroll 1974: J. H. Kroll, 'Numismatic appendix' (to V.R. Grace, 'Revisions in Early Hellenistic Chronology'), *MDAI(A)* 89 (1974), 201–03.
Kroll 1977a: J. H. Kroll, 'An archive of the Athenian cavalry', *Hesperia* 46 (1977), 83–140.
Kroll 1977b: J .H. Kroll, 'Some Athenian armor tokens', *Hesperia* 46 (1977), 141–47.
Kroll and Mitchel 1980: J. H. Kroll and F. W. Mitchel, 'Clay tokens stamped with the names of Athenian military commanders', *Hesperia* 49 (1980), 86–96.
Lang 1964: M. Lang, 'Part I: Weights and measures', in Lang and Crosby (1964), 1–68.
Lang and Crosby 1964: M. Lang and M. Crosby, *The Athenian Agora X: Weights, Measures and Tokens* (Princeton, 1964).
Laube 2006: I. Laube, *Thorakophoroi: Gestalt und Semantik des Brustpanzers in der Darstellung des 4. bis 1. Jhs. v. Chr.* (Tübinger Archäologische Forschungen 1) (Rahden, 2006).
Longo 2014a: F. Longo, 'L'Agorà del Ceramico e il Kolonos Agoraios', in Greco (ed.) 2014, 849–94.
Longo 2014b: F. Longo, 'L'Arsenale', in Greco (ed.) 2014, 941–43.
Matthaiou and Pitt (eds.) 2014: A. P. Matthaiou and R. K. Pitt (eds.), *ΑΘΗΝΑΙΩΝ ΕΠΙΣΚΟΠΟΣ. Studies in Honour of Harold B. Mattingly* (Ελληνική Επιγραφική Εταιρεία 16) (Athens, 2014).
Monaco 2004: M. C. Monaco, 'L'*Hipparcheion*, il lato settentrionale dell'Agorà di Atene e l'acquedotto cimoniano', *Workshop di archeologia classica* 1 (2004), 17–49.
Mørkholm 1991: O. Mørkholm, *Early Hellenistic Coinage. From the Accession of Alexander to the Peace of Apamea (366-188 B.C.)* (Cambridge, 1991).
Neils and Palagia (eds.) forthcoming: J. Neils and O. Palagia (eds.), *From Kallias to Kritias. Classical Culture: Athens in the Second Half of the 5th Century B.C. Proceedings of the International Conference, Athens, 6-8 June 2019* (Athens) (forthcoming).
Ober and Hedrick (eds.) 1993: J. Ober and Ch. W. Hedrick (eds.), *The Birth of Democracy: An Exhibition Celebrating the 2500th Anniversary of Democracy at the National Archives*, Washington, D.C., June 15, 1993 – January 2, 1994 (Athens, 1993)
Oliver 2007: G. J. Oliver, *War, Food, and Politics in Early Hellenistic Athens* (Oxford and New York, 2007).
Pélékidis 1962: Ch. Pélékidis, *Histoire de l'Éphébie attique des origins à 31 avant Jésus-Christ* (Trauvaux et mémoires, École française d'Athènes 13) (Paris, 1962).
Picón and Hemingway (eds.) 2016: C. A. Picón and S. Hemingway (eds.), *Pergamon and the Hellenistic Kingdoms of the Ancient World* (New York, 2016).
Postolacca 1868: A. Postolacca, 'Piombi inediti del Nazionale Museo Numismatico di Atene', *Annali dell'Instituto di Corrispondenza Archeologica* 40 (1868), 268–316 with illustrations (drawings) on tav. di aggiunti K and pl. LII in *Monumenti Inediti Pubblicati dall'Instituto di Corrispondenza Archeologica* 8 (1864–1868).
Pounder 1983: R. L. Pounder, 'A Hellenistic arsenal in Athens', *Hesperia* 52 (1983), 233–56.
Price 1991: M. J. Price, *The Coinage in the Name of Alexander the Great and Philip Arrhidaeus, A British Museum Catalogue* (2 vols.) (Zurich and London, 1991).
Pritchard (ed.) 2010: D. M. Pritchard (ed.), *War, Democracy and Culture in Classical Athens* (Cambridge and New York, 2010).
Pritchard 2018: D. M. Pritchard, 'The horsemen of Classical Athens: Some considerations on their recruitment and social background', *Athenaeum* 166 (2018), 439–53.
Rotroff and Lynch forthcoming: S. Rotroff and K. M. Lynch, 'The Crossroads Enclosure in the Athenian Agora: A preliminary report', in Neils and Palagia (eds.) forthcoming.
Sabin, van Wees and Whitby (eds.) 2007: Ph. Sabin, H. van Wees and M. Whitby (eds.), *The Cambridge History of Greek and Roman Warfare. Vol. 1: Greece, the Hellenistic World and the Rise of Rome, Part II: The Hellenistic World and the Roman Republic* (Cambridge, 2007).
Sauzeau and Compernolle (eds.) 2007: P. Sauzeau and Th. van Compernolle (eds.), *Les armes dans l'Antiquité. De la technique à l'imaginaire, Actes du colloque international du SEMA, Montpellier, 20 et 22 mars 2003* (Montpellier, 2007).
Schäfer 1997: Th. Schäfer, *Andres Agathoi. Studien zum Realitätsgehalt der Bewaffnung attischer Krieger auf Denkmälern klassischer Zeit* (Quellen und Forschungen zur antiken Welt 27) (München, 1997).
Schäfer forthcoming: M. Schäfer, ''Ερμῆς Ἵππιος. Hermes and his association with horses', in Valavanis and Moretti (eds.) forthcoming.
Schild-Xenidou 2008: V. Schild-Xenidou, *Corpus der boiotischen Grab- und Weihreliefs des 6. bis 4. Jahrhunderts v. Chr.* (MDAI, Athenische Abteilung, 20. Beiheft) (Mainz, 2008).
Sekunda 2007: N. V Sekunda, 'Military forces A. Land forces', in Sabin, van Wees and Whitby (eds.) 2007, 325–57.
Sekunda 2013a: N. V. Sekunda, 'Cavalry, Hellenistic', in Bagnall, Brodersen, Champion, Erskine, Huebner (eds.) 2013, 1388–89.
Sekunda 2013b: N. V. Sekunda, *The Antigonid Army* (Akanthina 8) (Gdańsk, 2013).
Serrati 2013: J. Serrati, 'The Hellenistic world at war: stagnation or development?', in Campbell and Tritle (eds.) 2013, 179–98.
Shear 1973a: T. L. Shear Jr., 'The Athenian Agora: excavations of 1971', *Hesperia* 42 (1973), 121–79.

Shear 1973b: T. L. Shear Jr., 'The Athenian Agora: excavations of 1972', *Hesperia* 42 (1973), 359–407.

Siedentopf 1968: H. B. Siedentopf, *Das hellenistische Reiterdenkmal* (Waldsassen, 1968).

Snodgrass 1999: A. M. Snodgrass, *Arms and Armour of the Greeks* (Reprint Baltimore and London, 1999).

Spence 1993: I. G. Spence, *The Cavalry of Classical Greece. A Social and Military History with Particular Reference to Athens* (Oxford, 1993).

Spence 2010: I. Spence, 'Cavalry, democracy and military thinking in Classical Athens', in Pritchard (ed.) 2010, 111–38.

Stampolides 1992: N. C. Stampolides, 'Ο θωρακοφόρος αρ. ΑΕ 268 της Κω', *ArchEph* 131 (1992), 129–62.

Stampolidis, Tsangari and Tassoulas (eds.) 2017: N. C. Stampolidis, D. Tsangari and Y. Tassoulas (eds.), *Money: Tangible Symbols in Ancient Greece* (Athens, 2017).

Svoronos 1900: I. N. Svoronos, 'Περὶ τῶν εἰσιτηρίων τῶν ἀρχαίων, Μέρος Δ'. Τὰ μολύβδινα σύμβολα', *JIAN* 3 (1900), 319–43.

Taylor 2016: M. J. Taylor, 'The battle scene on Aemilius Paullus's Pydna monument: a re-evaluation', *Hesperia* 85 (2016), 559–76.

Thompson 1942: M. Thompson, 'Coins for the Eleusinia', *Hesperia* 11 (1942), 213–29.

Tiverios 2001: M. A. Tiverios, 'Panathenäen und Makedonen. Panathenaische Preisamphoren aus dem nordgriechischen Raum', in Bentz and Eschbach (eds.) 2001, 41–54.

Tölle-Kastenbein 1980: R. Tölle-Kastenbein, *Pfeil und Bogen im antiken Griechenland* (Bochum, 1980).

Trundle 2010: M. Trundle, 'Light troops in Classical Athens', in Pritchard (ed.) 2010, 139–60.

Valavanis 1990: P. Valavanis, 'La proclamation des vainqueurs aux Panathénées', *BCH* 114 (1990), 325–59.

Valavanis and Moretti (eds.) forthcoming: P. Valavanis and J.-Ch. Moretti (eds.), *Hippodromes and the Equestrian Games in Ancient Greece, International Congress, 10-12/02/2016* (BCH Supplement) (Athens, forthcoming).

van Wees 2004: H. van Wees, *Greek Warfare. Myths and Realities* (London, 2004).

Wycherley 1978: R. E. Wycherley, *The Stones of Athens* (Princeton, NJ, 1978).

A RARE CLAY TOKEN IN CONTEXT: A FORTUNATE AND RECORDED DISCOVERY FROM THE NECROPOLIS OF TINDARI (MESSINA, 1896)[1]

ANTONINO CRISÀ

Introduction

Current research, performed at regional and state archives in Rome, Palermo and Syracuse, has revealed important data on the history of Sicilian archaeology during the post-Unification period (1861–1918). Sicily benefitted from an efficient archaeological safeguarding system, tested and perfected by the Bourbon authorities. The archaeologist Antonino Salinas played a leading role in exploring unknown sites and acquiring finds in provincial areas.

Among Salinas' long-standing research activity in the Messina province, excavations at Tindari's necropolis (1896) represent a crucial event in the history of Sicilian archaeology. Salinas performed extensive explorations at the site, discovering large Roman columbaria and substantial grave goods. Among them a clay token appears to have been neglected by scholars until now.

The scope of this article is to provide an analysis of the above-mentioned unpublished token, whose iconography shows remarkable connections with the coins and cults of ancient Tyndaris (fig. 1). Firstly, we provide a historical introduction to clay tokens, Tindari's site (fig. 2) and its local archaeology, considering the role of Salinas and Baron Sciacca della Scala, who were personally involved in the 1896 excavations. Secondly, we assess archival evidence, offering important information on the clay token and its discovery. Thirdly, an accurate description and analysis of the token are provided, revealing significant data concerning its iconography, production and dating. Lastly, we explain how the production and use of such tokens were connected to religion and civic life in the small community of Tyndaris.

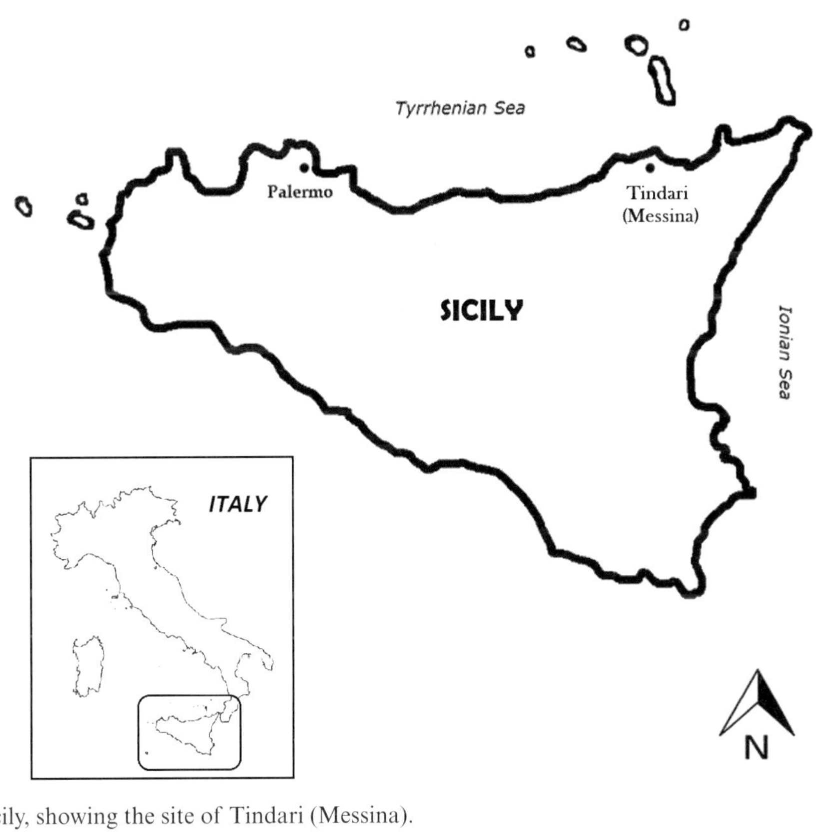

Fig. 1: Map of Sicily, showing the site of Tindari (Messina).

[1] I am thankful to Gabriella Tigano, 'Dirigente Responsabile U.O. 5, Soprintendenza per i Beni Culturali e Ambientali di Messina', who kindly authorised me to study this remarkable and neglected find from Tindari's excavations (protocol number 6110/V2777, 07 October 2014). I am also grateful to Maria Ravesi, the local inspector of the Soprintendenza, who I met in August 2015 in Tindari and who showed me the token at the Antiquarium of Tindari. Furthermore, Anna Maria Manenti, 'Funzionario Direttivo Archeologo', kindly helped me to trace the archival evidence of the token's acquisition at the 'P. Orsi' Museum in Syracuse in January 2017.

Fig. 2: Tindari – View of the promontory (from the south) and the sanctuary.

An overview of clay tokens in the ancient Mediterranean

Clay tokens (or *tesserae*), known since the nineteenth century, are commonly discovered in archaeological investigations, revealing a diverse and widespread production in the classical world.[2] These finds have created some interest among scholars in the past, although most specimens are still unpublished. They present a variety of iconography, which is closely connected with local religion, cults and traditions. The repertoire of images is quite varied and includes deities, heroes, animals, and objects from daily life, sporadically associated with Greek or Latin legends. Well documented are the so-called 'clay seals' or 'seal impressions', produced in the Hellenistic and Roman periods and attested, for instance, in Greece, Egypt and Turkey. Although they present similar iconography, these seals need to be considered as a different class of archaeological materials linked to trade.[3] There is also a rare specimen of a clay *spintria* showing a sex scene, found at Salona and now kept at the Museum of Split (Croatia).[4]

Clay *tesserae* from Palmyra (Syria), showing different shapes and images (e.g. local divinities, priests and religious symbols), are the best-known clay tokens and have been published by scholars in corpora and targeted studies.[5] We also know that a production of clay tokens is attested in Athens: artefacts have been discovered in the Agora and other urban areas since the nineteenth century. These bear a variety of images, like deities from the Greek pantheon, owls, amphorae, the name of commanders, etc.[6] As reported by Markypodi in this volume, many clay tokens are also missing an excavation context in Athens.

[2] Lenormant (1878–79), vol. 1, 215–16.
[3] Milne (1906), 32–45; Milne (1916), 87–101; McDowell (1935), 231–41; Davidson and Burr Thompson (1943), 107–08.
[4] Buljević (2008), 201–11. On *spintriae* see: Buttrey (1973), 52–63; Bateson (1991), 385–97.
[5] Ingholt, Seyrig, Starcky and Caquot (1955); Raja (2015), 165–86.
[6] Svoronos (1905), 323–38; Kroll (1977), 141–46; Kroll and Mitchel (1980), 86–96.

At Seleucia on the Tigris archaeologists found clay model discs of Seleucid coins, which represent coin types both on the obverse and the reverse. Similar artefacts, copying coins of Antioch, have been discovered in Syria (e.g. Palmyra) (fig. 3). Milne has argued that moulds used to make these pieces contained the original coins and small pieces of clay were pressed inside to obtain the discs. Scholars have argued that these tokens were produced – for instance – when the usual currency was in short supply due to a lack of materials, like silver and copper.[7]

Fig. 3: Clay Roman coin reproduction, found in Palmyra (Syria) (Ø 35mm) (Milne (1934): 24, fig. 1a–b).

Archaeological excavations have proved that clay tokens were also produced in Spain at Emporia and southern Italy.[8] Even if most finds are evidently still unpublished, some artefacts have been studied by scholars. Thanks to Mannino's works, we benefit from a series of papers on the so-called 'monete di terracotta' (terracotta coins) found in the ancient city of Metapontum (Matera), mostly in dump contexts of the Kerameikos quarter, an ancient manufacturing urban area. The small discs carry types taken from the local coinage of Magna Graecia and Sicily, like the grain-car, a common type on Metapontum's coinage. Imagery is also taken from the coinage of Caulonia, Leontinoi and Thurium. Mannino records a remarkable terracotta die showing a coin type of the Terina mint, which certainly testifies to a local production of these artefacts at the Kerameikos quarter in Metapontum.[9] Another Hellenistic token has been found at Monasterace Marina (Reggio Calabria), ancient Caulonia, reproducing the types of a bronze coin of Epizephyrian Locris.[10] Two significant sets of tokens found at Marcellina-Laos (175 specimens) and Sala Consilina (480 specimens), may testify to the local production of terracotta coins with an unknown 'exchange value'. Guzzo considered their production to form part of the early stage of the monetary economy of the Brettii in the area before the group began using real coins.[11]

Sicily had clay token production as well, although most of the finds are totally unpublished. A remarkable series is attested at ancient Makella (modern Marineo), a small town in the province of Palermo, not far from Corleone. Here archaeologists discovered a set of small clay discs depicting Demeter (or Hecate) carrying two torches; these finds have been provisionally dated by De Simone to the end of the fourth century BC. Further research is ongoing in order to understand how the tokens were used in the local community of Makella.[12]

Tokens have been also found at the so-called 'Sanctuary of Palikè' at Mineo (Catania), which developed during the fifth century BC. Tokens were produced utilising circular pottery sherds in the Hellenistic period, when the sanctuary was still operational. Only one carries a Greek legend (no. 580). Archaeologists interpreted these either as 'attendance tokens' to access the agora, or as *tesserae* for games. The latter, for instance, are also documented in Magna Graecia (e.g. Incoronata of Metaponto).[13]

[7] Milne (1934), 24–27; McDowell (1935), 241–50; Milne (1939), 93–95.
[8] Campo (1993), 204.
[9] D'Andria (1978), 409–12; D'Andria (1980), 418–20; Mannino (1993), 207–42; Mannino (1998), 61–71; Pedroni (1998), 5–10; Mannino (2002), 167–69, 286–87. At the beginning, D'Andria had even considered these terracotta tokens to be a joyful creation of the local ceramicists, who were copying circulating coins using clay (D'Andria (1978), 411: 'Non resta che pensare ad un gioco dei fornaciai che si divertivano ad imitare in argilla le monete metalliche circolanti').
[10] Gargano (2010), 6–8.
[11] Guzzo (1989), 111–12.
[12] De Simone (1997), 225–27; Spatafora and De Simone (2007), 36. The present author is currently studying and publishing all tokens found at Marineo (Palermo). For a preliminary analysis of Makella's finds see Crisà (2019).
[13] Franchi (1986), 177–78; Maniscalco (2008), 115–17, 238, nos. 580–83.

Introducing Tyndaris, a small ancient town in the Messina province

Historical sources provide us with a good record on ancient Tyndaris. Dionysius I, tyrant of Syracuse, founded the city in 396 BC to counter any potential Carthaginian advance from western Sicily.[14] After a few years, Tyndaris expanded to approximately 10,000 inhabitants. The Romans conquered the city in 254 BC, and it became a *civitas decumana*, paying 1/10 of its harvest to Rome.[15] Cicero's *Oratio in Verrem* offers detailed descriptions of Tyndaris in the first century BC. In fact, we know that Verres, praetor in Sicily between 71 and 69 BC, oppressed its inhabitants, seized their fine arts objects and punished Sopater, a local magistrate (*proagora*).[16] Tyndaris was also involved in the civil wars between Octavian and Sextus Pompeius and was re-founded as *Colonia Augusta Tyndaritanorum* in 22–21 BC. The city was prosperous during the Roman imperial period, as the archaeological evidence at insula IV and 'Cercadenari' quarter clearly testifies. Tyndaris became an episcopal see during the Byzantine period and was finally sacked by the Arabs in AD 836.[17]

After the Arab invasion, Tyndaris lost its importance and was progressively abandoned by its inhabitants, who probably moved to other neighbouring centres (e.g. Patti). Nevertheless, following a long abandonment, sixteenth century antiquarians (e.g. the well-known Sicilian author T. Fazellus (1498–1570)) became interested in the history and archaeology of Tindari. Substantial ruins and monuments, like the theatre and the Roman basilica, were still visible at that time. The remains also arose interest in the eighteenth century, as the detailed report by I. Paternò Castello (1719–86), Prince of Biscari, proves. In the first half of the nineteenth century a local antiquities market, incentivised by local collectors, travellers, diggers and even priests, made Tindari a remarkable centre for antiquarianism. For instance, E. Pirajno (1809–64), Baron of Mandralisca, visited the town and bought some archaeological finds to increase his collection of antiquities at Cefalù. Meanwhile, a branch of the Commission of Antiquities and Fine Arts – an antiquities safeguarding body of the Bourbon government that had its headquarters in Palermo – operated at Tindari. The site also had custodians to supervise the archaeological ruins.[18]

Social context at Tindari: D. Sciacca della Scala and A. Salinas

The noble family of Sciacca della Scala played a significant role in the history of Tyndaris, since the barons were often members of the local Commission, became mayors of nearby Patti, and owned vast lands within Tyndaris' archaeological site. More importantly, from the eighteenth century they had gathered a substantial collection of archaeological finds from Tindari, where they often performed excavations or acquired ancient artefacts from farmers. Finds included Latin and Greek inscriptions, vases, statues, bricks, urns and coins; collections were stored in the family castle at Scala (Patti, Messina) and many travellers were hosted by the barons. The Sciacca's archaeological collection markedly increased between the Bourbon (1816–60) and post-Unification period (1861–1918).

Domenico Sciacca della Scala (1846–1900) (fig. 4), the last antiquarian and collector of this Sicilian noble family, was a well-known politician, working as under-secretary at the Ministry of Agriculture, Commerce and Industry in Rome. He wrote some remarkable works, for example *La crisi agraria* (1885), *L'aumento di tassa e la cooperazione agricola* (1897) and *La tassa sullo zucchero indigeno* (1900). He suddenly died in 1900 without a will and his archaeological collection was largely distributed among his heirs.

The role of Antonino Salinas (1841–1914) is crucial in the history of post-Unification archaeology in Sicily. As director of the Museum of Palermo, the first Professor of Archaeology and a numismatist, Salinas shaped a new institution. The museum was to represent all phases of Sicilian history and promoted a regional identity in contrast to a national

[14] Diodorus Siculus, *Library of History*, XIV, 78, 5–6.
[15] Diodorus Siculus, *Library of History*, XXIII, 18, 5.
[16] Cicero, *Against Verres*, II, 4, 84–92.
[17] Spigo (2005), 15–18; Crisà (2008), 236–40; Gulletta (2011), 606–10.
[18] Crisà (2012), 38–42; Crisà (2018), 53–57.

identity supported by the Italian government. Salinas operated as an active archaeologist in the Messina province, also encouraging donations to the Palermo Museum from local collectors and performing surveys on largely unknown sites (e.g. San Fratello, San Marco d'Alunzio and Tripi). As we can argue from the 'Escursioni archeologiche' (*Notizie degli Scavi*) and archival records, Sciacca had a good relationship with Antonino Salinas, who often came to Scala to study his substantial numismatic and archaeological collection. We can therefore infer that these trips made Salinas interested in Tindari's archaeology. As a landowner, Sciacca could give Salinas permission to excavate on his properties on Tindari's promontory, where a vast area of ancient graveyards was totally unexplored. This sort of 'exchanging of favours' was very profitable. In fact, at the end of 1895 Salinas met Sciacca before beginning a new archaeological exploration.[19]

Fig. 4: Domenico Sciacca della Scala (1844–1900) (Crisà (2012), 160, fig. 22).

The necropoleis of Tyndaris: archaeological context and archival evidence

Before analysing the archival evidence relevant to the clay token, a brief description of Tindari's necropoleis (fig. 5) is essential to contextualise the 1896 excavations. Nevertheless, we do not possess thorough data on the necropoleis, because most of the previous and recent investigations, carried out by the Superintendency of Syracuse and Messina in 1956, 1974 and the early 2000s, remain largely unpublished.

Fig. 5: Tindari – Satellite view of Contrada Scrozzo (now Locanda) (necropolis) (Source: GoogleEarth).

[19] Salinas (1880), 191–200; Orsi (1915), 1–9; Cimino (1985), xxi–xl; Crisà (2012), 42–43; Spatafora and Gandolfo (2014), 12–30; Crisà (2018), 54–57, 73–79.

From the fourth century BC until the imperial age the ancient city benefitted from many graveyards which today cover vast areas, mostly outside the town's walls (south and east: Contrada Scrozzo and Santa Panta; south: Locanda). However, some tombs lay inside the outer town limits, especially in Contrada Cercadenari. Inhumation and incineration are both attested at Tindari. Grave goods are substantial and include Hellenistic and Roman pottery, lead and glass urns, coins, large clay medallions, etc. Antiquarian and archival sources report that bodies were often buried on a thick layer of marine sand. A wide range of graves, like 'cappuccina' tombs, columbaria and square monumental structures, were common at Tindari.[20]

Crucial documentation, previously neglected by scholars, has been recently discovered at the Central State Archive in Rome and the Archaeological Museum Archive in Palermo. A complete journal of excavations written by Salinas and his assistant 'in the field' Guido Scifoni, including a detailed inventory list, dispatches, letters and black and white pictures (fig. 6), sheds new light on the 1896 explorations and their impact on Tindari's local community. This community mostly comprises the state authorities, priests, custodians, skilful workers, women and even children, who were all involved in the excavation. Salinas employed a substantial local workforce to conduct a seven-month investigation from January to July 1896 in the ancient necropoleis and along the city walls, which he fully reinforced and cleared of wild vegetation.[21]

In particular, a few lines of the journal of the excavation record a short description of our clay token, which certainly generated interest among the workers and Scifoni, who did not discard it. In fact, according to late nineteenth century archaeological and antiquarian methods in Sicily, only a selection of finds was kept and inventoried. This, for instance, often excluded animal and human bones and fragmentary pottery. The token was preserved and properly described as follows:

Fig. 6: Tindari – Picture of the excavation and wall renovation, taken by A. Salinas (1896) (courtesy of Museo Archeologico Palermo) (Crisà (2018), 284, TIND.5.24).

[20] Giardina (1882), 161–62; Scaffidi (1895), 68–69; Spigo (2005), 89–92.
[21] Orsi (1896), 116–17; Crisà (2018), 73–79, TIND.7.90–91.

[p. 48] Dal 4 al 21 Maggio 1896 | Zappatori 9 Portacof(ani/e) 10 | Contrada Scrozzo | Proseguesi il lavoro di rinettamento e scavo del fronte S.O. della muraglia antica, e della torre esistente nella controindicata contrada, non che dell'altro fronte della stessa mura a N.E. delle quali se ne vanno restituendo alla luce molte parti del tutto sepolte. Lungo questo fronte rinvengonsi quà e là cinerari in terracotta, quasi addossati alle dette murara, ed a breve distanza si scovano di frequente scheletri interrati sotto tegole piane, alcune delle quali recano la marca di fabbrica.

È stato proseguito il lavoro di costruzione della maceria in secco, necessario per trattenere la scarpata di terra tagliata dinanzi le ripetute mure, ed oltre a questa, si è dovuto costruire un altro nel punto dove si depone la terra che mano mano va asportando, non essendo possibile, per considerevole volume di lasciarla sul posto.

È stato raccolto: [...] Terracotta Disco fittile col rilievo di due mezzi ellissi sostenenti ciascuno una croce. Diam. m. 0,038 – [257].

This passage provides us with much information on the token's discovery. First, we know that the artefact was found between 4 and 21 May 1896 in Contrada Scrozzo (fig. 7), where nine diggers (men) and ten basket carriers (women) were working along the southwest and northeast sections of the ancient walls. Workers excavated portions of the necropolis, discovering many graves, 'cappuccina' tombs and urns, including substantial grave goods, like coins, lamps and a Latin funerary inscription. Scifoni also collected and inventoried a small clay disc, showing two half ellipses and two crosses. It is evident Scifoni did not recognise the iconography of the Dioscuri caps. However, records prove that Scifoni submitted the journal of excavations to Salinas on a weekly basis. The latter repeatedly signed the report. Analysis of the finds was therefore postponed and ideally Salinas would have analysed all finds subsequently, but this never happened.

What was the final destiny of this tiny artefact after the 1896 excavations? In November 1896 most of the finds were packed into big wooden boxes and then moved from Tindari to Palermo by train. Salinas also donated a selection of archaeological objects to Sciacca as a

Fig. 7: Tindari – View of the ancient walls and area of the necropoleis.

reward for granting permission to excavate his lands at Tindari. The reward included vases, lead and glass urns, perfume containers, coins, bricks, etc. (fig. 8). Among them Sciacca probably obtained this token, accurately described in Scifoni's inventory list. The artefact was then preserved at Sciacca's palace in Scala di Patti until the early twentieth century. After Sciacca's death in 1900, his collection was progressively distributed amongst his heirs. However, the widowed princess Merlo, under the auspices of the archaeologist Paolo Orsi, donated some finds to the old Superintendence of Syracuse, including a fragmentary Nike sculpture.[22]

After a fortunate investigation at the 'P. Orsi' Archaeological Museum in Syracuse in January 2017, we discovered important and previously unknown archival evidence that helps us to understand the destiny of the clay token. The old museum inventory reports this short note:

> Altro piccolo lotto di terrecotte di Tindari, regalati, come altri precedenti dal rev. Padre Michele Cammisa (Aprile '17), cfr. n. 38209.
>
> 38280 | V | Medaglioncino fittile sul quale sono raffigurati in rilievo i due pilei dei Dioscuri sormontati da una specie di croce (diam. 34mm).

For some reason, which is still unknown, father Michele Cammisa, a local priest working at the Tindari's sanctuary, obtained a very small set of finds, which included our clay token. Cammisa donated these objects to the Syracuse Museum in April 1917. It can be argued that Paolo Orsi, who then was Director of the museum (1895–1934), personally obtained these finds during one of his visits to Tindari. We can also speculate that father Cammisa was interested in the clay token because it showed two crosses (even if they were stars). The artefact was inventoried at the former National Museum of Syracuse, now called 'P. Orsi'. Finally, all these finds moved to the small Antiquarium in Tindari, whose institution was promoted by Luigi Bernabò Brea in the late 1950s and which opened to the public in May

Fig. 8: Scala di Patti – Picture showing an assemblage of finds offered by Salinas to Sciacca della Scala (1896) (courtesy of Museo Archeologico Palermo) (Crisà (2018), 284, TIND.5.23).

[22] Orsi (1920), 345–47; Parisi (1949), 141–42; Spigo (1998), 144–45, 155; Crisà (2012), 42–43.

1960. Room V still preserves finds from Sciacca della Scala's collection, including the clay token.[23]

A remarkable clay token among coins and local cults

Soprintendenza ai Beni Culturali e Archeologici di Messina | Antiquarium di Tindari (Tindari, Patti – Messina), Room V | old inv. no. 38280 (ex-Museo Nazionale di Siracusa).

Ø: 34.59mm; weight: 7.18g; thickness: 4.46mm | Material: orange clay containing meagre sand elements | State of preservation: fairly good; the token does not have any fractures and the obverse is perfectly readable | Discovery date: 04–21/05/1896 | Find spot: Contrada Scrozzo (necropolis of ancient Tyndaris).

Side 1: The two small, stylised caps of the Dioscuri, formed by two ellipses (left: 9.13 x 19mm; right: 9 x 19mm) and two crosses representing stars on the top (left: 8.74 x 9mm; right: 10 x 9mm).

Side 2: Originally blank; it shows '38280' (black ink), which is an inventory number probably written by Paolo Orsi in early twentieth century.[24]

Date: end of the first century BC (?).

Bibliography: n/a.[25]

Fig. 9: Tindari, Antiquarium, Room V – Clay token (44–36 BC?) (Ø 34.59mm).

The clay token (fig. 9), which is a unique specimen at present,[26] carries the stylised iconography of the *pilei* of the sacred twins appearing in relief. Two ellipses represent the caps and two crosses symbolise the stars. In terms of production, the token's circular shape is regular, although the orange clay is not highly purified and shows sand elements. By contrast, light-brown highly refined clay was used to produce other Sicilian tokens showing Demeter/Hekate, found in Marineo (near Palermo). It is possible Tindari's tokens were produced by impressing a small clay 'flan' with a mould or struck using a die. As mentioned above, a rare terracotta die has been found in Metaponto that produced similar artefacts. We should however exclude the idea that another terracotta or lead/bronze token prototype might have been used, like the one published by Vajna and Vismara, because the relief of the *pilei* is quite prominent, the result of a presumed 'stamping' process.[27]

Castor and Pollux were frequently represented on Greek, Roman and provincial coinage. Their iconography was diverse and included, for instance, the sacred twins represented as horse riders, their juxtaposed heads wearing caps (fig. 10), or just the *pilei* and stars themselves. The long-standing and widespread adoption of imagery associated with the twins can be connected to their role as rescuers/saviours of soldiers and sailors in times of danger.[28]

Our clay token looks like a 'banal' small object. Nevertheless, it discloses important information on religion and daily life within the community of Tyndaris. The cult of the Dioscuri was markedly widespread in Laconia and Sicily, and it was a traditional cult at Tindari. Its founders even named the city in honour of Tyndareus, father of Castor and stepfather of Pollux. Tyndaris' coinage shows many connections with the Dioscuri. The images are either

[23] Bernabò Brea (1961), 209–10; Spigo (2005), 72, 78. On father Cammita see Reitano (1961), 96, 99, 121, 128; the author offers us little information on his activity at Tindari. We know that Cammita was responsible for supervising renovation works, commissioning new furniture and bells (1920), and reclaiming the old sanctuary's cemetery to build up a new public square. Finally, father Cammisa resigned from his duties on 3 July 1923 and moved to the USA to join his brother's family. I am grateful to Mairi Gkikaki regarding father Cammisa's interest in the clay token.

[24] The clay token does not have a current inventory number of the Superintendency of Messina.

[25] Only archival records have been fully copied and examined. In particular see Crisà (2018), TIND.7.90–91.

[26] The Superintendence of Messina reported that no tokens are currently kept at its local storehouses (letter of 23 November 2016, prot. no. 0007480). Thus the author could not perform a direct survey in local storehouses in Messina.

[27] De Simone (1997), 225–26; Vajna and Vismara (2001), 1018–20; Spatafora and De Simone (2007), 36. As already mentioned, Marineo's tokens will be fully published by the present author.

[28] Milne (1906), 33, no. 13; Savio (2002), 51–69; Rovithis Livaniou and Rovithis (2011–12), 10–11, 79–80.

Fig. 10: Silver denarius of Mn. Cordius Rufus (46 BC), Dioscuri with *pilei* and stars (Ø 18mm) (Classical Numismatic Group, Electronic Auction 163, lot no. 270).

'direct' references (standing and armed Dioscuri, the Dioscuri on horseback, heads of the Dioscuri, etc.) or 'indirect' (Helen of Troy, Zeus, caps, etc.), attested from the fourth to first century BC. In particular, stars are extremely common on Tindari's coinage; these allude indirectly to the sacred twins and their power to protect sailors in danger. A long continuity of cult is demonstrated by a mosaic (fig. 11), which shows two caps and stars and a bull, found in the apodyterium of the baths of insula IV and dated to the third century AD.[29]

The caps of the Dioscuri are not only attested on coins in the Greek world. For instance, among the published lead Hellenistic tokens found in the Agora of Athens is a specimen that shows the iconography of the Dioscuri's *pilei* (fig. 12), which appears on the obverse and reverse. Both caps are shown with a star of eight rays. These caps are more detailed than the *pilei* on our clay token, which can be seen only on the obverse.[30]

The dating of Tindari's clay token can only be achieved through iconographic and stylistic comparison, since Salinas and Scifoni did not perform stratigraphic excavations at Tindari in 1896, as is typical of late nineteenth century Sicily. Of course, Tyndaris' coinage offers much material for comparison. Some issues, generally dated to the 'Roman period' (or 'after 214 BC'), show more detailed caps and stars on one side and an eight-ray or nine-ray

Fig. 11: Tindari – Mosaic depicting the Dioscuri's caps at insula IV.

[29] Silius Italicus, *Punica*, 14.208; Spigo (2005), 52–54; Musti (2005), 141–43; Crisà (2006), 42–45; Crisà (2008), 240–41.
[30] Lang and Crosby (1964), 92, no. L59, pl. 21, no. L59 A–B (parallel provided by Mairi Gkikaki); see also Wilding's and Küter's articles in this volume on the interaction between tokens and coins.

Fig. 12: Lead token showing the Dioscuri's *pilei* found in Athens (inv. IL 812) (Ø 12mm) (courtesy of the Greek Ministry of Culture).

Fig. 13: Coin of Tyndaris, post 213–211 BC, eight-ray star and *pilei* (Ø 12mm) (Bertolami Fine Arts, ACR Auction 7, lot no. 207).

Fig. 14: Coin of Tyndaris, post 213–211 BC, Demeter and *pilei* (Ø 15mm) (Bertolami Fine Arts, ACR Auction 6, lot no. 356).

Fig. 15: Coin of Tyndaris, 44–36 BC (?), *pilei* and dolphin (Ø 20mm) (Classical Numismatic Group, Electronic Auction 364, lot no. 261).

Fig. 16: Coin of Tyndaris, 44–36 BC (?), *pilei* and rudder (Ø 14mm) (Bertolami Fine Arts, ACR Auction 6, lot no. 355).

star on the other with the ethnic legend T-Y-N-Δ-A-P-I-T-A-N (fig. 13).[31] On other occasions the *pilei* are paired with the veiled head of Demeter on the obverse (fig. 14).[32] This iconography is quite detailed: the stars are well defined with six-rays and the caps have a cuff on the bottom.

As already mentioned, our clay token shows a pair of Dioscuri caps that are simply outlined as ellipses (*pilei*) and crosses (stars). Thus, it is better to opt for two other coins, which offer a much more cogent iconographic point of comparison in order to obtain a more precise dating. In particular, C. Julius Longus, a local duovir (IIVIR), issued a coin showing two caps which have an ellipse shape along with chin straps and stars, associated with a dolphin and the legend EX D(ecreto) D(ecurionum) (fig. 15).[33]

Another coin (fig. 16) shows a rudder between the legend D-D on the reverse; this clearly alludes to navigation and, as we know, the Dioscuri traditionally protect sailors.[34] More importantly, the obverse offers a close iconographic link with our token. In fact, it represents not only a pair of similar caps, but the stars are even modelled as two stylised crosses, which are very similar to those on the clay *tessera*. This issue – as with the previous one – has been dated to 44–36 BC due to its legend (D-D). Thus, we can argue that the *tessera* might be produced in the same period – or generally speaking, at the end of the first century BC. This date roughly matches those of the Roman lamps and the Latin funerary inscription found by Scifoni and Salinas in the same area.

[31] Tyndaris, Æ, uncia, after 214 BC: Obv.: *Pilei* of the Dioscuri with stars; below IX; Rev.: Eight-ray star, T-Y-N-Δ-A-P-I-T-A-N; von Duhn (1876), 32, no. 21; Gabrici (1927), 194, no. 51; Minì (1979), 444, no. 28; Calciati (1983), vol. 1, 82, no. 23; Campana (2001–02), 78, no. 26, Crisà (2006), 43.

[32] Tyndaris, Æ, sextans, after 214 BC: Obv.: Veiled head of Demeter left; Rev.: TYNΔAPITAN, *pilei* of the Dioscuri with stars; von Duhn 1876: 30, no. 9; BMC Sicily: 236, no. 16; Gabrici (1927), 194, no. 42; Minì (1979), 444, no. 27; Calciati (1983), vol. 1, 82, no. 22; Campana (2001–02), 76, no. 21; Crisà (2006), 43.

[33] Tyndaris, Æ, fraction, late 1st century BC (44–36 BC?): Obv.: *Pilei* of the Dioscuri, C·IVLIVS C F. LONGVS II VIR; Rev.: Dolphin right, EX DD; von Duhn (1876), 32, no. 22; Gabrici (1927), 194, nos. 53–56; Minì (1979), 445, no. 33; Calciati (1983), vol. 1, 83, no. 27; RPC, vol. 1, 649; Crisà (2008), 244–48; RPC, suppl. 3, 19, Tyndaris; Villemur (2016), 437–38, no. 2 (the author has recently confirmed the attribution to Tyndaris).

[34] Tyndaris, Æ, fraction, late first century BC (44–36 BC?): Obv.: *Pilei* of the Dioscuri with highly stylised stars; Obv.: Rudder between D-D; Minì (1979), 445, no. 32; Calciati (1983), vol. 1, 83, no. 26; Villemur (2016), 439, no. 7.

Final remarks

Records have provided important data on our clay token from Tindari. The journal of excavations, written by Scifoni and Salinas in 1896, offers valuable information on the social context of the campaign, its workers, archaeological methods and activities in the field. Nevertheless, documentation is still lacking for some aspects. First, we only know the discovery area and do not have data on the exact find spot nor on the stratigraphy – this is, however, coherent with contemporary archaeological practice in late nineteenth century Sicily. But archival research in Rome, Palermo and Syracuse has shed new light on the collecting history of the clay token, which is now perfectly clear from its discovery in 1896 to its final move to the Antiquarium of Tindari. This information also confirms the role of priests (like father Cammisa), who worked at the sanctuary and were occasionally interested in collecting, acquiring or selling Tindari's antiquities from the late eighteenth century onwards.[35]

Salinas acted as director of Tindari's excavations. As a skilful numismatist and an expert in Sicilian numismatics, he had an interest in Tyndaris' coinage and certainly knew all its coin iconography, including the caps of the Dioscuri. Why then did Salinas not acquire the clay token to increase the collections of the Palermo museum and 'associate' the token with Tyndaris' coins, already studied and kept at his institution?[36] As Lenormant reported, Salinas was very interested in even writing a monograph on Sicilian tokens. It is therefore surprising that Salinas neglected the importance of our clay token in offering a selection of finds to Sciacca della Scala as a reward. Being extremely busy as a Museum director, it can be inferred that he probably did not have the chance (or time) to analyse the token before splitting all the finds between Sciacca and the Palermo Museum.[37]

How can we assess token production at Tyndaris? What was the role of clay tokens in the small ancient community in the Messina province? It is hard to provide 'definitive' answers to these questions, due to a lack of data and the uniqueness of our specimen. Nevertheless, we can provide some speculation on token production, use and final disposal, assessing all the evidence and advancing a hypothesis on the role of these apparently 'banal' artefacts at Tyndaris. First, following our overview of past scholarship and the close connections with local mintage, we can infer the Tyndaris tokens were produced for a very narrow circulation on the site – only one specimen is known so far. It is probably unlikely that these tokens were produced as 'terracotta coins', since the latter have normally two stamped sides, while our specimen has a blank reverse. Undoubtedly, further research needs to be conducted to understand the real extent of broader token production in Hellenistic and Roman Sicily and only a targeted analysis of finds can reveal new data on this phenomenon.

In this regard, we mention a significant comparison. A unique clay token (or *symbolon*) was discovered at Iaitas (Monte Iato) in the Palermo province. Dated to the second half of the fourth century BC, it bears a Greek inscription (ΔA) and Acheloos, an iconography also attested on Iaitas' coins since the late fifth century BC. The token, found in the local agora, can show a direct link with the civic, local life of the site.[38]

It is hard to comprehend the exchange value of the Tyndaris token, which clearly does not have any intrinsic value. It is certainly striking that our find reveals connections with Tyndaris' cults and traditions. In fact, it represents another artefact class, in addition to coins and mosaics, which demonstrates a long-standing local veneration of the sacred twins. Since religion and the civic sphere often overlapped in the Hellenistic and Roman periods, the small disc may have been produced as a token to obtain some privileges in a local festival dedicated to the Dioscuri. It is possible that someone who was carrying the token died and

[35] Crisà (2018), 112.
[36] Fraccia (1889), 52–53, nos. 221–26.
[37] Salinas (1880), 200: 'La numismatica tindaritana è pregevole per un buon numero di tipi non ancora pubblicati. Tacendo per ora di quelli, che mi erano già noti tanto dell'epoca greca che dell'epoca romana, e con nomi di magistrati, ricorderò soltanto quei che ricavai da questa recente visita; come la scoperta di una serie di riconî con tipi tindaritani (berretto de' Dioscuri; pura di nave etc.) [...]'. Lenormant (1895–96), vol. 1, 215: 'Le savant numismatiste sicilien M. Antonio Salinas [...] il annonce depuis plusieurs années l'intention d'y consacrer une monographie'.
[38] Frey-Kupper (2013), vol. 1, 85.

was buried in Contrada Scrozzo, close to the ancient walls. Unfortunately, no temples have been discovered in the region thus far; they probably lie under the new sanctuary of the Black Madonna, a modern and excessively coloured church whose construction in the 1950s–1960s irredeemably compromised any archaeological evidence in the acropolis area. A 'missing' temple of Zeus was seen by Fazellus on the Mongiove hilltop in the sixteenth century.[39]

Archaeological context is crucial in advancing an additional hypothesis on our clay token from Tindari. Since it comes from the ancient necropolis area, the token may have been buried in a grave. Thus, the artefact could have been used as Charon's obol, a small coin/token that was placed in the deceased's mouth to pay the ferryman in the underworld. This practice is attested in Sicily from the fourth and early third centuries BC.[40] Moreover, a 'terracotta coin' discovered in the necropolis area of Pizzica at Metaponto has been connected to ritual funerary practices.[41] Svoronos too had considered terracotta tokens as *charoneia nomismata* in his well-known article.[42]

This hypothesis, which cannot be proven due to a lack of data regarding the exact find spot, is suggested not only from archival records, but also from the iconography. As discussed, the clay token reproduces the same *pilei* and stars found on late first century BC low denomination coins of Tyndaris. This is certainly coherent with the common practice to use less valuable coins as Charon's obols.[43] Our clay token, which does not have any intrinsic value, may have been produced as an imitation of these coins to be used to pay the underworld ferryman. If it was not an obol, it might have been hypothetically placed in a grave as a 'talismanic' object, carrying a strong connection with the local cult of the Dioscuri. Only further finds can prove or contradict this hypothesis; other specimens may potentially be traced amongst old excavation materials, which are still unpublished, or new, desirable investigations in the field.

Bibliography

Adamesteanu, Mertens and D'Andria 1980: D. Adamesteanu, D. Mertens and F. D'Andria (eds.) (1980), *Metaponto I. Notizie degli Scavi di Antichità. XXIX. Supplemento 1975* (Rome, 1980).

Bateson 1991: D. J. Bateson, 'Roman *spintriae* in the Hunter Coin Cabinet', in Martini and Vismara (eds.) (1991), vol. 2, 385–97.

Bentz and Woznoik (eds.) 2019: M. Bentz and D. Woznoik (eds.), *Proceedings of the 19th International Congress of Classical Archaeology (AIAC), Cologne/Bonn, 22-26 May 2018* (Bonn, forthcoming).

Bernabò Brea 1961: L. Bernabò Brea, 'De l'art ancient a l'historie dans les Musées Archéologiques Italiens', *Museum (UNESCO)* 14 (1961), no. 4, 202–14.

Buljević 2008: Z. Buljević, 'Uz spintriju iz Salone u splitskom Arheološkom muzeju', *Archaeologia Adriatica* 2 (2008), no. 1, 201–11.

Buttrey 1973: T. V. Buttrey, 'The *spintriae* as a historical source', *NC* 23 (1973), 52–63.

Calciati 1983: R. Calciati, *Corpus Nummorum Siculorum: la monetazione di bronzo* (Mortara, 1983).

Campana 2001–02: A. Campana, '*Corpus Antiquae Italiae*, III. Sicilia: *Tyndaris* (ca. 354-21 a.C.)', *Panorama Numismatico* 18–19 (2001–02), nos. 150, 152, 159, 63–86.

Campo 1993: M. Campo, 'Objetos paramonetales y monedas objeto en *Emporion/Emporiae*', *RIN* 95 (1993), 193–205.

Cantilena 1995: R. Cantilena (ed.) (1995), *Caronte. Un obolo per l'aldilà. Atti del convegno, Salerno, 20–22 febbraio 1995. La Parola del Passato* (Naples, 1995).

Cimino 1985: G. Cimino, *Lettere di Antonino Salinas a Michele Amari* (Palermo, 1985).

Crisà 2006: A. Crisà, '*Tyndaris*: storia, studi numismatici e iconografia monetale dei Dioscuri', *Cronaca Numismatica* 18 (2006), no. 186, 36–46.

Crisà 2008: A. Crisà, 'La monetazione di Tindari romana con segni di valore e legende in lingua latina', *RIN* 109 (2008), 235–68.

Crisà 2012: A. Crisà, *Numismatic and Archaeological Collecting in Northern Sicily during the First Half of the Nineteenth Century* (Oxford, 2012).

[39] Giardina (1882), 181–82; Reitano (1961); Crisà (2006), 42–43.

[40] Cutroni Tusa (1995), 189–90, 195.

[41] Mannino (1993), 217–18; Mannino (1998), 67–69; Mannino (2002), 168.

[42] Svoronos (1905), 324–25.

[43] Stevens (1991), 215–16, 219–20; Cantilena (1995), 170–71.

Crisà 2018: A. Crisà, *When Archaeology Meets Communities: Impacting Interactions in Northern Sicily Over Two Eras (Messina, 1861-1918)* (Oxford, 2018).
Crisà 2019: A. Crisà, 'Tokens and the reproduction of divinities in Hellenistic and Roman Sicily: some preliminary case studies', in Bentz and Woznoik (eds.) (2019).
Cutroni Tusa 1995: A. Cutroni Tusa, 'La Sicilia', in Cantilena (ed.) (1995), 189–217.
D'Andria 1978: F. D'Andria, 'Metaponto-Fornaci (1977)', in VV.AA. (eds.) (1978), 409–12.
D'Andria 1980: F. D'Andria, 'Scavi nella zona del Kerameikos (1973)', in Adamesteanu, Mertens and D'Andria (eds.) (1980), 355–452.
Davidson and Burr Thompson 1943: G. R. Davidson and D. Burr Thompson, *Small Objects from the Pnyx: I, Hesperia Supplement* 7 (Princeton, 1943).
De Simone 1997: F. De Simone, 'La Montagnola di Marineo. Miscellanea', in VV.AA. (eds.) (1997), 225–35.
Fraccia 1889: G. Fraccia, *Antiche monete siciliane, pubblicate pel primo dal cav. Giovanni Fraccia* (Rome, 1889).
Franchi 1986: E. Franchi, 'Dischi di terracotta, pesi da telaio e rocchetti, fuseruole', in VV.AA. (eds.) (1986), 177–82.
Frey-Kupper 2013: S. Frey-Kupper, *Die antiken Fundmünzen vom Monte Iato 1971-1990. Studia Ietina X.1–2* (2 vols.) (Prahins, 2013).
Gabrici 1927: E. Gabrici, *La monetazione del bronzo nella Sicilia antica* (Palermo, 1927).
Gargano 2010: G. Gargano, 'Una «moneta di terracotta» dall'antica Caulonia', *SM* 60 (2010), 3–8.
Giardina 1882: N. Giardina, *L'antica Tindari: cenni storici* (Siena, 1882).
Giumlia and Rubinich (eds.) 2002: A. Giumlia and M. Rubinich (eds.), *Le arti di Efesto: capolavori in metallo dalla Magna Grecia. Catalogo della mostra, Trieste 2002* (Cinisello Balsamo, 2002).
Gulletta 2011: M. I. Gulletta, s.v. 'Tindari', in Nenci and Vallet (eds.) (2011), 606–54.
Guzzo 1989: P. G. Guzzo, *I Bretti. Storia e archeologia della Calabria preromana* (Milan, 1989).
Iachello (ed.) 1998: E. Iachello (ed.) (1998), *I Borbone in Sicilia (1734-1860)* (Catania, 1998).
Ingholt, Seyrig, Starcky and Caquot 1955: H. Ingholt, H. Seyrig, J. Starcky and A. Caquot, *Recueil des tessères de Palmyre* (Paris, 1955).
Kroll 1977: J. H. Kroll, 'Some Athenian armor tokens', *Hesperia* 46 (1977), 141–46.
Kroll and Mitchel 1980: J. H. Kroll and F. W. Mitchel, 'Clay tokens stamped with the names of Athenian military commanders', *Hesperia* 49 (1980), 86–96.
Lang and Crosby 1964: M. Lang and M. Crosby, *The Athenian Agora X: Weights, Measures and Tokens* (New Jersey, 1964).
Lenormant 1878–79: F. Lenormant, *La monnaie dans l'Antiquité* (Paris, 1878–79).
Maniscalco (ed.) 2008: L. Maniscalco (ed.), *Il santuario dei Palici. Un centro di culto nella valle del Magri* (Palermo, 2008).
Mannino 1993: K. Mannino, 'Le monete in terracotta', *RIN* 95 (1993), 207–42.
Mannino 1998: K. Mannino, 'Nuovi dati sulle monete di terracotta', *Studi di Antichità* 11 (1998), 61–71.
Mannino 2002: K. Mannino, 'Monete in terracotta da Metaponto', in Giumlia and Rubinich (eds.) (2002), 167–69, 286–87.
Martini and Vismara (eds.) 1991: R. Martini and N. Vismara (eds.), *Ermanno Arslan. Studia dicata* (2 vols.) (Milan, 1991).
McDowell 1935: R. H. McDowell, *Stamped and Inscribed Objects from Seleucia on the Tigris* (Ann Arbor, 1935).
Milne 1906: J. G. Milne, 'Clay-sealings from the Fayum', *JHS* 26 (1906), 32–45.
Milne 1916: J. G. Milne, 'Ptolemaic seal impressions', *JHS* 36 (1916), 87–101.
Milne 1934: J. G. Milne, 'Local currencies of East Syria under the Roman Empire', *Ancient Egypt and the East* 1 (1934), 24–27.
Milne 1939: J. G. Milne, 'Syriac substitute-currencies', *Iraq* 6 (1939), 93–100.
Minì 1979: A. Minì, *Monete di bronzo della Sicilia antica* (Palermo, 1979).
Musti 2005: D. Musti, 'Tindari. La città dei gemelli', *Sicilia Antiqua* 2 (2005), 141–43.
Nenci and Vallet (eds.) (2011), G. Nenci and G. Vallet (eds.), *Bibliografia Topografica della colonizzazione greca in Italia e nelle isole tirreniche* (Pisa and Rome, 2011), vol. 20.
Orsi 1896: P. Orsi, 'XV. Tindari. Scavi nella necropoli dell'antica città', *Notizie degli Scavi di Antichità* (1896), 116–17.
Orsi 1915: P. Orsi, 'Antonino Salinas', *Archivio Storico per la Sicilia Orientale* 12 (1915), 1–9.
Orsi 1920: P. Orsi, 'XXV. Tindari (Comune di Patti) – Frammento di Nike marmorea', *Notizie degli Scavi di Antichità* 17 (1920), 345–47.
Parisi 1949: G. Parisi, *Tindari. Storia, topografia, ricerche archeologiche* (Messina, 1949).
Pedroni 1998: L. Pedroni, '«Monete» greche di terracotta: una proposta interpretativa', *RN* 144 (1998), 5–10.
Raja 2015: R. Raja, 'Staging "private" religion in Roman "public" Palmyra. The role of the religious dining tickets (banqueting *tesserae*)', in Rüpke and Ando (eds.) (2015), 165–86.
Reitano 1961: A. Reitano, *Memorie sul santuario del Tindari* (Rome, 1961).
Rovithis Livaniou and Rovithis 2011–12: E. Rovithis Livaniou and F. Rovithis, 'Stellar symbols on ancient Greek coins (I-II)', *Romanian Astronomical Journal* 21–22 (2011–12), nos. 1–2, 1–12, 77–92.
Rüpke and Ando (eds.) 2015: J. Rüpke and C. Ando (eds.), *Public and Private in Ancient Mediterranean Law and Religion. Historical and Comparative Studies* (Berlin, 2015).
Salinas 1880: A. Salinas, 'Escursioni archeologiche a S. Marco d'Aluntio, S. Piero Patti, S. Fratello, S. Agata di Militello, Patti e Tindari', *Notizie degli Scavi di Antichità* (1880), 191–200.

Savio 2002: A. Savio, 'Il berretto frigio sulla moneta greca: un viaggio da oriente ad occidente', *RIN* 103 (2002), 51–69.

Scaffidi 1895: R. V. Scaffidi, Tyndaris*: storia, topografia, avanzi archeologici* (Palermo, 1895).

Spatafora and De Simone 2007: F. Spatafora and R. De Simone (eds.), *Makella. Montagnola di Marineo. Guida breve* (Palermo, 2007).

Spatafora and Gandolfo (eds.) 2014: F. Spatafora and L. Gandolfo (eds.), *Il Salinas ricorda Salinas, 1914-2014. "Del Real Museo di Palermo e del suo avvenire", Museo Archeologico Regionale "Antonino Salinas", Palermo 8 luglio-4 novembre 2014* (Palermo, 2014).

Spigo 1998: U. Spigo, 'Materiali per una storia degli studi archeologici nell'area dei Nebrodi e nelle Isole Eolie in età borbonica', in Iachello (ed.) (1998), 140–57.

Spigo 2005: U. Spigo (ed), *Tindari. L'area archeologica e l'Antiquarium* (Milazzo, 2005).

Stevens 1991: S. T. Stevens, 'Charon's obol and other coins in ancient funerary practice', *Phoenix* 44 (1991), 215–29.

Svoronos 1905: J. N. Svoronos, 'Αρχαία Ρήλινα Σύμβολοα και Εκμαγεία Νομισμάτων και Δακτυλιολίθων', *JIAN* 8 (1905), 323–38.

Vajna and Vismara 2001: E. Vajna and N. Vismara, '«Moneta» d'epoca tardo-repubblicana di «terracotta». Analisi metallografica e note per una discussione', *Annotazioni Numismatiche* 44 (2001), 1018–20.

Van Alfen, Bransbourg and Amandry (eds.) 2016: P. G. Van Alfen, G. Bransbourg and M. Amandry (eds.), *FIDES: Contribution to Numismatics in Honor of Richard B. Witschonke* (New York, 2016).

Villemur 2016: P. Villemur, 'De quelques émissions coloniales romaines en Sicile: retour à *Tyndaris*', in Van Alfen, Bransbourg and Amandry (eds.) (2016), 435–53.

von Duhn 1876: F. Von Duhn, 'Zur Münzkunde von *Tyndaris*', *ZfN* 3 (1876), 27–39.

VV.AA. (eds.) 1978: VV.AA., *Magna Grecia bizantina e tradizione classica. Atti del decimosettimo Convegno di studi sulla Magna Grecia, Taranto, 9-14 ottobre 1977* (Naples, 1978), 409–12.

VV.AA. (eds.) 1986: VV.AA. (eds.), *I Greci sul Basento: mostra degli scavi archeologici all'Incoronata di Metaponto, 1971-1984, Milano, 16 gennaio-28 febbraio 1986* (Como, 1986).

VV.AA. (eds.) 1997: VV.AA., *Archeologia e territorio. Beni Culturali Palermo* (Palermo, 1997).

ROMAN *TESSERAE* WITH NUMERALS: SOME THOUGHTS ON ICONOGRAPHY AND PURPOSE

ALEXA KÜTER

Introduction

The subject of this paper is the well-known but still mysterious group of Roman bronze tokens (*tesserae*) with numerals.[1] These *tesserae* recurrently form the focus of research as scholars try to solve their many puzzles only (it seems) to never reach a definitive answer. This contribution also cannot offer a final solution, but contributes some new thoughts on iconography and possible purpose, providing new stimulus to further research. The paper is divided into three parts: the first gives an iconographic overview of the three groups discussed. The second offers a short outline of previous research on these tokens and addresses their date. The third part provides a discussion.

Characteristics and place of production

With an average diameter of 18 to 23mm and a weight of ca. 4g, bronze tokens with numerals are larger than Roman quadrantes and smaller than asses, approximately corresponding to Roman semisses.[2] They belong to the Julio-Claudian period (27 BC–AD 68). While the beginning and end of the minting period cannot be determined with certainty, it is clear that a peak of production belongs to the reign of Tiberius, namely the year AD 23.[3] A few pieces are of later date (e.g. Claudius), but do not belong to the die-connected main group which this paper focuses on.[4]

Production has been attributed to the mint of Rome.[5] Apart from the general quality of the images, evidence for this has been sought in the material of the *tesserae*: orichalcum (brass), which is often held to be an imperial reserve.[6] Yet, it is far from certain that orichalcum was ever excluded from private use. It tended to replace bronze in other fields of use like metalwork.[7] It is striking, however, that the orichalcum tokens are a parallel product of the orichalcum coinage of AD 23 (see below). This coincidence makes a production in the mint of Rome likely. Together with the evidence of the excellent skills of the die-cutter, who obviously was familiar with imperial portraits, it seems at least likely that the *tesserae* with numerals were produced in the workshop near the temple of Juno Moneta, even though definitive evidence is lacking.

These *tesserae* have captured the imagination ever since they were first produced. Not only were they distributed throughout the Roman Empire after their production – as indicated by the find spots – they were imitated even in antiquity.[8] Later coins were transformed into tokens by erasing the reverse and incising a number, indicating a demand for this type of object.[9] During the Renaissance some pieces received private punch marks indicating the appraisal of their relative owners.[10] It is widely presumed that numerous modern fakes exist, which serve to satisfy the continuing appetite of collectors.[11] Even today sets of cheap imitations (recognisable as such) are available from commercial

[1] Special thanks go to Clare Rowan for publishing my paper. For help and suggestions, I am not only indebted to her but also to Stefanie Baars, Helle Horsnaes, Orla Mulholland and Klaus Vondrovec. Many of the *tesserae* cited here form part of the collection of the Münzkabinett, Staatliche Museen zu Berlin; for access to the Interactive Catalogue (IKMK), see http://ww2.smb.museum/ikmk. Coins and tokens from the Berlin collection will be referenced as IKMK followed by the object number. RIC 1^2= C. H. V. Sutherland and R. A. G. Carson, *The Roman Imperial Coinage I: From 31BC to AD 69* (London, 1984). Only a select bibliography can be provided here. For a general overview see Reis and Schindel (1998a–d) and Campana (2009), 43–96.

[2] See fig. 38. *Tesserae*: weight ca. 3.5–5g and diameter 18–23mm; quadrantes: weight ca. 2.9–3.3g and diameter ca. 15–18mm; semisses: weight ca. 4–5g and diameter 18–20mm; asses: weight ca. 9.5–11g and diameter ca. 27–29mm. For material see the samples from the IKMK.

[3] Küter (2016), 87 (for earlier references), 101–02.

[4] Claudius: Classical Numismatic Group, Auction 57, 4 March 2001, lot no. 1051. Die connections: Buttrey (1973), 54, pl. A–B; Göbl (1978), pl. 8.

[5] Göbl (1978), 31–32.

[6] Martini (1997), 5–10; Martini (1999), 13; Campana (2009), 54; Campana (2013), 66.

[7] Craddock (1978), 1; Bayley (1998), 9–13, 19–20. See below for tokens of orichalcum with the name of a private issuer, C. Mitreius.

[8] Findspots of these tokens are rare, but some are known from England, Italy, France (2 pieces), Croatia, Germany and Palestine. Ralite (2009), 193–97. For a 2010 find from the Thames in London, near Putney Bridge: http://finds.org.uk/news/story/227 (accessed 18/02/2018). Imitations: e.g. Roma Numismatics, E-Sale 3, 2 November 2013, lot no. 526.

[9] Numismatik Lanz München, Auction 105, 26 November 2001, lot no. 477.

[10] Punch marks of the families Gonzaga or Este, e.g. Gorny & Mosch, Auction 175, 9 March 2009, lot no. 319.

[11] Pesciarelli (2009), 31, no. 8.

sellers.[12] Yet, while the *spintriae* have seen die studies, and die links have been identified for other types, a complete study including all groups of *tesserae* with numerals is still missing, though some attempts have been made.[13]

This paper focuses on the group of *tesserae* with numerals on the reverse, which range from I to XVI (and sometimes bearing the additional letter A or even AVG).[14] These numerals are often surrounded by a laurel wreath with a central medallion.[15] Other tokens with a range up to XXV do not belong to this main group and are not included in the discussion here.[16]

Earlier research has placed these *tesserae* into different groups with the aim of achieving a better understanding of chronology.[17] This paper puts these tokens into groups as well, but with a focus on iconography. Three main iconographic themes can be determined: imperial portraiture, 'varia' (symbols, figures or complex scenes), and the so-called *spintriae* with depictions of *symplegmata*, e.g. erotic scenes of couples, both hetero- and homosexual.[18] In the first and second group, small or larger inscriptions may be added referring to the image.[19]

Iconography

The portrait group

Starting with the portrait group, various male members of the Julio-Claudian dynasty can be recognised. Heads of Augustus are present on at least half a dozen types. His portrait is shown facing right (fig. 1) or left, sometimes accompanied by a laurel wreath (fig. 2). Another type adds a short inscription to the portrait: FEL (fig. 3). This may mark the emperor as *felix* (lucky, happy), but it might also be explained as a general statement, *feliciter*, thus hinting at the 'happy times' the princeps brought to mankind.[20] Thus it would remind the owner of the new *saeculum aureum* (golden age) Augustus introduced in 17 BC, bringing a new age of felicity and prosperity to all Romans. Other tokens show the deified (Divus) Augustus with a radiate crown.[21] Further variation is provided by a thunderbolt that may accompany the image, comparing Augustus to the father of the gods, Jupiter, and reinforcing the divine character of the deceased emperor (fig. 4).[22] Augustus adorned with a laurel wreath, portrayed alongside his diademed wife Livia, demonstrates matrimonial concord (fig. 5).[23]

There are also two single female head types. Their identification is contentious. The first type shows a draped female bust facing right (fig. 6). There is a roll of hair (*nodus*) on the forehead and a second roll at the neck where the hair is tied together. The hair is twisted over the temples. The portrait has variously been identified as Octavia (the emperor's sister), as Julia (the only daughter of Augustus), and as Livia, the emperor's wife.[24] The second type, looking left and identified as Livia, is remarkably different, with only a *nodus* on the neck (fig. 7).[25] The rest of the hair is properly parted and flows in slight waves into a bun fastened

[12] See, for instance, https://www.amazon.com/Empire-Ancient-Brothel-Collection-Spintria/dp/B0167LSE2Q (accessed 04/12/2018).
[13] On the *spintriae* see Campana (2009); for a wider view on die links see n. 4. For the announcement of a full die study of all tokens with numerals (not completed), see Reis and Schindel (1998d), 53.
[14] IKMK 18203170.
[15] This border ornamentation has been identified as a *corona triumphalis*, connected to a triumph. See Campana (2009), 55; Pesciarelli (2009), 35.
[16] Differing in style and subject to this group, they are presumably of a later date or the result of misreading. Buttrey (1973), 52–53; Martini (1997), 5; Campana (2009), 54.
[17] Pesciarelli (2009), 33–40 with references to the older classifications of Buttrey (1973); Simonetta and Riva (1981).
[18] IKMK 18203125. The term *spintria* is a modern invention; see Jacobelli (1997), 2–3.
[19] See fig. 3 (Augustus, FEL), fig. 30 (gaming scene, MORA / MOLA), fig. 31 (dancers, legend illegible), figs. 18–20 (C MITREIVS L F MAG IVVENT).
[20] Contrarily, Pesciarelli (2009), 30, fig. 11, relates it to gambling fortune.
[21] IKMK 18203142, 18203146 and 18203158.
[22] Head of Augustus, bare: IKMK 18203147; laurel wreath: IKMK 18203134; radiate without thunderbolt: IKMK 18203142.
[23] Numismatica Ars Classica, Auction 40, 16 May 2007, lot no. 651; Göbl (1978), no. 75, pl. 8.
[24] Octavia: IKMK 18203139. De Belfort (1889), 84 pl. 3,6: 'Octavia?'' and ser. 1 pl. 3,8: 'Julia'. Livia: Buttrey (1973), pl. 4, type 12. Portraits of Julia with frontal *nodus*: Boschung (1993), 48–50 (Béziers-Kiel type) (Skizzen 17–18). Livia: Reis and Schindel (1998d), 51, no. 12.
[25] Classical Numismatic Group, Auction 57, 4 April 2001, lot no. 1045; Göbl (1978), 130, nos. 68–69, pl. 8; Reis and Schindel (1998d), 51, no. 13; Pesciarelli (2009), 30, fig. 12.

Fig. 1: Brass token. Augustus, bareheaded (4.39g) (Numismatica Ars Classica, Auction 64, 17 May 2012, lot no. 2448).

Fig. 2: Brass token. Augustus, wearing laurel wreath (3.21g, Ø 10mm) (Courtesy of the Münzkabinett, Staatliche Museen zu Berlin, IKMK 18203134) (photo: Lutz-Jürgen Lübke / Lübke & Wiedemann).

Fig. 3: Brass token. Augustus, wearing laurel wreath, and inscription FEL (5.48g) (Numismatica Ars Classica, Auction 72, 16 May 2013, lot no. 595).

Fig. 4: Brass token. Augustus, radiate, thunderbolt in left field (3.43g; Ø 21mm) (Courtesy of the Münzkabinett, Staatliche Museen zu Berlin, IKMK 1820313) (photo: Lutz-Jürgen Lübke / Lübke & Wiedemann).

Fig. 5: Brass token. Jugate busts of Augustus and Livia (4.76g) (Numismatica Ars Classica, Auction 78, 26 May 2014, lot no. 835).

Fig. 6: Brass token. Livia (?) (3.65g; Ø 20mm) (Courtesy of the Münzkabinett, Staatliche Museen zu Berlin, IKMK 18203139) (photo: Lutz-Jürgen Lübke / Lübke & Wiedemann).

at the neck. It may be assumed that these *tesserae* show two different members of the Julio-Claudian family.[26] Identification attempts should begin with the jugate busts of Augustus and Livia shown on fig. 5. Here Livia is depicted with a stephane and voluminous hair on her forehead. It is not clear whether this is a *nodus* or not.

Yet the *nodus* belongs to a well-known portrait style of Livia from the Augustan period.[27] There are two portrait types of Livia with a knot of hair on the forehead: the Marbury Hall type and the Copenhagen 615 type.[28] Under Tiberius a different hairstyle emerges, showing parted hair without a *nodus* (Ceres type).[29] It must be emphasised that on the basis of portrait types, either *tessera* could represent Livia. Unfortunately, any identifying sign – like the stephane of the jugate busts – is lacking. But looking at the facial features of the head facing left, this sober face with the distinctive nose is unlikely to represent Livia. Her fine features rather seem to be present in the portrait facing right. But given the very small material basis (one die for each type), the argument is not very strong and thus all conclusions remain preliminary.

Given that the draped bust with ornamental hairstyle probably represents Livia, the portrait facing left still needs identification. On the basis of the hairstyle, she might be either Antonia the Younger (mother of Drusus the Younger), or Livilla (wife of Drusus the Younger).[30] Livilla's portrait style emerged from a similar portrait type associated with her mother Antonia. The parted hair and the flat waves, flowing into a bun at the neck, fit with

[26] Contrarily, Reis and Schindel (1998d), 51, nos. 12–13, suggest that it is Livia in both images.

[27] For the portraits of Livia, see Winkes (1995), 206, no. 215 (Paris, Louvre); Boschung (1993), 45–47; Bartman (1999).

[28] Boschung (1993), 45–46 (Skizzen 10–11) (Marbury Hall) and 12–13 (Kopenhagen 615).

[29] Boschung (1993), 47 (Skizzen 14–15).

[30] For Antonia the Younger, see Boschung (1993), 51–52, Wilton House type (Skizzen 21–22). Julia, wife of Tiberius and daughter of Augustus, should be excluded: she had already died, disgraced and exiled, in 3 BC. Antonia the Younger, wife of Drusus the Younger, is a possibility, but after the death of her husband in 9 BC she was kept in the background. The wavy hair, lacking a *nodus* on the forehead, points to Livilla, wife of Drusus. For a comparison with sculptural portraiture, see Boschung (1993), 63–64, figs. 45–46 (Livilla, Leptis – Malta type).

Fig. 7: Brass token. Livilla (?) (6.17g) (Classical Numismatic Group, Auction 57, 4 April 2001, lot no. 1045).

Fig. 8: Brass token. Tiberius (3.43g; Ø 20mm) (Courtesy of Münzkabinett, Staatliche Museen zu Berlin, IKMK 18203144) (photo: Lutz-Jürgen Lübke / Lübke & Wiedemann).

Fig. 9: Brass token. Tiberius, wearing laurel wreath, *lituus* in front (4.83g; Ø 23mm) (Courtesy of the Münzkabinett, Staatliche Museen zu Berlin, IKMK 18203128) (photo: Lutz-Jürgen Lübke / Lübke & Wiedemann).

Fig. 10: Brass token. Cuirassed bust of Drusus the Younger (5.21g; Ø 23mm) (Courtesy of the Münzkabinett, Staatliche Museen zu Berlin, IKMK 18203145) ('Julio-Claudian prince') (photo: Lutz-Jürgen Lübke / Lübke & Wiedemann).

Fig. 11: Brass token. Cuirassed bust of Drusus the Younger (3.66g; Ø 19mm) (Courtesy of ANS 1944.100.76077).

Fig. 12: Brass token. Cuirassed bust of Drusus the Younger (4.02g; Ø 22mm) (Courtesy of the Münzkabinett, Staatliche Museen zu Berlin, IKMK 18203140) ('probably Germanicus') (photo: Lutz-Jürgen Lübke / Lübke & Wiedemann).

her hairstyle. Only the small framing locks ('Schläfchenlocken') that her sculptured portraits possess are lacking here.

Portraits of Tiberius are also found among the *tesserae*. His head appears bare (fig. 8) or with a laurel wreath and *lituus* in front (fig. 9).[31] The priestly staff marks him as a member of the augurs; but, above all, the *lituus* should be understood as a counterpart to the thunderbolt of Divus Augustus. Just as the *fulmen* (thunderbolt) is the attribute of the highest divine prestige (Divus Augustus), the *lituus* is the highest attribute that could possibly be given to a living human being (Tiberius), marking him as holder of *imperium* or power to command.[32]

Of special interest is the depiction of a young male member of the imperial family, preserved in two different iconographic types. One shows a youthful male bust facing left, clad in a cuirass and mantle (figs. 10–11).[33] It is difficult to identify. In the nineteenth century, the youth shown on the Berlin *tessera* was labelled as Nero while the specimen in the American Numismatic Society was identified as Caligula.[34]

The military dress is also found on a very similar but more elaborate type, which shows the individual from behind carrying a transverse spear (figs. 12–14). Usually identified as Germanicus, it has been shown elsewhere that this is probably a representation of Drusus the Younger as *promachos* (champion) and *exemplum virtutis* (a model of manliness).[35]

[31] IKMK 18203144, 18203128.

[32] *Lituus* as sign of *imperium*: Siebert (1999), 131. For the connection of emperor Tiberius and the *lituus,* see, e.g., the Great Cameo of France (Tiberius holding the augur's wand in his right hand). For its interpretation as a symbol of *imperium* (for Augustus and Tiberius) see Siebert (1999), 130.

[33] IKMK 18203145 and ANS 1944.100.76077 (3.66g, 19mm). While the head on the example from the ANS collection clearly wears a laurel wreath, the head on the piece from the Berlin Coin Cabinet might be bare. Yet, given the similarity of the scheme, the motif probably represents the same person.

[34] Nero: De Belfort (1889), 91, pl. IV, no. 13. Caligula: https://bit.ly/2RxykC3 (accessed 03/12/2018).

[35] Buttrey (1973), 62; Numismatica Ars Classica, Auction 64, 17 May 2012, lot no. 2453; Göbl (1978), 130, no. 82, pl. 8; Reis and Schindel (1998d), 51, no. 11; Pesciarelli (2009), 31, fig. 13. For an earlier study see Küter (2016), 96ff.

Fig. 13: Brass token. Cuirassed bust of Drusus the Younger (note the detail of the bulge of the *paludamentum* on the left shoulder) (4.36g) (Fritz Rudolf Künker GmbH & Co., KG 288, 13 May 2017, lot no. 394) ('Germanicus').

Fig. 14: Brass token. Cuirassed bust of Drusus the Younger (note the detail of the star on the back of the cuirass) (5.29g) (Classical Numismatic Group, Mail Bid Sale 57, 4 April 2001, lot no. 1048) ('Germanicus').

Fig. 15: Brass token. Twins of Drusus the Younger. (Courtesy of Helle Horsnaes, Kopenhagen, Nationalmuseen Reutze, inv. no. 2095).

Fig. 16: Sestertius of Tiberius (AD 23). Twin sons of Drusus the Younger (26.21g; Ø 36mm) (Courtesy of the Münzkabinett, Staatliche Museen zu Berlin, IKMK 18212918) (photo: Dirk Sonnenwald).

Fig. 17: As of Tiberius (AD 23). Drusus the Younger (11.27g; Ø 31mm) (Courtesy of the Münzkabinett, Staatliche Museen zu Berlin, IKMK 18212825) (photo: Dirk Sonnenwald).

The type is die-connected to another *tessera* (fig. 15), bearing the busts of two boys clad in tunics and adorned with two stars above their heads.[36] They have been identified as the twin sons of Drusus, Tiberius Gemellus and Germanicus Julius Caesar.[37] The stars mark them as Dioscuri. The motif of the twin heads seems to be drawn from sestertii coinage of AD 23 (fig. 16); here the busts (clad in tunics and adorned with *bullae*, necklaces worn by Roman children) are placed atop cornucopiae (horns of plenty) and complemented by a caduceus.[38] Asses were also issued with the depiction of Drusus the Younger at this time (fig. 17). This leads to the conclusion that the cuirassed bust on the tokens (figs. 10–14) must also represent Drusus, father of the twins Tiberius and Germanicus. Imperial coinage probably provided the model for the twin boys' depiction, and the bronze *tesserae* copied the scheme with some variation.

Reviewing the portrait group, it becomes clear that the tokens can be assembled into a family tree. No less than four generations are honoured here. Starting with Augustus and Livia as a couple, we move to Divus Augustus, whose deification lifted the entire family above all other Roman families into a divine sphere. The protagonist of the next generation is Tiberius as the current emperor. He lacks female company in the portrayals except, perhaps, for his mother Livia who – as an important nexus in the dynasty – is closely associated with the new emperor after the death of Augustus in AD 14.[39] The third level of this tree is dedicated to Tiberius' (living) offspring, namely Drusus the Younger as an active general. His wife Livilla is probably also shown. The fourth section of this genealogy consists of their sons, who are a promise to the upcoming generation: they are regarded as the guarantors of continuity, happiness and well-being.

[36] Buttrey (1973), 55, 62, no. 19; Göbl (1978), no. 82, pl. 8; Martini (1999), 24, no. II.3.C, fig. 39; Campana (2009), 47, fig. 2b; Reis and Schindel (1998a), 54. The pellet that connects the two busts is reminiscent of a *bulla* (cf. fig. 16).
[37] Buttrey (1973), 55; Göbl (1978), no. 77, pl. 8.
[38] Buttrey (1973), 55; Reis and Schindel (1998a), 54.
[39] For an iconographic connection see Bartman (1999), 102–21.

A mysterious sub-group of tokens concludes the portrait section (figs. 18–20). Consisting of three types, these specimens are listed in some catalogues, but are usually omitted from discussion of these *tesserae*. Yet, since some types of this group carry numerals on the reverse (figs. 18–19), they must be connected to this broader group in some way.[40] The common element of this small group is the obverse, which bears the inscription C(aius) MITREIVS L(ucii) F(ilius) MAG(ister) IVVENT(utis) (Gaius Mitreius, son of Lucius, *magister* of the youth). There exist at least three obverse dies that carry this legend alongside a bare male head. Whose portrait is this? The example from the Triton collection might suggest that it is Augustus who is depicted (fig. 18). Apart from the well-known physiognomy, there is a cornucopia shown beneath the portrait. The cornucopia is a typical emblem of the Augustan period, but it is by no means restricted to this time: the cornucopia might also be added to the portraits of Tiberius or Drusus.[41] This echoes the other small attributes like the *lituus*, *fulmen* or the inscription FEL that are found on other types mentioned above (figs. 3–4, 9) and gives some strength to the connection of these tokens to the imperial portrait group.

Yet a second obverse die (fig. 19) lacks the strong similarity to Augustus.[42] The fleshy cheeks show some similarity to Tiberian portraits or even Tiberius himself. An attribution of the portrait to a prince is equally possible, just as it may portray Mitreius, whose features are, unfortunately, unknown to us. As neither the legend nor the attribute differs, these tokens must show the same person. The same is true regarding the third die, this time not connected to a numeral, but to the depiction of a two-storey basilica (fig. 20), supplemented by a secondary incision, the numeral X.[43] In sum, the most obvious solution is to connect the portrait to Mitreius, as the legend indicates. Yet, regarding the cornucopia, a representation of a male member of the imperial family is equally possible.

The 'varia' group

Imperial symbols

Turning to the 'varia' group, the material can be organised thematically into several sub-groups. The first is connected to the portrait section, showing typical symbols belonging to the sphere of the Julio-Claudian imperial family: Victory (shown frontally), the Capricorn, Medusa, or Victoria in a *quadriga* (figs. 21–23).[44] These emblems are also typical pictorial motifs, frequently found on coins, militaria, lamps and other objects.

Fig. 18: Brass token. Obverse legend naming C. Mitreius (Classical Numismatic Group, Triton IV, 5 October 2000, lot no. 449).

Fig. 19: Brass token. Obverse legend naming C. Mitreius (Glendining & Co., Collection Hall 1950, part II, no. 2124).

Fig. 20: Brass token. Obverse legend naming C. Mitreius; reverse showing the Basilica of L. Sextilius (20mm; Ø 3.58g) (Courtesy of the Ashmolean Museum).

[40] Rowan (2017). A die link of this reverse to other tokens carrying numbers has not yet been found.

[41] For the token: Cohen (1892), 267, nos. 14–15; Rowan (2017). The cornucopia has a long tradition on coins and gems, starting in the early third century BC, denoting the concept of peace under an ideal ruler. Yet, it became very popular under Augustus who chose it as an emblem (e.g. aureus RIC I² Augustus 127). It also appears as the main motif on moneyers' issues (e.g. quadrantes RIC I² Augustus 422, 425). See Galinsky (1998), 111–18; Küter (2014), 299. On coins of Tiberius, it is not connected to the ruler himself but to the twins of Drusus (RIC I² Tiberius 42, see below).

[42] Glendining & Co., Collection Hall 1950, part II no. 2124; Göbl (1978), no. 67, pl. 8; Reis and Schindel (1998a), 54; Rowan (2017).

[43] Cohen (1892), 267, no. 12; Oxford, Ashmolean Museum (20mm, 3.58g); Rowan (2017). The legend on the structure ('L. SEXTILI S(uo) P(ecunia)') indicates that the basilica has been financed by L. Sextilius.

[44] Victoria (*quadriga*): Pesciarelli (2009), 36, fig. 17. Capricorn: Buttrey (1973), 62, fig. 18, pl. 4; Reis and Schindel (1998d), 52, no. 38. Medusa: Bernhart (1926), 12, pl. 32.7; Buttrey (1973), 62, no. 21, pl. 4; Göbl (1978), no. 96, pl. 9.

Fig. 21: Brass token. Victory (4.02g; Ø 22mm) (Numismatica Ars Classica, Auction 40, 16 May 2007, lot no. 652).

Fig. 22: Brass token. Capricorn (3.50g; Ø 21mm) (Courtesy of the Münzkabinett, Staatliche Museen zu Berlin, IKMK 18203161) (photo: Lutz-Jürgen Lübke / Lübke & Wiedemann).

Fig. 23: Brass token. Victory in *quadriga* (4.54g) (Gorny & Mosch Giessener, Münzhandlung 181, 12 January 2009, lot no. 2823).

Fig. 24: Brass token. Dionysus (6.50g) (Numismatica Ars Classica, Auction 64, 17 May 2012, lot no. 1096).

Fig. 25: Brass token. Maenad (3.98g) (Numismatica Ars Classica, Auction 64, 17 May 2012, lot no. 2455)

Fig. 26: Brass token. Maenad (Glendining & Co., Collection Hall 1950, part 2, no. 2122).

The Dionysiac group

The second group is filled with Dionysiac imagery. The god himself appears as a draped bust facing right (fig. 24).[45] The head has been identified as Drusilla or Apollo.[46] However, the distinctive ivy-wreath leaves no doubt that it is Dionysus, god of wine, who is shown here.[47] A companion to the god and part of his *thiasos* (retinue) is a Maenad, namely a female follower, represented on two types. One shows her with bare breasts holding a *thyrsus* (staff) (fig. 25).[48] On the second she is turning left and equipped with a *cantharus* (drinking cup) (fig. 26).[49]

A male companion to Dionysus is Silenus (or a satyr), riding a donkey or a mule to the right while holding a *thyrsus* (fig. 27).[50] His head is bent forward, leaving the impression that he is heavily drunk and almost sleeping on the back of his mount. The identification is secured by a small detail, namely the bell that is hanging from the neck of the animal – a common attribute of scenes of this kind.[51] Connected to this image is a type showing a *biga* of mules or donkeys (possibly pulling a triumphal chariot with two passengers).[52]

[45] Not mentioned in the catalogues of Buttrey (1973) or Reis and Schindel (1998). Gemini LLC, Auction 12, 11 January 2015, lot no. 338.

[46] Drusilla: Cohen (1892), 262.2; Numismatik Lanz München, Auction 94, 22 November 1999, lot no. 201; Fritz Rudolf Künker GmbH & Co., Auction 124, 16 March 2007, lot no. 8812. Apollo: Classical Numismatic Group, Auction 69, 8 June 2005, lot no. 1518.

[47] A further draped bust, adorned with wreath and long hair tied up at the neck, is difficult to identify. The bust is usually labelled as female and the wreath as made of ivy. Ceres is one suggestion, but the wreath of Ceres is usually made of corn ears. If it is an ivy wreath, then we may have a further example of a bust of Dionysus. See Buttrey (1973), 62, no. 20, pl. 4 (Ceres); Reis and Schindel (1998d), 51, no. 16 (Ceres).

[48] Not mentioned by Buttrey (1973) or Reis and Schindel (1998).

[49] Buttrey (1973), pl. 4, no. 22 (Maenad); Reis and Schindel (1998d), 51, no. 17; Martini (1997), 18, no. II.1.E ('mezza figura di Livia[?]-Menade[?]').

[50] Jacobelli (1997), 25, nos. 35–37; Jacobelli (2000), 28, fig. 46.

[51] On gems see Imhoof-Blumer and Keller (1889), 107, pl. XVII, no. 10.

[52] Milan, inv. M.0.9.32900 (much worn and thus not clearly readable); Paris, BN, inv. 17087; Martini (1997), 24–25, no. 38; Jacobelli (1997), 25, no. 38 ('i muli sembrano trainare una biga trionfale, il che attribuirebbe a questa scena un intento ironico' – see the definitely ironic type with triumphant apes on a camel, fig. 33 in this piece); Jacobelli (2000), 33, fig. 58. Campana (2009), 47, fig. 2c. The pieces are too worn to be discussed extensively.

Fig. 27: Brass token. Silenus (4.34g; Ø 21mm) (Courtesy of the American Numismatic Society, ANS 1944.100.76079).

Fig. 28: Brass token. Wine-making scene (6.27g) (Jaquier, Auction 40, 16 October 2015, lot no. 199).

A further theme can be added to this group: two males crushing grapes to make wine (fig. 28).[53] Grape vines rise to the left and to the right of a large tub in which two men are at work, indicating a country landscape. It is an exhilarating, amusing scene – the males look almost like dancers. One can imagine how slippery their work must be crushing grapes; they hold on to each other to keep their balance, the danger of falling into the slippery pulp ever present. The picture stimulates the imagination. Similar to Dionysus, the Maenads, and the riding Silenus, we have a motif frequently found elsewhere in Roman art, for example on sarcophagi.[54]

Playful and delightful scenes

The playful spirit of some of the *tesserae* mentioned above continues in other thematically diverse scenes. One type presents two male figures sitting together at a table (fig. 29). In the background, a high square pillar or a cupboard with the sculpture of a quadruped is visible. Depending on the transcription of the legend that might be MORA or MOLA, the figures are playing either *morra* (a finger game) or rather a board game. The round gaming pieces that are slightly visible on the table point to the latter case.[55] It would thus be the 'Nine Men's Morris' (mill) game, popular from antiquity until present times. The token is reminiscent of a lively pub scene. Similar depictions are known from graffiti in Pompeii, e.g. from the bar of Salvius (Pompeii VI.14.36), where two men are playing dice.[56]

A further type consists of three female figures in the style of the Three Graces, accompanied by a rather illegible legend (fig. 30).[57] The girls are properly dressed in tunics and mantles. Their cheeks are puffed up from playing the double pipe; they may or may not be shown wearing *phorbeia* (halters) to support their lips and cheeks. Their bending bodies suggest that they are dancing, obviously to their own tunes; as the two girls on the right are playing the *tibia* (double flute), they are a group of musicians. Such a representation is reminiscent of Maenads as part of the ecstatic retinue of Dionysus.[58] Given their dresses, however, they might rather represent *tibicinae* (professional flute players). Girls playing the double flute were often part of spectacles in the Roman theatre or in other festive entertainments. Female flute players also worked at bars or were hired at private dinner parties.[59] Here their business

[53] Jacobelli (1997), 28, cat. IV.4, no. 40, fig. 21; Martini (1997), 26, cat. II.3.D, no. 40; Jacobelli (2000), 28, fig. 48.
[54] Bielefeld (1997).
[55] See, for instance, Paris, BN, Département des Monnaies, Médailles et Antiques, no. 17088. Usually the legend is read as *mora*; see De Belfort (1892), 174ff., pl. VI, no. 13; Göbl (1978), nos. 71–72, pl. 8; Reis and Schindel (1998b), 54; Reis and Schindel (1998d), 52, no. 34; Pesciarelli (2009), 35, fig. 16 (Pesciarelli suggests that *morra* is the game that the *tesserae* with numerals belong to. Yet, *morra* is a simple finger game that could be played anywhere, anytime. There is no indication that any tokens were required). Clare Rowan encouraged me to consider the reading not *mor(r)a* but *mola*.
[56] The Pompeian graffito (CIL 04.03494 = Graff. Pomp. 00431, dated to AD 62–79) forms part of the painted decoration of the bar (*caupona*) of Salvius. The supporting graffito is similar to a modern comic, and provides the conversation of the two players. Man on the left (holding a dice cup): *Exsi*! ('I win!'). On the right: *Non tria, duas est*! ('No, it is not a three, it is a two!'). Clarke (1998–1999), 33, fig. 6 (http://www.pompeiiinpictures.eu/r6/6%2014%2036.htm) (accessed 17/12/2018).
[57] Glendining & Co., Collection Hall 1950, part II, no. 2123 ('THEOD – VINCAT'); Buttrey (1973), 62, fig. 23, pl. 4; Göbl (1978), nos. 91–92, pl. 8; Reis and Schindel (1998d), 52, no. 34 ('THEODORI. MVSA (?)'); Classical Numismatic Group, Mail Bid Sale 79, 17 September 2008, lot no. 1051 ('BAN HIL(?) – THEODHO(?)').
[58] On the Three Graces connected to Dionysus and the symposium see Pindar, *Odes*, 14.8.
[59] Varro, *Saturae Menippae*, 333; Aulus Gellius, *Attic Nights*, 13.11.1.

Fig. 29: Brass token. Players (Hess (1912), no. 467).

Fig. 30: Brass token. Musicians (6.15g) (Classical Numismatic Group, Mail Bid Sale 79, 17 September 2008, lot no. 1051).

Fig. 31: Brass token. Circus (?) *biga* (4.12g) (Numismatica Ars Classica, Auction 64, 17 May 2012, lot no. 1093).

was not restricted to music; the entertainment they provided was of a sexual nature as well. These professional *tibicinae* in service of upper-class men generally were of low social status.[60] The legend that accompanies the image is, unfortunately, not clear. It probably hints at the unknown context, which might be a musical competition or perhaps praises one of the girls ('Theod[ora?]').[61]

Another subject of the tokens is a circus (?) driver in a *biga*, galloping to the right (fig. 31).[62] Finally, a further *tessera* is such an eye-catcher that it deserves deeper discussion. It depicts a camel walking right, bearing on its back a chariot harnessed to the camel's head (fig. 32).[63] The 'driver' of this chariot holds a sceptre in his left hand, while his right hand is outstretched. Behind him a smaller figure raises its hand to the head of the driver. Two details, barely recognisable on the worn specimens that survive, create further puzzlement: the rear figure possesses a long tail, while the front figure has a ball-shaped belly. It is clear that this *tessera* shows a triumph scene – but one obviously of satiric character, as Luciana Jacobelli has rightly emphasised.[64] The elements of this *triumphus* are not a dignified *imperator* with a servant standing behind him in a chariot of horses. Rather we have a harnessed camel and two monkeys, riding the impressive animal in ridiculous perversion. The rear monkey imitates the state slave, whose task it was to hold the heavy *corona etrusca* above the head of the victorious general. Obviously, this picture demonstrates a good dose of humour. Not only is the triumph mocked but the token is almost funny: it is known that the servant whispered to the triumphator: 'Remember that you are only a human being' (*hominem te esse memento*!). But on this *tessera*, animals instead of humans are shown, though humanity is implicitly suggested. By this, one of the most venerable rituals of Roman culture becomes the target of humorous caricature.

One might think it impossible for the Romans to ridicule the ceremony of triumph. Still, such parodies are well-known from Roman antiquity.[65] A portion of self-irony can be demonstrated, for example, by the famous 'ape-Aeneas', a painting found in Pompeii.[66] In this 'monkey business', the male figures in the famous scene of Aeneas saving his father and son from Troy have turned into dog-headed apes with their penises on display.[67] Indeed, the token with the camel and monkeys may have a further meaning.[68] Some wealthy Romans kept trained monkeys as pets. Trained monkeys were also exhibited in theatres and circuses.[69] Being talented in mimicry of human beings, these creatures were put into costumes and

[60] Woeckner (2002), 69–70. It is important to emphasise that these musicians cannot have belonged to a ceremony of sacrifice or any occasion of dignity. It was the privilege of men (*tibicen*) to perform music at sacrifices, except for the few rites that were actually restricted to women. Wockner (2002), 70: '[...] While the *tibicen* was a member of a *collegium* or professional guild, the female *tibicina* was principally characterised as a drunken and promiscuous party girl'.

[61] See the *tessera* with inscription MORA (MOLA) (fig. 29), thus enlighting the context.

[62] Buttrey (1973), 62, no. 24, pl. 4; Reis and Schindel (1998d), 52, no. 33.

[63] IKMK 18203170; Buttrey (1973), 62, no. 25, pl. 4; Göbl (1978), no. 79, pl. 8; Jacobelli (1997), 26–27, cat. IV.3, fig 19; Martini (1997), 26, cat. II.3.E, no. 41; Jacobelli (2000), 24, 30, fig. 53; Pesciarelli (2009), 35.

[64] Jacobelli (1997), 26. Monkeys as a theme of burlesque: Voegtle (2013), 143ff. Rejecting the possibility of a parody of the Roman triumph: Reis and Schindel (1998a), 54.

[65] Voegtle (2013), 181–88.

[66] Pompeii IX 13.5; now in Naples, Museo Archeologico Nazionale, inv. 9089 (dated to AD 14–79).

[67] Maiuri (1950), 108–12, figs. 1–2; Voegtle (2013), 183–86, esp. 186; criticism on Maiuri by Brendel (1953–1954), 157, pl. 61.

[68] As insinuated, without further evidence, by Reis and Schindel (1998a), 54.

[69] Apuleius, *Metamorphoses*, 11.8.3.

Fig. 32: Brass token. Monkeys riding a camel (6.11g; Ø 22mm) (Courtesy of the Münzkabinett, Staatliche Museen zu Berlin, IKMK 18203170) (photo: Lutz-Jürgen Lübke / Lübke & Wiedemann).

Fig. 33: Brass token. Construction scene (5.36g; Ø 21mm) (Courtesy of the Münzkabinett, Staatliche Museen zu Berlin, IKMK 18203165) (photo: Lutz-Jürgen Lübke / Lübke & Wiedemann).

Fig. 34: Brass token. Construction scene (Courtesy of Klaus Vondrovec, Vienna, Kunsthistorisches Museum, inv. no. 32707; ex Collection Tiepolo 1821).

made people laugh by mirroring human behaviour while crossing moral frontiers. Evidence for this comes from wall paintings of Pompeii, where a monkey is shown wearing a jacket (perhaps a costume) while a boy trains him; monkeys dressed as gladiators also appear as lamp decorations.[70] Returning to our *tessera*, one might posit that the die-cutter not only imagined a monkey-triumph, but that he might have remembered such a circus scene from memory: as a side show during a performance, a camel might have been led though the arena, carrying a miniature chariot with trained monkeys dressed as a *triumphator* and a *servus*. Such a scene would certainly have made the audience laugh.

Another *tessera* can be added to the 'varia' group. It shows three figures, one of them in a large container (figs. 33–34). The motif is commonly referred to as a girls' swinging scene.[71] However, the basket in which the figure is seated is connected to four ropes that lead to a winch. The flanking figures are thus not pushing the individual in the basket, but rather pulling on the rope to lift the basket into the air. Much physical effort is needed for this task, as indicated by their posture. Rather than a swinging scene, the type depicts three men at a construction site. Scaffolding is clearly visible in the background, perhaps a ladder.

Similar construction site scenes are known from Roman reliefs and wall paintings.[72] The use of ladders and baskets for the transport of building materials in these reliefs is comparable to the *tessera* scene. A relief from Capua shows a tower crane or a treadmill; a winch and pulley are also used here.[73] Returning to the *tessera*, it seems that the winching of a figure in the basket is meant to add an element of fun to the token. Why does not the middle figure simply use the ladder, since the basket is supposed to transport bricks and tools? The raised arm might be a sign of joy due the unusual ride and the resulting troubles to his companions below.

Spintriae

This particular group, characterised by sexual imagery (*symplegma*), has been the focus of a significant amount of research whose conclusions will not be repeated here. Rather two points are emphasised: first, the lovers on these tokens are both heterosexual and homosexual (male and female).[74] Second, the playful, funny character of other tokens can also be found here, as demonstrated by a scene in which a whip is included (fig. 35). Since sadism or masochistic sexual practices are not documented in antiquity, Jacobelli might be right in interpreting this scene as a satire of the *manumissio vindicta*, a ceremony by which slaves

[70] Apes as actors: Lazenby (1949), 247–48; Toynbee (1973), 58; Voegtle (2013), 49.

[71] Bernhart (1926), 12, pl. 32, no. 4; Buttrey (1973), 62, no. 26; Göbl (1978), 130, no. 73, pl. 8; Jacobelli (1997), 24; Reis and Schindel (1998d), 52, no. 36; Jacobelli (2000), 20, 29, fig. 52; Pesciarelli (2009), 35.

[72] Folin (2014), 292–95; Kretschmer (1978), 22, fig. 27.

[73] Kretschmer (1978), 30, fig. 43: Capua, Museo Provinciale Campano, relief depicting the column factory of Lucceius Peculiaris.

[74] Scenes with homosexual content are difficult to detect, see Clarke (2003), 86–87. This is particularly the case for the smallish *tesserae*.

Fig. 35: Brass token. *Coitus a tergo* (4.20g) (Numismatica Genevensis, Auction 4, 11 December 2006, lot no. 144).

received their freedom (fig. 35).[75] In this sense the scene might evoke a playful release from 'slavery' by means of sexual intercourse.

To reiterate: the iconography of Roman bronze tokens with numerals can be divided into several groups. The portrait group focuses on the Julio-Claudian imperial family, showing a family tree. Much effort is put into adorning many of these images with attributes (*lituus*, thunderbolt, abbreviated legends) or particular modes of representation that give them a heroic and festive character. Few tokens seem to have a serious character (e.g. Capricorn and Victory); the majority of the imagery, like the monkeys riding a camel, was meant to make their owners smile. The *spintriae* add to the playful character. Their iconography is drawn from pattern books, using schemes that are widely known from many different types of object (mirrors, vases, wall paintings, reliefs, other small decorated items, etc.) from the classical period into the Roman Empire, thus proving their long-lasting popularity.[76] Clearly, the die cutters of the *tesserae* did not invent the motifs by themselves. In fact, they simply used well-known emblemata – not only for the *spintriae*, but also for the other scenes.

Dating, function and authority

Dating

On the function and exact dating of these tokens much research has already been performed, from the Renaissance to the present day.[77] The *tesserae* have predominantly been assigned to the reign of Tiberius (AD 14–37). Some types are thought to have been produced under Augustus (those showing the emperor without signs of deification); the end of production is generally assigned to the reign of Claudius.[78] Some scholars have proposed a Flavian date, particularly under Domitian (AD 81–96).[79] However, this later date can be excluded: the find of a gilded imitation of a *tessera* in a tomb in Modena (ancient Mutina) in 2003 with a closed context dating to the reign of Claudius means they must have been produced before the Flavians.[80] This context, as well as the iconographic repertoire of the group, indicates a Julio-Claudian date.

An even narrower time frame can be determined. Buttrey observed a close resemblance between some of the images on the tokens and motifs on the official Roman coinage of Tiberius (see below). It is a general rule that imperial coinage sets the example for emulation in types in other media, e.g. provincial coinage or glass pastes. This suggests that the parallel types on imperial coinage provide a *terminus post quem* for the

Fig. 36: Marble relief depicting the manumission of slaves (first century BC.) (Courtesy of Ad Meskens, Musée Royal de Mariemont).

[75] For the lack of sadomachism see Jones (1982), 113. For *manumissio vindicta*: Jacobelli (1997), 10–13; Campana (2009), 57, cat. D 1, no. 59.

[76] Pattern books for erotic depictions: Jacobelli (1995), 66–67, 83–84; cf. Trümpler-Ris (1982), 39–42 (mass production of *symplegma* scenes on ceramics).

[77] Paintings discovered in the Terme Suburbane of Pompeii appeared to be able to shed new light on these tokens, but the similarities between the images is mere coincidence. See Jacobelli (1995); Stumpp (2001), 201; Clarke (2003), 116–32.

[78] For an overview of the history of research see: Campana (2009), 44–48; Pesciarelli (2009), 31–32.

[79] Nadrowski (1906), 287–89; Simonetta and Riva (1981), 23.

[80] RIC I² Claudius 113. Benassi, Giordani and Poggi (2003), 263, no. 5. Dating of the as: according to RIC I², ca. AD 50–54 but lately a dating to AD 42–43 has been proposed by Besombes and Barrandon (2000), 161–88.

tokens. Given that *tessera* types like the radiate head of Divus Augustus, the twins of Drusus, or Drusus himself, appear on imperial coinage only in AD 23, this date can be taken as a starting point for the main group of tokens.[81] Moreover, as the official coins mention that Drusus is the holder of tribunician power for the second time (a position he had from March – April AD 23), and that he died suddenly on 25th June the same year – which would have made any mention of his role as heir obsolete – the coins and the *tesserae* were probably minted within this short three-month time span.[82]

Function

Multiple ideas have been proposed as to the purpose of tokens. Separate functions have been given to the different groups. But since Buttrey's 1973 article it is clear that any study has to account for the fact that the groups are die-linked: the imperial portraiture group, the 'varia' scenes and the *spintriae* all share dies. For that reason, it is impossible to deduce the purpose of tokens from their imagery. It is tempting, for example, to suppose that a token with a depiction of sexual intercourse served as a brothel token. But then what purpose would the imperial portrait serve, or the Capricorn? The various scenes were meant simply as decoration, not to indicate their field of use.[83] For this aspect, the most relevant and revealing feature are the numbers carried on the reverse.

There is no reason to suggest any connection to the military or triumphs since many of these tokens do not carry a laurel wreath as a border. Military victory and triumph form part of the themes, but these are found alongside other topics like the Dionysiac sphere. All in all, it is the same repertoire that can be found as common decoration in Roman private houses, from lamps to wall paintings. Motifs connected to the imperial house, myths, satire, and erotic encounters formed everyday decorative patterns displayed by their owners to demonstrate their high level of education and cosmopolitan nature.[84] Given the wide range of everyday themes and the highly lively iconography, the interpretation of these pieces as gaming tokens seems the most probable (at least for the moment).[85] The variety of esteemed portraits and funny or stimulating scenes fits within an ambience of leisure and gaming. Many of the topics address the interests of common people. It must be admitted, however, that gaming tokens are usually black or white and are undecorated.[86] What we know about them does not fit the characteristics of the tokens discussed here. Nevertheless, bone and ivory *tesserae* exist that bear numbers on one side (written in both Latin and Greek), combined with portraits of both the gods and Augustus.[87] These have been interpreted as gaming counters on the basis of their find spots.[88] These bone tokens and the brass *tesserae* with numerals discussed in this paper might have belonged to related games.

[81] RIC I² Tiberius 74–78, dupondii. Buttrey (1973), 55. Some tokens with numerals on the reverse probably bear portraits of Caligula and Claudius (e.g. Classical Numismatic Group, Auction 57, 4 April 2001, no. 1051; Göbl (1978), no. 94, tab. 9; IKMK 18203166). None of these, however, can be die-connected to the earlier group. It is important to stress that the Tiberian coinage of AD 23 provides a *terminus post quem* for the majority of types. This eliminates suggestions like that of Pesciarelli (2009), esp. 36, that the *tesserae* are not later than AD 17.

[82] For dating of the coins see Wolters (2016), 214–48. There is no need to assume that the tokens showing Augustus without a radiate crown were issued during the lifetime of the first emperor; these representations form part of the wide range of iconographic types of Augustus and are connected to the main group by dies.

[83] Bateson (1991), 392; Jacobelli (1995), 70; Pesciarelli (2009), 38.

[84] Clarke (1999), 721–25.

[85] Already Mowat (1898), 21; Buttrey (1973), 54; Benassi, Giordani and Poggi (2003), 261. There is no (board) game at hand that fits the needs of numerals up to XVI. For the games like 'XII *scripta*/*alea*', '*ludus latrunculorum*', mill or '*mancala*' see Widura (2015), 115–20.

[86] Holliger (1983), 5–24.

[87] For a complete set, found in 1903 in a child's grave in Russia, see Rostovtsew (1905), 110–24; Alföldi-Rosenbaum (1976), 205–39.

[88] One group dates to late Ptolemaic and early Roman Alexandria and is made of ivory (Holliger (1983), 11, fig. 4). Tokens of this type have been found all over the Roman Empire – just like the tokens with numerals. For a game counter (ivory) bearing a Roman numeral on the reverse (IIII), see Holliger (1983), 12, fig. 5. The obverse is undecorated.

Authority

An imperial gift to celebrate new coinage?

Close parallels in themes between *tesserae* and contemporary coinage have been stated. If there is, indeed, a close relation between the two media, a question arises: Who was responsible for the creation of the tokens?

Of particular interest is the coin emission of AD 23, dated to early summer by the second tribunician power of Drusus. The main aim of initiating a new series of coins was not just to serve economic needs, but to also communicate Tiberian family politics.[89] The emperor wanted to show whom he regarded as his possible heir, and that the future of the family was secured by male offspring (fig. 37). Tiberius chose Divus Augustus as the subject for dupondii (RIC I² Tiberius 74–78, obverse) and a sestertius issue (RIC I² Tiberius 49, reverse) and commemorated Livia on sestertii (RIC I² Tiberius 50–51, reverse). The emperor himself is shown on an as (RIC I² Tiberius 44, obverse). Drusus the Younger is honoured by a portrait on asses (RIC I² Tiberius 45, obverse), and his twin sons are shown on sestertii (RIC I² Tiberius 42, obverse).

This arrangement, which referenced to the past and the promising future of the ruling family, was valid for only a very short time span: with the death of Drusus it became obsolete. Nevertheless, the parallel arrangement of the motifs on coinage and the *tesserae* reveals a parallel genealogy.[90] Even more explicit on the tokens than on coinage, portraits and busts of fertile women, successful rulers and generals build up a genealogy. The 'portrait group' does not copy the coins, but obviously is inspired by them; it echoes and continues the themes. Therefore, it may be suggested that the tokens were created at the same time as the coins. This would give the main group of the tokens a small time frame, just like the coinage, of spring – early summer of AD 23. It is thus conceivable that the tokens might have been commissioned by the same authority as the coins.

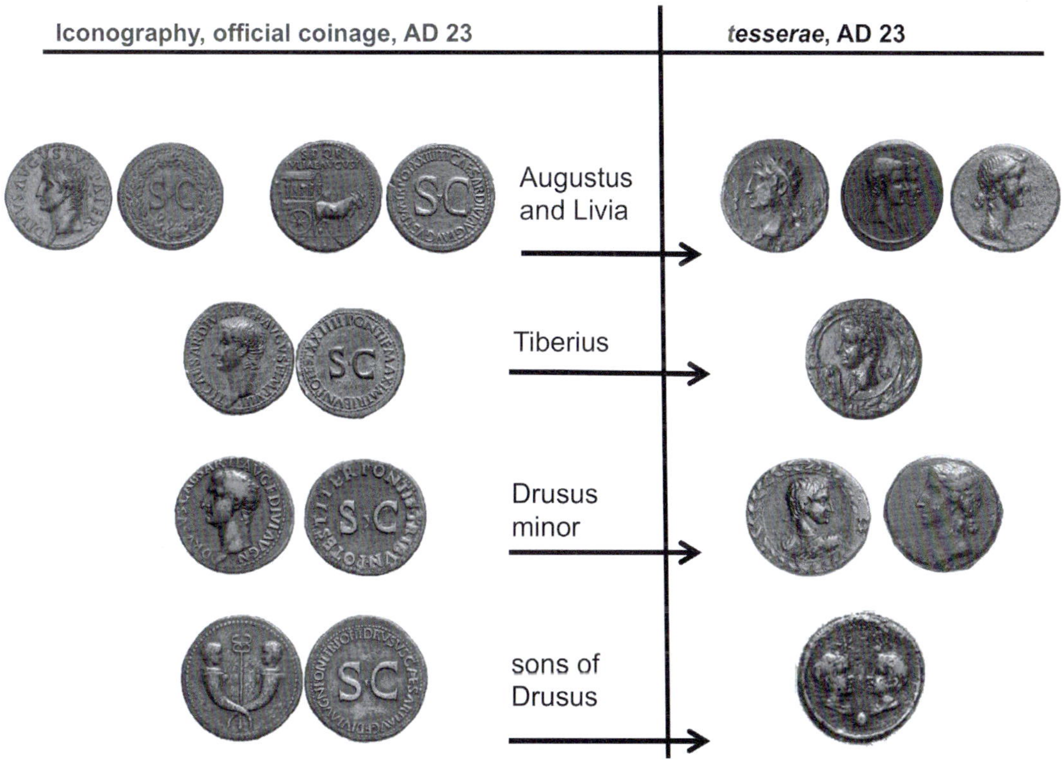

Fig. 37: Thematic and iconographic parallels between coinage and *tesserae*.

[89] Wolters (2016), 225.
[90] A similar presentation of genealogy is known, for instance, from the Great Cameo of France (Wolters (2016), 211).

Would Tiberius (or his inner circle) have commissioned these tokens as a parallel to official money? Looking at the denominations of Tiberius' coinage produced in AD 23, it is surprising that quadrantes, the smallest denomination, are entirely lacking.[91] But although it is tempting to see the *tesserae* as *pseudomonetae* filling a gap (fig. 38), one presumes that if small change had been needed it would have been properly produced, and not supplied by a group of heterogeneous tokens.[92] A better explanation could be that the issue of the sestertii, dupondii and asses was accompanied by the tokens as small give-aways – operating as gaming tokens that simultaneously communicated imperial ideology. The *tesserae* might have celebrated the new issue of money that had been important to Tiberius as a medium of communication.

A gift of Mitreius to the *iuvenes*?

An alternative scenario is also possible. It was noted above that within the mysterious Mitreius group (figs. 18–20), all tokens bear the inscription *magister iuventutis*, labelling C. Mitreius as head of a youth organisation (the *collegium iuvenum* / *iuventutis*).[93] The *collegia iuvenum* might be characterised as 'entertainment clubs, where people of age and mind could do military exercises, hunt or enjoy athletic contests'.[94] Since Mitreius is named on some tokens with numerals, declaring that he is responsible for their issue, it is a small step from here to suggest that Mitreius might have been the sponsor of the whole group of tokens. The *tesserae* might have been a gift of the *magister* to the *iuvenes*. This assumption would fit well with the partly educational (imperial portraits and symbols), partly entertaining character of these objects. In this case, Mitreius would probably have been inspired by contemporary imperial coinage, as well as genre motifs common in Roman daily culture, for the production of his set of tokens.

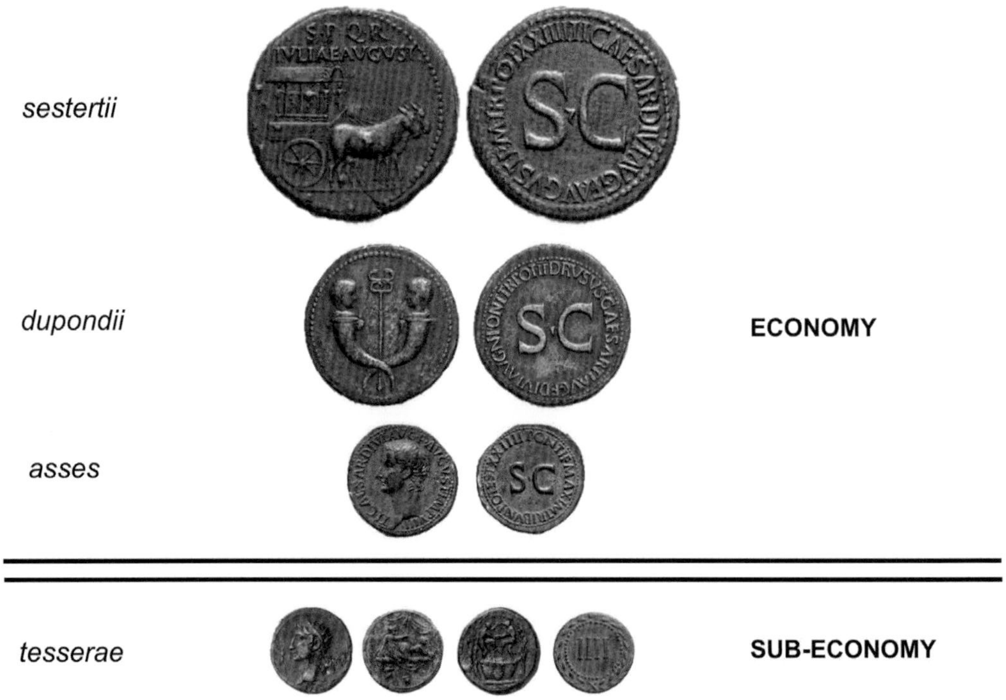

Fig. 38: Coinage (RIC I² Tiberius 42–51, AD 23) and *tesserae*: different economic levels?

[91] As noticed by Wolters (2016), 215.
[92] *Tesserae* as *pseudomonetae* (?): Reis and Schindel (1998c), 53.
[93] Kleijwegt (1994), 79–102.
[94] Kleijwegt (1994), 93.

Conclusion

While many possible explanations for these *tesserae* have been given in the past, the most probable solution is still that the tokens were counters in a game whose details are now lost. Further archaeological finds might be able to solve the case if *tesserae* were found in a context along with toys and/or other gaming pieces (and without coins, as was the case in Mutina). Such evidence is not available at the moment but might emerge in the future.[95] The same is true for the authority behind the production, which might be Tiberius or his personnel, or even C. Mitreius, who is the only person to provide his name within the whole group. Mitreius might be the key to our understanding of these pieces, but without further epigraphic evidence the case is better left open for the moment.

Bibliography

Alföldi-Rosenbaum 1976: E. Alföldi-Rosenbaum, 'Alexandriaca. Studies on Roman game counters III', *Chiron* 6 (1976), 205–39.

Bartman 1999: E. Bartman, *Portraits of Livia. Imaging the Imperial Woman in Augustan Rome* (Cambridge, 1999).

Bateson 1991: J. D. Bateson, 'Roman *spintriae* in the Hunter Coin Cabinet,' in Martini and Vismara (eds.) (1991), 385–97.

Bayley 1998: J. Bayley, 'The production of brass in antiquity with particular reference to Roman Britain', in Craddock (ed.) (1998), 7–26.

Benassi, Giordani and Poggi 2003: F. Benassi, N. Giordani and C. Poggi, 'Una tessera numerale con scena erotica da un contesto funerario di *Mutina*', *NumAntCl* 32 (2003), 249–73.

Bernhart 1926: M. Bernhart, *Handbuch zur Münzkunde der römischen Kaiserzeit* (Halle, 1926).

Besombes and Barrandon 2000: P. A. Besombes and J. N. Barrandon, 'Nouvelles propositions de classement des monnaies de «bronze» de Claude Ier', *RN* 155 (2000), 161–88.

Bielefeld 1997: D. Bielefeld, *Die antiken Sarkophagreliefs. Vol. 5, part 2, fasc. 2: Weinlese- und Ernteszenen* (Berlin, 1997).

Boschung 1993: D. Boschung, 'Die Bildnistypen der iulisch-claudischen Kaiserfamilie: ein kritischer Forschungsbericht', *JAC* 6 (1993), 39–79.

Brendel 1953–1954: O. Brendel, 'Der Affen-Aeneas', *RM* 60-61 (1953–1954), 153–59.

Buttrey 1973: T. Buttrey, '*Spintriae* as a historical source', *NC* 13 (1973), 52–62.

Campana 2009: A. Campana, 'Le *Spintriae*: tessere romane con raffigurazioni erotiche', in Morello (ed.) (2009), 43–96.

Campana 2013: A. Campana, 'Les *spintriae* et leur possible fonction ludique', *Archéothéma* 31 (2013), 66.

Cazzato, Roberto and Bevilacqua (eds.) 2014: V. Cazzato, S. Roberto and M. Bevilacqua (eds.), *La festa delle arti. Scritti in onore di Marcello Fagiolo per cinquant'anni di studi* (Rome, 2014).

Churchill, Brown and Jeffrey (eds.) 2002: L. J. Churchill, P. R. Brown, J. E. Jeffrey (eds.), *Women Writing Latin: From Roman Antiquity to Early Modern Europe* (vol. 1) (New York, 2002).

Clarke 1998–1999: J. R. Clarke, 'Look who's laughing: humor in tavern painting as index of class and acculturation', *MAAR* 43-44 (1998–1999), 27–48.

Clarke 1999: J. R. Clarke, 'Form, function, and meaning of *symplegmata* in Pompeian mosaics: the case for the "domestication" of sex', in Paunier (ed.) (1999), 721–25.

Clarke 2003: J. R. Clarke, *Roman Sex, 100 BC – 250 AD* (New York, 2003).

Cohen 1892: H. Cohen, *Description historique des monnaies frappées sous l'Empire Romain* (vol. 8) (Paris-London, 1892).

Craddock 1978: P. T. Craddock, 'The composition of the copper alloys used by the Greek, Etruscan and Roman civilizations: 3. The origins and early use of brass', *Journal of Archaeological Science* 5 (1978), 1–16.

Craddock (ed.) 1998: P. T. Craddock (ed.) *200 Years of Zinc and Brass* (British Museum Occasional Paper no. 50) (London, 1998).

De Belfort 1889: A. de Belfort, 'Essai de classification des tessères romaines en bronze', *ASFN* 13 (1889), 69–92.

De Belfort 1892: A. de Belfort, 'Essai de classification des tessères romaines en bronze', *ASFN* 16 (1892), 127, 171–79, 237–42, 265–73.

Folin 2014: M. Folin, 'L'immagine dell'architetto nell'iconografia romana di età imperiale', in Cazzato, Roberto and Bevilacqua (eds.) (2014), 292–95.

Galinsky 1998: K. Galinsky, *Augustan Culture. An Interpretive Introduction* (Princeton, 1998).

Göbl 1978: R. Göbl, *Antike Numismatik* (vol. 2) (München, 1978).

[95] See the numerous finds in graves or in military camps; e.g. in Vindonissa by 1983 more than 800 gaming pieces had been found (Holliger (1983), 5).

Holliger 1983: C. Holliger, 'Römische Spielsteine und Brettspiele', *Jahresbericht der Gesellschaft Pro Vindonissa* (1983), 5–24.

Imhoof-Blumer and Keller 1889: F. Imhoof-Blumer and O. Keller, *Tier- und Pflanzenbilder auf Münzen und Gemmen des Klassischen Altertums* (Leipzig, 1889).

Jacobelli 1995: L. Jacobelli, *Le pitture erotiche delle Terme Suburbane di Pompei* (Rome, 1995).

Jacobelli 1997: L. Jacobelli, *Tessere numerali bronzee romane nelle civiche raccolte numismatiche del comune di Milano* (Annotazioni Numismatiche, 10) (Milan, 1997).

Jacobelli 2000: L. Jacobelli, *Spintriae e ritratti giulio-claudii. Significato e funzione delle tessere bronzee numerali imperiali* (Milan, 2000).

Jones 1982: C. Jones, *Sex or Symbol? Erotic Images of Greece and Rome* (New York, 1982).

Kleijwegt 1994: M. Kleijwegt, '*Iuvenes* and Roman imperial society', *Acta Classica* 37 (1994), 79–102.

Kretschmer 1978: F. Kretschmer, *Bilddokumente römischer Technik* (Düsseldorf, 1978).

Küter 2014: A. Küter, *Zwischen Republik und Prinzipat: Die Münzmeisterprägung unter Augustus* (Berlin, 2014).

Küter 2016: A. Küter, '*Imitatio Alexandri* – the image of Drusus minor on brass tokens of the Münzkabinett, Staatliche Museen zu Berlin', *JAC* 31 (2016), 85–122.

Lazenby 1949: F. D. Lazenby, 'Greek and Roman household pets', *CJ* 44 (1949), 245–52.

Maiuri 1950: A. Maiuri, 'La parodia di Enea', *BdA* 35 (1950), 108–12.

Martini 1997: R. Martini, *Tessere numerali bronzee romane nelle Civiche Raccolte Numismatiche del Comune di Milano. Parte I: Considerazioni numismatiche. Catalogo* (Milan, 1997).

Martini 1999: R. Martini, 'Una tessera numerale bronzea con ritratto di Augustus in collezione privata. Tessera triumphalium (?): note per una discussione', *Annotazioni Numismatiche*, suppl. 13 (1999), 12–15.

Martini and Vismara (eds.) 1991: R. Martini and N. Vismara (eds.), *Ermanno A. Arslan Studia Dicata* (Milan, 1991).

Morello (ed.) 2009: A. Morello (ed.), *La Donna Romana. Immagini e vita quotidiana. Atti del Convegno, Atina, 7 marzo 2009* (Cassino, 2009).

Mowat 1898: R. Mowat, 'Contremarques sur des tessères romaines de bronze et de plomb. Les spintriennes', *RIN* 11 (1898), 21–42.

Nadrowski 1906: R. Nadrowski, 'Welchen Zweck hatten die römischen Spintrien?', *Berliner Münzblätter* 52 (1906), 287–89.

Paunier (ed.) 1999: D. Paunier (ed.) *La mosaique gréco-romaine, Tunis 3–7 octobre 1994* (Tunis, 1999).

Pesciarelli 2009: E. Pesciarelli, 'Nuovi contributi per la datazione delle *spintriae* e per la definizione degli scopi della loro coniazione', *Bollettino della Unione storia ed arte* 5 (2010), 27–42.

Ralite 2009: J.-C. Ralite, 'Une tessère érotique (*spintria*) découverte dans les ateliers de potiers de Sálleles (Aude) près de Narbonne (France, Aude)', *NC* 169 (2009), 193–97.

Reis and Schindel 1998a: L. Reis and M. Schindel, 'Kaiser – Huren – Spiele. Die römischen Messingtesserae mit Zahlzeichen', *Money Trend* 5 (1998), 52–55.

Reis and Schindel 1998b: L. Reis and M. Schindel, 'Kaiser – Huren – Spiele. Die römischen Messingtesserae mit Zahlzeichen', *Money Trend* 6 (1998), 52–54.

Reis and Schindel 1998c: L. Reis and M. Schindel, 'Kaiser – Huren – Spiele. Die römischen Messingtesserae mit Zahlzeichen', *Money Trend* 7–8 (1998), 51–53.

Reis and Schindel 1998d: L. Reis and M. Schindel, 'Kaiser – Huren – Spiele. Die römischen Messingtesserae mit Zahlzeichen', *Money Trend* 9 (1998), 51–53.

Rostovtsew 1905: M. Rostovtsew, 'Interprétation des tessères en os avec figures, chiffres et legends', *RA* 5 (1905), 110–24.

Rowan 2017: C. Rowan, 'Gaius Mitreius, Magister Iuventutis, and the Materiality of Roman Tokens' (http://blogs.warwick.ac.uk/numismatics/entry/gaius_mitreius_magister) (accessed 04/12/2018).

Schwarzer and Nieswandt (eds.) 2016: H. Schwarzer and H.-H. Nieswandt (eds.), *"Man kann es sich nicht prächtig genug vorstellen!" Festschrift für Dieter Salzmann zum 65. Geburtstag* (Marsberg, 2016).

Siebert 1999: A. V. Siebert, *Instrumenta Sacra: Untersuchungen zu römischen Opfer-, Kult- und Priestergeräten* (Berlin-New York, 1999).

Simonetta and Riva 1981: B. Simonetta and R. Riva, *Le tessere erotiche romane (spintriae)* (Lugano, 1981).

Stumpp 2001: B. E. Stumpp, *Prostitution in der römischen Antike* (Berlin, 2001).

Toynbee 1973: J. Toynbee, *Animals in Roman Art and Life* (London, 1973).

Trümpler-Ris 1982: C. Trümpler-Ris, 'Patrize für ein pergamenisches Reliefgefäß', *HASB* 8 (1982), 39–42.

Voegtle 2013: S. Voegtle, *Dein Gott ist ein Esel. Griechische und römische Tierkarikaturen als Spiegel antiker Wertvorstellungen* (Bern, 2013).

Widura 2015: A. Widura, *SpielRäume. Kulturhistorische Studien zum Brettspiel in archäologischen Kontexten* (Rahden-Westfalen, 2015).

Winkes 1995: R. Winkes, *Livia, Octavia, Julia. Porträts und Darstellungen* (Louvain-la-Neuve, 1995).

Woeckner 2002: E. Woeckner, 'Women's graffiti from Pompeii', in Churchill, Brown and Jeffrey (eds.) (2002), 67–81.

Wolters 2016: R. Wolters, 'Der Große Kameo von Paris und die Münzprägung des Tiberius', in Schwarzer and Nieswandt (eds.) (2016), 211–27.

LEAD TOKEN MOULDS FROM ROME AND OSTIA[1]

CLARE ROWAN

Introduction

The use of tokens in ancient Rome became spectacularly apparent to scholars in the eighteenth and nineteenth centuries, when thousands of lead monetiform objects were uncovered during urban renovation works in the city. The river Tiber and its banks proved a particularly fruitful location for these objects: hundreds of tokens were found here, as well as at least seven token mould halves.[2] Roman tokens, also known as *tesserae* in modern scholarship, exist in a variety of different shapes, but the majority of those from Rome are circular and roughly the same size as the smallest Roman coin denomination, a quadrans (ca. 14–18mm, fig. 1). Tokens also existed in other materials in the city (e.g. the bronze and brass pieces presented by Küter in this volume), but this contribution focuses on those produced in lead, which were cast from moulds.

Fig. 1: Example of a Roman cast lead token (Ø 16mm, 2.77g, 12h). Side A: Modius (container of grain). Side B: Three Graces. TURS 358 (pl. III, no. 57) (courtesy of Heberden Coin Room, Ashmolean Museum).

There have been several works examining Roman tokens.[3] Far less attention, however, has been given to the moulds used to create these objects, which shed light on the potential manufacturers, users and contexts of tokens. The following discussion makes reference to 61 token moulds with known find spots, listed at the end of the chapter as table 1. This list is not exhaustive, but forms a starting point to begin a detailed study of these objects.

Material and manufacture

Figure 2 shows a representative half of a Roman token mould made of palombino marble.[4] Roman token moulds are rarely found intact (with both halves). Figure 3a–b illustrates one such rare example, a quadrangular mould with one half possessing a central casting channel with 'branches' leading to the individual token moulds (fig. 3a), while the other half has only a central casting channel and no 'branches' (fig. 3b).[5] Another mould with both halves (no. 51), found in Ostia, is octagonal in shape and both halves contain a central channel and 'branches'; the difference in design here demonstrates there was no fixed approach to the manufacture of these objects. Both moulds used nails to fasten the two halves together (those that survive are made of iron); on fig. 3 one can see a nail remaining in the lower left and upper right corners. Placing nails through pre-made holes would not only serve to bind the moulds together, but would also ensure that each half of the design was correctly aligned. Small grooves that can be found on the sides of the Harvard mould and some other specimens

Fig. 2: Half of a palombino marble mould. The mould would have created seven circular tokens decorated with the image of the goddess Fortuna holding a cornucopia and rudder (108 x 76 x 29mm, 389.2g) (inv. no. 2008.118) (courtesy of Harvard Art Museums).

[1] The following abbreviations are used:
BMCRLT: *Roman Lead Tokens in the British Museum* (internal numbering system of the ancient lead tokens in the British Museum. A catalogue of these specimens is currently being prepared).
NSc.: *Notizie degli scavi di antichità* (1876–).
TURS: Rostowzew, M. (1903). *Tesserarum urbis Romae et suburbi*. St. Petersburg.

[2] Garrucci (1847), 1; Rostowzew and Prou (1900), 132; Rostovtsew and Vaglieri (1900); Dressel (1922).

[3] Ficoroni (1740), 77–85; Graillot (1896); Rostovtzeff (1897); Rostowzew (1905); Thornton (1980); Mitchiner (1984); Turcan (1988); Mlasowsky (1991); Overbeck (1995), 5–15; Virlouvet (1995), 309–24; Pensabene (2001–2003); Stannard (2015).

[4] Hirschland and Hammond (1968), 382.

[5] Cesano (1904a), 148–49.

Fig. 3a–b: A palombino marble mould with both halves, 93 x 96mm (inv. nos. 64247.2.1–2) (Vatican Museums). The tokens produced from these moulds would have ranged in size from 9–12mm. Figure 3a is engraved with an image of Fortuna, and Figure 3b with two different designs: an ant and two figures (Mars and Venus?) (Cesano (1904a), 148–9) (courtesy of Vatican Museums).

Fig. 4: Side of a token mould showing grooves (76 x 29mm) (inv. no. 2008.118) (courtesy of Harvard Art Museums, inv. no. 2008.118) (photo by author).

are suggestive of the use of wire (or a similarly strong material) to bind the two halves closely together (fig. 4).[6] Moulds used to cast coin flans have similar lines on their edges and it has been suggested these lines served to align both halves of the mould correctly.[7] The nails and grooves, then, may have served to both align the moulds and to ensure the two halves remained together under the pressure caused by the molten metal. The backs of token moulds are, for the most part, unworked rough stone.

The piece from Harvard Art Museums might also provide a clue as to how token designs were engraved. In the top left of the mould are two finely etched concentric circles (fig. 5). The inner circle is ca. 14mm in diameter, the size of the tokens this mould created. The outer circle may be an error or it may reveal that the size of the tokens was initially mapped out with two concentric circles before the engraver began to carve inwards (of the moulds personally inspected by the author to date, the Harvard mould is the only specimen to have this type of marking). The cutting of these circular impressions was achieved by a tool that left a deep central hole in the centre of each token cavity before the design was engraved – one can see a deep central hole on Fortuna's body in figures 2 and 5, and many Roman lead

[6] Pardini, Piacentini, Felici, Santarelli and Santucci (2016), 653. The octagonal mould from Ostia (no. 51) has no such grooves, again indicating variation.
[7] Ariel (2012), 61.

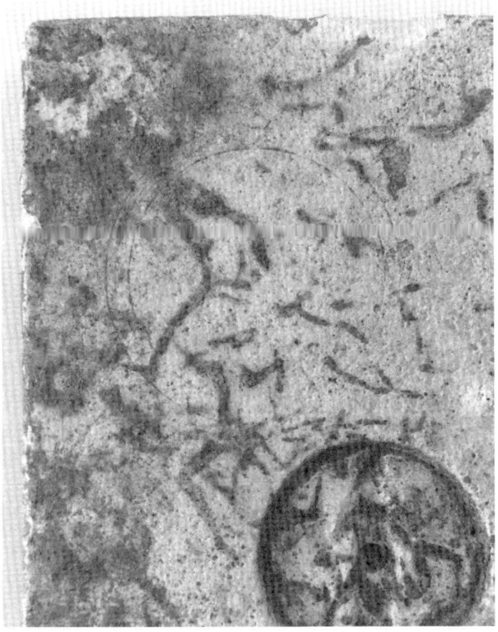

Fig. 5: Detail of the top left of a mould showing two concentric circles (inv. no. 2008.118) (courtesy of Harvard Art Museums) (photo by author).

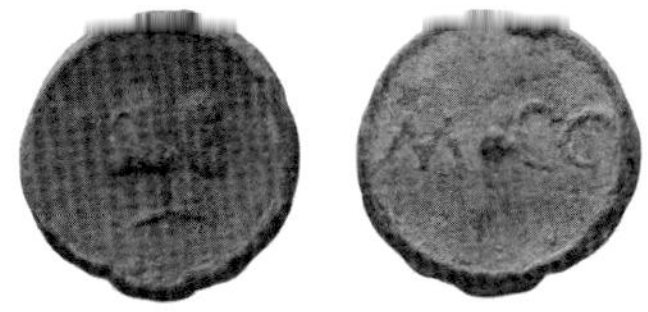

Fig. 6: Lead token demonstrating the central 'dot' resulting from the mould creation process (Ø 20mm, 3.95g, 12h). Side A: Head of Janus. Side B: MCC (Ficoroni 1740, part II, p. 120, XVII, no. 3) (courtesy of Heberden Coin Room, Ashmolean Museum).

tokens carry central protuberances that are the result of this manufacturing method (e.g. fig. 6).[8] On the other hand these cavities may have been part of the mapping process, enabling the artisan to space out the individual token moulds on the marble and ensure they aligned properly – this is suggested for the central cavities that are found on coin flan moulds excavated in Châteaubleau.[9]

Many of the moulds inspected by the author from Rome and Ostia are very similar to that presented in figs. 2–3 in terms of material, size, and design. There are, however, some variants. For example, a mould half now housed in the Altes Museum in Berlin and recorded by Rostovtzeff as TURS 3582 is made of what appears to be a very white limestone rather than palombino marble, and possesses worked, smooth edges and back.[10] Moulds 52 and 61 are made of Luna marble, a material that was prized in Rome for its colour, quality, and workability.[11] As with palombino, Luna marble allows fine detail.[12] While most moulds are rectangular in shape, octagonal (no. 51) and hexagonal (no. 48) shapes also exist.

The overall picture presented by the moulds is suggestive of a shared token making tradition around Rome and its environs: a common approach subject to some deviation. This, and the find spots of the moulds (discussed below), is suggestive of a distributed production rather than a centralised single workshop: tokens appear to have been created in multiple places by multiple individuals. The materials (easily workable stone, lead) were likely chosen because they were available and suited to the purpose. Palombino marble is perhaps best known for its use in Roman domestic decoration (in pavements and mosaics). The material properties of this marble means it is easy to work and carve with detail.[13] Lead was widely available and relatively cheap. Its low melting point (327.5 degrees Celsius) would have made it an ideal metal for this type of non-centralised production – the heat required to melt lead is much lower than copper (1085 degrees Celsius), for example, or silver (961.8 degrees Celsius).[14]

[8] Rostowzew (1905), 6; see also J. H. Kroll's *Unpublished Catalogue of the Roman Lead Tokens in Harvard Art Museums*, LT57.
[9] Pilon (2016), 56.
[10] A full publication of the moulds in the Altes Museum Berlin, along with the lead tokens in the Münzkabinett Berlin, is in progress.
[11] Strabo, *Geography* 5.2.5; Malacrino (2010), 25.
[12] http://www.artofmaking.ac.uk/explore/materials/6/Luna-Marble (accessed 07/06/2019).
[13] Pardini, Piacentini, Felici, Santarelli and Santucci (2016), 661.
[14] Boulakia (1972).

Studies of the use of moulds for the casting of coin flans have demonstrated that it is easier to remove cooled lead from stone moulds than from other materials. Stone also allows casting to be performed with the moulds upright (as suggested here by the placement of the channels), heat loss is minimised and oxidisation reduced. Stone moulds can also be reused.[15] The varying quality of the designs of Roman tokens is further evidence the moulds were not produced in a central workshop. The mould half now in the British Museum (no. 26), for example, has an array of different images of relatively good quality, whereas no. 61 has only a simple cross shape.

Although fig. 2 would have created tokens of identical imagery and shape, other examples demonstrate that a single mould might be used to produce tokens of different shapes and design. Number 9, for example, is a mould that was used to make circular tokens showing a ram as well as triangular tokens bearing the letters PR. Similarly moulds 4, 5, 13, 16, 20, 26, 28, 40, and 42 all created tokens with differing imagery and/or shapes. Number 28 was used to cast tokens that were in the form of a *tabula ansata* (a form of Roman tablet with dovetail handles that carried inscriptions, often used for votive offerings or in commercial contexts).[16] Since this token design also bears an inscription (MSA), one might interpret this as a playful representation that engages with the dialogues of monumentality and literacy in the Roman world.[17] Number 4 created tokens carrying the same letters (although these were at times joined together or ligate), but of differing sizes (17 and 9mm). Given the relatively large difference between the larger and smaller tokens made from this mould I would suggest that the different sizes were intentional, and that the diameter here must have been significant in some way, perhaps to distinguish between different values or different classes of bearer.

The intended design needed to be engraved as a mirror image and this was not successful in all cases. Errors are particularly noticeable on tokens carrying letters that are back to front (retrograde); here the engraver has simply engraved the letters as they would be written rather than allowing for the casting process.[18] The pairing of different designs, shapes and letters all within the one mould means that the current scholarly scheme of presenting Roman tokens is somewhat misleading; following on from Rostovtzeff tokens are largely presented according to 'themes' in modern scholarship (tokens referring to the emperor, for example, are grouped together, as are tokens showing ships, those carrying animals, etc). The moulds themselves indicate that often multiple 'themes' might be placed on tokens as part of a single production. But without a full corpus of moulds (and the known specimens are far fewer than the surviving variety of tokens) it is impossible to reconstruct what tokens might have been made together in every instance.

Find spots in Rome and Ostia

Many Roman token moulds are now housed in museums or reported in older publications and have no associated find spot.[19] Table 1 focuses on those moulds with find spots: it is not exhaustive, but nonetheless provides enough data to draw conclusions about the production and use of tokens in antiquity. The first observation is that moulds like this (and thus this particular method of manufacturing lead tokens) appear *only* to be found in Italy (and predominantly in Rome and Ostia) in antiquity. Although tokens of various sorts were used across the Roman world, the method of manufacture must have differed by region.

To my knowledge only two moulds have attributed find spots outside Rome and Ostia. The first is a mould half found in Como in northern Italy. During the construction of a palazzo at Via Plinio n. 4 in the late nineteenth century a mould was found inside an ancient

[15] Ariel (2012), 49. It is thought that flan production for the Roman mint was outsourced to private contractors, see Woytek (2019).
[16] A shape also known from TURS 1205, with Fortuna on one side and the legend DOM on the other.
[17] Eckardt (2017), 225.
[18] E.g. TURS 200, 659, 1352, 2904, 3081, 3357. Sometimes only a single letter is retrograde within a larger legend, e.g. TURS 1137 (pl. X, no. 74).
[19] E.g. Ficoroni (1740), 166, nos. 1–3; TURS 3572–99. Moulds have also begun to appear on the market; see Bertolami Fine Arts, Auction 44, 20 Apr 2018, lot no. 339.

edifice along the ancient city walls.[20] The mould, made of soapstone, measured 222 x 92 x 41mm, large in comparison to those from Rome and Ostia. Likewise, the circular designs for the tokens measure ca. 90mm in diameter, larger than those found in the capital. This mould created monetiform objects that carried Roman numerals (IV, V, V, VII, VIII, VIIII, IX, X, X, XI, XII, XII, XIII, XIII); above each numeral was a dot to indicate to the viewer how to interpret the piece (i.e. to tell the user to read IX instead of XI). These 'dots' possess similarities to the cavities discussed above and might have additionally served a similar function. Nogara suggested the mould might have created pieces of copper or lead; the author knew of no specimens that might have been produced from the object and nor do I. The second piece was recorded by Mommsen in the ninth volume of the *Corpus Inscriptionum Latinarum* (CIL) in the nineteenth century with a find spot of Telesia, which is located south of Rome.[21] Rostovtzeff also mentioned this piece, although it is clear he possessed some doubts about its authenticity.[22] One imagines that as these objects come to the attention of modern scholarship once more, further examples from elsewhere in Italy might come to light.

The finds with stratigraphy provide us with a date range during which these moulds were used. The most recent find of moulds (nos. 10–12) has a disposal date of the first century AD, whereas no. 52 suggests such moulds were still in use in the third century AD. Number 37 was found in the Casa dei Dipinti in Ostia, a Hadrianic apartment block still in use in the third century, while the finds associated with no. 44 also indicate a date in the second or third centuries AD. The surviving bricks from the theatre of Ostia are of the late second century AD (nos. 45–46).[23] These details correspond to the dates given to Roman lead tokens by scholars on the basis of style and design. Although lead tokens exist in Italy from the Republican period, in Rome they appear to be more of an imperial phenomenon, with designs referring to emperors from Augustus (27 BC–AD 14) to the emperor Carinus (AD 283–85).[24] Oddly, amongst the thousands of specimens gathered by Rostovtzeff, there is a lacuna in imperial representation between the Antonine dynasty (which ends AD 192) and Carinus.[25] This picture might change or be further clarified by future research.

Although most of the moulds listed here do not possess detailed stratigraphic information, the data that does exist enables further observation. The first is that *these moulds have been found*. Finds of coin dies from the Roman Empire are rare and largely occur outside Italy; it is presumed that dies were destroyed after use to prevent forgery.[26] By contrast, token moulds have been found in a relatively high number and certainly in much higher quantities than coin dies in Rome and Ostia.[27] This suggests that there was less concern that the moulds might be used for financial gain if they fell into the wrong hands. Rather, one gets the impression that these moulds were thrown away once they had served their purpose. And this purpose was likely one that was connected to a specific moment in time: either a single event or time period, after which the token would no longer have value. Indeed, although some of the moulds presented here exist only in fragments (nos. 5–6, 15, 33, 42, 53, 59–60), many are whole, although admittedly without their matching halves. Was each half of the mould intentionally deposited in a different area to prevent later fraud? Or, if one half of a mould broke, was the other simply thrown away? The nature of the archaeological record is such that it frequently possesses rubbish or abandoned items, although more work is needed before final conclusions are drawn.[28]

The temporary nature of lead tokens in Rome and Ostia may help to explain the bewildering array of images found on surviving specimens. If, as is suggested by some designs, a particular set of tokens were connected to a particular festival (e.g. the Saturnalia,

[20] Nogara (1917).
[21] CIL IX, 6087.
[22] TURS 3599 (pl. XII, no. 7); Rostowzew (1905), 82, n. 6.
[23] http://www.ostia-antica.org/dict.htm provides an overview of Ostia and its buildings (accessed 07/06/2019).
[24] Pedroni (1997).
[25] TURS 72–74.
[26] For a list of known coin dies from antiquity see Malkmus (2007).
[27] From the catalogue of Malkmus (2007) only one Roman period die (p. 134, no. V-27a) was found in Ostia, and none in Rome.
[28] No. 5 possesses some fractures in the marble, but it is impossible to know whether the stress of repeated casting or the manufacturing of the mould itself caused these.

a carnival type celebration during which social norms and hierarchies were inverted), one would imagine that the design of the tokens would change from year to year or celebration to celebration.[29] This would ensure that only the tokens created for a particular event could be used in a specific context; last year's tokens, so to speak, would no longer be valid. Once created, some moulds might have been reused over a longer period of time (as is known for more modern tokens), particularly in contexts like baths (nos. 39, 52).[30] Again it is possible that there was significant variation within a common framework. The data suggests very localised production of limited volume (the moulds are scattered rather than grouped together in a workshop, and would only have produced a handful of tokens at each casting), again suggestive of particular moments in time for particular communities or contexts.

For ancient Athens it has been suggested that a token might be countermarked once or more to enable to it to be reused; the rarity of this practice on tokens from Rome and Ostia suggests that in this region it was more common to prepare new tokens (and imagery) for each occasion.[31] This approach is similar to that found in Palmyra in Syria; here tokens are believed to have functioned as entrance tickets to sacred banquets. The archaeological record suggests that a particular token was created for a particular event: in the temple of the god Arsu, for example, a pot was found containing 125 tokens, all of the same type. These tokens were about to be distributed, or had already been gathered and then deposited in the vessel during the relevant event. As Raja concludes, these small objects were mini monuments attached to a specific event, serving both a practical and communicative function (they were tickets, but also bore imagery and text).[32] If we similarly view the tokens of Rome and Ostia as temporary monuments, then the use of lead becomes even more understandable. These were objects not intended to last (as with coinage); a soft, easily worked metal could be used. Unlike the example from Palmyra, however, the moulds from Rome and Ostia suggest that different imagery was used for the same context. Whether this was to differentiate between different types of users or goods, or simply because inhabitants of this region preferred a wider array of imagery, is a subject for further research.

A cultic context is possible for the three moulds found during excavations on the NE corner of the Palatine on a site identified as the *Curiae Veteres* (nos. 10–12). Roman authors detail that the *Curiae Veteres* (a sanctuary) was established by Rome's founder Romulus as he divided the people of Rome and its religious observances into 30 *curiae* or parts. The *curiae* corresponded to different regions of the city, providing inhabitants with a spatial or neighbourhood identity that was possibly also expressed on tokens.[33] When Rome's population grew a new building was constructed (*Curiae Novae*), but religious obstacles meant that some of the *curiae* remained in the old building.[34] It is likely that each individual *curia* in the city had a local structure associated with cultic feasting activity, but during particular festivals all the *curiae* assembled together in the central *Curiae* building in an act of city-unity. During the Fornicalia ('festival of the ovens'), for example, the priests of each *curia* assembled to determine the order in which each *curia* would perform their rites (this appears to have changed every year), a process that was likely performed by lot.[35] Moulds nos. 22 and 53 were also found at cultic sites: the 'Syrian sanctuary' on the Janiculum Hill in Rome and the Sabazeum in Ostia, both places associated with the worship of foreign cults.

The finds from the Baths of the Swimmer (Terme del Nuotatore) in Ostia provide an interesting case study for further exploration. In the same room (Ambiente XVI) as mould no. 52, which has a beetle design, but in an earlier layer (Stratum II, dated to the end of the second century and beginning of the third century AD) some lead waste was found. This scoria was damaged, but clearly had the shape of a central canal with branches emerging off

[29] TURS 501–10 for lead tokens referring to the Saturnalia. On the festival itself see Harrison (2001) and Dolansky (2011).
[30] For a parallel see Carradice (1994), who explores how only a change in benefactor led to a change in design for Scottish communion tokens.
[31] Crosby (1964), 116.
[32] Al-As'ad, Briquel-Chatonnet and Yon (2005); Raja (2015).
[33] TURS 490–93, interpreted by Rostovtzeff as referring to different regions in Rome. The author has not yet been able to verify all the descriptions given by Rostovtzeff. TURS 491 seems to have an alternative reading.
[34] Richardson (1992), 105; Steinby (1993), 337.
[35] Ovid, *Fasti* 2.527–32; Richardson (1992), 106.

each side; the logical conclusion is that this is waste from a token mould.[36] This would suggest that tokens were cast on site, though it is likely that it would also be possible to transport moulds to a local workshop for production.[37] One imagines that normally the tokens would be cut away from the 'branches' and then the remaining scrap metal would be melted down to make further tokens or other objects.[38] Ambiente XVI at this period has been identified as a wine bar or *popina*.[39] Excavations from taberna two in the theatre at Ostia revealed a set of poorly cast tokens still intact from the mould; here the casting may have been deemed too poor and this particular attempt thrown away, but it is further evidence that production was local and decentralised.[40] This taberna also yielded a token mould that was undecorated (no. 45), again suggesting that the engraving of these moulds was decentralised.[41] The existence of moulds in small shops suggests that some of these pieces may have been used in commerce or exchange in small economic circuits.

Also found in the Baths of the Swimmer were several lead tokens: in area 25 (Ambiente XXV), in stratum VA (dated to ca. AD 80–90, associated with the installation of the hydraulics), a token was found with a female figure on one side (probably Juno with patera and sceptre) and Fortuna on the other. From stratum III of this area (dated to ca. AD 190/200–225) two tokens were found of differing designs. The first carries the letters F C on one side with an unusual representation on the other; Rostovtzeff suggested that this was a *furca* (a pole used to carry the equipment of Roman legionaries), but the image also has similarities to the stylised representation of the caduceus found on tokens of late antiquity (fig. 7 is a different specimen with this same design).[42] The second token is decorated with a palm branch on one side and the letters PM (?) on the other.[43] The excavations thus reveal tokens with a variety of designs used across the lifetime of the baths (ca. AD 89–250). A further token was excavated more recently in the area NE of the bath complex showing Isis (or a priestess of Isis) on one side and a nude male figure on the other.[44]

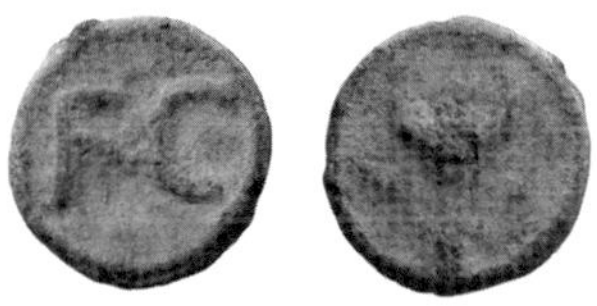

Fig. 7: Lead token (Ø 19mm, 5.14 g, 11h). Side A: F C. Side B: A *furca* or stylised caduceus with a star on either side. TURS 3065 (courtesy of Heberden Coin Room, Ashmolean Museum).

How precisely tokens were used in bathing complexes is still unknown, although they have been found in these contexts in Rome, Ostia and the provinces.[45] It has been suggested they might have functioned as entrance tickets, or that they acted as a form of money in an extremely local context, exchanged in return for particular goods or services once inside the complex.[46] The baths were another clear context where Roman tokens were used, which we should add to the shops and cultic/festival contexts already discussed. The multiple use contexts of these objects no doubt also contributed to the variety of designs.[47]

[36] Carandini and Panella (1977), 271. Further lead scoria from token moulds ('coduli') have been found in Ostia (Ostia Antiquarium inv. nos. 15732 a–f), although they have no find information. See Spagnoli (2001).
[37] This practice is known for Scottish communion tokens. See Wood (1904), 108.
[38] This is the suggestion for the medieval period. See Kool (2013), 303.
[39] Medri, di Cola, Carandini and Panella (2013), 20.
[40] *NSc.* (1912), 393.
[41] Mould no. 44 may also come from this same taberna, but the description is unclear and it may in fact come from another location in the theatre.
[42] Alföldi (1937), 20.
[43] TURS 691–92; Carandini and Panella (1977), 391.
[44] Pardini (2014), 43, from a stratum dated to AD 160–180/90.
[45] See most recently Spagnoli (2017) on an assemblage of tokens from the Terme dei Cisiarii in Ostia.
[46] Rostowzew and Prou (1900), 136–37; Rostowzew (1905), 102–03; Turcan (1987), 59; Turcan (1988), 626–30; Collingwood and Wright (1990), 2408.3; Lagóstena Barrios (1993), 308; Pedroni (1997), 209–10. Mora Serrano (2002), 52–53, wondered whether the specimens he presents from Alameda are connected with a nearby cultic site.
[47] Also suggested for Athenian tokens, Crosby (1964), 78.

Community cohesion and belonging

The tokens and token mould found in the Baths of the Swimmer do not bear images that a modern scholar might immediately associate with Roman bathing.[48] This cautions us of the dangers in using imagery alone to deduce the use contexts of Roman tokens. But the imagery meant that tokens had both a practical and communicative function. Indeed, the designs on tokens would have served to both create and reinforce group cohesion, a feeling of belonging.

Many of the moulds presented here carry letters on them, (in one instance in Greek rather than Latin, no. 42). These letters form combinations that we are hard pressed to decipher.[49] One presumes that these are abbreviations of words or phrases. Abbreviation occurs on Roman inscriptions and on Roman coinage, but in these contexts it was relatively standardised. The bewildering array of letter combinations on tokens, however, goes well beyond this repertoire. To elaborate: in contrast to many other media in the Roman world, the tokens in Rome and Ostia do not take efforts to explain their message to the user. Roman coinage, for example, often carries a legend that explains to the viewer the scene shown (e.g. the name of a deity or a reference to a particular ceremony). These clarifications are, for the most part, absent on tokens, which instead bear images without explanation, or, as mentioned above, letters that seem enigmatic. But this may have served to contribute to the feeling of belonging to a particular community. Tokens, after all, were created for a specific, very local group; one imagines that in this context little explanation of the design was necessary since the meaning would have been self-evident for the targeted user. The ability of users to understand the 'code' on the token, in contrast to those outside the group, likely contributed to a feeling of community, similar to the way that specific codes and complex images were used on the *jetons royaux* in France explored by Valin in this volume.

The banqueting tokens of Palmyra also worked in this way: these were everyday objects that, for a moment in time, controlled access to space – this too would have resulted in a dialectic of those on the 'in' (i.e. invited, with a ticket) and those on the 'out', a feeling of community further enhanced by the imagery and writing on the token.[50] From this perspective, tokens in Palmyra operated in an architectural sense, allowing cultic followers into a space and excluding strangers at a particular moment in time, an action akin to that of a door or fence.[51] If the tokens from Rome and Ostia associated with bathing complexes did serve to control access to these spaces (although the find locations provide no definitive clues in this regard), then both the design and use of the object contributed to feelings of belonging to a particular group. Here, however, the group may not have possessed a cultic focus, but was perhaps one based on a particular client or patronage networks.[52]

Conclusions

Token moulds very similar to those presented here are also known in Europe from the medieval period onwards (fig. 8).[53] The moulds from this later period are largely made of limestone, an easily workable material, with some created from slate.[54] Many of these later examples also possess casting channels and holes in the corners to ensure both halves are correctly aligned and remain bound together during the token creation process. The find spots of these moulds also indicate a very local production, by religious groups (e.g. communion tokens, which might be made by a single church) or other small communities.[55]

It is clear that more Roman moulds exist than was previously thought. Many questions remain unanswered, most notably *who* specifically carved these designs (a member of the

[48] By contrast, other token designs name baths or carry representations of the strigils and oil flask used during the process (e.g. TURS 886–904).
[49] Woytek (2015), 485 rightly draws attention to the fact they are epigraphic puzzles.
[50] Raja (2015), 179.
[51] Irvine, Hanks and Weddle (2013), 92, 102 explore this concept for sacred architecture.
[52] Pedroni (1997), 209 suggests that perhaps, in the case of Fregellae, a patron may have given bath access tokens to his clients as an act of euergetism. Turcan (1988), 630 suggests something similar for Roman lead tokens.
[53] Pozzi and Labrot (2008) (from Sondrio in Italy).
[54] Kool (2013), 303, n. 43.
[55] Kool (2013), 302.

Fig. 8: (Post)medieval stone mould for casting lead tokens (58.4 x 56.7 x 19.35mm) (courtesy of the Portable Antiquities Scheme, LON-E0BD25) (https://finds.org.uk/database/artefacts/record/id/745434; accessed 07/06/2019).

community? a local artisan?), how this method of manufacture spread throughout Rome and Ostia, and why this production technique does not appear to have moved beyond central and (perhaps) northern Italy. The production and use of lead tokens in this region appears to be very local: associated with individual bathhouses, shops, or festivals, for instance. But in tracing the history of this very local phenomenon, we can begin to better understand Roman society, and how the broader mediascape of impressive buildings, materials and images issued by the emperor and the elite might be utilised in the everyday.

Table 1: Roman lead token moulds with known find spots.

Unless otherwise stated, all entries are for a single mould half made of palombino marble. Full information for many specimens was not provided by the publications.

No.	*Description*	*Place*	*Context*	*Ref.*
1	99x88mm mould for 7 square tokens of ca. 12–14mm, all of the same design: **bird (dove?) standing right**.	Rome	Found on the Esquiline Hill in 1882 during construction works.	Cesano (1904a), 208.
2	110x62mm mould for 8 circular tokens of ca. 17mm, all of the same design: **ANTONI** (with some letters ligate).	Rome	As above.	Cesano (1904a), 209.
3	63x126mm mould for 15 triangular tokens of ca. 7mm, all of the same design: **C**	Rome	As above.	Cesano (1904a), 210.
4	120x70mm mould carrying two sets of casting channels. One is for 5 circular tokens of 17mm with **LVE,** and the second for 7 circular tokens of 9mm with a **monogram of LVE**.	Rome	As above.	Cesano (1904a), 211.
5	78x91mm fragment of a mould carrying two sets of casting channels. One is for 5 triangular tokens of ca. 10mm with **VC**, and the remnants of the second show triangular tokens (two visible) of ca. 13mm with **ST**.	Rome	As above.	Cesano (1904a), 212.
6	41x32mm fragment of a mould for a token of ca. 20mm showing a **nude male standing holding uncertain objects (bow and arrow?) in either hand**.	Rome	As above.	Cesano (1904a), 213.

No.	*Description*	*Place*	*Context*	*Ref.*
7	120x70mm mould for 9 square tokens, all of the same design: **Fortuna with rudder in one hand and cornucopia in the other**.	Rome	19th century excavations of the 'Monte delle Giustizia' near the Servian wall to make space for Termini train station.	*NSc.* (1877), 347–73.
8	No further details given.	Rome	'Monte delle Giustizia' near the Servian wall.	*NSc.* (1877), 357.
9	80x85mm mould for 3 circular tokens showing a **ram standing left** and four triangular tokens with the letters **PR**.	Rome	'Monte delle Giustizia'.	Ruggiero (1878), no. 4.
10	67x63x28mm mould for 9 circular tokens of ca. 7mm, all of the same design: **V F**.	Rome	Found in Area II of the NE Palatine excavations (*Curiae Veteres*), near the wall in a layer associated with the spoliation of the pre-imperial *curia* after the Neronian fire.	Pardini, Piacentini, Felici, Santarelli and Santucci (2016).
11	123x75x29mm mould for 9 square tokens of ca. 5mm all of the same design: **C**. Residue from the casting process was in the canal.	Rome	As above.	As above.
12	84x79x23mm mould for 9 circular tokens of ca. 6.5mm, all of the same design: **R F**.	Rome	Found in Area II of the NE Palatine excavations, in a medieval context associated with the spoliation of Neronian-Flavian material.	As above.
13	100x80mm mould for 15 tokens: 2 of **uncertain design**, 5 square tokens showing a **cantharus**, 8 circular tokens showing a **phallus**.	Rome	Aventine Hill.	Ruggiero (1878), no. 7.
14	105x75mm mould for 7 circular tokens of ca. 17mm, all of the same design: **The Three Graces standing nude**.	Rome	The Tiber. Found in the 19th century during the Lungotevere works.	Cesano (1904b), no. 1.
15	95x50mm fragment of a mould for 3 square tokens of ca. 12mm, all of the same design**: Fortuna standing right with rudder right hand and cornucopia in left**.	Rome	As above.	Cesano (1904b), no. 2
16	92x88mm mould for 4 circular tokens of ca. 30mm: 2 with a **dog standing right and CAP above**, 2 showing a **quadruped standing right** (goat or doe?).	Rome	As above.	Cesano (1904b), no. 3.
17	105x60mm mould for 9 circular tokens of ca. 8mm all of the same design: **a galley with oars and two people in it**.	Rome	As above.	Cesano (1904b), no. 4.
18	120x90mm mould for 5 square tokens, all of the same design: **S and palm branch**.	Rome	As above.	Cesano (1904b), no. 5.
19	80x90mm mould for 5 triangular tokens of ca. 14mm, all of the same design: **P above AF**.	Rome	As above.	Cesano (1904b), no. 6.
20	120x75mm mould for 5 tokens of ca. 16mm: 3 square tokens with the letter **L**, 2 triangular tokens with the letter **A**.	Rome	As above.	Cesano (1904b), no. 7.
21	Mould decorated with a **standing figure**, no further information.	Rome	Excavations associated with the construction of the Viale di Circonvallazione Gianicolense, near Trastevere train station.	Gatti (1926), 243.
22	Mould for 6 tokens, all of the same design**: two nude wrestlers with raised fists, an amphora between them and leaves blossoming around them**.	Rome	'Syrian Sanctuary' on the Janiculum Hill.	*NSc.* (1909), 410.

No.	*Description*	*Place*	*Context*	*Ref.*
23	142x98mm mould for 13 circular tokens of ca. 11mm, all of the same design: **horse standing right**.	Rome	No precise provenance, but Cesano was certain it was found during works in Rome.	Cesano (1904b), no. 8.
24	103x84mm mould for 8 circular tokens of ca. 13mm, all of the same design: **Hercules standing right holding cup in outstretched right hand and club in left**.	Rome	As above.	Cesano (1904a), no. 1.
25	125x90 mm mould for 7 triangular tokens of ca. 13mm, all of the same design: **PR above S**.	Rome	As above.	Cesano (1904a), no. 2.
26	Mould for 6 circular tokens: 2 of ca. 21mm showing **Fortuna, standing right, holding rudder in right hand and cornucopia in left**; 2 circular tokens of 20mm showing **Minerva, standing right, holding sceptre in left hand and resting right on shield**, and 2 circular tokens of ca. 20mm showing **Victory standing right, holding wreath in outstretched right hand and palm branch in left**. The mould appears to have originally been intended for 7 tokens, but the lower right of the mould was never incised.	Rome	British Museum accession record notes 'from Rome' (presented by the Rev. G. J. Chester), but no further information is provided.	British Museum 1890, 0514.1
27	112x70mm mould (material unreported) for 5 circular tokens of ca. 17mm, all of the same design, to produce tokens showing: **Minerva standing right holding spear in right hand and resting left on shield.**	Rome	Museo Nazionale di Napoli, part of the Borgia collection. Since Cardinal Borgia's collection was mainly assembled from objects found in Rome, these moulds are believed to come from the city.	Giglioli (1913), 3.
28	106x102mm mould for 3 square tokens of ca. 12.5x13mm carrying the legend **AF above P** and 3 tokens in the shape of a *tabula ansata* with the legend **MS above A**.	Rome	As above.	Giglioli (1913), 3.
29	140x70 mm mould for 9 circular tokens all of the same design: **Annona standing with corn-ears in one hand and a cornucopia in the other**.	Rome	The publication simply states 'from recent excavations in Rome'.	Ruggiero (1878), no. 1.
30	No further information given.		From a tufa quarry on the property of 'Cav. Piacentini', between the 8th and 9th kilometre to the left of the via Flaminia. A short distance away was the remains of walls in *opus reticulatum* and a mosaic floor, likely the remains of a Roman villa.	*NSc.* (1907), 348.
31	170x111mm mould for 11 circular tokens of (diameter not given), all of the same design: **CT**.	Ostia	Found in the fill during excavations on the street parallel to the Capitolium ('temple of Vulcan').	*NSc.* (1908), 332; Ostia Antiquarium inv. 589.
32	90x80mm mould for 7 circular (?) tokens of ca. 13mm all of the same design: **Fortuna standing with rudder and cornucopia.**	Ostia	Uncovered in the section of the decumanus up to the via della Pistrina (via dei Molini).	*NSc.* (1913), 216; Ostia Antiquarium inv. no. 7572.
33	145x125mm mould fragment for 11 circular tokens of 11mm (of which three are missing – the lower right corner has broken off), all decorated with the **head of Serapis**.	Ostia	Excavations along the via di Diana, including the SW corner of the House of Diana.	*Giornale degli Scavi*, vol. 8, (1915), 45; Ostia Antiquarium inv. no. 9535.

No.	*Description*	*Place*	*Context*	*Ref.*
34	80x81 mm mould for 8 circular tokens (no diameter given), all of the same design: **cornucopia within a wreath**.	Ostia	Finds from work on the northern side of the street that runs along the wall north of the Caserma dei Vigili.	*NSc.* (1912), 277; Ostia Antiquarium inv. no. 5776.
35	147x95mm mould for 9 circular tokens of 13mm, all of the same design: **F**.	Ostia	Excavations along the street and in the Caserma dei Vigili.	*NSc.* (1911), 367; Ostia Antiquarium inv. no. 4377.
36	135x95mm mould for circular tokens (number not specified) of ca. 15mm all of the same design: the letter **E**.	Ostia	Found while clearing the earth from a house on the via della Fontana ('casa della via della Fontana').	*NSc.* (1907), 18.
37	150x100mm mould for 7 square tokens of 13x12mm, all of the same design: **5 pellets**.	Ostia	Found above the covered corridor at the entrance of the casa dei dipinti along the via della Fontana.	*NSc.* (1913), 78.
38	110x110mm mould for 7 oval tokens of ca. 9mm of **uncertain design**.	Ostia	Found during the clearing of earth from the casa della via della Fontana.	*NSc.* (1907), 121.
39	Palombino mould for 9 square tokens of 8x8mm, decorated with **three pellets**.	Ostia	Excavations from the Terme Peristyle to the via della Fontana.	*NSc.* (1909), 200.
40	107x91mm mould for 5 tokens (shape not given, presumably circular). The three token moulds to the right of the central channel are decorated with **IV**, and the two on the left with a **palm branch**.	Ostia	Excavations of two *tabernae* (4, 5) along the decumanus between the via della Fontana and via dei Molini.	*Giornale degli Scavi*, vol. 7, (1914), 30; Ostia Antiquarium inv. no. 8701.
41	Mould for 7 tokens (shape not given, presumably circular), all of the same design: **an eagle**.	Ostia	Excavations of the land that formerly belonged to the Aldobrandini family and which was acquired through expropriation. This is in all probability Ostia Antiquarium inv. no. 12544, which is a mould for 7 circular tokens showing an eagle with wings spread and which has no associated find information.	*NSc.* (1918), 132. See also Spagnoli (2017), pl. VI, no. 4.
42	90x43mm mould fragment for 5 square tokens of ca. 7x6mm showing **a standing figure holding a sceptre in his left hand** and 5 triangular tokens of ca. 9mm with the design **ΦΛ**.	Ostia	Fill from the west side of via delle Corporazioni.	*NSc.* (1913), 132; Ostia Antiquarium inv. no. 7034.
43	110x100mm mould for 9 circular tokens of ca. 5mm, the design is **blank**.	Ostia	Piazzale delle Corporazioni: excavation of the portico behind the theatre on the east side of the piazzale.	*NSc.* (1912), 437; Ostia Antiquarium inv. no. 6309bis.
44	100x100mm mould with the outline of 7 square 10x10mm tokens sketched.	Ostia	Theatre. Found in the same stratum as a marble bust with an Antonine hairstyle.	*NSc.* (1913), 396; Ostia Antiquarium inv. no. 8367.
45	124x145mm mould for 9 round *tesserae* of 9mm, the design is **blank**.	Ostia	Theatre: at the back of the second taberna in the NE corner.	*NSc.* (1913), 132.
46	185mm mould for two series of (circular?) tokens of 10mm with the letters **IV**.	Ostia	Theatre: at the back of the third taberna, beginning from the NW corner. From a fire stratum that had a large quantity of dumped marble including the torso of a Nereid and other statues.	*NSc.* (1913), 296–99; Ostia Antiquarium inv. no. 8156

No.	*Description*	*Place*	*Context*	*Ref.*
47	125x95mm mould for 6 circular tokens, all of the same design: **P**.	Ostia	Excavation of the fill that came from around the theatre.	*NSc.* (1910), 185; Ostia Antiquarium inv. no. 2939.
48	152mm hexagonal mould for 9 tokens (shape not given, presumably circular), all of the same design: **C**	Ostia	From excavations associated with the installation of the railroad on the outside of the theatre and to the right of the sewer that came from the latrines.	*Giornale degli Scavi*, vol. 3, (1910), 162, Ostia Antiquarium inv. no. 3282.
49	145x72mm mould for 9 tokens (shape. not given, presumably circular), all of the same design: **L**	Ostia	As above.	*Giornale degli Scavi*, vol. 3, (1910), 163; Ostia Antiquarium inv. no. 3283.
50	161x90x15mm mould of Luna marble for 8 square tokens, all with the same design: **an anthropomorphic figure holding a sceptre (?), with a container (modius?) between the legs (?).**	Ostia	Insula delle Ierodule, found in a corridor in a stratum of abandonment.	Falzone and Pellegrino (2014), 364.
51	178x178mm octogonal-shaped full mould (both halves) for 11 circular tokens decorated with the letter **P** on each side.	Ostia	A workshop along the eastern side of the cardo maximus, opposite the Thermes du Phare (Baths of the Lighthouse).	Spagnoli (2001); Ostia Antiquarium inv. nos. 5920 a–b.
52	Fragment of a mould of Luna marble (no measurements given), for a single circular token of ca. 10mm showing a **beetle**.	Ostia	From Stratum I of Ambiente XVI of the excavations of the Terme del Nuotatore (stratum dated from the middle of the 3rd century to the end of the 4th century AD).	Carandini and Panella (1977), 271.
53	77mm mould fragment for 4 circular tokens of ca. 12mm decorated with a **small altar** (?).	Ostia	In the NE corner of the Sabazeum.	*NSc.* (1909), 23.
54	No further information given.	Ostia	Reported in the letters of Visconti, along with other small objects.	*Lettere di Visconti* 1855–1870, p. 131, 31 January 1866.
55	145x70mm mould of uncertain material for 9 circular tokens of ca. 10mm, all of the same design: **A**.	Ostia	No further information known.	TURS 3594
56	140x110mm mould of uncertain material for 9 circular tokens of different sizes (15–17mm) all of the same design: **lituus**.	Ostia	No further information known.	TURS 3596
57	165x145mm mould of uncertain material for 9 circular tokens of different sizes (13–15mm), all of the same design: **crossed cornucopiae**.	Ostia	No further information known.	TURS 3597
58	160x140mm mould of uncertain material for 9 circular tokens of ca. 15mm, all of the same design: **modius**.	Ostia	No further information known.	TURS 3598
59	Fragment of a mould half; the surviving fragment is for one circular token of 20mm decorated with **Aequitas holding cornucopia and a pair of scales**.	Ostia	No further information known.	Spagnoli (2017), pl. VI, no. 5; Ostia Antiquarium inv. no. 5905.

No.	Description	Place	Context	Ref.
60	Fragment of a mould half; the surviving fragment is for two circular tokens of 20mm decorated with **head of Serapis**.	Ostia	No further information known.	Spagnoli (2017), pl. VI, no. 6; Ostia Antiquarium inv. no. 12543.
61	120x80mm mould of Luna marble for 8 circular tokens of different sizes (7–12mm), all of the same design: **a cross**.	Ostia (?)[56]	Stray finds collected by individuals (including metal detectorists) from the earth moved to the surrounding fields of the city during earlier excavations.	Pensabene (2001–2003), 501.

Bibliography

Al-As'ad, Briquel-Chatonnet and Yon 2005: K. Al-As'ad, F. Briquel-Chatonnet and J.-P. Yon, 'The sacred banquets at Palmyra and the function of the *tesserae*: reflections on the tokens found in the Arsu temple', in E. Cussini (ed.) (2010), 1–10.

Alföldi 1937: A. Alföldi, *A Festival of Isis in Rome under the Christian Emperors of the IVth Century* (Budapest, 1937).

Ando and Rüpke (eds.) 2015: C. Ando and J. Rüpke (eds.), *Public and Private in Ancient Mediterranean Law and Religion* (Berlin, 2015).

Ariel 2012: D. T. Ariel, 'Judean perspectives of ancient mints and minting technology', *INJ* 7 (2012), 43–80.

Boulakia 1972: J. D. C. Boulakia, 'Lead in the Roman world', *AJA* 76 (1972), 139–44.

Butcher (ed.) 2019: K. Butcher (ed.), *Debasement. Manipulation of Coin Standards in Pre-Modern Monetary Systems* (London, 2019) (forthcoming).

Carandini and Panella (eds.) 1977: A. Carandini and C. Panella (eds.), *Ostia IV. Le Terme del Nuotatore. Scavo dell'ambiente XVI e dell'area XXV* (Studi Miscellanei 23) (Rome, 1977).

Carradice 1994: I. Carradice, 'Alexander Henderson and an early Scottish communion token', *NC* 154 (1994), 218–23.

Cesano 1904a: L. Cesano, 'Matrici e tessere di piombo', *Bullettino della commissione archeologica comunale di Roma* 33 (1904), 146–53.

Cesano 1904b: L. Cesano, 'Matrici e tessere di piombo nel Museo Nazionale Romano', *NSc.* (1904), 11–17.

Collingwood and Wright 1990: R. G. Collingwood and R. P. Wright, *The Roman Inscriptions of Britain Vol II: Instrumentum Domesticum* (Chester, 1990).

Crosby 1964: M. Crosby, 'Lead and clay tokens. Part II', in Lang and Crosby (1964), 69–146.

Cussini (ed.) 2010: E. Cussini (ed.), *A Journey to Palmyra. Collected Essays to Remember Delbert R. Hillers* (Leiden, 2010).

Descœudres (ed.) 2001: J.-P. Descœudres (ed.), *Ostia. Port et porte de la Rome antique* (Geneva, 2001).

Dolansky 2011: F. Dolansky, 'Celebrating the *Saturnalia*: religious ritual and Roman domestic life', in Rawson (ed.) (2010), 487–503.

Dressel 1922: H. Dressel, 'Römische Bleimarken', *ZfN* 33 (1922), 178–83.

Eckardt 2017: H. Eckardt, *Writing and Power in the Roman World. Literacies and Material Culture* (Cambridge, 2017).

Falzone and Pellegrino (eds.) 2014: S. Falzone and A. Pellegrino (eds.), *Scavi di Ostia XV: Insula delle Ierodule (c.d. Casa di Lucceia Primitiva: III, IX, 6)* (Rome, 2014).

Ferrandes and Pardini (eds.) 2016: A. F. Ferrandes and G. Pardini (eds.), *Le regole del gioco tracce archeologi racconti. Studi in onore di Clementina Panella* (Rome, 2016).

Ficoroni 1740: F. Ficoroni, *I piombi antichi* (Rome, 1740).

Garrucci 1847: R. Garrucci, *I piombi antichi raccolti dall'eminentissimo principe* (Rome, 1847).

Gatti 1926: E. Gatti, 'Notizie di recenti trovamenti di antichità in Roma e nel suburbio', *Bullettino della commissione archeologica comunale di Roma* 54 (1926), 235–69.

Giglioli 1913: G. Q. Giglioli, 'Due matrici di tessere plumblee', *Ausonia. Rivista della società italiana di archeologia e storia dell'arte* 7 (1913), 3–6.

Graillot 1896: H. Graillot, 'Une collection de tessères', *Mélanges d'archéologie et d'histoire* 16 (1896), 299–314.

Harrison 2001: G. W. Harrison, 'Martial on *sportula* and the *Saturnalia*', *Mouseion: Journal of the Classical Association of Canada* 1 (2001), 295–312.

[56] Although Pensabene publishes the find as from Ostia, the full (unpublished) corpus of the material suggests that the illegal excavations may have taken place over a broader region.

Hirschland and Hammond 1968: N. L. Hirschland and M. Hammond, 'Stamped potters' marks and other stamped pottery in the McDaniel Collection', *HSCPh* 72 (1968), 369–82.

Irvine, Hanks and Weddle (2013): R. D. G. Irvine, N. Hanks and C. Weddle, 'Sacred architecture: archaeological and anthropological perspectives', in Shankland (ed.) (2013), 91–117.

Kool 2013: R. Kool, 'Lead token money in the Kingdom of Jerusalem', *NC* 173 (2013), 293–339.

Lagóstena Barrios 1993: L. Lagóstena Barrios, 'Una tésera de plomo hallada en el yacimento romano de «Puente Melchor» Puerto Real (Cádiz)', *Habis* 24 (1993), 307–09.

Lang and Crosby 1964: M. Lang and M. Crosby, *The Athenian Agora X: Weights, Measures and Tokens* (New Jersey, 1964).

Malacrino 2010: C. G. Malacrino, *Constructing the Ancient World: Architectural Techniques of the Greeks and Romans* (Los Angeles, 2010).

Malkmus 2007: W. Malkmus, 'Ancient and medieval coin dies: catalogue and notes', in Travaini and Bolis (eds.) (2007), 75–240.

Medri, di Cola, Carandini and Panella 2013: M. Medri, V. di Cola, A. Carandini and C. Panella, *Ostia V. Le terme del nuotatore. Cronologia di un'insula ostiense* (Rome, 2013).

Mitchiner 1984: M. Mitchiner, 'Rome: Imperial portrait *tesserae* from the city of Rome and imperial tax tokens from the province of Egypt', *NC* 144 (1984), 95–114.

Mlasowsky 1991: A. Mlasowsky, *Die antiken Tesseren im Kestner-Museum Hannover* (Hannover, 1991).

Mora Serrano 2002: B. Mora Serrano, 'El depósito de plomos monetiformes de las termas de Alameda (?Vrgapa?), Màlaga', *Numisma* 246 (2002), 39–67.

Nogara 1917: B. Nogara, 'Matrici per tessere e coltello di età romana scavati in Como nella Piazza Cavour', *Rivista Archeologica della Provincia e antica Diocesi di Como* 73-75 (1917), 3–7.

Overbeck 1995: M. Overbeck, *Römische Bleimarken in der Staatlichen Münzsammlung München. Eine Quelle zur Sozial- und Wirtschaftsgeschichte Roms* (Munich, 1995).

Panella and Rizzo (eds.) 2014: C. Panella and G. Rizzo (eds.), *Ostia VI: Le Terme del Nuotatore* (Rome, 2014).

Pardini 2014: G. Pardini, 'Le monete', in Panella and Rizzo (eds.) (2014), 41–46.

Pardini, Piacentini, Felici, Santarelli and Santucci 2016: G. Pardini, M. Piacentini, A. C. Felici, M. L. Santarelli and S. Santucci, 'Matrici per tessere plumbee dalle pendici nord-orientali del Palatino. Nota preliminare', in Ferrandes and Pardini (eds.) (2016), 649–67.

Pedroni 1997: L. Pedroni, 'Tessere plumbee dalle terme di Fregellae', *Bollettino di Numismatica* 28–29 (1997), 203–10.

Pensabene 2001–2003: P. Pensabene, 'Su alcune tessere plumbee di uso commerciale', *Scienze dell'antichità. Storia archeologia antropologia* 11 (2001–2003), 479–510.

Pilon 2016: F. Pilon, *L'atelier monétaire de Châteaubleau. Officines et monnayages d'imitation du IIIe siècle dans le nord-ouest de l'Empire* (Paris, 2016).

Pozzi and Labrot 2008: L. Pozzi and J. Labrot, 'Una matrice medievale per la fusione di tessere rinvenuta a Sondrio', *Istituto Archeologico Valtellinese Notiziario* 6 (2008), 41–48.

Raja 2015: R. Raja, 'Staging "private" religion in Roman "public" Palmyra. The role of the religious dining tickets (banqueting *tesserae*)', in Ando and Rüpke (eds.) (2015), 165–86.

Rawson (ed.) 2010: B. Rawson (ed.), *A Companion to Families in the Greek and Roman Worlds* (Malden, 2010).

Richardson 1992: L. Richardson, *A New Topographical Dictionary of Ancient Rome* (Baltimore, 1992).

Rostovtsew and Vaglieri 1900: M. Rostovtsew and D. Vaglieri, 'Alveo del Tevere', *NSc.* (1900), 256–68.

Rostovtzeff 1897: M. Rostovtzeff, 'Étude sur les plombs antiques', *RN* 1 (1897), 462–93.

Rostowzew 1905: M. Rostowzew, *Römische Bleitesserae. Ein Beitrag zur Sozial- und Wirtschaftsgeschichte der römischen Kaiserzeit* (Leipzig, 1905).

Rostowzew and Prou 1900: M. Rostowzew and M. Prou, *Catalogue des plombs de l'antiquité* (Paris, 1900).

Ruggiero 1878: E. Ruggiero, *Catalogo del Museo Kircheriano* (Rome, 1878).

Shankland (ed.) 2013: D. Shankland, *Archaeology and Anthropology. Past, Present and Future* (London, 2013).

Spagnoli 2001: E. Spagnoli, 'VII.5-7-10', in Descœudres (ed.) (2001), 408–09.

Spagnoli 2017: E. Spagnoli, 'Un nucleo di piombi "monetiformi" da Ostia, Terme dei Cisiarii (II.II.3): problematiche interpretative e quadro di circolazione. Per un contributo di storia economica e di archeologia della produzione tra II e III secolo d.C.', *AIIN* 63 (2017), 179–234.

Stannard 2015: C. Stannard, 'Shipping *tesserae* from Ostia and Minturnae?', *NC* 175 (2015), 147–54.

Steinby 1993: E. M. Steinby, *Lexicon topographicum urbis Romae* (Rome, 1993).

Szaivert, Schindel, Beckers and Vondrovec (eds.) 2015: W. Szaivert, N. Schindel, M. Beckers and K. Vondrovec (eds.), *ΤΟΥΤΟ ΑΡΕΣΗ ΤΗ ΧΩΡΑ. Festschrift für Wolfgang Hahn zum 70. Geburtstag* (Vienna, 2015).

Thornton 1980: M. K. Thornton, 'The Roman lead *tesserae*: observations on two historical problems', *Historia* 29 (1980), 335–55.

Travaini and Bolis (eds.) 2007: L. Travaini and A. Bolis (eds.), *Conii e scene di coniazione* (Rome, 2007).

Turcan 1987: R. Turcan, *Nigra Moneta. Sceaux, jetons, tesseres, amulettes, plombs monétaires ou monétiformes, objects divers en plomb ou en etain d'époque romaine conservés au musée des Beaux-Arts de Lyon* (Lyon, 1987).

Turcan 1988: R. Turcan, 'Jetons romains en plomb: problèmes de datation et d'utilisation', *Latomus* 47 (1988), 626–34.

Virlouvet 1995: C. Virlouvet, *Tessera frumentaria. Les procédures de distribution du blé à Rome à la fin de la République et au début de l'Empire* (Rome, 1995).

Wood 1904: L. I. Wood, *Scottish Pewter-Ware and Pewterers* (Edinburgh, 1904).

Woytek 2015: B. Woytek, 'IO IO TRIVMP und A.P.P.F. Zu zwei Typen römischer Buntmetall-*Tesserae*', in Szaivert, Schindel, Beckers and Vondrovec (2015), (eds.), 479–98.

Woytek 2019: B. Woytek, 'Metal and system in Roman imperial mints. Flan production, quality control and the internal organisation of minting establishments during the Principate', in Butcher (ed.) (2019).

TOKENS OF ANTINOUS FROM THE ROMAN PROVINCE OF EGYPT

DENISE WILDING

Introduction

The tokens of Roman Egypt (30 BC–AD 380) are small, lead, monetiform objects that hold great potential for study in terms of their utilisation within everyday life. Tokens are found on sites throughout Egypt, and in a variety of different contexts, including the rubbish dumps of Oxyrhynchus, the Serapeum at Saqqara, the temple at Qasr Ibrim, the town of Karanis, and as far afield as a shipwreck on the Haifa coast.[1] Their exact purpose is not known conclusively, and it is likely that they served a variety of functions.[2] Their imagery is varied and often based on coin iconography influenced by both the classical and Egyptian worlds. Some clearly belong to the same series, such as those which depict Athena at Oxyrhynchus, or those that bear regnal dates and are heavily influenced by the Alexandrian coinage. These tokens have, however, been little studied in their own right since the work of Milne in the early twentieth century.[3] This paper aims to explore one subset of these tokens: those that depict Antinous, the favourite and lover of the emperor Hadrian (AD 117–138).

This study is a preliminary survey of tokens which depict Antinous from Roman Egypt, a full study being beyond the scope of this paper. The corpus comprises tokens from the three most comprehensive catalogues: Milne, Dattari and the University of Cologne collection.[4] Types which do not appear in these catalogues are collated from auctions, the Ashmolean Museum, the Yale University Art Gallery, the Petrie Museum, the collection of the American Numismatic Society, and one private collection.[5] Undoubtedly other examples exist, however the above have been chosen as they have either been studied first hand by the author (in the case of the museum collections), or the available images are of a high enough quality to undertake analysis (in the case of those from auctions). This study aims to examine the tokens of Antinous in order to assess how they sit alongside coins and medallions from Roman Egypt depicting Hadrian's favourite, as well as considering how their imagery and regnal dates can suggest a tighter chronology for their period of issue. This will then be placed in the wider context of their potential use within society in Graeco-Roman Egypt.

Antinous

Antinous was the lover of the emperor Hadrian who died prematurely while accompanying the emperor on a trip to Egypt in AD 130. Soon after, his image became ubiquitous across the Roman Empire and he was worshipped as a hero or god.[6] The events which resulted in Antinous' demise are not certain; while it is apparent that he drowned in the Nile, the exact circumstances surrounding this are not clear, and suggestion has been made that his death was a sacrificial act, self-imposed or otherwise.[7] Hadrian founded the city Antinoopolis, named after Antinous, whom he then deified, and created the cult of his worship. It seems that Antinous was not deified in the usual manner as was accorded members of the imperial family.[8] This is exemplified by the fact that Hadrian arranged for honours outside of Rome, but none at all within the city; official consecration was absent.[9] Hadrian encouraged the worship of Antinous, and this was embraced by the local provincial elite, exemplified by the distribution of festival coins of medallic character in Antinous' honour at Corinth by Hostilius Marcellus (a wealthy citizen who was given the liturgy 'Priest of Antinous'), and at

[1] The following abbreviations are used: RPC 3 = A. Burnett and M. Amandry, *Roman Provincial Coinage Volume III: Nerva, Trajan and Hadrian* (London, 2015). RPC 4 = *Roman Provincial Coinage Volume IV: Antoninus Pius to Commodus*. Online: http://rpc.ashmus.ox.ac.uk/.
Oxyrhynchus: Milne (1922), (1971); Saqqara: Longperier (1861); Qasr Ibrim: Frend (2004); Karanis: Kelsey Museum of Archaeology (unpublished); Haifa: Meshorer (2010).

[2] Wilding (*in prep.*) will consider how tokens in Roman Egypt may have functioned in general. See Milne (1908), (1915), (1922) and (1971), where tokens from Egypt are interpreted as a low denomination coinage.

[3] Milne (1908), (1922) and (1930).

[4] Dattari (1901); Milne (1971).

[5] Ashmolean Museum: previously published in Milne (1971); Petrie Museum: previously published in Milne (1915).

[6] Vout (2005), 82.

[7] Cassius Dio, *Roman History* 69.11.2–4; Aurelius Victor, *De Caesaribus* 14.5–7; Historia Augusta, *Hadrian* 14.5–7.

[8] Vout (2007), 114.

[9] Price (1987), 87.

Mantineia by Vetourios.[10] In Egypt, games in Antinous' honour (the *Megala Antinoeia*) were held for the first time in Antinoopolis in the spring of AD 131.[11] These were overseen by the Roman prefect of Egypt, rather than the local elite, which may account for their longevity into the third century.[12] The cult of Antinous was therefore created by the emperor, embraced by the elites, and became a religious cult with a mass following.[13]

After his deification Antinous was syncretised mainly with three different deities in Egypt: Hermes, Osiris and Dionysos, all gods associated with the underworld. In Egypt, Hermes was syncretised with Thoth, the Egyptian god connected with writing and wisdom, and who presided over the judgement of the souls of the dead.[14] Therefore Antinous' syncretisation with Hermes may also have extended to include Thoth in this region. His assimilation into Osiris-Antinous is evident from the inscription on the obelisk of Antinous now standing in Rome, where the dedication is to 'The god, Osiris-Antinous'.[15] This syncretism is probably due to the fact that both gods drowned in the Nile and were subsequently resurrected. Furthermore, both Dionysos and Hermes were also perceived as gods of fertility and had an association with the underworld. This, as well as the fact that the inscription on the obelisk mentioned above invokes Thoth to 'rejuvenate his spirit', indicates that although Antinous can be perceived as a god with chthonic associations, he also can also be equated with rebirth. His syncretism with previously existing deities therefore appears to be based on the cycle of life, death and rebirth.[16]

Alexandrian coinage and medals showing Antinous

In order to consider how tokens of Antinous were utilised and perceived in Roman Egypt it is also necessary to examine the Alexandrian coin issues that depicted him, which share iconographic similarities with both medallions and tokens portraying Antinous from Egypt. Coinage and medallions showing Antinous are prevalent elsewhere in the eastern provinces of the Empire, with over 30 cities striking in his honour.[17] Although these shall be taken into account where appropriate, the primary scope of this paper is limited to the material from Egypt.[18]

From Alexandria there were two coin issues, one dated to year 19 of Hadrian's reign and the other dated to year 21, which perhaps were struck to commemorate the four-year and six-year anniversaries of Antinous' death, and were possibly connected with the associated festivals held in his honour.[19] The issues depict the bust of Antinous on the obverse, draped and wearing the hemhem crown (a three-fold version of the atef crown, flanked by sheep horns and *uraei*, and with each of the three columns topped with a sun disc) and on the reverse Antinous riding or galloping on horseback, carrying a caduceus over his shoulder, although one issue depicts the caduceus alone.[20] Due to the presence of the caduceus, an attribute of Hermes, here Antinous should be viewed in terms of his syncretism with Hermes-Thoth, while the hemhem crown exemplifies his association with Osiris and his status as a god.[21]

Antinous' presence on the Alexandrian coinage is somewhat unexpected as its issues were more closely linked to the coinage of Rome than other Greek cities - he does not appear on Roman coins, but is shown on other Greek provincial issues. A hierarchy was also observed,

[10] Corinth: Amandry and Burnett (2015), 39; RPC, vol. 3, nos. 260–63; Mantineia: Amandry and Burnett (2015), 47; RPC, vol. 3, nos. 325–27.
[11] Birley (1997), 256.
[12] Boatwright (2000), 195.
[13] Opper (2008), 190.
[14] Derchain-Urtel (1981), 136–46; Fowden (1986), 22.
[15] Grimm, Kessler and Meyer (1994), 53.
[16] Dionysos and Hermes: Lambert (1984), 181; obelisk: Birley (1997), 256.
[17] Amandry (2015).
[18] von Mosch (2001); Amandry (2015); von Mosch and Klostermeyer (2015) for discussion of coins and medallions showing Antinous from elsewhere in the east.
[19] Blum (1914), 60; Amandry and Burnett (2015), 663.
[20] RPC, vol. 3, nos. 6062–64 ,6073–74, 6082, 6086, 6228, 6235, 6243.
[21] Pudill (2014), 23.

with members of the imperial family (Sabina and Aelius) appearing on Alexandrian silver and Antinous appearing on two issues only in bronze.[22] The frequent appearance of his image on tokens is therefore interesting given that there were so few coin issues. Perhaps, given this hierarchy in materials and limitation of issues, tokens provided another medium with fewer restrictions through which to strike monetiform objects in his honour.

Many of the coinages struck for Antinous in the east can actually be considered to be medallic issues, often struck for games and festivals. They do not have a denomination, were often manufactured from orichalcum, and frequently were larger in size than ordinary coin issues.[23] It is possible that medallions of Antinous did exist in Egypt, as a limestone mould, complete with channel to accommodate the poured metal (probably lead or bronze), was identified as a medallion mould by Jacobstahl.[24] However, if the mould were intended for the casting of medallions it would be a unique and unusual example. The imagery on the medallion mould is similar to that found on the coinage and on tokens; depicted in one hollow is Antinous-Hermes-Thoth on horseback, carrying a caduceus over his shoulder, while the other portrays the bust of Antinous – despite the break that runs through the mould, the curly hair and hemhem crown are just visible.[25] It seems that this was indeed intended to cast medallions or similar, rather than tokens, as at 40mm in diameter the object would have been unusually large to function as a token, most of which measure between 17 and 23mm (see catalogue below). Additionally, the erratic die axes of Antinous tokens from Egypt imply that they were perhaps struck rather than cast (for example, catalogue nos. 1a–e, which are all of the same type, but have different axes).[26]

These examples from Egypt and beyond demonstrate that there was wider contemporary use of paranumismatica depicting Antinous that did not function as money. This is useful for considering the variety of uses that monetiform objects had in the Roman Empire, and therefore for discerning how tokens may have functioned.

The tokens of Antinous

The tokens of Antinous from Egypt have received little attention aside from their inclusion alongside other tokens of Roman Egypt in Alexandrian coin catalogues.[27] Their potential has not been considered in studies of coinage depicting Antinous. For instance, in his examination of the coins showing Antinous, Blum mentions two tokens from Dattari's catalogue, but offers no discussion.[28] In his appendix focusing on the coins and gems of Antinous, Lambert does not mention the tokens, despite briefly referring to coarse lead copies of medallions, for which he provides no explicit details.[29] Pudill includes a brief summary of some token types in his publication on the iconography Antinous, but this discussion is not extensive.[30] No comprehensive study has therefore been undertaken focusing solely on the tokens which portray Antinous.

Many of the Antinous tokens are part of a larger corpus of tokens from Roman Egypt that are heavily influenced by the Alexandrian coinage. This subset shares similarities in terms of their style, and also imagery, and the types are interchanged and paired with each other in a variety of different combinations. Types paired with Antinous are therefore also paired with different imagery on other tokens. They are not as crude as some groups of tokens from Egypt, for example the Athena tokens of Oxyrhynchus. This suggests an element of sophistication in their manufacture, which when combined with their widespread

[22] Amandry and Burnett (2015), 544.
[23] Amandry and Burnett (2015), 856. The examples mentioned above from Corinth and Mantineia are listed in this category, as well as a full list of other issues.
[24] Jacobstahl (1905).
[25] Jacobstahl (1905), 77.
[26] This is in contrast to tokens cast in moulds, which often have regular die axes. See Rowan, this volume, for discussion of token moulds from Ostia and Rome which were affixed together tightly with nails, on the same orientation each time, resulting in tokens with regular die axes. Additionally, to date there are no token moulds from Egypt, in contrast to the emerging picture in Italy.
[27] Dattari (1901); Milne (1971); Geissen and Weiser (1983).
[28] Blum (1914), 57.
[29] Lambert (1984), 238–43.
[30] Pudill (2017), 187–90.

distribution throughout Egypt and the fact that they draw heavily on Alexandrian coinage, leads to the possibility that they were produced in Alexandria.

Therefore, the following discussion is undertaken with the indication that some tokens of Antinous, particularly those that are dated (nos. 1–11), are a small subset within the corpus of Alexandrian token types, themselves a subcategory within the corpus of tokens from Roman Egypt as a whole. Other Antinous tokens seem to belong to a different subset; those that carry the image of Antinous on one side and Zeus Ammon on the other and are inscribed with the legend ΕΠ ΑΓΑΘΩ (nos. 16–17) are significantly different to those clearly influenced by the Alexandrian coin types, and it is possible that they were manufactured by a different authority, or in a different workshop. Uniface examples in glass are also known, but their function as tokens is not certain, and therefore they are not included in the catalogue below.[31]

Antinous is depicted on one face of the tokens, although ascertaining whether this is the obverse or reverse is difficult due to the different range of types that are paired together without the regularity of the bust of the emperor on the obverse, as found on the contemporary coinage.[32] The portrait of Antinous depicted is often inspired directly by the Alexandrian coinage. For example, his bust is depicted on the obverse of Alexandrian coins draped and wearing the hemhem crown.[33] This is also the case for tokens (catalogue nos. 2, 5–6, 8–19, 24, figs. 1–3), although on the coinage he faces both left and right, while on the tokens he only faces right. On tokens he is sometimes accompanied by a crescent to the front, or

Fig. 1: Obverse: bust of Antinous right, crescent before. Reverse: Serapis standing facing, head left, wearing modius, right arm raised, sceptre in left hand (Ø 20mm; 3.29g; die axis: 12; metal: lead) (Milne (1971), no. 5446) (catalogue no. 12b) (Scale 2:1) (courtesy of the Ashmolean Museum, Heberden Coin Room).

Fig. 2: Obverse: Bust of Antinous right, wearing hemhem crown. Date: LH (Year 8). Reverse: Bust of Serapis Helios right. Date: LH (Year 8) (Ø 23mm; 4.50g; die axis: 8; metal: lead) (catalogue no. 8a) (Scale 2:1) (courtesy of Lee Toone).

[31] Glass example: Classical Numismatic Group, E-Sale 358, 26 August 2015, lot no. 258. Entwistle and Finney (2013), 135: similar objects from Roman Egypt have been interpreted as tokens, gaming pieces or counters.

[32] For purposes of consistency in this paper, the face portraying Antinous shall be referred to as the obverse. There is, however, an example on which he is possibly depicted on both faces (no. 16) and in this instance the side described as the obverse will remain consistent with the assignation of the collection in which the token is held.

[33] RPC, vol. 3, nos. 6062–64, 6073–74, 6082, 6086, 6228, 6235, 6243.

Fig. 3: Obverse: Bust of Antinous right, wearing hemhem crown, crescent before. Reverse: Nilus reclining right, holding reeds in right hand and cornucopia in left, crowned by Euthenia standing left (Ø 21mm; 8.84g; die axis: 1; metal: lead) (catalogue no. 13b) (Scale 2:1) (Classical Numismatic Group, E-Sale 353, 17 June 2015, lot no. 366).

with a caduceus over his shoulder. He is also depicted on tokens riding right on horseback with a caduceus over his shoulder (catalogue nos. 20–21, 26, fig. 4). This type is found on the reverse of Alexandrian coinage, paired with his bust on the obverse as discussed above.[34] Therefore, both observe and reverse types of Alexandrian coinage are utilised on tokens, although not on the same piece. A common distinguishing feature of tokens is the fact that their imagery is inspired by coinage, but they are never exact copies. The fact that the obverse and reverse types of the coinage are not found together on the tokens is a good example of the subtle variation between coinage and tokens.

Fig. 4: Obverse: Antinous-Hermes riding right, caduceus over shoulder. Reverse: Nike advancing left with wreath in right hand and palm in left (Ø 21mm; 4.24g; die axis: 1; metal: lead) (Milne (1971), no. 5420) (catalogue no. 20d) (Scale 2:1) (courtesy of the Ashmolean Museum, Heberden Coin Room).

Antinous is also portrayed on tokens paired with the bust of Isis (catalogue nos. 1, 3–4, 7, 22–23, 25, figs. 5–6). This imagery reflects an Alexandrian coin type where Isis is depicted opposite the bust of Serapis, a god who gained popularity under the Ptolemies and subsumed some of the aspects of Osiris.[35] This coin type can perhaps be interpreted as Isis and Osiris depicted in a classical style, and therefore in this context the imagery of Antinous should be read in terms with his syncretism with Osiris. Both Serapis and Osiris-Antinous had chthonic associations, so utilising the imagery of Antinous in this manner was in keeping with portraying a deity associated with death and rebirth, and the imagery of Osiris-Antinous can therefore be read in similar terms to that of Serapis. This is again an example

[34] RPC, vol. 3, 6062–63, 6073, 6082, 6228, 6235, 6243.
[35] Coin types: RPC, vol. 3, nos. 5902 and 6013; RPC, vol. 3, nos. 15530 and 14360–62; the god Serapis: Takács (1995), 28.

of how tokens were influenced by coin types, but the manufacturers had the freedom to adapt and change elements.

Antinous wears the hemhem crown when he is depicted on tokens, which provides further evidence that, as with the coinage, his image should be read in the context of his syncretism with both Hermes-Thoth and Osiris. The hemhem crown was the triple form of the atef crown and can be categorised a 'pre-sunrise crown', which is associated with cosmic regeneration. Both the hemhem and the atef crown are often depicted with deities who precede the sunrise, such as Osiris as ruler of the netherworld.[36] This attribute therefore is fitting with both an interpretation of Osiris-Antinous and Antinous-Hermes-Thoth on the tokens, and exemplifies his associations with the underworld, rebirth and regeneration.

The tokens of Antinous: dating

Tokens bearing regnal years and imagery clearly influenced by the Alexandrian coinage will provide the basis for this analysis, as these two elements comprise the best evidence for dating. The dates of these regnal years have not received any scrutiny. Tokens of Antinous are frequently attributed to the reign of Hadrian; for example, those in the collection of the Institute für Altertumskunde at the University of Cologne are dated from AD 130–138 (e.g. nos. 3584–87, catalogue nos. 20e–h), essentially from the year Antinous died until the end of Hadrian's reign.[37] Others have generally assumed that most of the dated tokens can be attributed to Hadrian's reign, while conceding that any date above year 22 (the last year of Hadrian's rule) must be from the reign of an emperor who ruled for longer.[38] Suggestion has also been made that the dates on tokens do not refer to the reign of an emperor, but instead refer to the number of years since Antinous' death.[39] However, through exploring the dates themselves, and the imagery on the tokens, it may be possible to tighten the date range for at least some of the series.

From the catalogue below it is apparent that regnal years are a common feature on tokens of Antinous. The date on each token is signified by the letter 'L' followed by the numeral in ancient Greek. This dataset is only a representative sample of the tokens of Antinous and is by no means comprehensive, however, some general conclusions can be drawn. Of the dated tokens, a pattern emerges of two-year increments pertaining to the lower numbers. Tokens are dated to year 2 (nos.1–2, fig, 5), year 4 (nos. 3–5), year 6 (nos. 6–7, fig. 6) and year 8

Fig. 5: Obverse: Bust of Antinous right, wearing hemhem crown, before bust of Isis facing left. Date: LB (Year 2). Reverse: Nilus riding right on hippopotamus, holding two corn-ears in right hand and cornucopia in left (Ø 20mm; 4.56g; die axis: 1; metal: lead) (catalogue no. 1f) (Scale 2:1) (courtesy of Yale University Art Gallery, inv. no. 2005.6.262).

[36] Goebs (2020), 19.

[37] See Institute für Altertumskunde online catalogue, e.g. no. 3585 (http://muenzen.uni-koeln.de/portal/databases/id/muenzen/titles/id/AL_3585.html?l=de) (accessed 24/05/2019).

[38] Pudill (2014), 91 for discussion of tokens dated to years 22 and 25.

[39] Pudill (2017), 187.

Fig. 6: Obverse: Bust of Antinous right, wearing hemhem crown, before bust of Isis left. Date: Lς (Year 6). Reverse: AN/TINO/OV (Ø 19mm; 3.06g; die axis: 7; metal: lead) (catalogue no. 7b) (Scale 2:1) (Classical Numismatic Group, E-Sale 353, 17 June 2015, lot no. 364).

(no. 8, fig. 2). It should be noted that tokens dated to intervening years, such as 3 and 5, do exist, however as far as the author is aware, they do not carry the image of Antinous.[40] The outliers seem to be those dated to year 18 (no. 9), year 20 (no. 10) and possibly year 25 (no. 11).

The coinage depicting Antinous was only struck in two years: 19 and 21 of Hadrian's reign. Hadrian died in his regnal year 22, which became regnal year 1 of Antoninus Pius' reign. It is therefore possible that the lower dates on the tokens are indicative that the token series took its lead from the coinage issues, and were struck in biennial intervals continuing onwards from the dates on the coins, resulting in years 19 and 21 of Hadrian for coin issues, followed by years 2, 4, 6 and 8 of Antoninus Pius for token issues. This would place at least some of the series at the beginning of Antoninus Pius' reign, particularly those which bear lower numbers. However, this is by no means conclusive given the small number of tokens within this dataset, and does not account for the undated tokens. It is therefore useful to examine the imagery and dates of tokens depicting Antinous and compare them to the Alexandrian coinage on which they are based. Of course, the tokens were by no means manufactured at exactly the same time as the coin types that they parallel, but the overview below will demonstrate that enough similarities are present between these tokens and coins to allow possible dates to be suggested. Three types will be examined, that of the facing busts of Antinous and Isis, that of Serapis standing with Cerberus, and that of Nilus riding on a hippopotamus. The latter two types are paired with an image of Antinous on the other face. Other imagery found on the tokens showing Antinous is not diagnostic enough to form a study. For instance, Nike appears on coinage over a broad temporal period, and therefore would not be a useful image to utilise for dating purposes.

The depiction of the bust of Antinous facing the bust of Isis (figs. 5–6) is paralleled by Alexandrian coin types that show the facing busts of Isis and Serapis. These types appear in year 18 and year 19 of Hadrian's reign.[41] Coins carrying these designs in the reign of Antoninus Pius are dated to years 5 and 23.[42] Tokens with the imagery are dated to years 2 (no. 1), 4 (nos. 3–4) and 6 (no. 7), as well as undated examples (nos. 22–23). A date for these tokens at the beginning of the reign of Antoninus Pius would therefore be plausible, inspired by types from the end of Hadrian's reign and the beginning of that of Antoninus Pius. Were this the case, they would be utilising types from the new and current coinage, thereby making the iconography of the tokens recognisable and in keeping with contemporary imagery.

The imagery of undated tokens showing Antinous is also able to provide a source of evidence in dating the Antinous types. For instance, a type depicts Antinous riding right on one face and on the other Serapis standing facing with head left, purse in right hand, sceptre in

[40] Geissen and Weiser (1983), 198, nos. 3572, 3577.
[41] Year 18: RPC, vol. 3, no. 5902, but placed above an eagle with wings spread; Year 19: RPC, vol. 3, no. 6013.
[42] RPC, vol. 4, nos. 15530, 14262.

left hand, Cerberus to the left (no. 21). The purse is an unusual attribute for Serapis, but the figure wears a kalathos ('grain measure') and is accompanied by the three-headed dog Cerberus, both of which were common attributes of the god. On the Alexandrian coinage the dog only appears in association with Serapis, aside from a few types where he appears dragged behind Heracles.[43] The figure on the token does not, however, bear any of the attributes of Heracles such as the club, and Cerberus is stood beside the figure rather than dragged behind him. Therefore, an identification of Serapis is more likely. The purse is usually an attribute of Hermes, so its appearance with Serapis could serve to highlight the association of Antinous with Hermes. This is particularly relevant as Antinous appears in the guise of Hermes-Thoth on the other face of the same token, thereby implying the image should be read in view of this syncretism. Therefore, it is possible that the deification of Antinous led to iconographic shifts in the representation of existing deities.

This type of Serapis standing facing with Cerberus to the left appears on the Alexandrian coinage from the reign of Trajan to the end of Antoninus Pius' reign. It is not possible that these tokens were struck during the reign of Trajan, as Antinous was only in his early childhood during Trajan's rule, and had not yet met Hadrian.[44] It is therefore more plausible that the imagery under Hadrian or Antoninus Pius provided the impetus for the imagery of the tokens. The type appears in years 11, 17, 18 and 19 of Hadrian's reign and then reappears in years 2, 4, 5, 8 and 21 of Antoninus Pius' reign.[45] The date clusters from the reigns of these emperors are in keeping with the dating of the iconography of Isis and Antinous discussed above, and a date at the end of Hadrian's reign or at the beginning of that of Antoninus Pius can be suggested.

Another type that appears on the reverse face of Antinous tokens is that of Nilus riding a hippopotamus left, holding two corn-ears and a cornucopia (no. 1, fig. 5). All of the tokens with this imagery also carry the regnal date year 2. This type only appears on Alexandrian coinage during Antoninus Pius' reign in years 1 and 2, and therefore it can be reasonably surmised that the tokens bearing this imagery date to a similar period as the coinage.[46] This is particularly plausible when we consider how the imagery discussed above was also current at the end of the reign of Hadrian and beginning of the reign of Antoninus Pius.

These Nilus types, and to some extent the Serapis types, also demonstrate that there is a conscious decision as to which aspects of imagery to keep from the coin types, and which to abandon. The legend found on the coin types of Nilus riding on a hippopotamus does not feature on the tokens of this type. It could be argued that this makes the inclusion of the date more relevant, and that it should refer to a specific year, rather than just being included on an arbitrary basis. It should also be taken into account that the absence of long legends on tokens in general from Roman Egypt could be an intentional design feature to distinguish them from coins. This again highlights the point that a common feature of tokens that differentiates them from coins is the variation in design and room for improvisation.

A comparison of the dies used to strike the Nilus riding hippopotamus tokens in this dataset is also useful in terms of considering the inclusion of the date (nos. 1a–f). Through a comparison of the images it is apparent that different dies have been utilised within this type of token. The placement of the date also varies: on nos. 1a–e the date is placed to each side of the busts, while on no. 1f it is placed below the busts. The fact that these tokens were not struck by the same die implies that the date was intentionally included, as it is always present even though its placement varies. Therefore, the actual date was intended to be communicated, and its presence was not an arbitrary inclusion. It is also interesting to note that

[43] RPC, vol. 4, nos. 15332, 16686.

[44] Birley (1997), 158. It is not known when Antinous was born, however the youthfulness of his portraits does not suggest an age much greater than late teens and therefore a possible date range for his time with Hadrian is AD 123–24 until his death in AD 130; the coin types do not appear until AD 134/35.

[45] Hadrian: RPC, vol. 3, nos. 5514, 5655, 5854, 5924, 6032; Antoninus Pius: RPC, vol. 4, nos. 13491, 14337, 15377, 15837, 16149.

[46] Year 1: RPC, vol. 4, nos. 15746, 15823; RPC, vol. 4, nos. 13531, 15378.

the date does not appear on the side of the token that depicts Nilus (as it does on coinage), instead it appears on the other face that depicts Isis and Antinous. Furthermore, other tokens carry the busts of Isis and Antinous, but do not bear a date (nos. 22–23) or bear different dates and do not feature the Nilus on hippopotamus reverse type (nos. 3–4, 7). This implies that the inclusion of dates on this type is influenced by the imagery of Nilus on hippopotamus as depicted on coins, even though image and date are split so that they appear on different faces of the tokens. This again suggests that the imagery and dates were not just blindly copied from the coinage, and that instead there was a conscious choice of what to include or exclude, and to some extent room for variation in the way that elements from coins were executed on tokens.

From an analysis of the above token types it is evident that they are influenced by coin types which share a common period of issue. The imagery of Isis and Antinous was adapted from a coin type of Isis and Serapis which was issued towards the end of Hadrian's reign and at the beginning of the reign of Antoninus Pius. This is also the case for the imagery of Serapis and Cerberus, although both of these types also appear at the end of the reign of Antoninus Pius. The Nilus riding on hippopotamus type is paralleled by coinage dating to year 1 and 2 of Antoninus Pius' reign, which perhaps allows for the most accurate dating. As all three of these examples date to a similar period, they therefore highlight the possibility that the tokens were struck over a short period extending from the end of Hadrian's reign to the beginning of that of Antoninus Pius. This implies a conscious utilisation of current and recognisable coin types on this series of tokens.

We cannot, however, rule out the possibility that tokens continued to be struck after this period, due to the presence of later dates, such as year 18 or 20 within the corpus. Additionally, we cannot entirely discount the potential for tokens to be struck later based on earlier coin types.

Discussion

Based on a preliminary investigation into the regnal dates and imagery, it is plausible that tokens, both dated and undated, which depict Antinous on one face were struck around the period ca. AD 134–44, with the potential for striking also at the end of the reign of Antoninus Pius. This date range means that tokens continued to use the imagery of the coin types struck biennially for Antinous after the coinage issues ceased (assuming that it was not in fact the tokens that influenced the coin types). This does not, however, indicate that the tokens were struck as an all-purpose coinage. There is a clear distinction between coins and tokens in that the Alexandrian coins in question were manufactured from bronze, whilst the tokens were made from lead. There is also significant enough variation between coins and tokens, both in terms of imagery and legends, to suggest that the manufacturers of the tokens consciously wanted to distinguish them from the coinage.

If the tokens (particularly those bearing low numbers as the regnal date) were struck at the beginning of the reign of Antoninus Pius, they formed part of the materiality of the cult of Antinous that continued to exist after the Hadrian's death. As stated above, Hadrian did not create the cult through official channels, instead constructing it from materiality and associated rituals and games. The tokens were perhaps part of this, and the fact that they might have been struck after Hadrian's death demonstrates how well the cult took hold and that there was room for appropriation of the imagery officially created during Hadrian's lifetime. The tokens adapt imagery found originally on the Alexandrian coinage. Antinous' syncretism with Hermes-Thoth and Osiris is in keeping with the ways in which Antinous was perceived within Egypt. The imagery on the tokens was therefore intended to be recognisable, with specific relevance to the province, and due to the similarity to coin types of this period, it can be inferred that the tokens were influenced by current and contemporary images. The iconography does, however, also parallel the imagery found on medallions of Antinous from elsewhere in the Empire. For example, a series of medallions from Bithynia exhibits reverses depicting the Arcadian myth of Hermes.[47] The imagery of Antinous-Hermes on tokens in Egypt is therefore also linked to myths associated with his homeland.

The prevalence of Nilus types paired with imagery of Antinous is noteworthy for considering the purpose tokens showing Antinous served in Roman Egypt (nos. 1, 3–4, 10, 13, 22, 26).[48] Nilus was the Graeco-Roman representation of the river Nile, and therefore signified fertility and the inundation, which was vital for the corn supply that Egypt provided to Rome. Antinous in his syncretism with Hermes and Osiris was also viewed as a god of rebirth and rejuvenation. It is therefore possible that the tokens within this series are associated with festivals celebrating these aspects.[49] In addition, the inscription ΕΠ ΑΓΑΘΩ found on some tokens (nos. 16–17) is translated as 'for good fortune', which would not be inconsistent with the sentiment of such festivals.

That tokens were utilised as part of festivals of the Nile, Osiris or Antinous cannot therefore be ruled out, particularly as Antinous' death coincided with the festival of Osiris. The fact that coins from elsewhere in the Empire (Corinth and Mantineia, as discussed above) have been interpreted as serving a medallic function for distribution at festivals and games demonstrates that numismatic objects depicting Antinous were utilised in these contexts, and therefore a similar purpose for tokens of Antinous in Egypt should be considered, in contrast to Milne's assertion that tokens in this province functioned as a low denominational coinage. It should be noted, however, that this theory needs testing against other tokens of the Alexandrian series, and integrated into a study of other token types, which will be explored by the author in the course of further research.

Conclusion

Through analysis of the regnal dates and imagery on the tokens of Antinous it can be postulated that at least part of the series was struck at the end of Hadrian's reign, or at the beginning of that of Antoninus Pius, thereby narrowing down the period of use for these tokens. Furthermore, they can be included in the materiality of the cult of Antinous, and show how this continued even after the death of Hadrian. The iconography depicted is also in keeping with the imagery of Antinous on coinage, and would therefore have been recognisable in terms of his assimilation to Hermes-Thoth and Osiris, and demonstrates his syncretism on Egyptian terms. It is also possible that tokens of Antinous, which also display imagery connected to rebirth, fertility and the life-giving waters of the Nile, were perhaps utilised within the context of festivals celebrating these qualities.

Catalogue[50]

Tokens bearing a date

1. Obverse: Bust of Antinous right, wearing hemhem crown, before bust of Isis left. Date: LB (Year 2).
   Reverse: Nilus riding hippopotamus left, holding two corn-ears in right hand and cornucopia in left.

   Specimens:

   a. Roma Numismatics, E-Sale 42, 06 June 2018, lot no. 376 (Ø 21mm; 4.1g; die axis: 4; metal: lead) (date in field to each side of busts).

[47] Von Mosch (2001).

[48] It should be noted, however, that the frequency of Nilus types may be accounted for in the fact that his imagery also occurred regularly on the Alexandrian coinage, which likely provided the impetus for the inclusion on tokens.

[49] Pudill (2017), 189–90 also has similar conclusions regarding the Nilus and Isis imagery found on Antinous tokens.

[50] Auction data current as of 31 March 2018. This paper presents an overview of the main types and specimens, collected from the sources outlined in the introduction. An exhaustive study is beyond the means of this paper. It should be noted that examples in Dattari (1901) resemble Antinous types, but are not catalogued as such. They are only included in this catalogue if an identification of Antinous is certain (nos. 6485, 6535). Dattari nos. 6437, 6443, 6445 are all possibly Antinous types, but are not included here, as certain identification is not possible.

b. Roma Numismatics, E-Sale 40, 28 October 2017, lot no. 355 (Ø 22mm; 6.75g; die axis: 2; metal: lead) (date in field to each side of busts).
c. University of Cologne Collection, no. 3569 (Ø 21mm; 4.65g; die axis: 3; metal: lead) (date in field to each side of busts).
d. University of Cologne Collection, no. 3570 (Ø 20mm; 6.08g; die axis: 6; metal: lead) (date in field to each side of busts).
e. American Numismatic Society (inv. no. 1944.100.79805) (Ø 19mm; 4.99g; die axis: 7; metal: lead) (date in field to each side of busts).
f. Yale Art Gallery (inv. no. 2005.6.262) (Ø 20mm; 4.56g; die axis: 1; metal: lead) (date below busts).

2. Obverse: Bust of Antinous right, wearing hemhem crown, crescent before. ΘΩ behind bust.
Reverse: Nike advancing left, holding wreath in right hand and palm in left. Date: LB (Year 2).

Specimens:

a. University of Cologne Collection (inv. no. 3567) (Ø 18mm; 2.85g; die axis: 9; metal: lead).
b. University of Cologne Collection (inv. no. 3568) (Ø 19mm; 2.76g; die axis: 4; metal: lead).
c. Classical Numismatic Group, E-Sale 353, 17 June 2016, lot no. 361 (Ø 17mm; 2.71g; die axis: 10; metal: lead).

3. Obverse: Bust of Antinous right, wearing hemhem crown, before bust of Isis left. Date (retrograde): LΔ (Year 4).
Reverse: Nilus reclining left, holding reeds in right hand and cornucopia in left, crocodile below, crowned by Euthenia, standing right.

Specimens:

a. Roma Numismatics, E-Sale 44, 03 March 2018, lot no. 407 (Ø 21mm; 4.62g; die axis: 9; metal: lead).
b. Roma Numismatics, E-Sale 43, 03 February 2018, lot no. 374 (Ø 19mm; 4.13g; die axis: 10; metal: lead).
c. Roma Numismatics, E-Sale 42, 06 January 2018, lot no. 377 (Ø 20mm; 4.67g; die axis: 10; metal: lead).
d. University of Cologne Collection (inv. no. 3575) (Ø 20mm; 3.86g; die axis: 9; metal: lead).
e. University of Cologne Collection (inv. no. 3576) (Ø 21mm; 4.12g; die axis: 3; metal: lead).

4. Obverse: Bust of Antinous right, wearing hemhem crown, before bust of Isis left. Date: LΔ (Year 4).
Reverse: Nilus seated right, holding reeds in left hand and cornucopia in right, crowned by Euthenia, standing left.

Specimens:

a. Roma Numismatics, E-Sale 40, 28 October 2017, lot no. 356 (Ø 19mm; 2.41g; die axis: 1; metal: lead).
b. University of Cologne Collection (inv. no. 3574) (Ø 20mm; 4.52g; die axis: 8; metal: lead).

5. Obverse: Bust of Antinous right, wearing hemhem crown, crescent before. Crowned by small figure of Nike flying left.
Reverse: Bust of Horus right, wearing headdress. Date: LΔ (Year 4).

Specimens:

a. American Numismatic Society (inv. no. 1944.100.79907) (Ø 21mm; 5.57g; die axis: 12; metal: lead).
b. University of Cologne Collection (inv. no. 3583) (Ø 21mm; 4.30g; die axis: 1; metal: lead).

6. Obverse: Bust of Antinous right, wearing hemhem crown.
Reverse: Bust of Horus right, wearing headdress. Date: LΔ (Year 6).

Specimen:

a. Roma Numismatics, E-Sale 42, 06 June 2018, lot no. 378 (Ø 22mm; 4.08g; die axis: 9; metal: lead).

7. Obverse: Bust of Antinous right, wearing hemhem crown, before bust of Isis left. Date: LΔ (Year 6).
   Reverse: AN/TINO/OV within wreath.

   Specimens:
   a. Roma Numismatics, E-Sale 40, 28 October 2017, lot no. 357 (Ø 20mm; 3.15g; die axis: 2; metal: lead).
   b. Classical Numismatic Group, E-Sale 353, 17 June 2015, lot no. 364 (Ø 19mm; 3.06g; die axis: 7; metal: lead).[51]

8. Obverse: Bust of Antinous right, wearing hemhem crown. Date LH (Year 8).
   Reverse: Bust of Serapis Helios right. Date: LH (Year 8).

   Specimens:
   a. Private collection (Ø 23mm; 4.50g; die axis: 8; metal: lead).[52]
   b. Roma Numismatics, E-Sale 41, 02 February 2017, lot no. 475 (Ø 22mm; 4.07g; die axis: no data; metal: lead).
   c. Cologne University Museum Collection (inv. no. 3579) (Ø 20mm; 3.54g; die axis: 9; metal: lead).

9. Obverse: Bust of Antinous right, wearing hemhem crown. Date LIH (Year 18).
   Reverse: Bust of Zeus Ammon right.

   Specimen:
   a. Naville Numismatics Ltd, Auction 30, 02 April 2017, lot no. 227 (Ø 22mm; 4.48g; die axis: no data; metal: lead).

10. Obverse: Bust of Antinous right, wearing hemhem crown, caduceus behind his shoulder.
    Reverse: Half-length figure of Nilus facing, head right. Date: LK (Year 20).

    Specimen:
    a. Classical Numismatic Group, Triton XXI, 09 January 2018, lot no. 100 (Ø 17mm; 3.04g; die axis: 6; metal: lead).

11. Obverse: Bust of Antinous right, wearing hemhem crown, crescent before.
    Reverse: Serapis standing facing, head left, raising right hand and holding sceptre in left. Date: LKE? (Year 25?).

    Specimen:
    a. Roma Numismatics, E-Sale 40, 28 October 2018, lot no. 358 (Ø 20mm; 4.86g; die axis: 6; metal: lead).

Tokens without a date

12. Obverse: Bust of Antinous right, wearing hemhem crown, crescent before.
    Reverse: Serapis standing facing, head left, raising right hand and holding sceptre in left.

    Specimens:
    a. Roma Numismatics, E-Sale 44, lot no. 408, 03 March 2018, (Ø 23mm; 5.48g; die axis: 12; metal: lead).
    b. Ashmolean Museum (Milne (1971), no. 5446) (Ø 20mm; 3.37g; die axis: 12; metal: lead).
    c. University of Cologne Museum (inv. no. 3559) (Ø 24mm; 11.23g; die axis: 7; metal: lead).
    d. Dattari (1901), no. 6535 (Ø 20mm; die axis: no data; metal: lead).[53]

[51] Catalogued at auction as AN/TINO/OC, however the specimen is quite worn, and a reading of ANTINO/OV is more likely, in line with specimen 5a.
[52] Many thanks to Lee Toone for bringing this specimen to my attention, and providing the relevant information.
[53] Identified in Dattari (1901) only as a 'young man', but after comparison with other tokens an identification of Antinous is certain.

13. Obverse: Bust of Antinous right, wearing hemhem crown, crescent before.
Reverse: Nilus reclining right, holding reeds in right hand and cornucopia in left, crowned by Euthenia standing left.

Specimens:

a. Roma Numismatics, E-Sale 42, 06 January 2018, lot no. 379 (Ø 20mm; 6.13g; die axis: 12; metal: lead).
b. Classical Numismatic Group, E-Sale 353, 17 June 2015, lot no. 366 (Ø 21mm; 8,84g; die axis: 1; metal: lead).

14. Obverse: Bust of Antinous right, wearing hemhem crown, crescent before.
Reverse: Nike advancing left, holding wreath in right hand and palm in left.

Specimen:

a. Roma numismatics, E-Sale 42, 06 January 2018, lot no. 380 (Ø 21mm; 5.14g; die axis: 11; metal: lead).

15. Obverse: Bust of Antinous right, wearing hemhem crown, crescent before. ΘѠ behind bust.
Reverse: Nike advancing left, holding wreath in right hand and palm in left.

Specimen:

a. Roma Numismatics, E-Sale 40, 28 October 2017, lot no. 359 (Ø 17mm; 2.64g; die axis: 9; metal: lead).

16. Obverse: Bust of Antinous right, wearing hemhem crown, ΕΠ ΑΓΑΘѠ.[54]
Reverse: Bust of Zeus Ammon right, [...]ΟΛΕΙ.

Specimens:

a. Mitchiner (1984), no. 10 (Ø 23mm; 4.4g; die axis: no data; metal: lead).
b. American Numismatic Society (inv. no. 1944.100.79801) (Ø 22mm; 8.25g; die axis: 12; metal: lead).
c. Roma Numismatics, Auction 6, 29 September 2013, lot no. 922 (Ø 17mm; 2.53 g; die axis: 11; metal: lead).
d. Roma Numismatics, E-Sale 37, 24 June 2017, lot no. 266 (Ø 21mm; 4.3g; die axis: 2; metal: lead).

17. Obverse: Bust of Antinous right, wearing hemhem crown, Ε[Π ΑΓ]ΑΘѠ.
Reverse: Bust of Antinous right, wearing hemhem crown(?), illegible legend.

Specimen:

a. American Numismatic Society (inv. no. 1944.100.79912) (Ø 30mm; 11.86g; die axis: 9; metal: lead).

18. Obverse: Bust of Antinous right, wearing hemhem crown, crescent before. Uncertain legend.[55]
Reverse: Bust of Serapis right, wearing modius.

Specimen:

a. Mitchiner (1984), no. 11 (Ø 21mm; 4.08g; die axis: no data; metal: lead).

19. Obverse: Bust of Antinous right, wearing hemhem crown.
Reverse: Bust of Serapis right, wearing modius.

Specimen:

a. American Numismatic Society (inv. no. 1944.100.79806) (Ø 22mm; 9.73g; die axis: 12; metal: lead).

[54] Nos. 16a and 18a were previously identified as Serapis, but comparison with Antinous' portrait on tokens and other numismatic objects leads to a certain identification of Antinous.

[55] Possibly a variation on ΕΠ ΑΓΑΘѠ.

20. Obverse: Antinous-Hermes riding right, wearing hemhem crown and holding caduceus.
Reverse: Nike advancing left, holding wreath in right hand and palm in left.

Specimens:

a. Roma Numismatics, E-Sale 44, 03 March 2018, lot no. 409 (Ø 20mm; 4.78g; die axis: 6; metal: lead).
b. Yale Art Gallery (inv. no. 2001.87.21807) (Ø 19mm; 6.02 g; die axis: 5; metal: lead).
c. Roma Numismatics, E-Sale 41, 02 December 2017, lot no. 478 (Ø 20mm; 4.78g; die axis: 6; metal: lead).
d. Ashmolean Museum (Milne (1971), no. 5420) (Ø 21mm; 4.24g; die axis: 1).
e. University of Cologne Museum (inv. no. 3584) (Ø 20mm; 4.35g; die axis: 7; metal: lead).
f. University of Cologne Museum (inv. no. 3585) (Ø 18mm; 2.33g; die axis: 3; metal: lead).
g. University of Cologne Museum (inv. no. 3586) (Ø 20mm; 2.95g; die axis: 3; metal: lead)
h. University of Cologne Museum (inv. no. 3587) (Ø 20mm; 2.83 g; die axis: 1; metal: lead).

21. Obverse: Antinous-Hermes riding right, wearing hemhem crown and holding caduceus.
Reverse: Serapis standing left, holding purse in right hand and sceptre in left; Cerberus to left.

Specimen:

a. Roma Numismatics, E-Sale 40, 28 October 2017, lot no. 360 (Ø 22mm; 3.96g; die axis: 11; metal: lead).

22. Obverse: Bust of Antinous right, wearing hemhem crown, before bust of Isis left.
Reverse: Nilus seated right, holding reeds in left hand and cornucopia in right, crowned by Euthenia, standing left.

Specimens:

a. Roma Numismatics, E-Sale 41, 02 December 2017, lot no. 476 (Ø 19mm; 2.95g; die axis: 8; metal: lead).
b. Dattari (1901), no. 6485 (Ø 20mm; die axis: no data; metal: lead).[56]
c. Milne (1971), no. 5433 (Ø 23mm; 1.99g; die axis 4; metal: lead).[57]

23. Obverse: Bust of Antinous right, wearing hemhem crown, before bust of Isis left.
Reverse: Nike advancing left, holding wreath in right hand and palm in left.

Specimen:

a. Milne (1971), no. 5432 (Ø 19mm; 2.62g; die axis: 7; metal: lead).[58]

Unclear/illegible date

24. Obverse: Bust of Antinous right, wearing hemhem crown, crescent before.
Reverse: Bust of Serapis right wearing modius, squared C behind left shoulder, unclear legend to right.

Specimen:

a. Petrie Museum (inv. no. UC55756) (Ø 17mm; 2.73g; die axis: 12; metal: lead).

25. Obverse: Bust of Antinous right, wearing hemhem crown, before bust of Isis left.
Reverse: Nike advancing left with wreath in right hand and palm in left. Unclear date.

Specimen:

a. Petrie Museum (inv. no. UC55761) (Ø 20mm; 2.66g; die axis: 12; metal: lead).

[56] Identified as Hermes and Harpocrates, but an identification of Antinous and Isis is more plausible.
[57] Identified as Hermanubis and Harpocrates, but an identification of Antinous and Isis is more plausible.
[58] Identified as Hermanubis and Harpocrates, but an identification of Antinous and Isis is more plausible.

26. Obverse: Antinous-Hermes riding right, wearing hemhem crown and holding caduceus. L in field to right.
    Reverse: Nilus seated right, holding reeds in left hand and cornucopia in right, crowned by standing figure left.

    Specimen:

    a. American Numismatic Society (inv. no. 1944.100.79803) (Ø 22mm; 5.2g; die axis: 3; metal: lead).

Bibliography

Amandry 2015: M. Amandry, 'Numismatique romaine impériale: Iconographie du pouvoir impérial et des identités civiques', *Annuaire de l'École pratique des hautes études (EPHE), Section des sciences historiques et philologiques,* 146 (2015) (http://journals.openedition.org/ashp/1706; accessed 25/05/2019).

Amandry and Burnett 2015: M. Amandry and A. Burnett, *Roman Provincial Coinage Volume III: Nerva, Trajan and Hadrian* (London, 2015).

Birley 1997: A. R. Birley, *Hadrian. The Restless Emperor* (London, 1997).

Blum 1914: G. Blum, 'Numismatique d'Antinoos', *JIAN* 16 (1914), 33–75.

Boatwright 2000: M. T. Boatwright, *Hadrian and the Cities of the Roman Empire* (Princeton, 2000).

Cannadine and Price (eds.) 1987: D. Cannadine and S. Price (eds.), *Rituals of Royalty: Power and Ceremonial in Traditional Societies* (Cambridge, 1987).

Dattari 1901: G. Dattari, *Monete imperiali greche. Numi augg. Alexandrini. Catalogo della collezione G. Dattari, compilato dal proprietario* (Cairo, 1901).

Derchain-Urtel 1981: M-T. Derchain-Urtel, *Thot. À travers ses épithètes dans les scènes d'offrandes des temples d'époque gréco-romaine* (Bruxelles, 1981).

Eggler and Uehlinger (eds.) 2020: J. Eggler and C. Uehlinger (eds.), *Iconography of Deities and Demons in the Ancient Near East* (forthcoming).

Entwistle and Finney 2013: C. Entwistle and P. C. Finney, 'Late Antique glass pendants in the British Museum', in Entwistle and James (eds.) (2013), 131–77.

Entwistle and James (eds.) 2013: C. Entwistle and L. James (eds.), *New Light on Old Glass: Recent Research on Byzantine Mosaics and Glass* (London, 2013).

Fowden 1986: G. Fowden, *The Egyptian Hermes: A Historical Approach to the Late Pagan Mind* (Cambridge, 1986).

Frend 2004: W. H. C. Frend, 'Qasr Ibrim 1974: The coins', *JEA* 90 (2004), 167–92.

Geissen and Weiser 1983: A. Geissen and W. Weiser, *Katalog Alexandrinischer Kaisermünzen der Sammlung des Instituts für Altertumskunde der Universität zu* Köln (vol. 4) (Opladen, 1983).

Goebs 2020: K. Goebs, 'Crown (Egypt)', in Eggler and Uehlinger (eds.) (2020), 1–30 (https://www.academia.edu/11958136/Crown_Egypt_for_IDD_) (accessed 24/05/2019).

Grimm, Kessler and Meyer 1994: A. Grimm, D. Kessler and H. Meyer, *Der Obelisk des Antinoos* (München, 1994).

Jacobstahl 1905: P. Jacobstahl, 'Eine Gußform mit dem Bilde des Antinoos', *Zeitschrift für Ägyptische Sprache und Altertumskunde* 42 (1905), 76–90.

Lambert 1984: R. Lambert, *Beloved and God. The Story of Hadrian and Antinous* (London, 1984).

Longperier 1861: A. Longperier, 'Monnaies du Serapeum de Memphis. Trouvaille de Myt Rahineh', *RN* 6 (1861), 1–24.

Meshorer 2010: Y. Meshorer, 'A coin hoard from a third century shipwreck off the Carmel Coast', *Antiqot* 63 (2010), 111–35.

Milne 1908: J. G. Milne, 'The leaden token coinage of Egypt under the Romans', *NC* 8 (1908), 287–310.

Milne 1915: J. G. Milne, 'Leaden tokens from Memphis', *Ancient Egypt* (1915), 107–21.

Milne 1922: J. G. Milne, 'The coins from Oxyrhynchus', *JEA* 8 (1922), 158–63.

Milne 1930: J. G. Milne, 'Egyptian leaden tokens', *NC* 10 (1930), 300–15.

Milne 1971: J. G. Milne, *Catalogue of Alexandrian Coins* (Oxford, 1971).

Mitchiner 1984: M. Mitchiner, 'Imperial portrait *tesserae* from the city of Rome and Imperial tax tokens from the province of Egypt', *NC* 144 (1984), 95–114.

Opper 2008: T. Opper, *Hadrian: Empire and Conflict* (London, 2008).

Price 1987: S. Price, 'From noble funerals to divine cult: The consecration of Roman Emperors', in Cannadine and Price (eds.) (1987), 56–105.

Pudill 2014: R. Pudill, *Antinoos - Münzen und Medaillons* (Regenstauf, 2014).

Pudill 2017: R. Pudill, *Göttlicher Antinoos: Ein Idealbild jungendlicher Schönheit* (Regenstauf, 2017).

Takács 1995: S. A. Takács, *Isis and Serapis in the Roman World* (Leiden, 1995).

von Mosch 2001: H.-C. von Mosch, 'Die Antinoos-Medaillons von Bithynion-Klaudiopolis', *SNR*, 80 (2001), 108–28.

von Mosch and Klostermeyer 2015: H.-C. von Mosch, and L.-A. Klostermeyer, 'Ein Stempelschneider auf Reisen. Die Antinoosmedaillons des Hotilios Markellos und Hadrians Reise im Jahr 131/2 n. Chr.' In Wartenberg and Amandry (eds.) (2015), 285–325.

Vout 2005: C. Vout, 'Antinous, archaeology and history', *JRS* 95 (2005), 80–96.

Vout 2007: C. Vout, *Power and Eroticism in Imperial Rome* (Cambridge, 2007).

Wartenberg and Amandry (eds.) 2015: U. Wartenberg and M. Amandry (eds.), *ΚΑΙΡΟΣ. Contributions to Numismatics in Honor of Basil Demetriadi* (New York, 2015).

Wilding *in prep.*: D. Wilding, *Tokens and Communities in the Roman Provinces: An exploration of Egypt, Gaul and Britain*. PhD thesis, University of Warwick (Coventry) (*in prep.*).

TOKENS IN THE ATHENIAN AGORA IN THE THIRD CENTURY AD: ADVERTISING PRESTIGE AND CIVIC IDENTITY IN ROMAN ATHENS[1]

MAIRI GKIKAKI

Introduction

Athens is the earliest classical city in the ancient Mediterranean to have employed tokens on a significant scale, using these objects from the middle of the fourth century BC until the latter part of the third century AD.[2] These tokens were, from their very beginnings, indispensable for the workings of Athenian democracy. *Symbola*, the Greek word for *tesserae*, had the form of clay plates cut along a jigsaw line in the fifth century BC. They bore the names of tribes and demes and were employed in allotment procedures. These procedures were indispensable for the distribution of magistracies among the citizenship and the workings of the participatory democracy.[3] Taking on a monetiform appearance from the fourth century BC onwards, *symbola* were used as evidence of attendance at the law courts, the Assembly (*ekklesia*) and the Council (*boule*); they also operated as *theōrika* (the entrance fee to the Greater Dionysia and other festivals). Tokens were also distributed to be exchanged for wheat, as a rare testimony preserved on an honorific decree of the mid-third century BC testifies.[4]

Nevertheless, for quite a long period of time Athenian tokens were primarily studied as pieces in museums or private collections; the implications of this are discussed in Makrypodi's paper in this volume. Crosby's publication in *The Athenian Agora* vol. X (1964) has been an important step forward in the study of these objects, since it mapped tokens against find contexts, data invaluable for addressing questions of chronology and function.

The find

The present contribution examines a hoard of 60 tokens and 30 closely related pieces.[5] This is one of the largest token hoards excavated in Athens to date. The find was previously published by Crosby in the catalogue of the Athenian Agora tokens but the implications of this hoard for Athenian history have yet to be discussed.[6]

In a small pit (D 11:6 in the Athenian Agora Excavations reference system) dug into the bedrock at the northeast corner of what has been named Room II of a 'Roman House', 60 lead tokens were unearthed (cat. nos. 1–60). The 'Roman House' once stood on the south slope of the hill of Agoraios Kolonos, on which the marble temple of Athena and Hephaistos still stands. No pottery or datable finds were recorded in pit D 11:6. It belongs to 'section ΠΘ' or 'D 10–12' according to the most up-to-date classification of the site plan of the Athenian Agora.[7] The architectural remains excavated there in 1935 under the direction of T. Leslie Shear have been regarded as part of a house,[8]

[1] I am very grateful to Clare Rowan for organising the conference, at which this paper was first presented. I am also grateful to John H. Kroll (Oxford), Christina Kuhn (Oxford), Kenneth Sheedy (Sydney), Stamatoula Makrypodi (Athens) and Brian Mertens (Athens and Oxford) for helpful discussions. Sylvie Dumond has greatly facilitated my study at the American School of Classical Studies at Athens and a particular debt of gratitude is owed to her. I also wish to thank the Ephorate of the Antiquities of the city of Athens for providing me with access to the material. Finally, I thank the anonymous reviewers.
The following abbreviations are used:
IG = *Inscriptiones Graecae* (1873–).
SEG = *Supplementum epigraphicum Graecum* (1923–).
SNG = *Sylloge Numorum Graecorum.*

[2] Lang and Crosby (1964), 75–130, in particular p. 76: 'Athens would seem to be the only city in which they were in abundant use in the Hellenistic period' and pp. 83–85 for the chronological conspectus. For earlier tokens outside the classical period see Schmandt-Besserat's paper in the present volume.

[3] *SEG* (1923), 36.232, 38.50; Lang (1959), 80–89; Crosby (1964), 77; Staveley (1972), 48–51, 69–72; Rhodes (1981), 690; Whitehead (1986), 277–90.

[4] *SEG* (1923), 57.33; Crosby (1964), 77.

[5] See the complete catalogue at the end of this paper.

[6] Crosby (1964), 112–13, 137.

[7] Frantz, Thompson and Travlos (1988), pl. 3.

[8] Shear (1936), 14–19 with the plan on fig. 13 showing the cistern and only two of the excavated rooms because the excavation at that point had not progressed further. In this preliminary excavation report the tokens found were designated as 'seals'.

although there are no compelling reasons to come to this conclusion.[9] The vicinity to other securely identified Roman houses in the valley further south between the Pnyx and the Areopagus made the identification seem probable.[10]

Five rooms were excavated and two more can be conjectured by the presence of fragmentary walls and floors that are aligned with the better-preserved structure (fig. 1). If the structure were a house, the extant rooms would have belonged to its NW corner. A nearby well, which was in operation until about the mid-third century AD and presumably belonged to the house, might be used to provide an idea of the location of the courtyard. The house size is hard to calculate but it is well known that the majority of the Athenian houses throughout antiquity ranged between 120 and 150m^2, whereas a few from the Roman period reached 335–420m^2.[11] Eight further tokens were contained in a stratum (D 11:7) on the northern side of the house in Room I (cat. nos. 61–68). The fill here also included 23 coins, the latest of which was an issue of Probus (AD 276–282). The coins remain unpublished.[12]

In the nearby cistern (D 10:1) located 12m NW of the 'Roman House' and connected to it through a rock-cut channel (D 11–12), 22 further tokens were discovered (cat. nos. 69–90).[13] The fill in the cistern (which included pieces of sculpture and a large quantity of painted plaster and iron fragments) was the result of the sack of the city by the Heruli in AD 267. The latest coins were those of Gallienus (AD 253–268) and Postumus (AD 258–267).[14] The

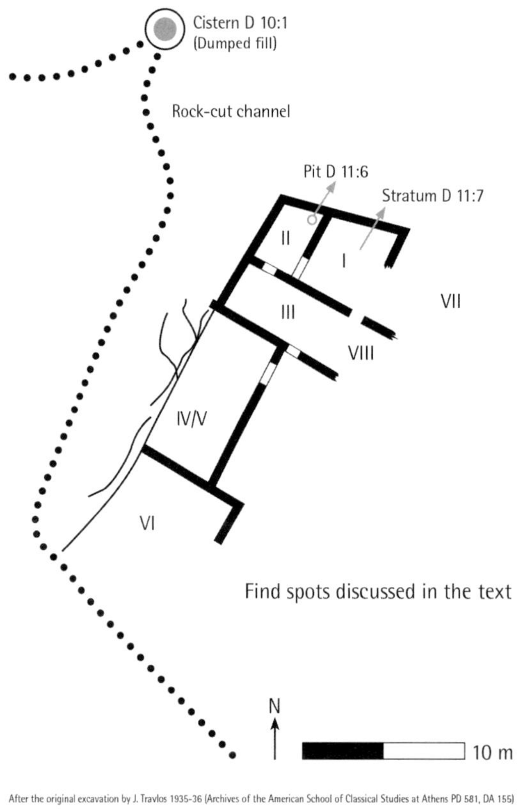

Fig. 1: Plan of the find spots of the tokens discussed in the text (digitally mastered by Matthias Demel (Kürnach, Germany) after the plan by John Travlos (1935–36) in the Archives of the American School of Classical Studies at Athens PD 581, DA 155).

[9] Crosby (1964), 137; Thompson and Wycherley (1972), 228.
[10] Young (1951), 272–79.
[11] Frantz, Thompson and Travlos (1988), 37.
[12] Crosby (1964), 137.
[13] The cistern is aligned with the eleventh column of the Hephaistos temple and is 58.20 metres south of the stylobate. The tokens and their types according to Crosby (1964): IL1074 (type L202), IL201, IL203–04, IL209, IL212, IL253, IL258 (type L250), IL199 (type L251), IL200, IL202, IL205–08, IL211, IL213, IL215 (type L263), IL257 (type L265), IL240 (type L272), IL286 (type L289), IL241 (type L290).
[14] Crosby (1964), 137.

cistern is thought to belong to the house not only because of the rock-cut channel but also because tokens of the same design were found both in the stratum from Room I (D 11:7) and in the cistern (D 10:1). A dolphin countermark is found on tokens from all three deposits (cat. nos. 1–47, 52–53, 58, 65–66, 86–87, 89).

Numerous finds in the cistern provide indications of the decoration of the interior. Two ivory furniture attachments depicting the Muses were found there.[15] A herm of Herakles in *rosso antico* and a feminine-looking head crowned with an ivy wreath, probably Dionysos, were also found.[16] The deep red marble of the herm would have been a rare extravagance at Athens. The Dionysos head, a work of the second century AD, standing just under a metre tall, would have probably been a part of a group composition, perhaps with a satyr. Five bronze statuettes were also recovered from the cistern. They depict Pan, Herakles of the Farnese type, Hermes, a bull representing either Zeus or Apis, and the snake-daimon Glykon.[17] A portrait herm was also discovered.

This inscribed portrait herm deserves particular attention.[18] The honorary dedication commemorates 'Moiragenes, son of Dromokles, of the deme Koile, *eponymos* of the tribe Hippothontis'. The portrait head is smaller than life size and depicts a clean-shaven man of mature age gazing forward solemnly. On stylistic and technical grounds, the portrait is considered to be a work of the Hadrianic or early Antonine period (second century AD).[19] As *eponymos*, Moiragenes was a prominent and wealthy citizen who donated the funds to cover the prytany's sacrifices.[20] The Koile lies within the city *trittys* of the tribe Hippothontis (the *trittyes* were a divisional system used in the city). But the house where the herm was found lies within the boundaries of Melite, a deme from the tribe Kekropis. Melite had always been inhabited by reputable citizens, such as Antiphon, Epicurus, Callias, Phocion and Themistocles. As with Koile and Kollytos, which were all situated to the west of the Acropolis and within the city walls, this was a prominent deme.[21]

Moreover, the walls of the house were brightly plastered in light green and pink to resemble panels of marble revetment. Floors laid in *opus reticulatum* and pebble mosaic would have lent further prestige to the interior. Mention should also be made of the location itself, which provided residents with close access to the heart of the city, as well as sought-after views of the square of the Agora below and the Acropolis and Areopagus above.

Among the 90 tokens discussed here two pieces stand apart because of their Hellenistic date. One was found in the cistern (D 10:1) and carries the representation of a kantharos (cat. no. 69 = fig. 23). The other is decorated with a palmette (cat. no. 62 = fig. 19) and was found in the stratum of debris in Room I (D 11:7).[22]

The architecture

Only a small part of the original structure of the 'Roman House' is preserved (fig. 1). A long wall running approximately eight metres NE to SW forms the continuous back wall of Rooms II and III (fig. 1). Room II is almost square in shape, ca. 12m^2 and is accessible through the much bigger trapezoidal-shaped Room I (ca. 20m^2), which functions as an antechamber. Room III (25m^2), lying to the SW of Rooms I and II, is rectangular and was connected to Room I via a doorway. Another door provided access to the SE and another access to the SW. The extremities of the preserved walls betray that once they would have continued forming more rooms. But their partial preservation does not provide much clarity

[15] Agora BI 166 and BI 167: Shear (1935), 444, fig. 8; Shear (1936), 17, fig. 15.

[16] Herakles (Agora S 590): Harrison 1965, 173, n. 230. Dionysos (Agora S 589): Shear (1935), 444–47, fig. 9. The androgynous head was identified as a maenad, presumably because of the chignon and the Venus rings at the neck, both of which appear in youthful, languid images of the god. See Gasparri (1986), nos. 119–26.

[17] Shear (1936), 15–19.

[18] Agora S 586: Harrison (1953), 35–37, no. 25, pl. 17; Geagan (1964), 199, no. H372.

[19] Smith (1998), 83–84.

[20] On the *eponymos*: Oliver (1941), 3; Geagan (1967), 99–101; Meritt and Traill (1974), 21.

[21] Lohmann (1999), 1190.

[22] For palmette parallels: Postolacca (1868), nos. 683–702; Crosby (1964), 106, cat. nos. L210–11. There are no known parallels for this particular type of kantharos on other tokens.

as to what existed to the east of Room III. To the south, Room IV, which runs from NE to SW, is delimited by the natural rise to the NW, and had a door providing access to the rest of the structure, which is not preserved.[23]

After examining the relationship of the pit (D 11:6) to the architectural remains, the conclusion can easily be reached that the pit was a true hiding place, not visible to anyone who might have glanced through the door of Room II. It is a space providing controlled access. Moreover, Room II is accessible only through an antechamber (Room I). This would qualify Room II as belonging to the 'second layer of depth' in the building, according to current terminology, because it would have been designated for 'inhabitants' and not 'visitors'.[24]

The remains hinder an exact comparison with known examples of different building types. Nevertheless, the hierarchical arrangement of space – some spaces being generally accessible and others possibly accessible only to a limited group – is a special feature typical of the seats of cult associations.[25]

Interpretation of the types

The 90 tokens from Agoraios Kolonos are closely interconnected. Forty-six specimens belong to the same uniface series, displaying a Hermes bust right (cat. nos. 1–44, 65–66, figs. 3–7). The remaining 44 specimens are distributed over an additional 23 types, catalogued at the end of this piece. We can observe that the tokens exhibit mostly gods, both established deities (Athena, Hermes and Poseidon) and 'new' gods, who acquired significance in the Hellenistic period (Serapis and Alexander the Great). Here only the most significant in terms of imagery will be discussed.

The bust of Athena on a ship (cat. no. 48 = fig. 9, cat. no. 49) might be interpreted as the vessel carrying Athena, or the goddess piloting it. The image refers to the dedication of the *peplos* (Athena's garment), which was suspended on the mast of the Panathenaic ship and during the Panathenaia festival was brought from Kerameikos to the foot of the Acropolis.[26] This is not the only case of a festive procession portrayed on a token. Two well-known specimens of the Roman imperial period, one excavated in the Agora and one in the Hallerstein Collection (now at the University Museum of Göttingen) depict a cart driven by horses and carrying a stylis (mast); this is the cart of Dionysos which featured at the Anthesteria (fig. 2).[27] Tokens, which were introduced in the Late Classical period in Athens in order to facilitate participation of the citizen body in governance, came to be used for a broader range of uses in the course of the last centuries BC and the first centuries AD.[28] First and foremost in the Roman period, tokens seem to have been connected with participation in festivals, and the sharing of gifts and benefits associated with these celebrations, as the iconography of these specimens indicates.[29]

Fig. 2: Courtesy of the Archaeological Institute of Goettingen University. Photo: Stephan Eckardt. Reproduced at 2:1.

All the 'Hermes bust' examples are countermarked with the design of a dolphin swimming right. This dolphin punch is deeply impressed on the specimens, which exhibit a thin and particularly wide flan. As a result small holes have often developed in the area of the countermark. It seems that the 'Hermes bust' examples may have been reused because they exhibit thin, spread flans. Overstrikes cannot be ascertained because no

[23] The architectural remains were recorded by John Travlos: PD 581 (DA 155), kept in the Agora in Athens and digitised on ascsa.net.

[24] Markus (1993), 169–244; Irvine, Hanks and Weddle (2012), 91–117.

[25] Egelhaaf-Gaiser (2002), 125–28.

[26] Deubner (1932), 32–34; Shear (2001), 143–54.

[27] Benndorf (1875), 612 no. 4, plate X, no. 51; Crosby (1964), 95, cat. no. L88.

[28] Bubelis (2010), 182–83.

[29] This conclusion is easily reached when comparing the iconography of the Hellenistic tokens and the iconography of the Roman period tokens of Athens.

Fig. 3: Agora Museum/ Ephorate of Antiquities of the city of Athens IL220 (cat. no. 2, Ø 22mm) (courtesy of the Hellenic Ministry of Culture).

Fig. 4: Agora Museum/ Ephorate of Antiquities of the city of Athens IL222 (cat. no. 3, Ø 21mm) (courtesy of the Hellenic Ministry of Culture).

Fig. 5: Agora Museum/ Ephorate of Antiquities of the city of Athens IL236 (cat. no. 15, Ø 21mm) (courtesy of the Hellenic Ministry of Culture).

Fig. 6: Agora Museum/ Ephorate of Antiquities of the city of Athens IL263 (cat. no. 30, Ø 23mm) (courtesy of the Hellenic Ministry of Culture).

Fig. 7: Agora Museum/ Ephorate of Antiquities of the city of Athens IL269 (cat. no. 34, Ø 22mm) (countermark on the left, which obliterated the *kerykeion*) (courtesy of the Hellenic Ministry of Culture).

Fig. 8: Agora Museum/ Ephorate of Antiquities of the city of Athens IL221 (cat. no. 47, Ø 25mm) (courtesy of the Hellenic Ministry of Culture).

traces of the older types – if they have ever existed – are discernible. The softness of the material could possibly account for the fact that the details of any earlier die are lost.[30] The preservation of most of these specimens makes it impossible to conduct a full die study, but the 17 pieces where such examination could take place were found to be distributed over five dies. The *kerykeion* or caduceus has a curved staff on at least six tokens (IL217, IL220 = fig. 3, IL226, IL228, IL232, IL238, IL270) and this is probably the first die. The pleats of the neck-line and the straight stem of the *kerykeion* are all very similar on a number of tokens (IL222 = fig. 4, IL225, IL234, IL245, IL264) and this is probably another die. Two more tokens have a distinctly small head and belong to yet another die (IL235–36 = fig. 5). Specimens IL227, IL263 (fig. 6), IL269 (fig. 7) and IL278 can be distributed over two distinct dies respectively.

Hermes, the herald god, is not a stranger to tokens. The *kerykeion*, his divine badge, frequently occurs on the Hellenistic tokens of the city. It is found, for example, on early Hellenistic lead letter-tokens, pieces connected with the allotment of jurors and other state functionaries.[31] The *kerykeion* is also found accompanied by the legends ΑΓ or ΑΓΟΡ and ΠΕΝ.[32] The former legends refer to the *agoranomoi* (market overseers) and their functions or the administration of the *agorastikon* fund, while the latter references the workings of the Council of the Five Hundred. Quite a few Hellenistic tokens carry a *kerykeion* combined with an ear of wheat (at times also accompanied by a poppy head), suggesting that this device was employed in the context of wheat distributions.[33]

There are particular aspects of Hermes that make him a suitable presence for procedures involving communality and participation. It is in the god's specific nature to preside over

[30] Overstriking is well known for the Late Classical bronze dikast tickets, probably some sort of 'recycling'. For bronze tokens struck on earlier issues of bronze tokens see Svoronos (1923–1926), pl. 100, no. 31. There are also bronze tokens which have been overstruck on Syracusan bronze coins: Svoronos (1898), 50, no. 48 (1), pl. Δ.12, 48 (3), 50 (δ), 51, nos. 58 (α), 58 (δ), 59 (α), (β), (ε), 60 (α), 61 (δ), 63 (γ) pl. Δ.25, 52, no. 67 (α), pl. Δ.28; Boegehold (1995), 72, no. 18.

[31] Svoronos (1900), 324, no. 37 pl. I, 22, no. 51, pl. I, 31, 325, no. 69 pl. I, 49; Crosby (1964), 87, cat. nos. L7, 88, L19.

[32] ΑΓ or ΑΓΟΡ: Svoronos (1900), 332, nos. 159–62, pl. III, nos. 4, 5, 7; Crosby (1964), 102, cat. no. L170; Bubelis (2010), 186. On the *agorastikon* fund: Bubelis (2013), 122–6. ΠΕΝ: Svoronos (1900), 198. On the contrary Dumont (1870) thought the type was associated with festivals and ΠΕΝ refers to Penteteris. More obscure is the meaning of the legend ΕΡΧΟ and ΕΡΧΟΥ, which also accompany images of the *kerykeion*.

[33] Engel (1884), 20, cat. no. 200; Crosby (1964), 102–03, cat. nos. L172–73.

distributions. In the *Homeric Hymn to Hermes* the god performs a sacrifice followed by the allocation of 12 shares on equal terms.[34] Hermes is thus associated with spaces where honours are defined and sharing takes place. The theology is a deeply social one, because the sharing of honours is closely connected to reciprocity. Hermes' works find resonance in the broader frame of the city-state as a political and religious community since here too specific procedures are instituted so that repartitions are realised and decisions are reached.[35]

A major trend observed among the tokens of the hoard is their imitation of coin types. The 'Hermes bust' series bears a close resemblance to fractions of Athenian civic issues of the imperial period.[36] The 'standing Hermes / standing Serapis' tokens (fig. 24) constitute a pasticcio of two distinct reverses found on Roman imperial coinage of the third century AD, specimens of which have been found in the Athenian Agora.[37] Standing Hermes was a design also employed on Athenian provincial coins of the imperial period.[38]

The 'head of Athena / boukranion' series (cat. no. 52 = figs. 11, cat. no. 53) is likewise probably inspired by Athenian drachms of the second century AD. The 'Serapis bust / prow' series closely copies – in a simplified manner – Roman provincial issues of the cities of Asia Minor.[39] Alexander the Great (cat. no. 58 = fig. 15, cat. no. 88 = fig. 27) is likewise well known from the civic issues of cities of imperial Asia Minor and also appears on lead tokens from Roman Ephesos.[40] The type of the mature, bearded head with hair gathered in a bun and revered expression likely represents the personified *Demos* (cat. no. 88 = fig. 27).[41] The similarity between the design of coins and tokens has already attracted the attention of scholars.[42]

The lion head tokens (cat. nos. 45–47, fig. 8) relate to architecture and are representations of waterspouts. These specimens are remarkable because they are mould-made, a technique rarely used for Athenian tokens.

The countermark

The dolphin countermark found on 52 tokens is the link that associates the finds of all three deposits: those in the pit of Room II (D 11:6), those in the destruction debris in Room I (D 10:1), and those in the cistern (D 11:7). There are two distinct punches for the dolphin countermark. The smaller is found on the 'Lion head with tenon' series. It is only 8mm long and possesses a rill around the dolphin. The larger punch is approximately 11mm long (including the free space left around the dolphin) and was used on the extensive 'Hermes bust' series (with the punch placed consistently at 3h) as well as on tokens carrying the types of 'Athena bust on ship', 'Athena / boukranion', 'bearded head right', 'head of Alexander the Great', 'bust of Poseidon' and 'helmet'. On the majority of the 'Hermes bust' series the countermark is placed consistently on the right (41 out of a total of 46), which suggests that they were all countermarked within a short period of time and possibly from the very beginning of their manufacture. On the whole, 53 out of 60 tokens contained in the pit D 11:6 were countermarked with the dolphin (one of either of the punches). Crosby has suggested that the repetition of the same countermark on different types suggests that all these tokens

[34] *Homeric Hymn to Hermes*, lines 126–29.

[35] Jaillard (2007), 237–41.

[36] Svoronos (1923–26), pl. 92, nos. 30–34, pl. 99, nos. 42, 44.

[37] Crosby (1964), 112 mentions five coins from the Antioch mint with this Hermes design on the reverse: two of Valerian (AD 253–260) (Thompson (1954), 379) and three of Gallienus (AD 253–268) (Thompson (1954), 487, 498). Four examples of Roman coins carrying Serapis reverses are known from the Athenian Agora: one of Caracalla (Thompson (1954), 216 = BMC, vol. 5, 455, no. 126), one of Gordian III (Thompson (1954), 306 = RIC IV.3, no. 30) and two of Gallienus (Thompson (1954), 468).

[38] Svoronos (1923–1926), pl. 92, nos. 27–29.

[39] Bricault (2017), 229–31, pl. 24, nos. 26–31 (Magnesia ad Maeandrum, Smyrna).

[40] Civic issues: *SNG* France 2326 (Hadrian, Aegeae, Cilicia); Waddington, Babelon and Reinach (1904–1912), 288, pl. LXXIV.26 (rev.) (Marcus Aurelius or Commodus, Nicaea, Bithynia). Tokens: Gülbay and Kireç (2008), 133, no. 188a, 136–38, nos. 195–200.

[41] Martin (2013), 10–69.

[42] Postolakas (1880), 7; Crosby (1964), 77; Bubelis (2010), 182–88; de Callataÿ (2010).

Fig. 9: Agora Museum/Ephorate of Antiquities of the city of Athens IL224 (cat. no. 48, Ø 20mm) (courtesy of the Hellenic Ministry of Culture).

Fig. 10: Agora Museum/Ephorate of Antiquities of the city of Athens IL219 (cat. no. 50, Ø 25mm) (courtesy of the Hellenic Ministry of Culture).

Fig. 11: Agora Museum/Ephorate of Antiquities of the city of Athens IL274 (cat. no. 52, Ø 23mm) (courtesy of the Hellenic Ministry of Culture).

Fig. 12: Agora Museum/Ephorate of Antiquities of the city of Athens IL268 (cat. no. 54, Ø 19mm) (courtesy of the Hellenic Ministry of Culture).

Fig. 13: Agora Museum/Ephorate of Antiquities of the city of Athens IL283 (cat. no. 55, Ø 20mm) (courtesy of the Hellenic Ministry of Culture).

Fig. 14: Agora Museum/Ephorate of Antiquities of the city of Athens IL261 (cat. no. 56, Ø 20mm) (courtesy of the Hellenic Ministry of Culture).

Fig. 15: Agora Museum/Ephorate of Antiquities of the city of Athens IL265 (cat. no. 57, Ø 21mm) (courtesy of the Hellenic Ministry of Culture).

Fig. 16: Agora Museum/Ephorate of Antiquities of the city of Athens IL244 (cat. no. 58, Ø 20mm) (courtesy of the Hellenic Ministry of Culture).

Fig. 17: Agora Museum/Ephorate of Antiquities of the city of Athens IL272 (cat. no. 59, Ø 17mm) (courtesy of the Hellenic Ministry of Culture).

Fig. 18: Agora Museum/Ephorate of Antiquities of the city of Athens IL279 (cat. no. 60, Ø 18mm) (courtesy of the Hellenic Ministry of Culture).

Fig. 19: Agora Museum/Ephorate of Antiquities of the city of Athens IL284 (cat. no. 61, Ø 11mm) (courtesy of the Hellenic Ministry of Culture).

Fig. 20: Agora Museum/Ephorate of Antiquities of the city of Athens IL288 (cat. no. 62, Ø 15mm) (courtesy of the Hellenic Ministry of Culture).

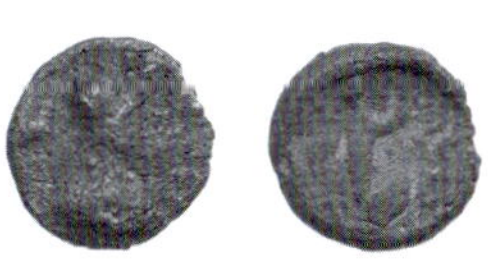

Fig. 21: Agora Museum/Ephorate of Antiquities of the city of Athens IL290 (cat. no. 63, Ø 14mm) (courtesy of the Hellenic Ministry of Culture).

Fig. 22: Agora Museum/Ephorate of Antiquities of the city of Athens IL289 (cat. no. 64, Ø 17mm) (courtesy of the Hellenic Ministry of Culture).

Fig. 23: Agora Museum/Ephorate of Antiquities of the city of Athens IL1074 (cat. no. 69, Ø 13mm) (courtesy of the Hellenic Ministry of Culture).

Fig. 24: Agora Museum/Ephorate of Antiquities of the city of Athens IL213 (cat. no. 77, Ø 19mm) (courtesy of the Hellenic Ministry of Culture).

Fig. 25: Agora Museum/Ephorate of Antiquities of the city of Athens IL209 (cat. no. 82, Ø 20mm) (courtesy of the Hellenic Ministry of Culture).

Fig. 26: Agora Museum/Ephorate of Antiquities of the city of Athens IL257 (cat. no. 77, Ø 20mm) (courtesy of the Hellenic Ministry of Culture).

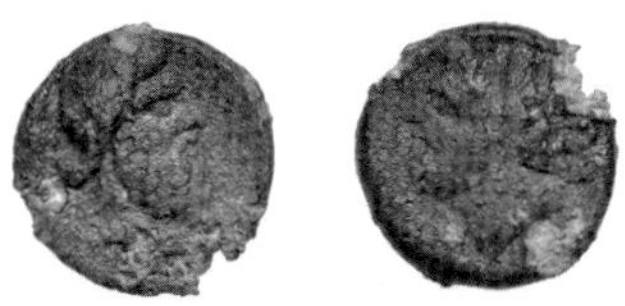

Fig. 27: Agora Museum/Ephorate of Antiquities of the city of Athens IL240 (cat. no. 88, Ø 17mm) (courtesy of the Hellenic Ministry of Culture).

Fig. 28: Agora Museum/Ephorate of Antiquities of the city of Athens IL286 (cat. no. 89, Ø 22mm) (courtesy of the Hellenic Ministry of Culture).

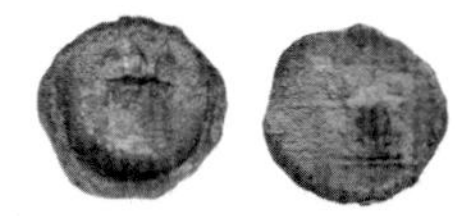

Fig. 29: Agora Museum/Ephorate of Antiquities of the city of Athens IL241 (cat. no. 90, Ø 15mm) (courtesy of the Hellenic Ministry of Culture).

were all issued by the same authority, who presided over all stages of the tokens' use: distribution, authentication, and the collection of the tokens back.[43]

On Palmyrene tokens, which are generally made of clay and two-sided, space was deliberately left on one of the sides for the addition of a small design made on a separately attached piece of clay and carrying a stamp, sometimes produced by impressing a gem. While the designs of the two sides were taken from the ready-made patterns manufactured at the workshop and offered to the commissioners, this third aspect, the punch, was the personal badge of the commissioner. It was carefully prepared and attached as pastillage. The private punches safeguarded the authenticity of the tokens and prevented their counterfeiting.[44]

In this case, the dolphin countermark bears a connection to the commissioners of the tokens, the people who occasioned their use and distribution. Saying that, the different designs of the faces could signify a variety of occasions. Therefore, the 'Hermes bust' series, which is more abundantly preserved, may be linked with the most recent occasion. This is a tentative interpretation because while in Palmyra specimens of the same type bear different private punches, in Athens specimens of different dies have the same countermark. This is a phenomenon that may be related to the coherence of the lot and the circumstances of the discovery.

Similarly, the countermark of a stork and lizard is placed on 15 of the types found together on the floors of the shops in the Stoa of Attalos, as well as the Stoa's environs. The find is contemporary to the Agoraios Kolonos tokens.[45] Although the exact meaning of the countermarks still escapes us, it is evident that they helped regulate a complex system of token distribution.

Interpretation: functions and meanings of Athenian tokens

The evidence presented above permits the formulation of some hypotheses concerning the possible roles – religious, political, social – played by these tokens. Specimens of the 'Hermes

[43] Crosby (1964), 83.
[44] Ingholt, Seyrig, Starcky and Caquot (1955), iv–v; du Mesnil du Buisson (1962), 18–20; Makrypodi (2016), figs. 1–2, 6.
[45] Mylonas (1901), 119–22, pl. 7; Crosby (1964), 116.

bust', 'Hermes / Serapis' and 'Lion with tenon' series have also been found in the Bouleuterion Plateia, the most conspicuous spot of Athenian politics, which suggests a connection with the works and aspirations of the civic elite, and particularly elite euergetism.[46] The politics of elite euergetism were intended to result in the praise and admiration of the citizenry and were translated into prestige and status.[47] The considerable expense linked to the magistracies and offices of Roman Imperial Athens (e.g. the sacrifices financed by the eponymous archon, the hoplite general, the prytanising tribe) and the related distributions of money, food (including grain) and gifts gave the incentive for token distribution.[48]

Parallel situations can be found elsewhere in the Roman Empire. In Ephesos the imagery and legends on tokens suggest they were connected to festivals, serving to enhance the status of the elite, who issued the tokens and sponsored the activities. Of importance here is the use of abbreviated names and monograms of wealthy and influential individuals, which functioned as symbols to communicate with token-users.[49] Caius Vibius Salutaris' endowment to the citizenry of Ephesos was such a case. The gifts would have been distributed with the aid of tokens.[50] In Palmyra, tokens used as entrance tickets to sacred banquets carried the representation of one or more of the priests responsible for the celebration. Banqueting was obviously a means of negotiating social power and civic identity. The image of the donor or donors, accompanied by their name, would have circulated on tokens among the beneficiaries, in other cases among the members of an association; these objects must have been much sought-after for the benefits of attending a one-time event as well as for the access and prestige associated with exclusive spheres of societal life.[51]

In Athens of the Second Sophistic concerns for elite status and identity were apparent.[52] Clans, an archaic organisation that was revived under Augustus, provided the candidates for priesthoods and magistracies as well as governing bodies (the Council of the Five Hundred and the Council of Areopagus). Magistracies and priesthoods were no longer elected but had transformed into life-long positions, to which members of the clans were appointed.[53] The plague and the economic crisis under the Antonines meant that the expense of holding an office became more acute. The intentional resemblance of tokens to well-known coin types may have been chosen as an abstract allusion to the funds donated and a more concrete appeal for increased prosperity in view of the crisis of the Severan period in the early third century AD.

In AD 212, when the *Constitutio Antoniniana* granted Roman citizenship to almost all in the Empire, the Athenian clans must have felt prompted to accentuate their status in a much more ostentatious way. Reference to venerable ancestors was one way of differentiating their own citizenship, based on noble ancestry, from the *en masse* citizenship granted by imperial degree. An honorific epigram of AD 240 (*IG* II^2 3679) records that the *Claudii* of Melite claimed descent from illustrious personalities of the past: the general Conon and Alexander the Great.[54] The emphasis on status and ancestry of the family can be glimpsed in a dedicatory inscription from ca. AD 200, where on the occasion of an intermarriage between the *Casiani* of Steiria (a deme on the east coast of Attica) and the *Claudii* of Melite, the ancestry of the honorands is meticulously inscribed with the former family claiming even Perikles among its ancestors, counting 21 generations backwards.[55] The *Casiani* of Steiria were of the *genos* of the *Eumolpidai*, which claimed descent from Poseidon and were traditionally

[46] Crosby (1964), 112. 'Hermes/Serapis' (IL699) from Bouleuterion Plateia F10 and one un-inventoried specimen from northwest of Bouleuterion (F8), 'Hermes bust' (IL58) from near Bouleuterion deposit F 12:4 (third to fourth century AD); 'Lion's head with tenon' (IL127–28) from the northwest corner of the Bouleuterion Plateia; 'Hermes head right / head right' (IL129) from near the northwest corner of Bouleuterion Plateia (F10).

[47] Veyne (1990), 214–16; McHugh (2017), 124–34.

[48] Geagan (1967), 6–8, 18–31.

[49] Gülbay and Kireç (2008); Kuhn (2014).

[50] Wankel (1979), 167–249, no. 27.

[51] Seyrig (1985); Kaizer (2002), 116–20, 255–58; Al-As'ad, Briquel-Chatonnet and Yon (2005); Raja (2015).

[52] For the Second Sophistic in general: Borg (2004); Whitmarsh (2013); Johnson (2017).

[53] Geagan (1967), 75, 81; Woloch (1969); Oliver (1980); Oliver (1981), 83–88; Camia (2014).

[54] Clinton (2004), 55–56.

[55] The Athenian Agora I 7483: Clinton (2004), 39–56, figs. 1–5, particularly 54–55. The 21 generations are compatible with the actual date of the inscription by a reckoning of thirty years to a generation.

hierophants, the highest priesthood in the Eleusinian cult.[56] The family of the *Claudii* of Melite, contemporaries to *Casiani*, were of the *genos* of *Kerykes* and occupied the *daduchia* priesthood, second in importance after the hierophants.[57] It is tempting to think that the issue and distribution of the tokens of Agoraios Kolonos were managed by members of the Athenian elite and that the designs represented the divine ancestry and celebrated the priesthoods of these families, advertising their connections in the same way as these inscriptions.

The predilection for Hermes and Alexander the Great on the tokens of Agoraios Kolonos can only partially be explained as adaptations of contemporary coinage in and outside Athens. Instead they are linked to the self-consciousness and self-portrayal of the elite. The 44 'Hermes bust' tokens form a coherent ensemble and point to a particular event, which could have been initiated by a man of the *genos* of *Kerykes*, because this group claimed descent from Hermes himself. The dolphin countermark is connected to the final phase of this event. It is of some significance that the dolphin countermark is found on all 'Hermes bust' specimens but is not restricted to them. Was the same authority responsible for the various series of tokens, the related events, and the countermarking? Could the initiator behind the dolphin countermark have been a priest of Poseidon-Erechtheus? It is nevertheless tempting to see the dolphin design and the way that it almost obliterates Hermes' face as an expression of the competition between the elite families for status and priesthoods.[58] Tokens and the events associated with them were instruments in the elite's quest for primacy. The types commemorate family priesthoods, divine forefathers and historical ancestors. They bear witness to the elite's concern to gain the praise of the citizenry and preserve their prestige. Similar to Ephesos, endowments are also attested for Athens: Claudius Atticus' endowment for example (Herodes Atticus' father),[59] and the so-called Eleusinian endowment.[60]

The meticulous design of Hermes' bust – the winged cap, the draped neckline, the *kerykeion* resting on the god's shoulder – betray a particular admiration and knowledge of classical antiquity. The 'lion with tenon' tokens are similarly classical in design and almost archaic in appearance. Similar observations can be made for the rest of the series. The absorption of the Greek world into the Roman Empire resulted into a particular attachment to the past, mythical genealogy, and local history, which ultimately affected social memory.[61]

The iconography of the heavy bronze wreathed coinage of the second century AD can be explained as a product of the same conditions and has also been related to the cultural and societal activities of the Athenian elite. The coin types commemorate divine forefathers and historical ancestors. Issued by influential Athenian families, they were probably used for distributions of money to the Athenian citizenry upon the holding of the eponymous archonship and other high offices of the city.[62]

Conclusion

The hoard of 60 tokens along with the 30 closely related pieces discovered in the Herulian debris on the southwest slope of the Agoraios Kolonos brings to light the roles these objects played in social life. The above analysis clearly demonstrates the powerful networks of political and sacred affairs that likely prompted the issuing and use of tokens. The imagery and find spots of these pieces suggest tokens were issued by wealthy magistrates with high aspirations. The imagery points to the ambitions of the Athenian elite to preserve their distinguished status in a continuously changing environment.

Close analysis succeeded in placing the tokens in the complex society of imperial Athens and demonstrated how tokens enabled the maintenance of an exclusive community with

[56] Mylonas (1961), 167–68, 230–31.
[57] Follet (1976), 274–78; Clinton (1992), 78; Byrne (2003), 153–59.
[58] An example is the enmity between the *Claudii* of Melite and the *Claudii* of Marathon: Clinton (1974), 61–62.
[59] Oliver (1949), 302–03.
[60] Oliver (1952), 381–99.
[61] Swain (1996), 65–131; Alcock (2001), 323–50.
[62] Kroll (1997).

connections to the broader political, religious and cultural network of the Roman Empire. The acceptance and circulation of the pieces created bonds between issuers and users, and close examination and control of these objects were procedures that shaped social life. Their divine iconography has proven to be more earthly in nature, with the imagery of tokens connected to identities and ancestry, celebrating priesthoods, shaping relations and contributing to the continuity of primacy among the elite.

Catalogue

60 tokens found in Pit D 11:6 (hoard)

Bust of Hermes right in a round incuse, with winged cap on his head and *kerykeion* on right shoulder. Countermarked with a dolphin (11mm) facing right with a long tail. Uniface.[63]

cf. cat. nos. 65–66. Unless specified the countermark is in the right field.
Bibliography: Crosby (1964), 112, cat. no. L264.

1. **IL217**, Ø 21mm, 4.46g.
2. **IL220 (fig. 3)**, Ø 22mm, 4.63g.
3. **IL222 (fig. 4)**, Ø 21mm, 3.69g.
4. **IL223**, Ø 20mm, 2.73g (1/3 broken off), countermark obliterated Hermes' face.
5. **IL225**, Ø 22mm, 5.92g, countermark obliterated Hermes' face.
6. **IL226**, Ø 22mm, 6.00g, countermark obliterated Hermes' face.
7. **IL227**, Ø 21mm, 5.95g, countermark obliterated the lower part of the face and the neck.
8. **IL228**, Ø 21mm, 4.59g, countermark obliterated Hermes' face.
9. **IL229**, Ø 23mm, 7.09g.
10. **IL230**, Ø 22mm, 7.38g, countermark obliterated Hermes' face.
11. **IL232**, Ø 20mm, 4.77g.
12. **IL233**, Ø 22mm, 5.69g.
13. **IL234**, Ø 21mm, 3.83g.
14. **IL235**, Ø 23mm, 5.22g.
15. **IL236 (fig. 5)**, Ø 21mm, 2.80g, countermark on the left.
16. **IL237**, Ø 22mm, 4.57g.
17. **IL238**, Ø 20mm, 4.57g, countermark obliterated Hermes' face.
18. **IL239**, Ø 23mm, 6.98g, countermark obliterated Hermes' face.
19. **IL242**, Ø 20mm, 3.23g.
20. **IL243**, Ø 20mm 3.80g.
21. **IL245**, Ø 20mm, 3.78g, countermark obliterated Hermes' face.
22. **IL246**, Ø 22mm, 5.69g.
23. **IL247**, Ø 21mm, 4.89g, countermark obliterated Hermes' face.
24. **IL248**, Ø 17mm, 2.92g. A piece on the left is broken off, probably in the area of countermarking, and almost 1/3 is missing.
25. **IL249**, Ø 20mm, 4.19g.
26. **IL250**, Ø 21mm, 5.69g, countermark obliterated Hermes' face.
27. **IL251**, Ø 20mm, 4.16g, countermark obliterated Hermes' face.
28. **IL259**, Ø 21mm, 4.83g.
29. **IL260**, Ø 19mm, 4.80g, countermark obliterated Hermes' face.
30. **IL263 (fig. 6)**, 23mm, 6.81g.
31. **IL264**, Ø 19mm, 4.45g, countermark obliterated Hermes' face.
32. **IL266**, Ø 20mm, 4.74g, countermark obliterated Hermes' face.
33. **IL267**, Ø 22mm, 6.85g.
34. **IL269 (fig. 7)**, Ø 22mm, 4.54g. Countermark on the left, which obliterated the *kerykeion*.
35. **IL270**, Ø 21mm, 5.09g.
36. **IL271**, Ø 22mm, 6.04g, countermark partially erased Hermes' face.
37. **IL275**, Ø 21mm, 5.35g, countermark obliterated Hermes' face.
38. **IL276**, Ø 21mm, 5.13g.
39. **IL277**, Ø 23mm, 4.71g.
40. **IL278**, Ø 21mm, 3.18g, countermark on the left.

[63] Crosby (1964), 112–13, L264 lists 45: 44 + the radiate bust IL283 with no countermark, which was mistaken for Hermes.

41. IL280, Ø 20mm, 3.47g, small part broken off.
42. IL281, Ø 23mm, 6.16g, countermark partially erased Hermes' face.
43. IL282, Ø 21mm, 4.44g, countermark on the right.
44. IL285, Ø 22mm, 6.85g.

Other specimens of the same type found in the Agora: IL335 from Kolonos Agoraios (A–F 9–15) (Ø 21mm, 5.91g). The countermark on the right partially erased Hermes' face. **IL158** (deposit F 12:4) (Ø 23mm, 3.10g) (half of it broken off), countermark on the right.

Lion's head seen from above with tenon, dolphin countermark. The countermark is 8mm with a rill that delineates the dolphin. Uniface.

Bibliography: Crosby (1964), 115, cat. no. L291.
These tokens are mould made, with solid robust flans and flat backs.

45. IL218, Ø 21mm, 6.66g. The countermark is at 12h.
46. IL231, Ø 28mm, 11.79g. The countermark is at 12h.
47. IL221 (fig. 8), Ø 25mm, 9.55g. The countermark is at 6h.

Other specimens of the same type found in the Agora: IL127 from the northwest corner of the Bouleuterion Plateia (F10) (Ø 22mm, 10.32g). The countermark is at 12h and a small piece is broken off. **IL128** from the northwest corner of the Bouleuterion Plateia (F10) (Ø 26mm, 9.58g). The countermark is at 12h. **IL1203** from the Southwest Area (Ø 23mm, 7.03g). The countermark is at 6h.

Bust of Athena with Corinthian helmet left on ship, the oars are denoted with incisions, star in field right. Just below the ship, countermark of a dolphin facing right (11mm). From pit D11:6. Uniface.

Bibliography: Crosby (1964), 111, cat. no. L256.

48. IL224 (fig. 9), Ø 20mm, 2.71g. The countermark is at 9h.
49. IL273, Ø 24mm, 4.95g. The countermark is at 10h.

Side A: Bust of Serapis right. Side B: Prow (right).

Bibliography: Crosby (1964), 113, cat. no. L268.

50. IL219 (fig. 10), Ø 25mm, 4.81g, 6h.
51. IL262, Ø 21mm, 5.52g, 3h.

Other specimens of the same type found in the Agora: **IL590** (Ø 20mm, 5.14g, 3h) and **IL1215** (Ø 19mm, 4.96g, 12h).

Side A: Head of Athena right. Side B: Filleted boukranion with countermark of a dolphin above (11mm).

Bibliography: Crosby (1964), 110, cat. no. L251.

52. IL274 (fig. 11), Ø 23mm, 6.45g, 9h.
53. IL294, Ø 17mm, 3.32g, 9h.

Specimen of the same type found in the Agora: **IL1440** from Agoraios Kolonos (Ø 25mm, 6.48g, 3h), dolphin countermark on the reverse at 1h.

Side A: Head of Hermes right in incuse. Side B: Male head right in slight incuse.

Bibliography: Crosby (1964), 113, cat. no. L273. Cf. the finds in stratum D 11:7.

54. IL268 (fig. 12), Ø 19mm, 5.92g, 9h.

Radiate male bust right. Uniface.

Bibliography: Crosby (1964), 112–13, cat. no. L264.[64]
55. IL283 (fig. 13), Ø 20mm, 6.05g.

[64] IL273 was originally mistaken as the same type as L264. But the bust bears a radiate crown, no *kerykeion* is visible, and there is no countermark.

Side A: Bust of Poseidon right. Side B: Prow right, square object in field above. Border of dots 13mm in diameter.

Bibliography: Crosby (1964), 113, cat. no. L267.

56. IL261 (fig. 14), Ø 20mm, 5.33g, 3–4h.

Bearded male bust right, club in field left, dolphin countermark facing upwards (11mm) behind the bust. Uniface.

Bibliography: Crosby (1964), 113, cat. no. L271.

57. IL265 (fig. 15), Ø 21mm, 7.19g.

Diademed head of Alexander the Great right, dolphin countermark facing downwards (11mm) in the field right. Uniface.

Bibliography: Crosby (1964), 114, cat. no. L 275.

58. IL244 (fig. 16), Ø 20mm, 5.79g, countermark in right field.

Side A: Deer standing right. Side B: Prow right, square object in field above.

Bibliography: Crosby (1964), 114, cat. no. L280.

59. IL272 (fig. 17), Ø 17mm, 3.88g, 6h.
Specimen of the same type found in the Agora: IL1439, Ø 18mm, 5.21g, 5–6h.

Filleted thyrsus (?). Uniface.

Bibliography: Crosby (1964), 115, cat. no. L298.

60. IL279 (fig. 18), Ø 18mm, 3.91g, small piece broken off.
8 tokens found in stratum D 11:7

Palmette. Uniface.

Bibliography: Crosby (1964), 107, cat. no. L212.

61. IL284 (fig. 19), Ø 11mm, 2.33g.

Draped figure standing left, left arm forward and down, uncertain symbols in field left and right. Uniface.

Bibliography: Crosby (1964), 97, cat. no. L102.

62. IL288 (fig. 20), Ø 15mm, 2.46g.

Side A: Bust of Athena right in crested Corinthian helmet, owl behind head. Side B: Demeter standing in cart drawn right by two serpents; upraised arms perhaps carrying torch and grain.

Bibliography: Crosby (1964), 110, cat. no. L245.

63. IL290 (fig. 21), Ø 14mm, 2.42g, 6h.

Side A: Pegasus galloping right, in field below dolphin right (no countermark), all in square incuse. Side B: Bacchus.

Bibliography: Crosby (1964), 114, cat. no. L282.

64. IL289 (fig. 22), Ø 17mm, 4.72g, 12h.

Bust of Hermes right in round incuse, winged cap on his head, *kerykeion* on his shoulder, countermark of a dolphin facing right with long tail. Uniface.

Cf. the 44 pieces in pit D 11:6 above: cat. nos. 1–44.
Bibliography: Crosby (1964), 112, cat. no. L264.

65. IL255, Ø 21mm, 5.49g. The countermark on the right partially erased Hermes' face.
66. IL256, Ø 22mm, 4.18g. The countermark is on the *kerykeion* at 7h.

Side A: Hermes turned slightly left; cap, winged shoes, and chlamys falling from left arm. Moneybags in right hand, *kerykeion* in left. In field, lower right, a star; lower left, indeterminate object. Border of dots 14mm in diameter. Side B: Serapis, semi-draped, wearing modius, head turned to left. Right arm outstretched, staff in left hand. In field lower left, star. Border of dots 14mm in diameter.

Bibliography: Crosby (1964), 112, cat. no. L263. Cf. the finds in Cistern D 10:1: cat. nos. 70–78.

67. IL292, Ø 17mm, 5.81g, 1h.

Side A: Head of Hermes right in incuse. Side B: Male head right in slight incuse.

Bibliography: Crosby (1964), 113, cat. no. L273. Cf. the finds in pit D 11:6: cat. no. 54.

68. IL287, Ø 18mm, 5.42g, 9h (thick robust flan).

Specimen of the same type found in the Agora: **IL129** (Ø 19mm, 4.34g) from near the northwest corner of Bouleuterion Plateia (F10).

22 tokens found in cistern D 10:1

Ribbed flaring kantharos.
Bibliography: Crosby (1964), 105, cat. no. L 202.

69. IL1074 (fig. 23), Ø 13mm, 2.50g.

Side A: Hermes turned slightly left; cap, winged shoes, and chlamys falling from left arm. Moneybags in right hand, *kerykeion* in left. In field, lower right, a star; lower left, indeterminate object. Border of dots 14mm in diameter. Side B: Serapis, semi-draped, wearing modius, head turned to left. Right arm outstretched, staff in left hand. In field lower left, star. Border of dots 14mm in diameter.

cf. the finds in stratum D11:7: cat. no. 67. Bibliography: Crosby (1964), 112, cat. no. L263.

70. IL200, Ø 19mm, 6.63g, 6h.
71. IL202, Ø 21mm, 6.48g, 9h.
72. IL205, Ø 20mm (disintegrated).
73. IL206, Ø 18mm, 5.07g, 12h.
74. IL207, Ø 21mm, 5.93g, 6h.
75. IL208, Ø 20mm, 5.71g, 9h (a small part is broken off).
76. IL211, Ø 22mm, 7.26g, 1h.
77. IL213 (fig. 24), Ø 19mm, 5.23g, 3h.
78. IL215, Ø 21mm, 6.26g, 12h.

Head of Athena right in crested Corinthian helmet in linear circle. Uniface.

Bibliography: Crosby (1964), 110, cat. no. L250.

79. IL201, Ø 23mm, 7.20g.
80. IL203, disintegrated.
81. IL204, Ø 21mm, 4.82g.
82. IL209 (fig. 25), Ø 20mm, 4.42g.
83. IL212, Ø 19mm, 3.94g.
84. IL258, Ø 19mm, 5.46g.
85. IL253, Ø 16mm, 2.94g.

Side A: Head of Athena right. Side B: Filleted boukranion with countermark of dolphin (11mm) above.

Bibliography: Crosby (1964), 110, cat. no. L251.
Cf. the finds in the pit D 11:6: cat. nos. 52–53.

86. IL199, Ø 18mm, 4.06g, 9h.

Bust of Poseidon right, in field right trident with dolphin entwined around it, dolphin countermark left (11mm). Uniface.

Bibliography: Crosby (1964), 113, cat. no. L265.

87. IL257 (fig. 26), Ø 20mm, 4.22g.

Side A: Head of the personified *Demos* right. Side B: Head of Alexander the Great left.

Bibliography: Crosby (1964), 113, cat. no. L272.

88. IL240 (fig. 27), Ø 17mm, 5.34g, 6h.

Helmet, dolphin countermark (11mm) left and yet another countermark (12mm) right. Uniface.

Bibliography: Crosby (1964), cat. no. L289.

89. IL286 (fig. 28), Ø 22mm, 6,26g,

Side A: Kalathos or altar. Side B: Kalathos or altar.

Bibliography: Crosby (1964), cat. no. L290.

90. IL241 (fig. 29), Ø 15mm, 4.44g, 6h.

Bibliography

Al-As'ad, Briquel-Chatonnet and Yon 2005: K. Al-As'ad, F. Briquel-Chatonnet, and J.-P. Yon, 'The sacred banquets at Palmyra and the function of the *tesserae*: reflections on the tokens found in the Arsu temple', in Cussini (ed.) (2005), 1–10.

Alcock 2001: S. Alcock, 'The reconfiguration of memory in the eastern Roman Empire', in Alcock, D'Altroy and Morrison (eds.) (2001), 323–50.

Alcock, D'Altroy and Morrison (eds.) 2001: S. Alcock, T. D'Altroy and K. D. Morrison (eds.), *Empires. Perspectives from Archaeology and History* (Cambridge, 2001).

Ando and Rüpke (eds.) 2015: C. Ando and J. Rüpke (eds.), *Public and Private in Ancient Mediterranean Law and Religion* (Berlin, 2015).

Benndorf 1875: O. Benndorf, 'Beiträge zur Kenntnis des Attischen Theaters', *Zeitschrift für die Österreichischen Gymnasien* 26 (1875), 579–618, 730.

Boegehold 1995: A. Boegehold (ed.), *The Athenian Agora XXVIII: The Lawcourts at Athens: Sites, Buildings, Equipment, Procedure and Testimonia* (Princeton, 1995).

Borg 2004: B. E. Borg (ed.), *Paideia. The World of the Second Sophistic* (Berlin, 2004).

Bricault 2017: L. Bricault, 'Serapis au droit des monnaies provinciales Romaines d'Asie Mineure et de Thrace', *NC* 177 (2017), 213–44.

Bubelis 2010: W. Bubelis, 'Tokens and imitation in ancient Athens', *Marburger Beiträge zur Antiken Handels-, Wirtschafts-, und Sozialgeschichte* 28 (2010), 182–88.

Bubelis 2013: W. Bubelis, 'The Agorastikon of Hellenistic Athens: not a market-tax', *ZPE* 185 (2013), 122–26.

Byrne 2003: S. G. Byrne, *Roman Citizens of Athens* (Leuven, 2003).

Camia 2014: F. Camia, 'Political elite and priestly posts during the Roman Imperial period: some considerations', *ZPE* 188 (2014), 139–48.

Clinton 1974: K. Clinton, 'The sacred officials of the Eleusinian mysteries', *TAPhA* 64 (1974) 1–143.

Clinton 1992: K. Clinton, *Myth and Cult: The Iconography of the Eleusinian Mysteries, The Martin P. Nilsson Lectures on Greek Religion, Delivered 19-21 November 1990 at the Swedish Institute at Athens* (Stockholm, 1992).

Clinton 2004: K. Clinton, 'A family of *Eumolpidai* and *Kerykes* descended from Pericles', *Hesperia* 73 (2004), 39–57.

Crosby 1964: M. Crosby, 'Lead and clay tokens. Part II', in Lang and Crosby (1964), 69–146.

Cussini 2005: E. Cussini (ed.), *A Journey to Palmyra. Collected Essays to Remember Delbert R. Hillers* (Leiden, 2005).

de Callataÿ 2010: F. de Callataÿ, 'Les plombs à types monétaires en Grèce ancienne: monnaies (officielles, votives ou contrefaits), jetons, sceaux, poids, épeuves ou fantaisies?', *RN* 167 (2010), 219–55.

Deubner 1932: L. Deubner, *Attische Feste* (Berlin, 1932).

du Mesnil du Buisson 1962: R. du Mesnil du Buisson (comte), *Les tessères et les monnaies de Palmyre* (Paris, 1962).

Dumont 1870: A. Dumont, *De plumbeis apud Graecos tesseris* (Paris, 1870).

Egelhaaf-Gaiser 2002: U. Egelhaaf-Gaiser, 'Religionsästhetik und Raumordnung', in Egelhaaf-Gaiser and Schäfer (eds.) (2002), 123–72.

Egelhaaf-Gaiser and Schäfer (eds.) 2002: U. Egelhaaf-Gaiser and A. Schäfer (eds.), *Religiöse Vereine in der Römischen Antike. Untersuchungen zu Organisation, Ritual und Raumordnung* (Tübingen, 2002).

Engel 1884: E. Engel, 'Choix de tessères grecques en plomb', *BCH* 8 (1884), 1–21.

Follet 1976: S. Follet, *Athènes au IIe et au IIIe siècle av. J.-C.: Études Chronologiques et Prosopographiques* (Paris, 1976).

Frantz, Thompson and Travlos 1988: A. Frantz, H. A. Thompson, and J. Travlos, *The Athenian Agora XXIV: Late Antiquity: A.D. 267-700* (Princeton, 1988).

Gasparri 1986: C. Gasparri, s.v. 'Dionysos', *Lexicon Iconographicum Mythologiae Classicae*, 3 (1986), 435–36.

Geagan 1964: D. Geagan, *The Athenian Agora XVIII: Inscriptions: The Dedicatory Monuments* (Princeton, 1964).
Geagan 1967: D. Geagan, D. Geagan, *The Athenian Constitution after Sulla, Hesperia Supplement* 12 (Princeton, 1967).
Gülbay and Kireç 2008: O. Gülbay and H. Kireç, *Efes Kurşun Tesseraelari. Ephesian Lead Tesserae* (Istanbul, 2008).
Harrison 1953: E. B. Harrison, *The Athenian Agora. Portrait Sculpture. Vol. I* (Princeton, 1953).
Harrison 1965: E. B. Harrison, *The Athenian Agora. Archaic and Archaistic Sculpture. Vol. XI* (Princeton, 1965).
Ingholt, Seyrig, Starcky and Caquot 1955: H. Ingholt, H. Seyrig, J. Starcky, and A. Caquot, *Recueil des tessères de Palmyre* (Paris, 1955).
Irvine, Hanks and Weddle 2012: R. Irvine, N. Hanks and C. Weddle, 'Sacred architecture: archaeological and anthropological perspectives', in Shankland (ed.) (2012), 91–117.
Jaillard 2007: D. Jaillard, *Configurations d'Hermès. Une «theogonie hermaïque»* (Kernos Supplement 17) (Liège, 2007).
Johnson 2017: W. A. Johnson (ed.), *The Oxford Handbook of the Second Sophistic* (New York, 2017).
Kaizer 2002: T. Kaizer, *The Religious Life of Palmyra. A Study of the Social Patterns of Worship in the Roman Period* (Stuttgart, 2002).
Kroll 1997: J. H. Kroll, 'The Athenian imperials: results of recent study', in Nollé, Overbeck and Weiss (eds.) (1997), 61–69.
Kroll 2015: J. H. Kroll, 'Small bronze tokens from the Athenian Agora: *symbola* or *kollyboi*?', in Wartenberg and Amandry (eds.) (2015), 107–16.
Kuhn 2014: C. Kuhn, 'Prosopographical notes on four lead *tesserae* from Roman Ephesos', *ZPE* 190 (2014), 137–40.
Lang 1959: M. Lang, 'Allotment by tokens', *Historia* 8 (1959), 80–89.
Lang and Crosby 1964: M. Lang and M. Crosby, *The Athenian Agora X: Weights, Measures and Tokens* (Princeton, 1964).
Lohmann 1999: H. Lohmann, s.v. 'Melite [5]', in *Der Neue Pauly* (Stuttgart, 1999) (vol. 7, Lef-Men), 1190.
Makrypodi 2016: S. Makrypodi, 'The tokens (*tesserae*) of Palmyra. New data from the collections of the Numismatic Museum (Note 1)', *Archaeology and Arts*, 13 June 2016 (https://www.archaeology.wiki/blog/2016/06/13/tokens-tesserae-palmyra/; accessed 06/06/2019).
Markus 1993: T. A. Markus, *Buildings and Power: Freedom and Control in the Origin of Modern Building Types* (London, 1993).
Martin 2013: K. Martin, *Demos, Boule, Gerousia: Personifikationen Städtischer Institutionen auf kaiserzeitlichen Münzen aus Kleinasien* (Bonn, 2013).
McHugh 2017: S. McHugh, *Renewing Athens. The Ideology of the Past in the Roman East*. PhD thesis, University of Oxford (Oxford, 2017).
Meritt and Traill 1974: B. D. Meritt and J. S. Traill, *The Athenian Agora XV: Inscriptions: The Athenian Councillors* (Princeton, 1974).
Mylonas 1901: K. D. Mylonas, 'Αττικά Μολύβδινα Σύμβολα', *ArchEph* 40 (1901), 119–22.
Mylonas 1961: G. E. Mylonas, *Eleusis and the Eleusinian Mysteries* (Princeton and London, 1961).
Nollé, Overbeck and Weiss (eds.) 1997: J. Nollé, B. Overbeck and P. Weiss (eds.), *Internationales Kolloquium zur Kaiserzeitlichen Münzprägung Kleinasiens, 27-30 April 1994 in der Staatlichen Münzsammlung* (München, 1997).
Oliver 1941: J. H. Oliver, *The Sacred Gerusia, Hesperia Supplement* 6, (Princeton, 1941).
Oliver 1949: J. H. Oliver, 'Patrons providing financial aid to the tribes of Roman Athens', *AJPh* 70 (1949), 299–308.
Oliver 1952: J. H. Oliver, 'The Eleusinian endowment', *AJA* 21 (1952), 381–99.
Oliver 1980: J. H. Oliver, 'From *gennētai* to *curiales*', *Hesperia* 49 (1980), 30–56.
Oliver 1981: J. H. Oliver, 'Civic status in Roman Athens. Cicero, *Pro Balbo* 12,30', *GRBS* 22 (1981), 83–88.
Postolacca 1868: A. Postolacca, 'Piombi inediti del Nazionale Museo Numismatico di Atene', *Annali dell' Instituto di Corrispondenza Archeologica* 40 (1868), 268–316 with illustrations (drawings) on tav. di aggiunti K and pl. LII in *Monumenti Inediti Pubblicati dall'Instituto di Corrispondenza Archeologica* 8 (1864–1868).
Postolakas 1880: A. Postolakas, 'Κερμάτια Συμβολικά', *Αθήναιον* 9 (1880), 7–50.
Raja 2015: R. Raja, 'Staging private religion in Roman public Palmyra. The role of the religious dining tickets (banqueting tesserae)', in Ando and Rüpke (eds.) (2015), 165–86.
Rhodes 1981: P. G. Rhodes, *A Commentary on the Aristotelian Athenaion Politeia* (Oxford, 1981).
Seyrig 1985: H. Seyrig, 'Les tessères Palmyreniennes et le banquet rituel', *Scripta Varia. Mélanges d'archéologie et d'histoire* (Paris, 1985), 313–22.
Shankland (ed.) 2012: D. Shankland (ed.), *Archaeology and Anthropology. Past, Present and Future* (London 2012).
Shear 1935: T. L. Shear, 'Archaeological Notes: The Agora Excavations', *AJA* 39 (1995), 437–47.
Shear 1936: T. L. Shear, 'The campaign of 1935', *Hesperia* 5 (1936), 1–42.
Shear 2001: J.L. Shear, *Polis and Panathenaia: The History and Development of Athena's Festival* (PhD Thesis-University of Pennsylvania, Ann Arbor, 2001).
Smith 1998: R. R. R. Smith, 'Cultural choice and political identity in honorific portrait statues in the Greek East in the second century AD', *JRS* 88 (1998), 56–93.

Staveley 1972: E. S. Staveley, *Greek and Roman Voting and Elections* (London, 1972).
Svoronos 1898: I. N. Svoronos, 'Περί των Εισιτηρίων των Αρχαίων. Μέρος Α΄ Εισιτήρια του Λυκούργειου Διονυσιακού Θεάτρου και της Κλεισθενείου Εκκλησίας των Αθηναίων', *JIAN* 1 (1898), 37–84.
Svoronos 1900: I. N. Svoronos, 'Κατάλογος των Μολύβδινων Συμβόλων του Εθνικού Νομισματικού Μουσείου', *JIAN* 3 (1900), 322–43.
Svoronos 1923–26: I. N. Svoronos, *Les Monnaies d'Athenes* (Munich, 1923–1926).
Swain 1996: S. Swain, *Hellenism and Empire. Language, Classicism and Power in the Greek World AD 50-250* (Oxford, 1996).
Thompson 1954: M. Thompson, *The Athenian Agora II: Coins: From the Roman through the Venetian Period* (Princeton, 1954).
Thompson and Wycherley 1972: H. A. Thompson and R. E. Wycherley, *The Athenian Agora XIV: The History, Shape and Uses of an Ancient City Center* (Princeton, 1972).
Veyne 1990: P. Veyne, *Bread and Circuses. Historical Sociology and Political Pluralism* (translated by B. Pearce) (London, 1990).
Waddington, Babelon and Reinach 1904–1912: W. Waddington, E. Babelon and T. Reinach, *Recueil général des monnaies grecques d'Asie Mineure* (Paris, 1904–1912).
Wankel 1979: H. Wankel, *Die Inschriften von Ephesos Teil 1.A. Inschriften Griechischer Städte aus Kleinasien, Band 11.1* (Bonn, 1979).
Wartenberg and Amandry (eds.) 2015: U. Wartenberg and M. Amandry (eds.) *KAIROS. Contributions to Numismatics in Honor of Basil Demetriadi* (New York, 2015).
Whitehead 1986: D. Whitehead, *The Demes of Attica, 508/7-ca. 250 BC* (Princeton, 1986).
Whitmarsh 2013: T. Whitmarsh (ed.), *Beyond the Second Sophistic: Adventures in Greek Postclassicism* (Berkeley, 2013).
Woloch 1969: M. Woloch, 'Four leading families in Roman Athens (AD 96-191)', *Historia* 18 (1969), 503–10.
Young 1951: R. S. Young, 'An industrial district of Ancient Athens', *Hesperia* 20 (1951), 135–288.

USING AND REUSING TOKENS: SOME REMARKS ABOUT CHRISTIAN GRAFFITI ON CONTORNIATES[1]

CRISTIAN MONDELLO

Introduction

In 1943 András (Andreas) Alföldi asserted that 'Vielleicht gibt es in dem ganzen, mächtig großen Gebiet der antiken Numismatik keine einzige Gruppe von Prägungen, die für die politisch-historischen, religiösen, künstlerischen und geistesgeschichtlichen Probleme ihrer Zeit so viel zu sagen haben wie die spätrömischen Medaillons, welche die italienischen Humanisten nach der an ihrem Rande umlaufenden Furche (*contorno*) 'Kontorniaten' genannt hatten'.[2]

Named after their turned-up edges, contorniates are bronze medallions produced – perhaps only in Rome – from the mid-fourth to the late fifth century AD. Both struck and cast, contorniates bear a great variety of depictions with a high proportion of subjects related to the games and the circus. However, the thematic connection between the obverses and reverses, as well as the function, authority and context of these specimens is far from clear. According to Alföldi, contorniates were distributed as *Propagandamittel* at the New Year festival games by the Roman senatorial aristocracy as an act of opposition to the intolerance and the new ideology of the Christian regime. This idea was supported by various depictions on the contorniates (e.g. Roman emperors, Graeco-Roman deities, some figures of writers) interpreted by the Hungarian scholar as 'pagan' symbols, which were chosen by those responsible for the production in order to promote paganism and evoke the happiness of the 'good old days'.[3] Although the idea enjoyed tremendous popularity in parallel with the 'conflict model' of understanding relations between pagans and Christians in this period, Alföldi's interpretation has been harshly criticised in recent decades. These criticisms highlight the lack of empirical evidence to support the connection of these specimens with the New Year festival, as well as the lack of evidence as to their value as a propaganda instrument of the 'pagan reaction'.[4]

The purpose of this contribution is to analyse a series of largely neglected graffiti on the contorniates related to Christian imagery, which are portrayed on some specimens alongside the multi-faceted Graeco-Roman iconographic repertoire. As opposed to Alföldi's thesis, these motifs allow us see the use and reuse of contorniates, whose function continues to defy comprehension despite the rich scientific literature on the subject.

In this paper, I will examine the typology, technique and style of the Christian and Graeco-Roman graffiti occurring on contorniates, and I will discuss the problem of identifying those responsible for their execution as well as their possible chronology. I will then conduct an iconographic analysis of Christian graffiti by considering the meaning of the symbols represented in the broader context of Roman late antique material culture; on the basis of the evidence, I will suggest a possible interpretation of the graffiti depicted on contorniates. Finally, an appendix including the specimens bearing Christian graffiti will be provided at the end of the contribution.[5]

Christian and Graeco-Roman graffiti on contorniates

Christian graffiti reproducing the Chi Rho and Chi monograms as well as the cross are placed on the surface of a certain number of contorniates, generally in small dimensions next to the main types.

[1] I wish to thank the editorial board of this volume and the anonymous reviewer for providing helpful suggestions and references. In addition, special thanks to Clare Rowan for patiently responding to questions on scientific and practical aspects of the text preparation and the matter of obtaining and using illustrations, respectively.

[2] Alföldi (1942–1943), 3: 'Perhaps there is no group of coins within the whole, mighty field of ancient numismatics which has so much to contribute to the political-historical, religious, artistic and ideological problems of their time as the late antique medallions which were called 'contorniates' by the Italian humanists according to their circular hollow [*contorno*]'.

[3] Alföldi's thesis, supported in 1942–1943 in his first publication on the contorniates, was reaffirmed without any significant changes in the larger and updated work on the contorniates, which was published in two volumes at a later time by the Hungarian scholar and, after his death in 1981, by his wife: see Alföldi and Alföldi (1976); Alföldi and Alföldi (1990), 25–63.

[4] A severe reassessment of Alföldi's interpretation was already made by Toynbee (1945), 115–21. For the reaction of the scientific community to Alföldi's thesis more recently see Mittag (2015), 259–68.

[5] In discussing the contorniate specimens, this paper takes into account the most recent classification of the series of contorniates proposed by Mittag (1999), while reference to single specimens is related to the catalogues of Alföldi and Alföldi (1976) and Alföldi and Alföldi (1990).

Fig. 1: Æ contorniate (inv. no. 35727/66) (Ø 34mm, 20g) (Appendix no. 3) (courtesy of the Museo Nazionale Archeologico di Firenze).

Fig. 2: Æ contorniate (Ø 40mm, 19.64g) (Appendix no. 4) (courtesy of CGB Numismatique Paris) (https://www.cgb.fr/trajan-medaillon-contorniate-b-,brm_328725,a.html) (accessed 21/05/2019).

The Chi Rho appears four times on the so-called 'regular' contorniates (AD 355/360–395/423), alongside the portrait of the Roman emperor on the obverse (Nero, Vespasian, Trajan) (Appendix 1–4, figs. 1–2). The Chi monogram, combined upside down with the PE monogram below a racehorse and on the right of a palm branch, is scratched on the reverse of a specimen probably attributable to the so-called 'Graviert/Eingelegt' series (Appendix 5, fig. 3). The cross, in both Greek and Latin variants, is depicted on 12 pieces of the 'regular' contorniates, in combination with the types of Alexander the Great, Olympias/Omphale, the Roman emperor (Nero, Vespasian, Trajan, Caracalla) (Appendix 6–14, figs. 4–6), and one or two charioteers on the obverse (Appendix 18–20, fig. 7). The cross also occurs three times on the so-called 'Kaiserserie' (AD 379–472), where it is represented as a small-sized symbol beside or sometimes over the portrait of the Roman emperor (Honorius, Theodosius II, Valentinian III) (Appendix 15–17).

Furthermore, Christian graffiti also occur on the contorniates as the main iconography, occupying the whole field on one of the two sides. A Chi Rho monogram surrounded by a double circle is engraved on the reverse of one of the 'regular' contorniates; on the obverse, the bust of Alexander the Great is accompanied, in right field, by an incuse solar symbol, at the centre of which is the letter S (Appendix 21, fig. 8). A Chi Rho with a tiny circle in the middle, surrounded in turn by a larger circle, is engraved on one side of a specimen, while on the other side is a spiral surrounded by five palm branches (Appendix 22, fig. 9).

Fig. 3: Æ contorniate (Ø 37mm, 25.86g) (Appendix no. 5) (Gemini Numismatic Auctions, Auction 5, 6 January 2009, lot no. 863).

The interpretation of Christian graffiti occasionally appearing on contorniates raises the issue of the dating as well as the

Fig. 4: Æ contorniate (inv. no. MACBo 15365) (Ø 36.5mm, 23.75g) (Appendix no. 9) (courtesy of the Museo Civico Archeologico di Bologna).

Fig. 5: Æ contorniate (inv. no. MACBo 15388) (Ø 38.5mm, 24g) (Appendix no. 11) (courtesy of the Museo Civico Archeologico di Bologna).

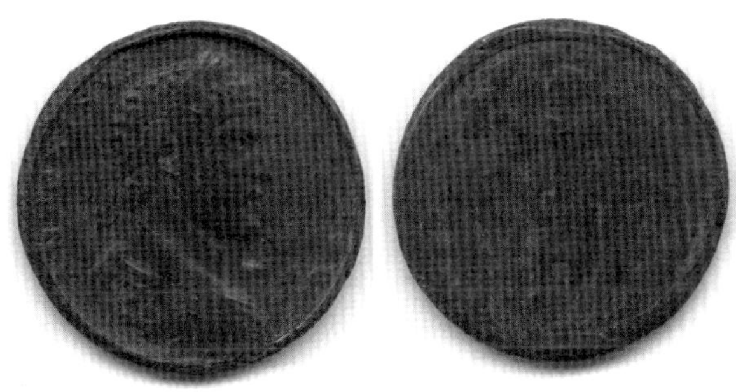

Fig. 6: Æ contorniate (inv. no. MACBo 15421) (Ø 37.5mm, 24.65g) (Appendix no. 14) (courtesy of the Museo Civico Archeologico di Bologna).

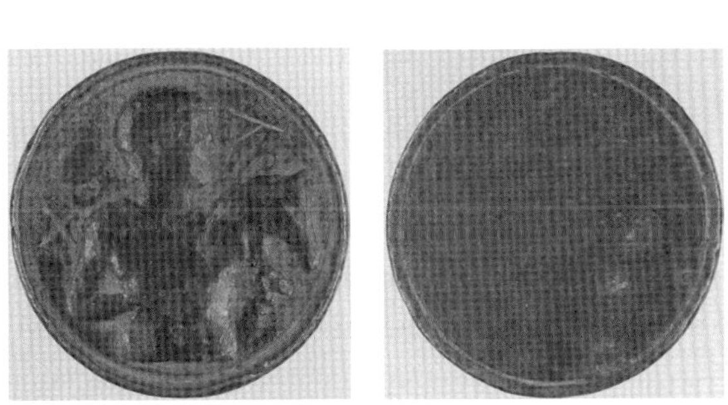

Fig. 7: Æ contorniate (inv. no. MAN 2011/101/61) (Ø 36mm, 25.33g) (Appendix no. 18) (courtesy of the Museo Arqueológico Nacional de Madrid).

authenticity of these signs, due to the fact that they were included on the surface of the specimens only after their striking. This question must be considered in the broader framework of small-sized additional symbols belonging to the Graeco-Roman tradition, which are frequently engraved on one or both sides of contorniates alongside the main images. These motifs were analysed by Sheila Campbell and Elizabeth Alföldi-Rosenbaum in the second volume of *Die Kontorniat-Medaillons* (1990), which was published after the death of A. Alföldi.[6] The classification of additional symbols on the contorniates was made – taking into account the notes of A. Alföldi – according to the type and its occurrences, the techniques used, and drawings for each subject were provided. However, many symbols were not included, some drawings are missing and, generally, the interpretation needs updating on the basis of new specimens which have appeared in the last thirty years.

The overall revision of the 'Die Beizeichen der Kontorniaten' section of Campbell – Alföldi-Rosenbaum has demonstrated the following numerical distribution concerning the more frequent additional symbols on the contorniates (I–VI), which are distinguished according to their typology and technique (table 1).

Table 1: Frequent additional symbols on contorniates (revised and updated from Alföldi and Alföldi (1990)).

	Engraved	*Scratched*	*Stippled*	*Inlaid*	*Traces visible*	*Erased*	*Other*	*Total*
(I.) Palm branch	589	23	1	• Ag: 57 • Uncertain: 5	1	41	8	**725**
(II.) Monogram PE	531	18	9	• Ag: 62 • Au/Ag: 1 • Cu: 1 • Brass: 1 • Uncertain: 5	5	18	8	**659**
(III.) Leaf	52	1	7	• Ag: 21 • Brass: 1 • Uncertain: 2		1		**85**
(IV.) Cross	11	2		• Ag: 2				**15**
(V.) Swastika	2			• Ag: 1				**3**
(VI.) Solar symbol	23			• Ag: 3			4	**30**

Table 2 summarises the distribution of occasional symbols, which were grouped within a single entry (VII) by Campbell and Alföldi-Rosenbaum,[7] as well as those that were intentionally eradicated (VIII), whose morphology could not be identified.

This shows that the most recurring additional symbols on the contorniates are the palm branch, represented on 725 pieces, and the PE monogram, portrayed on 659 specimens. The next frequent are the leaf (85), a solar symbol (30), the cross (15), animals (9), while the Chi Rho as a symbol is documented on six specimens. Moreover, on a large amount of pieces there are various motifs currently unclassified (ca. 100 types) reproducing letters, names, flowers, fruits, objects and other signs that are difficult to interpret.

The morphology, technique and style of these graffiti are not uniform: some symbols are engraved, scratched or stippled, either carefully or approximately (figs. 10a–d). Many others are carried out by expert hands or by professional tools (figs. 10e–h). On many specimens, these small-sized motifs are inlaid with different metals (figs. 10i–l). The silver inlay in the form of a palm branch is documented on at least 57 pieces. The PE monogram appears variously inlaid in silver (62), gold and silver (1), copper (1), brass (1), and in an unspecified metal (5); the leaf is inlaid in silver (21), brass (1), or another metal (2); in addition, metal inlays are used to adorn even the rarest types, such as the solar symbol (3), the swastika (1),

[6] The chapter is entitled 'Die Beizeichen der Kontorniaten', in Alföldi and Alföldi (1990), 241–353.

[7] For specimens carrying the Chi Rho (A.) design, I have included new pieces that have been published since the analysis of Campbell and Alföldi-Rosenbaum. This includes the Chi Rho as a small sized symbol and as a main type. For all other types the numbers represented are those published in Alföldi and Alföldi (1976).

Table 2: Occasional additional symbols on contorniates (revised and updated from Alföldi and Alföldi (1990).

(VII.)	Occasional symbols:	*Engraved*	*Scratched*	*Stippled*	*Inlaid*	*Traces visible*	*Erased*	*Other*	*Total*
(A.)	Chi Rho	4	2						**6**
(B.)	Trident	1			• Ag: 1				**2**
(C.)	Millet	2							**2**
(D.)	Caduceus	3							**3**
(E.)	Phallus	1							**1**
(F.)	Amphora or Kantharos	1							**1**
(G.)	Laurel wreath				• Ag: 1				**1**
(H.)	V or globule	1							**1**
(I.)	Victoria with palm branch	2							**2**
(K.)	Amor with wreath	1							**1**
(L.)	Sol				• Ag: 1				**1**
(M.)	Animals	7			• Ag: 2				**9**
(N.)	Varia								***c.*100**
(VIII.)	**Eradicated symbols**						236		**236**

and the trident (1). In certain cases, the metal insert originally applied to the surface of specimens has undoubtedly fallen out.[8]

The techniques used and the differences in quality imply that these graffiti were created after the striking or casting process. Who added these additional symbols and when? Although the data is small, some observations can be made. In the case of those symbols roughly punched onto the surface, whose design and outlines are rudimentary or strongly irregular, it can be argued that they were the work of inexperienced individuals. In other cases, the high technical and graphic execution of the additional motifs, as well as the insertion of metal inlays, imply the work of specialists with professional skills. In this sense, the evidence agrees with Mittag's idea that the authors of these graffiti should be distinguished into two different groups: private persons and specialised artisans.[9] In the former it is possible to recognise the temporary owners of the specimens, who – for reasons to be established – clumsily reproduced graffiti mostly by hand or using a punch and a hammer.[10] It is much more complex to evaluate those responsible for the high quality symbols, because of the difficulty of establishing the presence of craftsmen and private workshops in the city of Rome in the second half of the fourth century, when contorniate production started. Even though the existence of private mints in Rome at this time has been denied,[11] these additional symbols seem to testify at least to the presence of trained and experienced artisans working on coins and coin-like objects, although it is not easy to say whether this happened within private workshops or the Roman mint. On the other hand, it is hard to believe that these small-sized secondary symbols, placed on low value and unofficial issues, could be commissioned from the official mint of Rome by private individuals. The variety of the designs and the style of the symbols added by both untrained and skilled hands on

[8] See Alföldi and Alföldi (1990), 241.

[9] Mittag (1999), 172.

[10] The hypothesis that the temporary owners of contorniates added such graffiti on their own or commissioned them from professional craftsmen is corroborated by the presence, on some specimens, of letters or names that are engraved, scratched, or in some cases inlaid in silver or another metal: e.g. see Alföldi and Alföldi (1976), cat. no. 114, 2 (CHRYSOPOLVS), cat. no. 223, 2 (CALVO), cat. no. 307, 4 (CAL-PVRNI), cat. no. 360, 28 (NAT[a]L[is]?), cat. no. 381, 13 (BICTORINVS).

[11] Thus, Holden (2008), 124, with regard to the location of contorniate production, today largely ascribed to the official Roman mint which continued to operate during the fourth century under the supervision of the *Comes sacrarum largitionum*, even though Rome had ceased to be the locus of the imperial court. However, poor quality and recurring inconsistencies on the contorniates (e.g. incongruous obverse-reverse combinations, frequent errors in titular legends) could suggest that the production of the series was made most likely by private *officinae*. For this possibility see Mittag (1999), 213–14; Sánchez Vendramini (2013), 94–95.

contorniates seem to exclude the possibility that their realisation was executed in a single context.

However, graffiti added on tokens as something 'mass-produced' are attested on a series of brass Roman *tesserae*. A token kept in the Ashmolean Museum bears a male portrait surrounded by the legend C. MITREIVS L. F. MAG. IVVENT (*'Gaius Mitreius, son of Lucius, master of the youth')* on the obverse, and the depiction of a two-storey basilica on the reverse, which is supplemented by the incised numeral X in the exergue.[12] The legend on the building – L. SEXTILI· S(*uo*) P(*ecunia*) (*'Lucius Sextilius, at his own expense')* – indicates that the basilica was financed by a certain L. Sextilius. Other similar specimens belonging to the same series carry the numbers IIII and VIIII incised in the exergue, and the building on the reverse varies on different examples. This suggests that the attribution of a certain value or meaning (that is, that indicated by the Roman numeral) to this series of brass tokens occurred after they were struck, probably to simplify their manufacture.[13] Graffiti also occur on official Roman coins that were transformed into *tesserae* in antiquity by erasing their reverses and engraving Roman numerals on the surface instead, often in a very crude style. These specimens probably served as an imitation, made by private individuals, of the *tesserae* with numerals belonging to the Julio-Claudian period (27 BC–AD 68).[14]

How can these graffiti be dated? The practice of countermarking is well attested on Roman coins. The only guarantee that this operation was not carried out in modern times are the specimens found in excavation, although, even in this case, the lack of contextual data can affect our knowledge of the precise moment in which the engraving took place. For the contorniates – for which we usually do not have contextual data – the only observations that can be made are from the analysis of the pieces themselves. From such an analysis it is clear that additional symbols can be added multiple times. For example, on the obverse of the same specimen there are often two different palm branches, made by different hands and with non-uniform techniques (engraving, scratching, silver inlay), and this implies different moments for their execution.[15] Two identical types (e.g. two crosses or two PE monograms), apparently made by the same person, may be found on the same piece,[16] as well as two different symbols (a heart-shaped leaf and a PE monogram) distinguished by an heterogeneous style, probably added at two different times.[17] There is also the case of symbols being placed over previous motifs, which have been partially erased: this occurs for the palm branch engraved over the PE monogram and vice versa.[18] In addition, about 236 eradicated symbols, not replaced by further motifs, are attested on the contorniates published by A. Alföldi and Elizabeth Alföldi-Rosenbaum.[19]

In regard to the Christian graffiti, the Chi Rho and Chi monograms were both engraved or scratched on the surface, next to the main iconography, after the striking of the pieces. The cross, as well as being engraved and scratched, is also inlaid with silver in two cases. However, the Chi Rho that appears as the main type on the reverse of a contorniate (Appendix 21, fig. 8) is almost certainly a countermark made with a burin (or another professional instrument). Before the application of the countermark the original design was erased and the surface smoothed: indeed, according to Alföldi's catalogue, the specimen is part of the series showing Alexander the Great (XI, no. 40), whose reverse was originally occupied by a race scene in the Circus Maximus. For Alföldi's specimen no. 287, 2, portrayed on plate 121, 3 (Appendix 3, fig. 1), it is not possible to say if the Chi Rho and the letter A were engraved at the same time, as proposed by Guarducci, who interpreted the

[12] Oxford, Ashmolean Museum, 20mm, 3.58g. Rostovtzeff (1905), 60.

[13] For a discussion of this series of brass Roman tokens see Rowan (2017). See also Küter's contribution in this volume. Brass is often held to be an imperial reserve – see e.g. Martini (1999), 13 – but the use of this material for the production of these *tesserae* as well as tokens with numerals bearing imperial portraits does not exclude private use.

[14] See Mondello (2018).

[15] Alföldi and Alföldi (1976), cat. no. 34, pl. 12, 3, cat. no. 79, 3, pl. 27, 3, cat. no. 181, 4, pl. 67, 1, cat. no. 230, 4, pl. 94, 4, cat. no. 250, 4, pl. 108, 12.

[16] Alföldi and Alföldi (1976), cat. no. 457, 2, pl. 187, 7, cat. no. 640, pl. 205, 1.

[17] Alföldi and Alföldi (1976), cat. no. 345, 16, pl. 141, 1.

[18] Alföldi and Alföldi (1976), cat. no. 118, 2, pl. 40, 2, cat. no. 121, 1, pl. 40, 10, cat. no. 346, 1, pl. 141, 4, cat. no. 360, 29, pl. 149, 1.

[19] Alföldi and Alföldi (1990), 341–53.

Fig. 8: Æ contorniate (inv. no. Ctn.Rom.Imp.3) (Ø 40mm, 23.35g) (Appendix no. 21) (courtesy of the Biblioteca Apostolica Vaticana).

Fig. 9: Æ contorniate (30.39g) (Appendix no. 22) (Paul-Francis Jacquier Numismatique Antique, Auction 39, 12 September 2014, lot no. 812).

association of these two graffiti as an expression of 'Christ-Life':[20] the letter A is in fact engraved on contorniates alone or, in some cases, in connection with other symbols or letters.[21] The only Chi Rho depicted as an original type, not as an additional symbol, is probably the one represented on a specimen whose two sides are exclusively occupied by engraved iconographies (Appendix 22, fig. 9): this specimen may be attributed to the series of engraved and inlaid contorniates which, according to Mittag, may have been produced in the Rhine and Danubian areas in the fourth century.[22]

From this overview, it is likely that the additional symbols were, in most cases, engraved by the recipients of the contorniates not long after production. This is suggested by various clues: the graffiti are always placed on the obverse, and they are attested on a high proportion of specimens with different provenances; the PE monogram is even occasionally embossed (e.g. Appendix 20), and this suggests it belonged to the original iconographic repertoire of the contorniates;[23] lastly – as will be explained below – the motifs reproduced on the surface of the contorniates frequently occur also on other Roman and late Roman artefacts. Overall these data are noteworthy and cannot be considered accidental: engraving graffiti on contorniates appears as a uniform practice in its contents and general character, which was spread within the same social and cultural atmosphere, probably in the last centuries of the Roman Empire.[24]

[20] Guarducci (1958), vol. 1, 450–51.
[21] See e.g. Alföldi and Alföldi (1976), cat. no. 122, 2, pl. 41, 2, cat. no. 180, 16, pl. 66, 8, cat. no. 199, 27, pl. 76, 5, cat. no. 223, 2, pl. 89, 9, cat. no. 496, 1, pl. 195, 11.
[22] Mittag (1999), 33, 180.
[23] Thus, with regard to the PE monogram on contorniates, Guarducci (1958), vol. 1, 426 noted that it appeared embossed in some cases and was therefore certainly contemporary with the striking or casting process ('[…] in alcuni casi ci appare a rilievo, ed è quindi certamente contemporaneo al conio o alla fusione'). For other specimens see: Alföldi and Alföldi (1976), cat. no. 87, 3, pl. 29, 6, cat. no. 231, pl. 94, 5, cat. no. 344, 7, pl. 139, 8.
[24] For these same reasons, the antiquity of the metal inlays – used almost exclusively for additional symbols on the obverses, and on contorniates with various origins – is plausible, although this can only be determined by an in-depth technical analysis.

Symbols of Christian faith and contorniates: an interpretation

The role played by the additional symbols on the contorniates has not been particularly defined, unlike the possible meaning of specific motifs (such as, for example, the PE monogram). This aspect should be examined in terms of the iconographic repertoire as well as the function of contorniates.

The graffiti – engraved on several of the struck, cast and engraved/inlaid series – have generally been interpreted as apotropaic signs and omens of good luck, mainly connected to the context of *ludi* (games) and their attendant *spectacula* (spectacles). The iconography on the contorniates, related to games, the circus and the amphitheatre, mostly allude to this context. Such additional symbols would hence be 'allusions to the victories of favourites, or the prizes [...] which successful competitors had actually received [...]'.[25] Alternatively, they might be explained as 'glückbringende oder übelabwehrende Symbole' ('good luck or apotropaic symbols'),[26] or as attachments 'die übel abwehren und Glück symbolisieren sollten' ('to ward off evil and symbolise happiness'), an interpretation that corresponds with the hypothesis that the contorniates were produced as amulets or auspicious gifts.[27]

Undoubtedly, most of the incised signs reproduce symbols that possess a lucky and propitious value, well documented on many works of art and everyday objects before contorniate production. The palm branch, the laurel wreath, and Victoria with a palm branch, refer to the notion of victory and the desire for victory, as is commonly represented in Greek and Roman imagery. The personification of Victoria also occurs on bronze tokens with Roman numerals (where she is shown frontally or in a *quadriga* as an Augustan or 'imperial' symbol) as well as on coins, militaria and other objects.[28] The solar symbol and the swastika can be interpreted as favourable symbols communicating happiness,[29] as well as the leaves, which are often depicted with this meaning on mosaics, door thresholds, coins, *tabulae lusoriae* (gaming boards), and funerary inscriptions.[30] An apotropaic value (not only a religious or ornamental significance) can be recognised in Dionysian attributes such as grapes, ivy, and the kantharos, which are all images that also appear with this meaning on gems and intaglios.[31] Moreover, some of the obverses of the earlier imperial bronze tokens with Roman numerals often bear Dionysiac imagery. Types include Dionysus, the bust of a maenad with bare breasts holding a thyrsus or carrying a kantharos, as well as Silenus riding a donkey or a mule.[32]

The PE monogram, formed by the ligature of the letters P and E or P and F, has not yet been fully clarified, despite intense scientific research since the seventeenth century. Variously resolved as *palma emerita*, *praemia emerita*, *palma et laurus*, *palma feliciter*, or *praemiis feliciter remunerabimur*, the monogram too would invoke victory, more precisely that one was victorious in agonistic and sporting competitions. Use of the monogram is documented – well before the contorniates – on the so-called proto-contorniates (first century BC – fourth

---

On the traces of gilding on the contorniates, Mittag (1999), 178, believes it is conceivable that contorniates were inlaid with gold in antiquity ('Grundsätzlich ist des denkbar, daß in der Antike einige Kontorniaten vergoldet wurden').

[25] Thus, Toynbee (1945), 120, who explained the contorniates as mementoes, reminiscences, luck-bringing gifts distributed during games, shows, performances, and ceremonies of all kinds. The preponderance of the subjects connected to the games has frequently led scholars to link the function of the contorniates to the *ludi* and their attendant entertainments, variously as awards for winners in the games (Morellius (1695), 45), as *tesserae* to enter the games (Pinkerton (1784), 100–05), as mementoes for the public attending the games (Haverkamp (1722), 158; Robert (1882), 97–135, 364–92), or as chips for table games (Gnecchi (1895), 31–51, 277–306; King (1871), 210–18; Toynbee (1986²), 235).

[26] Alföldi and Alföldi (1990), 340. Previously, Alföldi (1942—1943), 36 argued that such apotropaic signs guaranteed that the pieces bearing them were lucky New Year talismans with an anti-Christian function, used by recipients in a version of 'heads or tails'.

[27] Mittag (1999), 178.

[28] See Küter's contribution in this volume.

[29] The *crux gammata* ('swastika'), as well as the solar emblem used in various cultural contexts since the fourth millennium, are assimilated to the cross in Christian epigraphy: see, for instance, Ferrua (1941), 172–73. Nevertheless, given the variety of semantic and religious values the swastika had acquired, it cannot be considered as a definitive Christian sign, and consequently it is excluded here from the series of Christian graffiti.

[30] Mittag (1999), 177.

[31] Alföldi and Alföldi (1990), 340. For example, see the two intaglios decorated with grapes published by Mastrocinque (2014), 210–11, nos. 591–92. See also Mastrocinque (2014), 142, no. 373.

[32] See Küter's contribution in this volume. This bust on bronze tokens with Roman numerals has been identified as Drusilla by Cohen (1892), 262, 2, or Apollo (see Classical Numismatic Group, Auction 69, 8 June 2005, lot no. 1518).

Fig. 10a: Æ contorniate (Ø 40.5mm, 25.13g, 12h) (Classical Numismatic Group, Electronic Auction 401, 12 July 2017, lot no. 570) (scale 2:1).

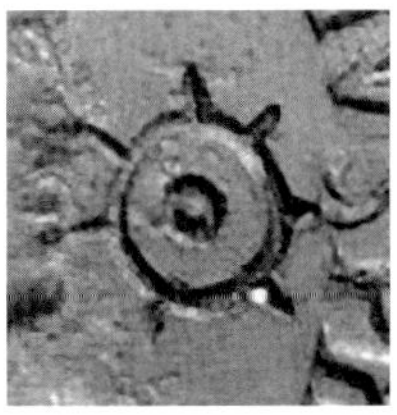

Fig. 10b: Æ contorniate (49.81g) (Numismatica Ars Classica, Auction 72, 16 May 2013, lot no. 803) (not to scale).

Fig. 10c: Oricalchum contorniate (Ø 39mm, 23.51g) (Gemini, LLC, Auction 5, 6 January 2009, lot no. 857) (scale 2:1).

Fig. 10d: Æ contorniate (23.43g.) (Jean Elsen & ses Fils S.A., Auction 128, 12 March 2016, lot no. 177) (not to scale).

Fig. 10e: Æ contorniate (30.43g) (Numismatica Genevensis SA, Auction 4, 11 December 2006, lot no. 288) (not to scale).

Fig. 10f: Æ contorniate (25.44g) (Numismatica Ars Classica NAC AG, Zürich, Auction 29, 11 May 2005, lot no. 674) (not to scale).

Fig. 10g: Æ contorniate (Ø 37mm, 22.67g, 7h) (Classical Numismatic Group, Inc., Auction Mail Bid Sale 75, 23 May 2007, lot no. 1151) (scale 2:1).

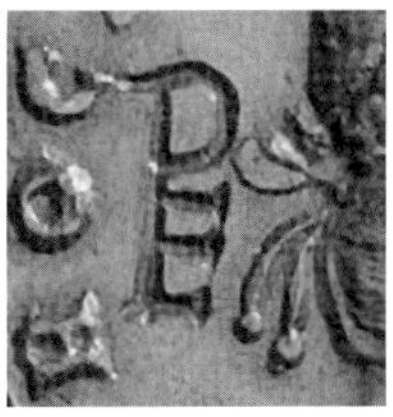

Fig. 10h: Æ contorniate (Ø 41mm, 18.01g) (Numismatica Genevensis SA, Auction 7, 27 November 2012, lot no. 339) (scale 2:1).

Fig. 10i: Æ contorniate (Ø 36mm, 24.81g, 12h) (Classical Numismatic Group, Inc., Auction Triton IX, 9 January 2006, lot no. 1606) (Scale 2:1).

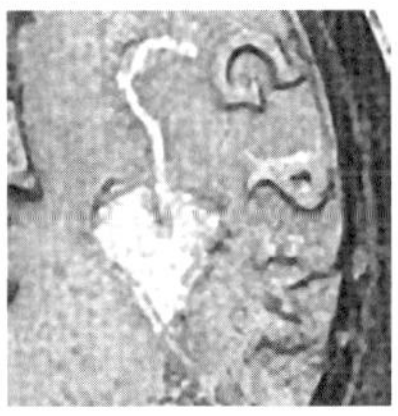

Fig. 10j: Oricalchum contorniate (Ø 39mm, 26.18g) (Gemini, LLC, Auction V, 6 January 2009, lot no. 854) (scale 2:1).

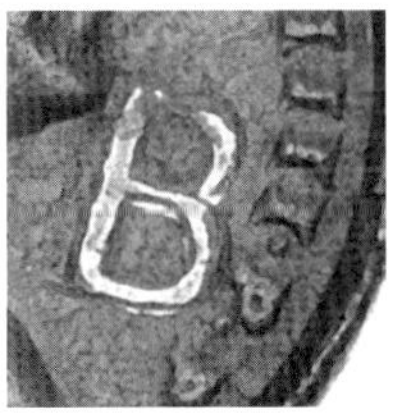

Fig. 10k: Æ contorniate (Ø 39mm, 23.68g, 6h) (Classical Numismatic Group, Inc., Auction Triton XVI, 8 January 2013, lot no. 1209) (scale 2:1).

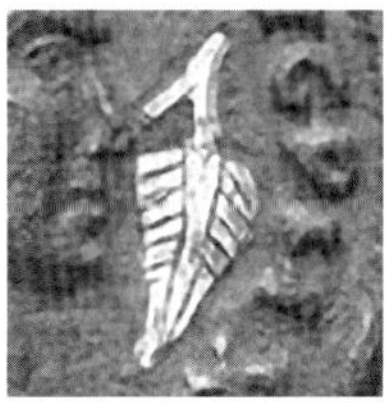

Fig. 10l: Æ contorniate (Ø 42mm, 39.03g, 6h) (Roma Numismatics Limited, Auction E-Sale 8, 31 May 2014, lot no. 862) (scale 2:1).

century AD?), inscriptions, *tabulae lusoriae* and *instrumenta domestica* (domestic implements).[33] Not all the graffiti on contorniates refer to this propitious semantic field: letters, names and monograms of various kinds seem rather to express a sense of property, that is, ownership of the specimens on which they were engraved.

It is noteworthy that signs relating to the symbolism and iconographic language of early Christians also appear in this context. Although the Chi Rho and Chi monograms (often inscribed in a circle) constitute well-attested Christograms in late antiquity, we cannot state that the cross had a Christian meaning in all cases given the plurality of religious and non-religious contexts in which it was employed.[34] It is probably to be identified as a Christian emblem on the obverse of a contorniate of the 'Kaiserserie', which bears two Latin crosses inlaid with silver on either side of a portrait of the eastern Roman emperor Theodosius II (AD 408–450) (Appendix 16), which lend the piece a particular religious and decorative connotation. Moreover, the Christian cross occurs embossed on contorniates in at least two cases: a specimen with the bust of Nero accompanied by the legend IMP NERO CAESAR AVG PMX on the obverse and a long cross surrounded by the incuse inscription LVBIANVS V-ELENI VIVA on the reverse,[35] and on an obverse type, documented by two pieces, which shows the pearl-diademed bust of Majorian (AD 457–461), wearing a *toga triumphalis*, holding a *mappa* in his raised right hand and a sceptre surmounted by the *globus cruciger* (cross-bearing orb) in his left.[36]

How can we explain the presence of Christian signs on contorniates, whose imagery reveals a traditional, polytheistic milieu? It is necessary to make allowances for the social, religious, and political transformation that affected Roman society before and during the period of contorniate production, which began in the middle of the fourth century and continued until the AD 470s. If the struggle between 'pagans' and Christians characterised the intellectual, political and legislative arena, the forty-year period after Julian's death also continued to be an uninterrupted era of religious and cultural syncretism, in which different groups ('pagans', Christians, and Jews) interacted in a variety of spheres. There was conflict on occasion, but also competition and, above all, coexistence. This is evidenced, inter alia, by the process of 'hellenisation' of Christianity throughout the imperial age as well as, in turn, the syncretistic attempts by the Graeco-Roman world to absorb the figure and religion of Christ. Late Roman mosaics from villas in Roman Britain (Hinton St Mary and Frampton) represent the Chi Rho and various components of Christian and Gnostic imagery within iconographic plans that include depictions of other gods, mythological scenes and symbols belonging to Graeco-Roman tradition.[37]

The name of Christ is often invoked in magical Greek papyri, in the *phylakteria* and is assimilated to Egyptian deities (Horus and Harpocrates) on late Roman Egyptian gems, demonstrating syncretistic popular piety.[38] The relations between Christianity and polytheistic cults outside of inflexible official positions in late antiquity suggest a two-way exchange with reciprocal social and religious assimilation, which cannot solely be explained by the once-dominant notion of overt pagan-Christian conflict.[39]

From the fourth century AD the cross and Chi Rho were not only signs of religious identity, but, with the gradual change introduced by Constantine, they were suggestive of victory and became an icon of political power and the successful face of the Church. Like the Chi Rho, the image of the cross, a symbol of the triumph of Christianity, is perceived as a powerful relic, a talisman able to heal and protect against demonic forces, and it was found

[33] For a *status quaestionis* about the PE monogram and its meaning see Mittag (1999), 173–77. An overview of the numerous monuments and artefacts carrying the PE monogram is provided by Marrou (1941–1946), 109–31 and Alföldi and Alföldi (1990), 307–12.

[34] In any case, it is reasonable to maintain that in the second half of the fourth century AD the cross was mainly recognised within late Roman society as symbol of Christian religion and the Passion of Christ.

[35] H. P. Hall Sale, Glendining & Co. Ltd., 16—21 November 1950, Part II, lot no. 2144, from the Froehner collection (apparently unpublished in the standard references).

[36] Alföldi and Alföldi (1976), pl. 192, 4; Alföldi and Alföldi (1990), pl. 228, 12.

[37] Smith (1969), 71–125; Perring (2003), 74–83.

[38] Barb (1964), 1–22. On late antique and early Christian gems see Spier (2007).

[39] See, e.g., Cameron (2011); Salzman, Sághy and Lizzi Testa (2016), 1–8.

everywhere: painted on coins, on sarcophagi, on standards and weapons, embroidered on clothes, or tattooed on bodies.[40]

The combination of the cross and the Chi Rho (or other Christian symbols) with the PE monogram is frequent during the fourth and fifth centuries, and this could be significant for understanding the function of these signs. The PE monogram, accompanied by motifs evoking a Christian context, is represented on a number of clay lamps: it appears, for example, surmounted by a cross,[41] or paired with the apocalyptic letters A and Ω.[42] On two funerary epigraphs from the catacomb of Cyriaca, the PE monogram is associated with the *chrismon* and two palms,[43] and is combined with the staurogram or monogrammatic cross, which is flanked by the letters A and Ω.[44] On the fastening in the bricks of a *loculus* in the catacombs of Priscilla, the PE monogram is portrayed to the right of a hooked cross and below two small graffiti interpreted as an amphora and a citron.[45]

One of the most significant documents contemporary with the contorniates is the Roman epitaph of Eleutheria, mother of Pacatianus, dating to the fourth consulate of Julianus and Sallustius (AD 363) (fig. 11).[46] The first nine of the thirteen lines of the inscription (mutilated on the left side) end with a series of symbols – six of which are also depicted on contorniates – in the following order: a palm branch, a wreath of leaves (or a solar symbol), a Chi Rho, a PE monogram, another palm branch, a swastika, a vase (or a tripod), an Omega, a Pythagorean Upsilon. The combination of these signs, which have no textual connection

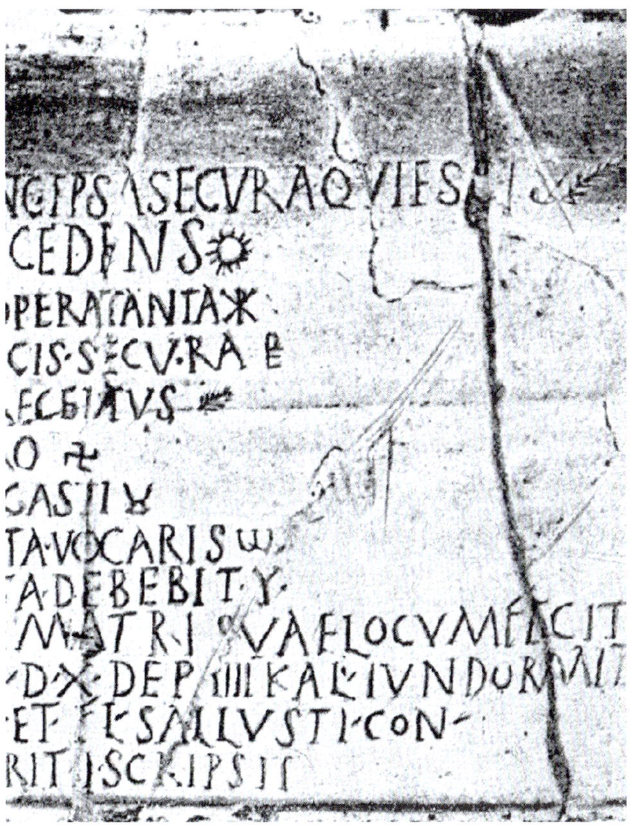

Fig. 11: Epitaph of Eleutheria (AD 363) (Marrou (1941–1946), 117) (courtesy of the École Française de Rome)

[40] On the cross as a symbol of triumph in late antiquity see Filoramo (2011), 393–97.
[41] De Rossi (1888—1891), 85–86.
[42] *Corpus Inscriptionum Latinarum* XV, no. 6767. See also Paleani (1993), cat. no. 4, 6. The PE monogram is engraved along with a palm branch and a Christian monogram on a bronze lamina edited by Pignorius, see Eckhel (1798), vol. 8, 280.
[43] Bruzza (1877), 58–72, pl. FG, no. 22.
[44] Bruzza (1877), 58–72, no. 25.
[45] Wilpert (1906), 16, fig. 4.
[46] Diehl (1924—1931), 3359 (= De Rossi (1857—1861), 159). See de Longpérier (1865), 412–15; Dölger (1929), 299–315.

with the corresponding lines of the funerary epigraph, implies that they were emblems with positive meaning, probably interchangeable, well known at the time of the first period of contorniate production and used outside of games contexts. Additionally, the presence of the PE monogram, associated with the Chi Rho and traditional symbols of victory, reveals that it was also adopted by Christians, who perhaps reinterpreted it as a 'symbole de victoire encore, mais d'une victoire plus noble, celle de l'âme chrétienne, rachetée par le Christ, sur les forces du péché et de la mort'.[47] The symbols represented in the epigraphic field, probably alluding to victory after death, were figuratively integrated into the epitaph at the end of each line, contributing to the portrayal of the deceased Eleutheria as a victorious athlete, a victorious charioteer.[48]

In the late Roman empire, the Christian cross and the Chi Rho communicated the mystery of deliverance and redemption, also gaining an apotropaic and cosmic meaning; they were no longer ignominious symbols (particularly the cross) but universal *signa victoriae* (signs of victory), in line with patristic exegesis from the second to the fifth century.

The fact that contorniates were personalised by their owners by means of engraved crosses, Christian monograms, and more common Graeco-Roman symbols of good omen and victory, might suggest that at least a part of the production was created in order to be used and (at a later stage) reused as charms and gifts with amuletic properties.[49] Because of their typological and morphological features (coin-like objects, large diameter and weight, absence of a mintmark), as well as their imagery, contorniates were likely appropriate presents and special gift medallions. The creation of coin-like amulets and the transformation of ancient coins into talismans (usually pierced and fastened at the neck by way of a *funiculum* or cord) was a rather widespread custom among the Romans.[50] Evidence of similar habits in terms of syncretism and magical use are documented for early Christians by literary sources and some late antique tokens, which present significant parallels to contorniates. For instance, the so-called 'Asina coins', a group of fourth–fifth century AD tokens combine pagan iconography (e.g. Alexander the Great, Hercules-Minerva, Providentia) and epigraphic elements related to Christian religion, and have been interpreted as Christian or Gnostic amulets.[51]

In support of his model of the private production of 'regular' contorniates as amulets, Mittag has argued that some of the subjects on the obverse (Alexander the Great, Apollonius of Tyana, Apuleius) and the reverse (Alexander the Great, Cybele and Attis, the Mother Goddess, Apollo, the Dioscuri, Isis, the Circus Maximus, the victorious charioteer, Pythagoras) would have been interpreted as allusions to magic and apotropaic use, in accordance with the data found in literary sources and papyri.[52] Likewise, the perforation of several specimens – a hole is sometimes made in the centre or at the edge of a contorniate specimen, but also a series of symmetrical holes (numbering from two to six) are found on the flan in some cases – was intended to turn the contorniates into amulets, probably due to the magical function of their iconography.[53] However, the imagery depicted on 'regular' contorniates does not solely communicate magical or theurgical notions. It is also necessary

[47] Marrou (1941–1946), 122: 'A symbol of victory again, but of a nobler victory, that of the Christian soul, redeemed by Christ, over the forces of sin and death'. The depiction of the Chi Rho amongst the symbols accompanying the epitaph suggests that Eleutheria was probably a Christian.

[48] de Longpérier (1865), 415.

[49] The reuse of contorniates for the same purpose is suggested by the erased symbols and the symbols placed over previous graffiti.

[50] E.g. see Perassi (2011a), 223–74.

[51] Thus, Cavedoni (1857), 309–14, pl. VIII. *Contra* Alföldi (1951a), 57–66; Alföldi (1951b), 92–96. Coins reused with an amuletic function within the Christian community of Antioch are mentioned in a sermon of John Chrysostom, who condemns those who 'tie bronze coins of Alexander the Great around their head and feet': John Chrysostom, *Ad illuminandos catechesis* 2, 5 (= *Patrologia Graeca*, 49, 240). Apart from Chrysostom's theological considerations, the disapproval of this custom suggests that a certain number of Christians at that time used amulets and magical *praxeis*; on this point see Kahlos (2016), 162–77; de Bruyn (2017). On the images of Alexander the Great as *portafortuna* in the fourth century Roman West see Historia Augusta, *Triginta Tyranni* 14, 2, 6.

[52] Mittag (1999), 147–71.

[53] The pierced pieces represent 6.63% of struck contorniates and 3.93% of cast specimens: see Mittag (1999) 167–71. On pierced contorniates bearing the types of Alexander the Great see also Fulghum (2001), 139–47. More generally, see Perassi (2011b).

to take into account the preponderance of subjects related to games and the circus, Roman emperors, as well as narratives from early Roman history and Greek myth, in order to understand the function of contorniates.[54] In light of this, it is likely that the contorniates, which can be divided into various subgroups, were given as gifts to a variety of recipients in several contexts, and were multifunctional.

Conclusions

The meaning of Christian graffiti represented on contorniates is probably to be explained in relation to the *Glückssymbolik* ('good luck symbols') that were added after manufacturing. However, it cannot be excluded that these incisions, at least in some cases, were engraved by the temporary owners of the specimens as an expression of personal faith.

The typology of the additional signs from the Graeco-Roman and Christian tradition shows that the iconographic repertoire of contorniates was shared by pagans and Christians alike. In contrast to the anti-Christian function proposed by Alföldi, the coexistence of pagan and Christian imagery on a single object is of great significance in understanding the changing religious atmosphere in this period. Indeed, the evidence of domestic artefacts is increasingly proving that the shift from a pagan to a Christian culture was extremely complex and multifaceted in other social and geographical fields as well, since the Christian impact on late antique material culture was gradual and not immediately visible.[55] Moreover, shaping, appropriating and manipulating traditional symbols of memory and identity is a typical feature of power struggle and ideological and military subjugation.[56]

Christian graffiti on contorniates furnish proof of the reception and circulation of contorniates in Christian environments, perhaps to serve as good luck gifts, not unlike other amulets and prophylactic *instrumenta* that were severely condemned in the fourth and fifth centuries by the Fathers of the Church.

Appendix[57]

Chi Rho / Chi monogram (as a symbol)

1. Obv.: NERO CLAVD CAESAR AVG GER P M TR P IMP P, laureate head of Nero (VI) r.; Chi Rho inside a circle is engraved in l. field.
Rev.: OLYMPI NIKA, charioteer holding whip, driving a *quadriga* r.
References: Alföldi and Alföldi (1976), cat. no. 150, 1, pl. 50, 8 (Milan: Museo Teatrale al Teatro della Scala).

2. Obv.: IMP CAES VESPASIAN AVG COS III, laureate bust of Vespasian (II) r., drapery on left shoulder; a motif, probably a Chi Rho, engraved in r. field.
Rev.: Helmeted Mars Propugnator advancing r., holding standard, shield and resting foot on galley prow.
References: Alföldi and Alföldi (1976), cat. no. 238, 6, pl. 104, 1 (20.67g) (Tübingen: Archäologisches Institut der Universität).

3. Obv.: DIVO NERVAE – TRAIANO AVG, laureate, draped, cuirassed bust of Trajan (VII) r.; symbols engraved on either side, a Chi Rho in l. field, the letter A in r. field.
Rev.: DOM NINVS, charioteer holding whip, driving *quadriga* r.
References: Alföldi and Alföldi (1976), cat. no. 287, 2, pl. 121, 3 (Ø 34mm; 20g) (Florence: Museo Nazionale Archeologico).

[54] See Holden (2008), 123: 'Mittag's conclusions need not invalidate standard interpretations of the contorniates but rather can suggest that the contorniates may not have been exclusively related to games'. In any case, the apotropaic function of the contorniates would have been secondary to their function as tokens given out at games: see Holden (2008), 123, n. 12. On this point, see also the reenactment of Sánchez Vendramini (2013), 95.

[55] Lavan and Mulryan (2011); Salzman, Sághy and Lizzi Testa (2016).

[56] For instance, during the German occupation of the Channel Islands (1940–1945), Guernsey, Jersey and British coins were used and manipulated by both Germans and islanders to proclaim German ownership, military might and power as well as to protest against German appropriation and occupation of the islands: see Carr (2012).

[57] Where the information is available, diameter and weight of the specimens are provided.

4. Obv.: IMP CAES NERVAE TRAIANO OPTIMO AVG GER DAC P M TR P COS V P P, laureate, draped, cuirassed bust of Trajan l., seen from three quarters behind; a Chi Rho engraved in l. field.
Rev.: Bacchus reclining r. in *biga* drawn by panthers l.; to r., Cupid flying l., holding bunch of grapes; to l., Satyr standing r., holding a *pedum*; two maenads in background; in exergue, rhyton, *pedum*, satyr mask, bunch of grapes, Selinus mask, and amphora.
Reference: CGB Numismatique Paris (Ø 40mm, 19.64g).

5. Obv. (?): Charioteer standing facing, holding wreath and whip in extended r. hand and palm in l. hand.
Rev. (?): Racehorse standing l., palm above head; in field below, palm branch and an eradicated, upside down monogram combining PE and X.
Reference: Gemini Numismatic Auctions, Auction 5, 6 January 2009, lot no. 863 (Ø 37mm, 25.86g).

Cross (as a symbol)

6. Obv.: ALEXXAN – DER MAG, bust of Alexander (VIII) r., wearing lion's skin; cross engraved in r. field.
Rev.: Emperor on horseback over a fallen lion.
Reference: Alföldi and Alföldi (1976), cat. no. 23, 9, pl. 211, 3 (31.13g) (Boston: Museum of Fine Arts).

7. Obv.: ALEXA – NDER, bust of Alexander (XI) r., wearing lion's skin over head, its paws knotted on his chest; cross engraved in r. field.
Rev.: Four chariots racing around the *spina* of the Circus Maximus.
Reference: Alföldi and Alföldi (1976), cat. no. 40, 16, pl. 14, 10 (22.49g) (New York: American Numismatic Society).

8. Obv.: No legend, bust of Olympias/Omphale (III) l., with veiled head, holding the sceptre in r. hand. In r. field, a rectangle inlaid in silver, above which is an engraved cross.
Rev.: Hercules fighting a centaur.
References: Alföldi and Alföldi (1976), cat. no. 66, 3, pl. 23, 11 (25.70g) (The Hague: Koninklijk Kabinet van Munten en Penningen, 1967, no. 206).

9. Obv.: NERO CLAVDIVS CAESAR AVG GER P M TR P IMP P P, laureate bust of Nero (II) r.; a cross is engraved over his neck.
Rev.: Bacchus reclining r. in *biga* drawn by panthers l.; to r., Cupid flying l., holding bunch of grapes; to l., Satyr standing r., holding a *pedum*; two maenads in background; in exergue, rhyton, *pedum*, satyr mask, grape bunch, Selinus mask, and amphora.
References: Alföldi and Alföldi (1976), cat. no. 130, 8, pl. 44, 2 (Ø 36.5mm, 23.75g) (Bologna: Museo Civico Archeologico).

10. Obv.: NERO CLADIVS (sic!) CAESAR AVG GER P M TR P IMP P P, laureate bust of Nero (X) r.; cross engraved in r. field.
Rev.: AVRELIANVS, charioteer holding whip, driving *quadriga* r.
References: Alföldi and Alföldi (1976), cat. no. 181, 5, pl. 67, 2 (25.78g) (London: British Museum).

11. Obv.: IMP NERO CAESAR AVG P MAX, laureate bust of Nero (XVI) r.; cross engraved in r. field.
Rev.: Four chariots racing around the *spina* of the Circus Maximus.
References: Alföldi and Alföldi (1976), cat. no. 209, 20, pl. 84, 3 (Ø 38.5mm, 24.00g) (Bologna: Museo Civico Archeologico).

12. Obv.: IMP CAES VESPASIAN AVG COS III, laureate bust of Vespasian (II) r., drapery on left shoulder; cross engraved in r. field.
Rev.: Hunter with a dog attacking a wild boar.
References: Alföldi and Alföldi (1976), cat. no. 242, 4, pl. 105, 4 (25.51g) (Vienna: Bundesslg. von Münzen, Medaillen und Geldzeichen).

13. Obv.: DIVO TRAIA – NO AVGVSTO, laureate, draped, cuirassed bust of Trajan (XXIII) r.; an inclined Latin cross is engraved on his neck.
Rev.: Olympias reclining l. on a *kline*, extending hand to serpent coiled at feet.
References: Alföldi and Alföldi (1976), cat. no. 343, 4, pl. 138, 10 (25.80g) (Vienna: Bundesslg. von Münzen, Medaillen und Geldzeichen).

14. Obv.: ANTONINVS – PIVS AVG, laureate and cuirassed bust of Caracalla (III) r.; in r. field a palm branch is engraved, and perhaps even a cross below.
Rev.: Inexplicable scene ('Augur'?).
References: Alföldi and Alföldi (1976), cat. no. 418, 4, pl. 176, 8 (Ø 37.5mm, 24.65g) (Bologna: Museo Civico Archeologico).

15. Obv.: HONORIO – AVGVSTO, pearl-diademed, draped, cuirassed bust of Honorius (II), r.; in r. field a palm branch is engraved, in l. field a Latin cross.
Rev.: ARTEMI VINCAS INVNDATOR PENNA, charioteer in facing *quadriga*.
References: Alföldi and Alföldi (1976), cat. no. 450, 8, pl. 186, 8 (MMAG Basel).

16. Obv.: D N THEODO – SIVS P F AVG, diademed, draped, cuirassed bust of Theodosius II (II) r.; one Latin cross in r. field and one in l. field, inlaid with silver.
Rev.: BONIFATIVS, charioteer driving *quadriga*, seen from front; on each side of the charioteer there is a circle, inlaid in silver.
References: Alföldi and Alföldi (1976), cat. no. 457, 2, pl. 187, 7 (Serrure, April 1908, 155).

17. Obv.: D N PLA VALENTI – NIANVS P F AVG, diademed, draped, cuirassed bust of Valentinian III (I); in r. field, there is a cross engraved above a previous eradicated symbol.
Rev.: Smoothed; pellet in circle incuse.
References: Alföldi and Alföldi (1976), cat. no. 467, 3, pl. 189, 9 (36.78g) (Columbia, MO: University of Missouri, Museum of Art and Archaeology).

18. Obv.: Half-length figure of charioteer (III) r., seen from front, holding whip in r. hand and race-horse by reins in l. hand; in l. field a helmet, below which is an engraved cross; in r. field, the letter A is incised.
Rev.: Blank or erased.
References: Alföldi and Alföldi (1976), cat. no. 496, 1, pl. 195, 11 (Ø 36mm, 25.33g) (Madrid: Museo Archeológico).

19. Obv.: Half-length figure of charioteer (IX) r., seen from front, holding whip in r. hand and racehorse by reins in l. hand; in l. field an incised cross; in r. field, a palm branch.
Rev.: Blank or erased.
References: Alföldi and Alföldi (1976), cat. no. 515, 1, pl. 201, 5 (29.28g) (London: British Museum).

20. Obv.: Two standing charioteers (X), seen from front; in r. field, there is a PE monogram; in l. field two palm branches, one next to the edge and the other between the two charioteers. These motifs are embossed. In addition, a scratched cross is between the heads of the figures.
Rev.: DOMNINVS IN VENETO; charioteer holding whip, driving *quadriga* r.
References: Alföldi and Alföldi (1976), cat. no. 518, pl. 201, 10 (Milan: Museo Teatrale al Teatro della Scala).

Chi Rho monogram (as a type)

21. Obv.: ALEXA – NDER, bust of Alexander (XI) r., wearing lion's skin over head, its paws knotted on his chest; in r. field an incuse solar symbol, at the centre of which is the letter S.
Rev.: engraved Chi Rho within a double circle.
References: Alföldi and Alföldi (1976), cat. no. 42, pl. 15, 9 (Ø 40mm, 23.35g) (Vatican City: Biblioteca Vaticana, Medagliere).

22. Obv. (?): Spiral (labyrinth?) surrounded by five palm branches.
Rev. (?): Chi Rho with a tiny circle in the middle, surrounded in turn by a circle.
References: Paul-Francis Jacquier Numismatique Antique, Auction 39, 12 September 2014, lot no. 812 (30.39g).

Bibliography

Alföldi 1942–1943: A. Alföldi, *Die Kontorniaten. Ein verkanntes Propagandamittel der stadtrömischen heidnischen Aristokratie in ihrem Kampfe gegen das christliche Kaisertum* (Leipzig, 1942–1943).

Alföldi 1951a: A. Alföldi, 'Asina. Eine dritte Gruppe heidnischer Neujahrsmünzen im spätantiken Rom', *SM* 2 (1951), 57–66.

Alföldi 1951b: A. Alföldi, 'Asina II. Weitere heidnische Neujahrsmünzen aus dem spätantiken Rom', *SM* 2 (1951), 92–96.

Alföldi and Alföldi 1976: A. Alföldi and E. Alföldi, *Die Kontorniat-Medaillons. Teil 1: Katalog* (Berlin, 1976).

Alföldi and Alföldi 1990: A. Alföldi and E. Alföldi, *Die Kontorniat-Medaillons. Teil 2: Text* (Berlin-New York, 1990).
Asirvatham, Pache and Watrous (eds.) 2001: S. R. Asirvatham, C. O. Pache and J. Watrous (eds.), *Between Magic and Religion. Interdisciplinary Studies in Ancient Mediterranean Religion and Society* (Lanham, 2001).
Barb 1964: A. A. Barb, 'Three elusive amulets', *Journal of the Warburg and Courtauld Institutes* 27 (1964), 1–22.
Bruzza 1877. L. Bruzza, 'Della interpretazione del monogramma PE che si trova nei contorniati e nelle iscrizioni', *Annali dell'Istituto di Corrispondenza Archeologica* 49 (1877), 58–72.
Cameron 2011: A. Cameron, *The Last Pagans of Rome* (New York, 2011).
Carr 2012: G. Carr, 'Coins, crests and kings: symbols of identity and resistance in the Occupied Channel Islands', *Journal of Material Culture* 17 (2012), 327–44.
Carr, Swift and Weekes (eds.) 2003: G. Carr, E. Swift and J. Weekes (eds.), *TRAC 2002: Proceedings of the Twelfth Annual Theoretical Archaeology Conference, Canterbury 2002* (Oxford, 2003).
Cavedoni 1857: C. Cavedoni, 'Médailles du temps d'Honorius portant des signes chrétiens mêlés à des types païens', *RN* (1857), 309–14.
Cohen 1892: H. Cohen, *Description historique des monnaies frappées sous l'Empire Romain*, vol. VIII (Paris-London, 1892).
de Bruyn 2017: Th. de Bruyn, *Making Amulets Christian. Artefacts, Scribes, and Contexts* (Oxford, 2017).
de Longpérier 1865: A. de Longpérier, 'Observations sur trois médaillons romains de bronze', *RN* 10 (1865), 401–17.
De Rossi 1857–1861: G. B. De Rossi, *Inscriptiones christianae urbis Romae septimo saeculo antiquiores*, vol. 1 (Rome, 1857–1861).
De Rossi 1888–1891: G. B. De Rossi, *Bullettino di Archeologia Cristiana* 4, VI (1888–1891), 85–86.
Diehl 1924–1931: E. Diehl, *Inscriptiones Latinae Christianae Veteres (ILCV)* (3 vols.) (Berlin, 1924–1931).
Dölger 1929: F. J. Dölger, 'Eine christliche Grabinschrift vom Jahre 363 mit exorzistischen Zeichen als Zeilensicherung', *Antike und Christentum* 1 (1929), 299–315.
Eckhel 1798: J. Eckhel, *Doctrina numorum veterum* (vol. 8) (Vindobonae, 1798).
Ferrua 1941: A. Ferrua, 'Simboli pagani nelle catacombe cristiane', *Roma* 19 (1941), 167–76.
Filoramo 2011: G. Filoramo, *La croce e il potere. I cristiani da martiri a persecutori* (Rome-Bari, 2011).
Fulghum 2001: M. M. Fulghum, 'Coins used as amulets in late antiquity', in Asirvatham, Pache and Watrous (eds.) (2001), 139–47.
Gnecchi 1895: F. Gnecchi, 'Cos'erano i contorniati', *RIN* 8 (1895), 31–51, 277–306.
Guarducci 1958: M. Guarducci, *I graffiti sotto la confessione di San Pietro in Vaticano* (vol. 1) (Città del Vaticano, 1958).
Haverkamp 1722: S. Haverkamp, *Dissertationes de Alexandri Magni numismate et de nummis contorniatis* (Leiden, 1722).
Holden 2008: A. Holden, 'The abduction of the Sabine women in context: the iconography on late antique contorniate medallions', *AJA* 112 (2008), 121–42.
Kahlos 2016: M. Kahlos, '*Artis heu magicis:* the label of magic in fourth-century conflicts and disputes', in Salzman, Sághy and Lizzi Testa (eds.) (2016), 162–77.
King 1881: C. W. King, 'On the true nature of the contorniate medals', *The Archaeological Journal* 28 (1871), 210–18.
Lavan and Mulryan (eds.) 2011: L. Lavan and M. Mulryan (eds.), *The Archaeology of Late Antique 'Paganism'* (Leiden-Boston, 2011).
Marrou 1941–1946: H. I. Marrou, '*Palma* et *laurus*', *Mélanges d'Archéologie et d'Histoire* 58 (1941–1946), 109–31.
Martini 1999: R. Martini, 'Una tessera numerale bronzea con ritratto di Augustus in collezione privata, *Tessera triumphalium* (?): note per una discussione', in *Scritti in ricordo di V. Candellieri. Annotazioni numismatiche*, suppl. 13 (Milan, 1999), 12–15.
Mastrocinque 2014: A. Mastrocinque, *Les intailles magiques du department des Monnaies, Médailles et Antiques* (Paris, 2014).
Mittag 1999: P. F. Mittag, *Alte Köpfe in neuen Händen: Urheber und Funktion der Kontorniaten* (Bonn, 1999).
Mittag 2015: P. F. Mittag, 'Alföldi and the contorniates', in Richardson and Santangelo (eds.) (2015), 259–68.
Mondello 2018: C. Mondello, 'Converting Roman coins into *tesserae*: development and value', *Coins at Warwick Blog* (https://blogs.warwick.ac.uk/numismatics/entry/converting_roman_coins/) (accessed on 21/05/2019).
Morellius 1695: A. Morellius, *Specimen Universae Rei Nummariae Antiquae* (Lipsiae, 1695).
Paleani 1993: M. T. Paleani, *Le lucerne paleocristiane* (Roma, 1993).
Perassi 2011a: C. Perassi, 'Monete amuleto e monete talismano. Fonti scritte, indizi, *realia* per l'età romana', *NAC* 40 (2011), 223–74.
Perassi 2011b: C. Perassi, 'Monete romane forate. Qualche riflessione su «un grand thème européeen» (J.-P. Callu)', *Aevum* 85 (2011), 257–315.
Perring 2003: D. Perring, 'Deconstructing the Frampton pavements: Gnostic dialect in Roman Britain?', in Carr, Swift and Weekes (eds.) (2003), 74–83.
Pinkerton 1784: J. Pinkerton, *Essay on Medals* (London, 1784).
Richardson and Santangelo (eds.) 2015: J. H. Richardson and F. Santangelo (eds.), *Andreas Alföldi in the Twenty-First Century* (Stuttgart, 2015).
Rivet (ed.) 1969: A. L. F. Rivet (ed.), *The Roman Villa in Britain* (London, 1969).

Robert 1882: Ch. Robert, 'Médaillons contorniates', *RBN* 38 (1882), 97–135, 364–92.

Rostovtzeff 1905: M. Rostovtzeff, *Römische Bleitesserae. Ein Beitrag zur Sozial- und Wirtschaftsgeschichte der römischen Kaiserzeit* (Leipzig, 1905).

Rowan 2017: C. Rowan, '*Gaius Mitreius, Magister Iuventutis*, and the materiality of Roman tokens', *Coins at Warwick Blog* (https://blogs.warwick.ac.uk/numismatics/entry/gaius_mitreius_magister/) (accessed 21/05/2019).

Salzman, Sághy and Lizzi Testa 2016: M. Salzman, M. Sághy and R. Lizzi Testa (eds.) *Pagans and Christians in Late Antique Rome. Conflict, Competition, and Coexistence in the Fourth Century* (Cambridge-New York, 2016).

Sánchez Vendramini 2013: D. Sánchez Vendramini, 'Los contorniatos: características, función e importancia', *ÓMNI. Revista Numismática* 6 (2013), 85–96.

Smith 1969: D. J. Smith, 'The mosaic pavements', in Rivet (ed.) (1969), 71–125.

Spier 2007: J. Spier, *Late Antique and Early Christian Gems* (Wiesbaden, 2007).

Toynbee 1945: J. M. C. Toynbee, 'Review of Andreas Alföldi 1942-1943', *JRS* 35 (1945), 115–21.

Toynbee 1986²: J. M. C. Toynbee, *Roman Medallions* (New York, 1986²).

Wilpert 1906: J. Wilpert, *Römische Quartalschrift* 20 (1906), 16.

THE HOLME CULTRAM ABBEY SERIES: ENGLISH MEDIEVAL TOKENS AND A CISTERCIAN USE CASE

KATE RENNICKS

Introduction

English medieval lead tokens are under-researched and poorly understood, particularly outside London. Invariably, before the late Tudor period, they carry no dates or maker's marks and their designs only exceptionally give scope for any narrative beyond bare description.[1] In 2015, 43 lead tokens were recovered during excavation at the Cistercian abbey of Holme Cultram in West Cumbria (table 1). This new series is significant in quantity, rich in its detail and unusually offers the opportunity to pose hypotheses on their usage and function in society. This article considers medieval token finds that have been recorded since the last great review of English tokens[2] and sets the Holme Cultram tokens into a framework of usage, both locally and in the wider monastic context.

Holme Cultram Abbey: A brief historical background

Holme Cultram Abbey is situated on a low plain in the modern village of Abbeytown, between the Solway Firth and the Lake District. It was founded in 1150 by Prince Henry of Scotland, son of King David I, and populated from Melrose. The medieval cartulary was arranged in the 1920s and offers glimpses of a rich development.[3] In the thirteenth and fourteenth centuries, Holme Cultram consolidated much of the west Cumbrian plains within its estates and maintained holdings in Galloway, Newcastle, Hartlepool and Boston in Lincolnshire for the distribution of wool and salt products. Situated within a few miles of the coast and with a daughter house (Grey Abbey) at Strangford Loch in Northern Ireland,[4] the Abbey boasted particularly strong trading links across the Irish Sea communities, enjoying freedom from tolls during the reigns of three Manx Kings.[5]

Much of present-day Cumbria was ceded to Henry II of England in 1157 and the abbey's foundation has been seen as a political manifestation of Scottish control of the western part of the border.[6] Following repeated Scottish raiding, Henry II and Pope Innocent issued penalties for any person that 'troubled the monks'.[7] Robert the Bruce (father of King Robert I) was buried at the abbey in 1294, although this did nothing to stem attacks by his son. Edward I used the abbey as a base for his Scottish campaigns of 1299 and in July 1307 spent his last living night there. Raiding and the threat of violence continued periodically through to its surrender at the Dissolution in 1538.

From an archaeological perspective, Holme Cultram has been largely ignored.[8] The site looks unassuming today and while extant remains are visible above ground (the current village church of Abbeytown has been formed from the original nine bay nave),[9] little now suggests that this abbey was formerly of comparative size and stature to the great Yorkshire abbeys of Fountains and Rievaulx.[10] Neglect and lack of funds led to the collapse of the tower in 1600 and by 1630 the church was said to have been in 'great ruin'. Excavation from 2008 to 2017 has demonstrated systematic dismantling of the structures associated with the abbey and by 1703, only the church remained standing.[11]

[1] Egan (2006), 590.
[2] Mitchiner and Skinner (1983); Mitchiner and Skinner (1984).
[3] Grainger and Collingwood (1929).
[4] Founded 1190.
[5] Bull and Rennicks (2013).
[6] Jamroziak (2008b).
[7] Grainger and Collingwood (1929), 212, 280.
[8] The same is true from an historical perspective. See Jamroziak (2008a).
[9] The villagers petitioned Thomas Cromwell to use the abbey as the parish church in 1538. See Gilbanks (1900), 106–30.
[10] Thanks to Glyn Coppack, who recently calculated the height of the nave.
[11] Walker and Graham (2013). A hoard of 81 silver coins dated to the fourteenth century was recovered at Holme Cultram in the late nineteenth century while digging a grave, although it is unlikely that these were related to the token finds described here. See North (1975).

The tokens

Thirty-four of the excavated tokens were located by metal detector in spoil heaps or unstratified contexts in the area identified through recent excavation as the chapter house, adjacent to the dorter. Nine were found in stratified contexts but these were either topsoil or demolition debris.[12] Nine different types of token were found, ranging from 13–16mm in diameter and around 1mm thick. A review of several thousand published tokens has determined that there are no examples known with designs that match those from Holme Cultram and therefore they can be interpreted as two distinct and previously unknown local series.[13]

Table 1: Summary of token types found at Holme Cultram and their designs.

Type	*Obverse*	*Reverse*	*Powell Classification*	*Nos. found*
1	Hammer, tongs and horseshoe	Letters - SEVIL+	21: inanimate objects	3
2	A stylised ship (possibly weighing scales or salt pan)	Letters - SEL with a superscript abbreviation mark	6: Ship	30
3	Flower with five petals	Letters - possibly INLE or HIC?	17: trees, plants and their produce	1 or 2
4	A pollarded tree or stag's head with antlers	A 'h' or 'p' with a dot or star in the middle (possibly a crozier)	17: trees, plants and their produce or 19: animals	1
5	A leaping stag	Letters- FLE with a subscript dot beneath the 'L'	19: animals, including fish and insects	1
6	*Fleur de lys*	The letters VIO A?	4: lis	2
7	A stag or cow's head with antlers	indecipherable lettering	19: animals, including fish and insects.	1
8	Indecipherable design	Letters - MAB	Unknown	1
9	A crowned letter 'R'	Blank	25: miscellaneous objects, royal	1

Manufacture

The Holme Cultram tokens are cast and at least four have obvious casting sprues. An associated mould has not been recovered yet but there is good archaeological evidence of token manufacture available from other excavations (discussed later).

There has been a lack of care and attention with the finishing and some are miscast or untrimmed, indicating local manufacture.[14] Casting sprues can be seen at 12 o'clock and 6 o'clock on at least four examples. Some have a heavier relief design and some are slightly ovoid as if too much metal has been poured into the mould or it has not been properly closed. Several of the ship motif designs are pierced but given their crude manufacture, this is more likely to string them together for transportation than for use as decoration. Though they may have been roughly manufactured, their intrinsic value to the bearer warranted safekeeping. It is also likely that there is more than one mould for the type 2 tokens, so it could be that one type of token was more important than others or was required in greater quantities.

Metallic analysis - X-Ray fluorescence testing

Seven tokens were tested in total with X-Ray fluorescence, to try to establish whether all the different designs could be considered as of the same token issue (table 2).

[12] Walker and Graham (2013) demonstrated that the outer monastic buildings were subject to systematic, organised demolition in the post reformation years.
[13] For a complete register of all tokens found including inventory numbers, see Walker and Graham (2016), 87.
[14] Saunders and Saunders (2001), 102.

Table 2: Results of the XRF analysis and breakdown of the component metals within the tested samples.

Sample No. or Element	*% & STD*	*Pb*	*Fe*	*Sn*	*Ti*	*Zr*	*Se*	*Mn*	*Ag*	*Au*	*Cu*	*As*	*Mo*
28	%	97.8	1.5	0.3	0.2	0.1	0.1	0					
	STD	0.085	0.017	0.021	0.043	0.0042	0.0032	0.0087					
16 obverse	%	0.4	3	0.5				0.2	94.5	0.9		0	
	STD	0.021	0.0024	0.016				0.014	0.09	0.0072	0.0056	0.0085	
16 reverse	%	0.1	1.6	0.3					97.4		0.6		0
	STD	0.0012	0.018	0.016					0.089		0.0063		0.0013
24	%	98.9	0.6	0.2		0.1	0.1	0					
	STD	0.086	0.011	0.021		0.0041	0.0031	0.011					
63	%	99.4		0.4		0.1	0.1	0					
	STD	0.086		0.021		0.004	0.0031	0.011					
72	%	98.7	0.5	0.4		0.1	0.1	0					
	STD	0.087	0.012	0.022		0.0043	0.0033	0.012					
65	%	97.5		2.1		0.2	0.1	0			0.1		
	STD	0.085		0.03		0.0042	0.0032	0.01			0.0035		
62	%	99.1		0.6		0.1	0.1	0					
	STD	0.086		0.022		0.0041	0.0032	0.011					

The results demonstrate that there are two different types of token at Holme Cultram. Sample 16 (the crowned R) is both stylistically and physically different to the other examples. It is the only uniface piece and it is a similar weight to the other examples but its surface is primarily made of silver with trace amounts of gold on one side. Yet, physical examination does suggest that the primary metal is lead with surface gilding and this, coupled with the find location (in the same place as the others), plus the piece's similarity in size to the other tokens, suggests that it is indeed a token but with a different purpose than the others (perhaps more value based).

The rest of the tokens are almost pure lead. The results have been kindly reviewed by Peter Northover who commented that some of the impurities in the data may be a quirk of the automatic peak recognition software (e.g. for zirconium, selenium and manganese).[15] The iron, possibly the manganese and the titanium may essentially be earthy elements in the surface encrustation. The tin is likely to be a real component of the melt showing that this is workshop scrap rather than newly smelted and refined lead. This suggests that not only was lead smelting happening at the abbey (or at least within its locality) but that there was waste enough to manufacture secondary products. Use of scrap for making tokens has also been seen at Fountains Abbey, where a series of square tokens give the impression that they had been made from a sheet of spare or leftover lead, possibly roofing material that had then been stamped and crudely cut to size. Like the piercing, the crude manufacture coupled with high volumes indicates that their function was more important than their physical form to both those who commissioned their manufacture and those who used them.

Possible dating

Mitchiner and Skinner analysed 476 tokens using X-Ray fluorescence and determined some broad dating rules based on the proportion of lead to tin.[16] They demonstrated that tokens were usually made of pewter until the early fourteenth century, when the metal composition changed from 62% tin to pure lead in a single step. It is possible that this resulted from a shortage of tin (although pilgrim badges produced for ecclesiastical usage continued to be made of pewter) or the rise of a new source of manufacture.[17] Tin was reintroduced in tokens in the 1480s as a fairly abrupt change and is probably to be linked with the slump in London's pewter exports during the last quarter of the fifteenth century.[18] If we fit the Holme Cultram series within this metal composition date range, we see a date range for manufacture of these tokens of between 1300–1480. Stylistic analysis in view of Mitchiner and Skinner's published series is consistent with the 'small neat tokens' of late Plantagenet type, dated 1425–1490 (particular details include the raised circular borders to the designs, crude ship depictions, and imagery suggesting trading commodities such as a blacksmith's hammer) although the London samples tend to be around 2mm smaller than the Holme Cultram series.[19]

There are also some minor stylistic similarities with the style of the lettering that is shown on some of the ecclesiastical issues with some of their 'Early Tudor' tokens dated ca. 1490 to 1545 but as a rule, the early Tudor tokens have far more complexity to the designs; the metallic composition of these later types tends to have far greater quantity of tin and the size tends to be around 5–7mm wider in diameter than the Holme Cultram series. Caution is exercised, since Mitchiner and Skinner's study is heavily London-centric, but in the absence of secure stratigraphy the dating of 1300–1490 is preferred for manufacture, although there is a possibility that these tokens were used later into the sixteenth century and up to the

[15] University of Oxford, Oxford Materials Characterisation Service.
[16] Mitchiner and Skinner (1983); Mitchiner and Skinner (1984).
[17] Tin production in Devon and Cornwall declined by 20–40% between 1430s and 1460s. See Hatcher (1973), 158.
[18] Mitchiner and Skinner (1983), 40–41.
[19] Mitchiner and Skinner (1984), 87–94, 142–44.

Dissolution of the Monasteries in 1536.[20] The crowned 'R' token (type 9) is likely to have been a distinct token series.

Designs

Some of the Holme Cultram tokens have comparator designs that are worthy of note. Rievaulx Abbey boasts a particularly attractive token with the letters WELB on one side and a ship's wheel or a star design on the other. The raised Lombardic lettering spelling WELB on the token shown in figure 1 is similar in form and style to the lettering on the Holme Cultram tokens, in particular the closed 'E'. This letterform may also assist with dating both examples. Bertram's work on inscriptions in Oxfordshire has demonstrated that Lombardic script, characterised by a closed 'C' and 'E', appeared in the third quarter of the thirteenth century and dominated until the mid-fourteenth century, with only occasional later usage.[21] This unpublished token is currently on display at the new exhibition at Rievaulx, and has in the past been erroneously interpreted by English Heritage as a reference to the abbey's monastic grange at Welbeck.[22] The arrangement of designs with particular lettering does suggest that the designs of these tokens had a meaning that was not just arbitrary decoration. It is also possible to postulate meaning for some of them.

Fig. 1: The WELB token from Rievaulx (inv. no. 860032) (courtesy of English Heritage, Susan Harrison).

Crowned R

The 'crowned R' (fig. 2) is quite different to the other tokens, both in style and surface composition, made primarily from lead but with silver gilt and incised with secondary decoration. It is included as a token in this series because it was found in the same location as the rest of the series and is of the same shape and size. It is also suggested that despite differences in composition, its functionality is that of a token. The abbey is dedicated to Mary and its seal features the Virgin Mary standing, so the crowned R could stand for 'Regina Coeli', or Mary Queen of Heaven.[23] Similar designs are found on finger rings in the medieval period, thought to be seals.[24] A crowned 'R' is found in the Jerusalem Chamber of the Cheneygates (the medieval house of the Abbots of Westminster) and is thought to be the royal cypher of Richard II in whose reign the chamber was constructed.[25] There are a number of associations with royal 'R's in the charter evidence, notably in connection with royal grants of forestry by Richard I at Inglewood, although the King did not visit the abbey.[26] Crowns also appear on other letters, such as S, D or Y, which have no overtly royal connection so the crown as a signifier of royal association is by no means sure. The crown may be used as reinforcement – the adding of one talismanic device to another to emphasises its importance.[27]

Fig. 2: The crowned R token (type 9) (Small Find Reference 16) (photo by the author).

[20] Holme Cultram surrendered to Thomas Cromwell's commissioners on 6th March 1538. See Grainger and Collingwood (1929), 156–57.
[21] Bertram (2003), 29. As he points out, the study of medieval epigraphy has been much neglected. His work focusses on Oxfordshire, so dating is suggested with caution, pending a more national (or at least northern) study.
[22] Thanks to Glyn Coppack and Michael Carter for pointing out that this interpretation is in fact incorrect, for Rievaulx did not have a grange called Welbeck.
[23] Gilbanks (1900), 88.
[24] Dalton (1912), 57, 60–66; Cherry (1991), 46; Spencer (1998), 156–57.
[25] http://www.westminster-abbey.org/our-history/jerusalem-chamber (accessed 05/06/2019).
[26] Grainger and Collingwood (1929), 45–47.
[27] Spencer (1998), 319.

'R' motifs are readily available for comparison on the extant remains at Holme Cultram (although they do not feature a crown). Carved stones can be found on the abbey porch, showing a chained bear and the initials of Abbot Robert Chamber, as well as on Chamber's tomb (fig. 3). There is some similarity between these characters and the design of the token 'R': note the foot of the upright and the kick of the tail on the token (although there is difference in the upper flick of the upright). Chamber was one of the great builder abbots of the late medieval period. He carried out extensive building works at the abbey and his initials appear prolifically in carving in a number of places at the abbey and through the parish.[28] While his works were at the later end of our proposed date range, this token is so different to the others that it can be considered a different series and may have been manufactured at a different time.

Fig. 3: Abbot Chamber's initials on his tomb (note the Lombardic closed 'C') (photo by the author).

Some tokens from monastic contexts have been interpreted as signs of the abbot's favour or intent. At Waltham Abbey, Essex, a token was found with fifteenth century pottery in an oyster midden in the garden, bearing an alternative blazon for the abbey.[29] At Ramsay Abbey, Cambridgeshire, an unusual late medieval token was found, featuring a letter R on the obverse and a bird pecking a fish on the reverse.[30] Both have been interpreted as a symbol of authority. It is possible that this token could have travelled from another abbey, such as Rievaulx, yet it is tempting to associate it with Abbot Chamber. The lavish nature of his building work seems to accord with the ostentation of the precious metal composition of this token. It might have been a demonstration of the abbot's authority or served as a method of showing that the bearer was 'trusted'. Sadly though, this association must remain speculation.

Ship / SEL

The ship token with the SEL lettering (type 2, fig. 4) is by far the most numerous design recovered, although the reason for the unusually high volume is not clear. The ship motif is a relatively common phenomenon in token design, although the Holme Cultram examples are simpler and more stylised than others. Mitchiner and Skinner record similar late Plantagenet and early Tudor designs from London and one is held in Bristol museum (unpublished).[31] All these examples show the same curved bottomed boat with rigging above in an equilateral triangle but are far more detailed in design than the simple line drawing of the Holme Cultram series, but no examples of ship tokens found elsewhere have associated lettering on the reverse.

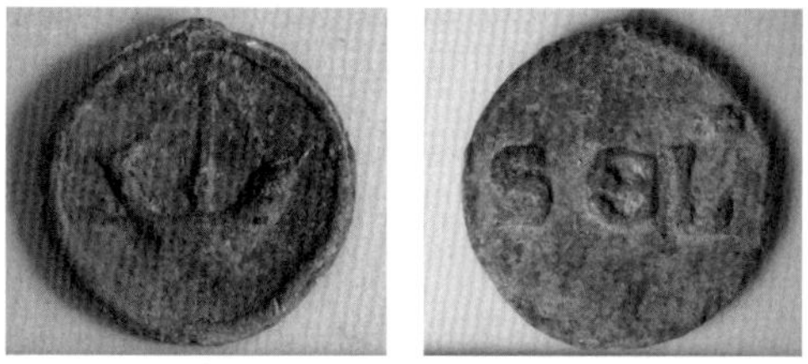

Fig. 4: A ship / SEL token (type 2) (Small Finds Reference 72) (photo by the author).

The lettering SEL, French for salt, could be associated with the abbey's extensive salt production activities along the Solway (it held salt pans at nearby Saltcoates). The abbey was close to the Irish Sea and charters also contain repeated

[28] His accession was in 1489, he received the right to pontifical privileges in 1508 and was replaced by his successor, Matthew Deveys, in 1531. Walker and Graham (2016), 6.
[29] Huggins (1976), 126–27.
[30] Spoerry, Atkins, Macauley and Shephard Popescu (2008), 193.
[31] Mitchiner and Skinner (1985), 143, 149.

Fig. 5: Stag's head tokens; far left and far right (Small Finds Reference 62 and 65) are examples of Holme Cultram tokens types 4 and 7 featuring a stag's head. The centre token is the stag's head token from Rievaulx (inv. no. 860034) (photo by the author).

references to the abbey receiving and dispatching ships between Ireland, the Isle of Man and Scotland.[32] This could be a token for exchange at the port or alternatively, the ship could be the sign for the local tavern, which would make the token an indication of the right to a measure of ale at the local watering house (this is also one interpretation for the Winetavern series).

Stag or cow's head

One of the most interesting comparative examples for type 7, the stag or cow's head, comes from late medieval contexts at Rievaulx Abbey in Yorkshire (fig. 5). This example bears a notable resemblance to Holme Cultram types 4 and 7, featuring a horned animal's head (cow or stag) on the obverse. While the Rievaulx and Holme Cultram designs are not from the same mould, they are so similar as to suggest a common template for the creator of the mould, emphasising the link between the two Cistercian houses. A match can also be seen in the design of the crozier of the type 4 design with a similar example at Fountains Abbey, another closely linked Cistercian house. The Holme Cultram stag / crozier token is unusual in that the reverse would normally feature letters, so perhaps the crozier signifies something belonging to or associated with the abbey.

Tying function with place - Leaping stag / FLE; Blacksmith motif / SEVIL; Lys / VIO

There is an extensive collection of charters at Holme Cultram and it is through their reading that a sense of tokens associated with particular places can be glimpsed. For example, the leaping stag / FLE type (type 5, fig. 6), could easily be a reference to the abbey's lands at Flemingby (now known as Flimby). Forestry rights at Flemingby were confirmed by Richard I and it is possible that the deer symbolises the right to hunt or a right to a certain amount of meat.[33] If the image is a tree, as might be possible on type 4, the token might indicate rights to wood. A similar pattern can be seen with the type 1 tokens (blacksmith tools / SEVIL+, fig. 7), where the name harks to the hamlet of Sevill (Seaville) only a mile or so from the abbey. It is conceivable that this token is a grant for a blacksmithing service from Sevill. The *fleur de lys* was a common medieval design. The lily is traditionally considered to

Fig. 6: The leaping stag / FLE token (type 5) (Small Finds Reference 63) (photo by the author).

Fig. 7: Token with hammer, tongs and horseshoe and SEVIL+ (type 1) (Small Finds Reference 24) (photo by the author).

[32] Grainger and Collingwood (1929), 94–95.
[33] Grainger and Collingwood (1929), 18–21.

be the flower of innocence and is particularly associated with the annunciation of the Virgin Mary.[34] Holme Cultram was dedicated to Saint Mary so this sign could be symbolic of the abbey itself and communicate a right to particular goods or charity.[35]

This function and themes connected to place are echoed in a find from another Cistercian house, Roche Abbey. Like the Holme Cultram series, it features both letters and depictions, although both are on the same face of the token.[36] The design shows the letters ARRA, with depictions of rats around the letters. An interpretation for ARRA is elusive but it is reasonable to suggest that it may have been something to do with rats, perhaps the name of the rat catcher or the location of his dwelling, with the token given for the service of rat catching. Perhaps each token was given for the capture of the two rats depicted and could then be exchanged elsewhere for other goods or services.

Token research up to the 1980s and finds from recent excavations

In order to better understand how the tokens from Holme Cultram may have been used, a review of medieval English tokens has been carried out. Token research over the last 30 years has not been extensive, yet as Egan pointed out,[37] excavations at medieval sites regularly produce tokens, suggesting sustained and common usage from the twelfth to the sixteenth century.[38] The most important research on tokens so far was a wide-ranging study in two parts by Mitchiner and Skinner in 1983 and 1984, which analysed over 1250 English tin, pewter or lead tokens, issued between 1200 and 1672. Find spots were primarily from the Thames foreshore or from East Anglia and very few from outside of London were studied.[39] This is perhaps one of the drawbacks of their work and it has partly led to a belief that tokens are a southern and eastern phenomenon. This can now be challenged, with a wealth of available finds now known from the north and west of England.

Mitchiner and Skinner's assessments of token functionality derive from continental parallels and they conclude that the principal user of the earliest tokens was the church before tokens spread to a more secular circulation. At Notre-Dame in Paris, chaplains received tokens for attending church services; at Bethune near Calais, tokens were issued to the poor in times of need in the fifteenth century; at St Omer, tokens were distributed to workmen that could be exchanged for food and drink at inns in the town approved by the chapter. The inn-keeper would then redeem from the chapter, on presentation of the token, the price of the food; at Nevers, tokens conferred on those who possessed them the exclusive right to cry, carry and sell certain commodities.[40]

Many of the finds available to Michiner and Skinner were located in ports, such as London, Dublin or Paris. The Dublin 'Winetavern' series excavated in 1962–1963 is notable for its volume (the largest cache ever found at over 2,000 items) and for the suggestion that this was a manufacturing location.[41] Some tokens from the Winetavern mould were also recovered in a collection of around 50 tokens from excavations at Trig Lane, London, dating from the thirteenth to fifteenth centuries, showing that some tokens did have value that could translate outside their immediate locality, perhaps as trading aids.[42] While some have seen international trade as the common denominator for the use of tokens,[43] this interpretation may not provide the whole picture. After all, no lead tokens were recovered in the extensive excavations at Southampton, one of the busier medieval ports.[44]

[34] Spencer (1998), 157.
[35] The *fleur de lys* also appears on tiling recovered in excavation. See Hodgson (1907); Walker and Graham (2013).
[36] Powell (2015), 3.
[37] Egan (2006), 589.
[38] References to lead tokens in literature have been discussed elsewhere. See Courtenay (1972); Grierson, (1972); Given-Wilson (et al.) (2005).
[39] See Rigold's discussion of the boy bishop series (1982), which seems to have been related to a festive custom in local monastic houses akin to the lord of misrule.
[40] Mitchiner and Skinner (1983), 29–33.
[41] Dolley and Seaby (1971).
[42] Rigold (1982).
[43] Schofield and Vince (2003), 131.
[44] Platt and Coleman Smith (1975).

Archaeological research since 1984

It is clear that there is a great deal of under reporting of tokens in the archaeological research to date. Vast quantities are recovered by metal detectorists, some publish prolifically on the topic and significant volumes are in private hands.[45] In 2011, one detectorist claimed to have recovered over 1,000 tokens from a few fields in Shropshire, far more than most museums hold.[46] The British Museum boasts around 3,500, mostly recovered from mud larking on the Thames foreshore.[47] A search string of 'medieval lead token' via the Portable Antiquities Scheme website shows records of 1,747 known lead tokens at the time of writing (February 2018), suggesting massive under reporting. It is surprising just how few tokens are recorded in museum collections. MOLA only shows 68 pieces on its online catalogue; Bristol holds only seven lead tokens, Salisbury holds 29 (including some interesting depictions showing genitalia, likely to be brothel tokens) and Cambridge 120. Given their crude appearance, they have hitherto not been seen as that important, so there are also examples where they have not been listed in excavation records or remain uncatalogued in museums. For instance, two crude tokens were recovered during excavations in the guesthouse at the Cistercian abbey of Kirsktall in 1979–86 and at the time of writing were as yet unpublished.[48]

Over 30 years on from Mitchiner and Skinner's studies, there is far more information available from English excavations, particularly with the benefit of the digitisation of archaeological records. The breadth of geographical locations and different types of sites in which tokens are found does suggest a variety of functions dependent on circumstance. Some of the earliest known tokens identified were recovered in Gloucester at St Mary de Lode church, where three lead tokens were found in stratigraphically sound contexts from the late eleventh century.[49] This is significant, given that Mitchiner and Skinner record a hiatus in tokens during the Anglo-Saxon and Norman periods in England.[50] In 1991, at Vintners Place, London, several lead tokens were recovered from pre–1250 deposits from what is considered to be one of the most extensive assemblages of eleventh and twelfth century Anglo Norman metal work.[51] Excavations at Montgomery Castle in Mid Wales recovered eleven uniface tokens in sealed contexts dating from 1260–1280 in the outer ditch and middle ward of the castle. They were interpreted as receipts for tolls or chits to allow the drawing of items from the quartermaster's stores.[52] More recently, divers have recovered 125 tokens from the bed of the River Wear.[53] During the late-medieval period, the area adjacent to the river thronged with pubs, dyers, bakers, candle makers and butchers, and these tokens have been interpreted as a form of small change, where one token would equate to a particular commodity such as a joint of pork or a few candles. All these tokens are, as a rule, very sparse and are usually only decorated with a collection of lines or dots. None have any similarity to the Holme Cultram series, yet they attest to the many uses that tokens could have.

Token moulds are known in England throughout the medieval period from the thirteenth to fifteenth centuries and some have been recently discovered. One from the Cistercian abbey of Dundrennan in the Scottish borders, found in the nineteenth century, was used for early beaded pictorial tokens and can be stylistically dated from 1200–1250.[54] The Dundrennan designs bear a striking stylistic similarity to the famous Winetavern tokens from Dublin[55] and also to one token found at Rievaulx Abbey (now at the English Heritage store at Helmsley). Moulds from Farnham in Surrey and Bedern in York can be stratigraphically

[45] See David Powell's enthusiastically curated http://www.mernick.org.uk/leadtokens and the Lead Token Corresponding Society (http://thetokensociety.org.uk/; accessed 05/06/2019).
[46] Radsall (2011).
[47] David Powell's personal comments.
[48] Thanks to Katherine Baxter at Leeds Museum for searching through the collection.
[49] Bryant and Heighway (2003), 212.
[50] Mitchiner and Skinner (1983), 29. Also see Egan (2006) for a discussion on early tokens found in the 20 years since Mitchiner and Skinner's work.
[51] Nenk, Margeson and Hurely (1992), 240.
[52] Knight (1993).
[53] Gary Bankhead's personal comments.
[54] Anderson (1874–1876), 79.
[55] Dolley and Seaby (1971).

dated to the early to mid-thirteenth century and one at Winchester was recovered from a fifteenth century context.[56] All were multi token moulds, showing between three and ten different designs that could be cast at any one time. The example from Bedern was usable on two sides, possibly part of a mould 'stack'.[57] Again, none of these moulds have any similarity to the Holme Cultram series but the moulds do attest to geographical distribution on a more national (as opposed to southern and eastern) level and that some tokens were meant to be created in high volumes.[58]

Tokens from Cistercian houses

Research into museum and English Heritage collections have revealed a host of previously unrecorded and unpublished tokens from Cistercian abbeys that have close ties with Holme Cultram (table 3, fig. 8). Six were found at Rievaulx Abbey during site clearances in the 1920s and 1930s (these provide close comparators to the Holme Cultram series); at Fountains Abbey three round and over 100 square tokens were located during Glyn Coppack's excavations in the 1980s.

Table 3: Tokens and find spots at Cistercian abbeys.

Abbey	*Founded*	*Filiation*	*Nos.*	*Location of token*	*Dating*
Dundrennan	1142	Rievaulx	Mould	unknown	Stylistically 13th century.
Fountains	1132	Clairvaux	>100	Reredorter drain	unknown
Holme Cultram	1150	Melrose	43	Chapter house	unknown
Kirkstall	1147	Fountains	7	Abbey guest house	unknown
Newminster	1138	Fountains	2	Robber trench in the nave	unknown
Rievaulx	1132	Clairvaux	6	Site clearances 1920s and 1930s, dorter sub vault and to the south of the reredorter	One stylistically 13th century, the others are unknown
Roche	1147	Fountains	1	unknown	unknown
Tintern Parva			2	Monastic drain	Stratigraphically dated to 1250–1300

One of the drawbacks of looking at Cistercian sites and considering common ground is the fact that so few have been excavated and of those that have, few have been excavated extensively. For the most part, tokens have been recovered in small quantities from Cistercian sites. We have already established that tokens were a common feature in medieval life and so perhaps a few tokens should be expected at an excavation. However, on the basis of volume, stylistic similarity, find location and the well-attested links between these monastic houses (in particular Holme Cultram, Fountains, Rievaulx and potentially Roche Abbey), a common interpretation of their function can be proposed.

Despite the lack of confirmed stratigraphy, the location of the token find spots against the abbeys' known ground plans is significant in their interpretation. At Holme Cultram, the tokens have all been recovered in the vicinity of the chapter house and the northern end of the dorter. At Fountains Abbey, similar tokens were recovered from the reredorter drain; at Rievaulx Abbey the find spots were the dorter sub vault and south of the reredorter. At Kirkstall Abbey, the finds hailed from the guesthouse. Those from the sub vault of the monk's sleeping quarters at Fountains could be associated with storage space below the dorter. The fact that they appear within domestic structures points to the tokens being used by the monks and the community, as well as their guests. The Holme Cultram tokens (alongside Rievaulx and Roche) were created for monastic use and may well have been distributed or issued for transactions by monks. None of the designs are exactly the same as those at

[56] Farnham: Poulton (1998), 139–41; Bedern: Ottoway and Rogers (2002), 2712–13; Winchester: Biddle (2012), 658–61.

[57] For reproductions of the images of the token moulds listed here, see Rennicks (2016).

[58] For further discussion of token moulds see Rowan's chapter in this volume. Note that the method of making cast tokens in moulds has altered little since the Roman period.

Fig. 8: Map showing locations of Cistercian abbeys in which tokens have been recovered (created by the author).

other Cistercian houses but some are similar, and the volumes found at houses with close affinity is sufficient to suggest that their function could have been the same.

The function of the Holme Cultram tokens

Low level fiduciary transactions may well have been carried out using tokens in other parts of the country, but the quite specific depictions on some of the Holme Cultram tokens and the possible geographic association with the abbey's holdings suggest that interpretation as a straight monetary substitute is over simplistic. A better way to look at these objects is as credit, given out by the abbey in exchange for goods and services. Tokens could be given to furnish proof that 'something' had happened, but this could be variable from place to place. Examples might have included a toll, consumable, or a service that could later be redeemable against a fee or alternative service.[59]

[59] Sargent and Velde (2002), 217.

Courtenay's valuable work on tokens discussed their use in the administration of charity. Tokens marked with an item of necessity (such as bread, wine, meat or charcoal) acted as an IOU or a way to pay the provider of a service in kind, for example with commodities that may have been controlled or produced by the issuing body.[60] The recipient could redeem the token against the commodity depicted at a time of their choosing, the issuer could control the number of recipients at any one time and crucially for Holme Cultram (suffering as it did from repeated Scottish aggression) such a system allowed them to defer the expenditure of resources. This may have been important to an issuing body that was suffering from cash flow problems or a reduction in the amount of small change (as brought on by the bullion famines of the fifteenth century).[61]

We have seen at Holme Cultram and at other Cistercian houses that an association can be made between function and place by looking at the relationship between letters and designs. Building on Courtenay's work, someone who had carried out work for the abbey could be paid in tokens that could then be redeemed for goods from a specific place. Tokens with lettering and non-commodity designs are less easy to interpret but could have been charity based (for example the lys or the crozier could indicate a grant of charity, for example in the form of meat for food), as opposed to a grant of meat or permission to hunt in exchange for rendered services. The crowned R token is different and can be seen as a token of conferred power by the abbot.

All of these things form a picture of estate management, whether of goods or people, with tokens acting as the transactional mechanism. The practice of using tokens valued in kind (whether for charity or for trade) may have been to preserve close ties between the donor and recipient. Moreover, on a monastic estate such as Holme Cultram or Rievaulx, that was producing diverse commodities for sale, the use of tokens between granges and landholdings would have ensured that goods continued to circulate and the local economy continued to flow. It is plausible to see a scenario in which a token was given in charity or in exchange for a service that allowed the redeemer to access a different service or commodity elsewhere on the abbey's lands – meat from abbey holdings at Flemingby, ale from the tavern, salt from the salt pans at Saltcoates or iron goods from Sevill.

Management rather than control

It is proposed that the tokens at Holme Cultram were a mechanism for management and communication of need. They assisted in the free exchange between monastic estates, movement of goods from those estates, sustenance of local people and most importantly, management of relationships. This is echoed by the interpretation of similar finds from Rievaulx, Fountains and Roche Abbeys. Holme Cultram was a monastic house that may have been wealthy at times, but like its sister houses at Rievaulx and Fountains, it encountered serious hardship through Scottish attacks, famine and the decline of its population. Use of tokens is symptomatic of these local conditions. They are a means of getting by, of sustaining those living in the monastic house itself as well as local people.

This review has considered new finds and tested them against old conclusions, bringing them together to develop a narrative of use. Tokens are evidence of local adaption in the absence of prescribed systems and so the development of broad theories of use or manufacture is almost impossible. Tokens should be celebrated for their multiplicity of style and function rather than ignored by archaeologists.

Addendum

At the time of submission of this article (May 2019), further excavations were on-going at Holme Cultram Abbey, part of a Heritage Lottery Funded project exploring Holme Cultram

[60] Courtenay (1972).
[61] A dearth in small change is also evidenced over the fourteenth and fifteenth centuries by the proportionately higher number of cut halfpence and farthings recovered in excavation in comparison to pennies. See Bolton (2012), 232–40, 271–72.

Harbour. One of the trenches was sited over the northern end of the chapter house and a further 31 tokens have been recovered, including three previously unknown designs (a five pointed star / lettering ALO, a double crown / lettering SAN and a set of cast triangular tokens featuring the letter R on the obverse and a series of dots on the reverse). It is too early at this stage to provide a full analysis although many of these tokens did come from stratified contexts within the chapter house. The triangular tokens are particularly of interest as no known examples of triangular tokens have been seen elsewhere.

These new tokens will be discussed in the forthcoming excavation report once full site analysis has taken place but at this stage, the find spot locations within the chapter house add weight to the argument that these were tokens for monastic use. A number of new questions have been raised by these recent excavations, including the motivation for using both circular and triangular tokens contemporaneously; why we have both triangular and circular tokens featuring a letter 'R'; the meanings of the lettering and designs on the new circular tokens and why they have been found within the mortar of the chapter house floor surface. We have much to learn.

Bibliography

Anderson 1874-1876: J. Anderson, 'Notes on «Pilgrims' Signs» of the Middle Ages, and a stone mould for casting leaden tokens, found at Dundrennan Abbey', *Proceedings of the Society of Antiquaries of Scotland* 11 (1874-1876), 62–80.

Bertram 2003: J. Bertram, 'Medieval inscriptions in Oxfordshire', *Oxoniensia* 68 (2003), 27–53.

Biddle 2012: M. Biddle, *Winchester Studies 8: The Winchester Mint and Coins and Related Finds from the Excavations of 1961-71* (Oxford, 2012).

Bolton 2012: J. L. Bolton, *Money in the Medieval English Economy* (Manchester, 2012).

Bryant and Heighway 2003: R. Bryant and C. M. Heighway, 'Excavations at St Mary de Lode Church, Gloucester, 1978-9', *Transactions of the Bristol and Gloucestershire Archaeological Society* 121 (2003), 97–178.

Bull and Rennicks 2013: P. Bull and K. S. Rennicks, 'The historical background', in Walker and Graham (eds.) (2016), 1–8.

Cherry 1991: J. Cherry, 'Rings', in Saunders and Saunders (eds.) (2001), 46.

Cook and Williams (eds.) 2006: B. Cook and G. Williams (eds.), *Coinage and History in the North Sea World, c. 500-1250* (Boston, 2006).

Courtenay 1972: W. J. Courtenay, 'Token coinage and the administration of poor relief during the Late Middle Ages', *The Journal of Interdisciplinary History* 3 (1972), 275–95.

Dalton 1912: O. M. Dalton, *Catalogue of the Finger Rings in the British Museum* (London, 1912).

Dolley and Seaby 1971: M. Dolley and W. A. Seaby, 'A find of thirteenth-century pewter tokens from the National Museum excavations at Winetavern Street, Dublin', *NCirc* 79 (1971), 446–48.

Egan 2006: G. Egan, 'The earliest English lead tokens', in Cook and Williams (eds.) (2006), 589–600.

Gilbanks 1900: G. E. Gilbanks, *Some Records of a Cistercian Abbey* (London, 1900).

Given-Wilson (et al.) 2005: C. Given-Wilson, P. Brand, S. Phillips, M. Ormrod, G. Martin, A. Curry and R. Horrox (eds.), 'Henry IV: September 1402', in *Parliament Rolls of Medieval England.* British History Online (http://www.british-history.ac.uk/no-series/parliament-rolls-medieval/september-1402 (accessed 05/06/2019).

Grainger and Collingwood 1929: F. Grainger and W. Collingwood, *The Register and Records of Holme Cultram* (Cumberland and Westmorland Antiquarian and Archaeological Society Record Series 7) (Kendal, 1929).

Grierson 1972: P. Grierson, 'Notes on early Tudor coinage', *BNJ* 41 (1972), 80–94.

Hatcher 1973: J. Hatcher, *English Tin Production and Trade before 1550* (London 1973).

Hodgson 1907: T. H. Hodgson, 'Excavations at Holme Cultram', *Transactions of the Cumberland and Westmoreland Antiquarian and Archaeological Society* 7 (1907), 262–68.

Huggins 1976: P. J. Huggins, 'The excavation of an 11th-century Viking hall and 14th-century rooms at Waltham Abbey, Essex, 1969-71', *Medieval Archaeology* 20 (1976), 75–133.

Jamroziak 2008a: E. Jamroziak, 'Holme Cultram Abbey: A story of success?', *Northern History* 45 (2008), 27–36.

Jamroziak 2008b: E. Jamroziak, 'Border communities between violence and opportunities: Scotland and Pomerania compared', in Unger (ed.) (2008), 123–35.

Knight 1993: J. K. Knight, 'Excavations at Montgomery Castle, Part II, The finds', *Archaeologia Cambrensis* 142 (1993), 182–242.

Milne and Milne (eds.) 1982: G. Milne and C. Milne (eds.), *Medieval Waterfront Development at Trig Lane, London: An Account of Excavations at Trig Lane, London 1974-76 and Related Researches* (Special Paper no. 5) (London, 1985).

Mitchiner and Skinner 1983: M. Mitchiner and A. Skinner, 'English tokens 1200 to 1425', *BNJ* 53 (1983), 29–77.

Mitchiner and Skinner 1984: M. Mitchiner and A. Skinner, 'English tokens 1425 to 1672', *BNJ* 54 (1984), 86–163.

Nenk, Margeson and Hurely 1992: B. S. Nenk, S. Margeson and M. Hurley, 'Medieval Britain and Ireland in 1991', *Medieval Archaeology* 36 (1992), 184–308.

North 1975: J. J. North, 'An unpublished fourteenth century hoard', *NCirc* 81 (1975), 332–33.

Ottoway and Rogers 2002: P. Ottoway and N. Rogers, *Craft, Industry and Everyday Life: Medieval finds from York - The Archaeology of York: The Small Finds* (York, 2002).

Platt and Coleman Smith 1975: C. Platt and R. Coleman Smith, *Excavations in Medieval Southampton 1953-1969. The Finds* (vol. 2) (Leicester, 1975).

Poulton 1998: R. Poulton, 'Farnham: excavations between Castle Street and Bear Lane', *Surrey Archaeological Collections* 85 (1998), 97–157.

Powell 2010: D. Powell, *Powell Classification System for Lead Tokens* (http://www.mernick.org.uk/leadtokens/Classification_System.pdf; accessed 05/06/2019).

Powell 2015: D. Powell, 'Money from the monastery: some Yorkshire examples', *Leaden Tokens Telegraph* 102 (2015), 1–3.

Radsall 2011: C. Radsall, 'Tokens galore', *Treasure Hunter* (May 2011), 19–21.

Rennicks 2016: K. S. Rennicks, *The Function and Purpose of Lead Tokens in Medieval England: A Case Study at Holme Cultram Abbey, Cumbria*. B.A. (Hons) thesis, University of Bristol (Bristol, 2016).

Rigold 1982: S. E. Rigold, '4. Jettons and tokens', in Milne and Milne (eds.) (1982), 97–104.

Sargent and Velde 2002: T. J. Sargent and F. R. Velde, *The Big Problem of Small Change*, (Princeton, 2002).

Saunders and Saunders (eds.) 2001: P. Saunders and E. Saunders, *Salisbury and South Wiltshire Museum Medieval Catalogue. Part 3* (Salisbury, 2001).

Schofield and Vince 2003: J. Schofield and A. Vince, *Medieval Towns, the Archaeology of British Towns in the European Setting* (London, 2003).

Spencer 1998: B. Spencer, *Pilgrim Souvenirs and Secular Badges* (London, 1998).

Spoerry, Atkins, Macauley and Shephard Popescu 2008: P. Spoerry, R. Atkins, S. Macauley, E. Shepherd Popescu, 'Ramsey Abbey, Cambridgeshire: excavations at the site of a Fenland monastery', *Medieval Archaeology* 52 (2008), 17–210.

Unger (ed.) 2008: R. Unger (ed.), *Britain and Poland-Lithuania: Contact and Comparison from the Middle Ages to 1795* (Boston, 2008).

Walker and Graham 2013: J. Walker and M. Graham, *St. Mary's Abbey, Holme Cultram, Abbeytown, Cumbria: Archaeological and Historical Investigations* (Bowness on Windermere, 2013).

Walker and Graham 2016: J. Walker and M. Graham, *An Interim Report on Archaeological Excavations at Holme Cultram Abbey Season 2015 NGR: NY1774 5075* (unpublished) (Abbeytown, 2016).

HOW ROYAL TOKENS CONSTITUTED AN ART MEDIUM THAT PARTICIPATED IN THE MONARCHICAL SYSTEM BETWEEN 1610 AND 1661

SABRINA VALIN

Introduction

Primarily used in accounting ('to do the books'), royal tokens (*jetons royaux*) gradually came to be manufactured to also commemorate significant achievements of the French government. In fifteenth century France, the duke of Burgundy Philippe le Bon began to use these objects as commemorative items that glorified his government, and which were delivered to the subjects of the court.[1] In the sixteenth century, Charles V ordered tokens struck with his own coat of arms or his bust and a Latin inscription dedicated to him.[2] Moving beyond a utilitarian function, these tokens have often been confused with medals: both media glorified the power of the sovereign but were very different objects. Tokens were produced in more volume and are smaller than medals: they measure 2.7cm in diameter, whereas medals measure 6cm across.[3] And in contrast to medals, tokens possessed an intrinsic value linked to the weight of the metal they contained, which was very important in estimating their monetary value (they were not exchanged for merchandise). In France, tokens delivered annual gifts and *les jetons de presence* given to individuals as an attendance fee in different academies can be considered as a monetary exchange.[4] In England, tokens had an exclusively commercial use and were manufactured for traders, craftsmen, companies and local authorities, who exchanged their tokens for goods. Furthermore, in the seventeenth century, tokens were used when the quantity of silver and copper was insufficient. The last characteristic that separated tokens and medals concerns the iconography of their reverses. The meaning of the mottos found on the reverse of tokens was intentionally difficult to interpret, whereas the representations on medals were very clear.[5]

This paper sets out what is distinctive about these tokens and explores their variety. Token exchanges between 1610 and 1661 will be also analysed. Generally, tokens show the coats of arms of France and Navarre or the king's bust on the obverse, and a commemorative iconography on the reverse. The first category examined is the annual gifts to the king and the members of his family, who were also his private councillors. The second concerns tokens struck to reward officers of the royal institutions and their chiefs. Finally, I will examine ceremonial tokens, which were thrown to common people during coronations or weddings. In view of the discussion and rich documentation, it will be demonstrated that these items constituted a way for the crown to strengthen the relationship between the king, his officers and the people. The delivery of royal tokens materialised the loyalty of members of the royal institutions towards the king, and the king's gratitude towards his subjects.[6] This contribution will demonstrate that the exclusivity of this bond was not only founded on the value of this gift, but above all on the interpretation of an aristocratic 'language', difficult to understand.[7] The lower classes could not access the different levels of meaning carried by the imagery on these tokens, which created inequalities of understanding. They would have experienced tokens as they were thrown to crowds in royal ceremonies. Thus the final section of the chapter proves that the ritual of the delivery of ceremonial tokens to common people, as well as the precious metal (gold and silver) they contained, were almost as important as their iconographic content.

The following abbreviations are used :
BnF = The Bibliothèque nationale de France.
Arch. Nat = Archives nationales, Paris.

[1] Pastoureau (1984), 15.
[2] van Loon (1732), foreword.
[3] Burke (1995), 245.
[4] Guéant and Prieur (2007), 8; Sarmant and Ploton-Nicollet (2010), 16.
[5] Marin (1981), 157.
[6] Furetière (1727), 837; Sarmant and Ploton-Nicollet (2010), 12–14.
[7] Boureau (1985), 119.

The annual gifts to the king, his relatives and his treasurer

Every year or month, the king and a part of his family received a purse of 100 gold tokens that commemorated the most glorious events of the government.[8] Even if the function of these items became more and more glorifying, they kept their initial accounting use. Indeed, Louis XIV needed a set of 100 tokens to do the books, according to the imperial tradition.[9] Between 1610 and 1614, the two main recipients were Louis XIII and his mother Marie de Médicis; they received 210 tokens.[10] Four years after their wedding in 1615, Louis XIII and his wife Anne d'Autriche received 212 tokens, in addition to Marie de Médicis, who collected a purse of 100 tokens.[11] Following the birth of Louis Dieudonné in 1638, the new king, his mother Anne d'Autriche, and his father Louis XIII received a generous sum of 312 tokens as gifts.[12] In 1643, following the death of Louis XIII, his brother Gaston d'Orléans received a purse of tokens instead of the monarch, while Louis Dieudonné and Anne d'Autriche received 212 tokens.[13] During the minority of Louis XIV, Jean Warin fulfilled an order of 312 royal tokens dated to 1646 for the king, his mother, and his brother Philippe d'Orléans.[14] This document proves that the number had not changed since 1619, when Pierre Regnier was an officer of the workshop of *la Monnaie du Moulin.*[15] Although gifts regularly included a sum of 312 tokens, archival documents provide no reason why this particular number should be so popular.

Apart from royal marriages or deaths, which occasioned changes in the number of tokens given, the number of tokens in purses remained constant at 100 throughout the seventeenth century, demonstrating an almost ritual nature to these remittances. Who was responsible for the production of these royal tokens? Under Henry IV, it was the Duke of Sully, the general treasurer (*trésorier général*), who ordered tokens from the engraver. At the beginning of each year, in the morning, the Duke gave a purse of tokens to the king and his wife:

> 'Every year, the first day of the month of January, Sully gave to the king and the queen purses of tokens in the morning and then, there were little funny scenes with a naïve story'.[16]

Under the reign of Louis XIII, the patron of royal tokens also appears to be a treasurer, but a treasurer with a different remit, the treasurer of savings (*trésorier de l'Épargne*). An extract from a document dated to the 27th December 1638 records this:

> 'The treasurer of savings commissioned from Jean Warin the quantity of three hundred and twelve tokens for the king, the queen and the Dauphin. These tokens weighed eleven marcs three ounces two gros. Besides, Jean Warin was the author of eight thousand tokens in silver to be delivered to the treasurer himself'.

They weighed nine, twenty, thirteen marcs, six ounces.[17] The text reveals that the patron of royal tokens here was a treasurer, like the Duke of Sully mentioned above. He was probably

[8] Furetière (1690), 837 in Sarmant and Ploton-Nicollet (2010), 13–14.

[9] Mahudel (1729); Feuardent (1904), 6.

[10] Arch. Nat., Z[1b] 399: 27th February 1614. Certificate given by the court of moneys to Pierre Regnier for the tokens of the Council of State.

[11] Arch. Nat., Z[1b] 401: Certificate dated 1st March 1619, quoted by Mazerolle (1902–1904) vol. 1, 240.

[12] Arch. Nat., Z[1b] 407: 27th December 1638; 12th–13th January 1639. Information about the tokens ordered by the treasurer of savings, distributed to the king and the treasurer savings in 1639, manufactured by Jean Warin.

[13] Arch. Nat. Z1b 409: Request for the supply of State council tokens dated 19th December 1643 (1644), quoted by Mazerolle (1902–1904) vol.1, 76.

[14] Arch. Nat., Z[1b] 409: Request addressed to Jean Warin and dated 3rd January 1646, quoted by Mazerolle (1902–1904) vol. 1, 78.

[15] Arch. Nat., Z[1b] 401: Certificate dated 1st March 1619 given by the court of moneys to Pierre Régnier for the tokens of the Council of State, quoted by Mazerolle (1902–1904) vol. 1, 240.

[16] Prévôt de Longpérier (1863), 425: '*Chaque année, au premier jour de janvier, Sully offrait au roi et à la reine des bourses de jetons qu'il leur portait de bon matin, et il s'ensuivait des petites scènes dont le récit naïf est véritablement fort amusant*'.

[17] Arch. Nat., Z[1b] 407: 27th December 1638; 12th–13th January 1639: '*L'an mil six cens trente huict, le XXVIIe décembre, nous Nicolas Frénicle, conseiller du Roy en sa Cour des monnoyes, assisté de maître Nicolas Delaistre, greffier de lad. ville sur le réquisittoire à nous faict par Maître Jehan Varin, maître garde et conducteur des engins de la monnoye du Moulin de ceste ville de Paris feuilles transportéz de lad. Monnoye du Moulin au logement dud. Varin, nous auroit esté par iceluy Varrin, cy présenté la quantité de troys cens douze jettons desd. lesquels led. Varrin nous auroit dict avoir du commandement du Sieur Trésorier de l'Espargne de faire fabriquer pour estre par luy déslivréz au Roy, à la Reyne et à Monseigneur le dauphin et poidz fait desd. jettons pezant onze marcs trois onces deux gros d'iceluy. De plus, nous a esté représenté par led. Varrin la quantitté de huict mil jettons d'argent pour estre aussy par luy déllivréz aud. sieur Trésorier de l'espargne poids faict iceux le sont trouvéz pezant neuf, vingt, treize, marcs, six onces*'.

Bertrand de La Bazinière.[18] The high number of tokens ordered under his control (more than 8,000) would have been justified by the number of members of the treasury of savings (*trésor de l'Épargne*) and the goods he had to manage. The monarch and his officers had excellent benefits (the cardinal of Richelieu, for instance, received a plot of land). The treasurer of savings (*trésorier de l'Épargne*) was responsible for managing the incomes of the court, enabling royal expenditure. There were two or three treasurers of savings who worked on a rota during a period of three years.[19] Generally, one of these treasurers of savings ordered and delivered these purses of tokens to the royal family.

Even if the treasurer of savings had to deliver his own tokens to the members of the institution of which he was the chief, these 8,000 tokens could be considered a gift. Sully, for example, received 'a box of diamonds with a royal portrait, a perfume chain set with diamonds and bracelets very precious' for having delivered tokens to the king.[20] And Bertrand de la Bazinière benefited by having 8,000 of these little medal-like objects carrying the king's portrait and the memory of past achievements of the monarch.

The aesthetic quality of the royal tokens strengthened the social link between the king and his officers. The design was an 'expression of social qualities' according to Norbert Elias.[21] An archival document connected to the production of the tokens ordered from Jean Warin by the *trésorier de l'Épargne* mentioned above shows the care taken with the design of these pieces, making specific mention of the hallmarks used by the engravers:

> 'A hallmark of three lines of high on four of wide representing a woman bent to the ground and another woman who carries a basket was used with the hallmark inventoried under the number 472. We added a horn of plenty which spreads at the top of the sky and these words DIVITIAS DIIDANT E JVRA FRVENDI above these figures and in the exergue: 1639. There is, on the other side of this token, the name and the portrait of King Louis XIII'.[22]

This description from the inventory of hallmarks and coins by Nicolas Delaunay is enlightening when considering our example (fig. 1). Each hallmark of these tokens seems to be engraved by Jean Warin because they were manufactured with precision. The quality of these tokens, in comparison to others, can be understood by a consideration of the wider context of the time. In 1639, Jean Warin was chosen by Louis XIII to conduct a monetary reform that included the introduction of more regular, more circular currency, reintroducing a mechanical press for production.[23] This reform implies a change also took place in the manufacture of tokens delivered to the king by the treasurer – they too were now manufactured by machine. The beauty of the tokens, like the now regularised coinage, were connected with the function of the treasurer, and the King's council sought the advice of an engraver for their tokens. This phenomenon appears in 1643 when the intendant of mottos (*intendant des devises*) Dubuisson-Aubenay was commissioned for token design.[24] Dubuisson-Aubenay was man of letters who could not provide advice to the council on artistic composition, so Jean Warin was called upon.

The tokens themselves show a cornucopia (horn of plenty) that pours out wealth onto farmers picking up these goods (fig. 1). This picture is surrounded by an inscription: '*Divitias dii dant et iura fruendi*' which means 'both give goods and the right to enjoy it'.[25] This motto

[18] Mousnier (2005), 760; Vignal Souleyreau (2013), 378.

[19] Charlet (1996), 67.

[20] Prévôt de Longpérier (1863), 17: '*Une boëte de diamans où estoit le portrait du roi, une chaîne de parfum enrichie de diamans et des bracelets fort riches*'.

[21] Elias (1991), 38: '*L'expression hautement différenciée de certaines qualités sociales*'.

[22] Arch. Nat., KK 960: *Inventaire des poinçons et carrés de la Monnaie des médailles, dressé après l'érection de la charge de directeur du balancier des médailles, 'establi sous la grande galerie du Louvre' en faveur de Nicolas de Launay*, par édit de juin 1696, fol. 473: 'Inventory of the hallmarks and coins of La Monnaie des médailles, drawn up after the erection of the office of director of the mechanical press, 'establi dans la grande galerie du Louvre' in favour of Nicolas de Launay by an edict of June 1696'. fol. 473: '*Un poinçon de trois lignes de haut sur quatre de large représentant une femme courbée jusqu'*à terre et une autre qui emporte un panier. Pour servir avec le poinçon inventorié ci devant n. *472 à des jettons où l'on a ajouté au-dessus de ces quatre figures une corne d'abondance qui se répand du haut du ciel et ces mots DIVITIAS DIIDANT E JVRA FRVENDI et dans l'exergue: 1639. Il y a de l'autre côté du jetton le nom et le portrait du Roi Louis XIII*'.

[23] Arch. Nat., Z^{1b} 538: Letters patent dated the 24th December 1639 quoted by Mazerolle (1932), vol. 1.

[24] Juren (1976), 156–70.

[25] BnF, Département des Manuscrits, Clairambault 281, fol. 595.

refers to the prosperity of the government and alludes to the duties of the treasurer who gave a purse of these tokens to the king in 1639. In this way, the royal power and treasurer's competences are both communicated by this token. The reverse design is, of course, connected to the royal portrait on the obverse. The king is represented in an ancient Roman style, clothed with a paludamentum and wearing a laurel wreath. Through this token Louis XIII was connected to a long line of Roman emperors, who also had agricultural and industrial holdings.

Fig. 1: Silver token of Louis XIII, on the reverse a horn of plenty above four farmers (1639) (Ø 27mm, 6.18 , 12h) (BnF, MMA, JR. 982).

Even if these tokens served to highlight the treasurer's skill, the social gap between the two recipients was indicated by the material chosen. The royal tokens intended for the monarch were made of gold and the treasurer's tokens of silver. This material distinction is strengthened by the quality of the purses that contained these tokens. Some payment orders show that royal purses were generally made in red velvet and contained gold embroidery.[26] This was characteristic of royal clothes and their embroidery, like the mantles of the Bourbon dynasty with golden lilies.[27] Worn during royal ceremonies, this attire marked the hierarchical relationship between the king and his subjects within the royal court.

An award for the officers related to the manufacturing of tokens

This difference between the tokens delivered to the king and those given to the treasurer is connected to the function of these items. The first were manufactured to satisfy the king, who could see the glory of his reign through these little medal-like objects, and the second essentially constituted an award for the work of the officer. The treasurer received tokens as a payment for his delivery of royal tokens and, above all, for having served the government. Beyond this pecuniary function, this delivery was considered a form of gratefulness for his good behaviour towards the king. This particular function of tokens continues today: tokens supported by a block chain reward particular behaviours.[28] Tokens rewarded, above all, the treasurer for his will and his capacity to translate the thoughts of the monarch through the mottos inscribed on the tokens.[29] Sully was the first treasurer who was well known for this, under the reign of Henry IV. His zealousness is visible through his memoirs when he wrote that the reverses of tokens were created 'as his majesty had given him the subject'.[30] He created token designs from topics that the king chose. A conversation between the king and Sully illustrates this relationship:

> 'Rosny, you will have to remember to adapt a motto to a topic selected in the presence of Monsieur de Montpensier and the cardinal de Joyeuse, when they were talking about an argument with Messieurs de Bouillon, de la Trimouille and their consequences that we all know, like leaks. I answer them that my subjects were wrong to span my reign with worries, because I don't have more pleasure than to make them happy and to be loved by everybody. I ordered you to try to make me happy and according to my will like you do'.[31]

The token shown in fig. 2 captures the essence of this conversation, communicating the unity between the king and his subjects. The reverse shows an open pomegranate whose

[26] BnF, Département des Manuscrits, Nouv. Acqu. fr. 165: order of payment of the tokens provided to the Council of State January–March 1639. Fol. 76, quoted by Mazerolle (1932) vol. 2, 74.

[27] Sternberg (2014), 40.

[28] See the contribution of Maurer in this volume.

[29] Babelon (1982–1983), 23.

[30] Prévôt de Longpérier (1863), 11: '*Tels que Sa Majesté lui avait donné le sujet de les devoir faire*'.

[31] Prévôt de Longpérier (1863), 15: '*Rosny vous serez-vous souvenu d'y approprier une devise sur le sujet que je vous dis en présence de Monsieur de Montpensier et du cardinal de Joyeuse, lors qu'ils me parloient des brouilleries de Messieurs de Bouillon, de la Trimouille et de leur sequelle que nous cognoissons tous dont l'on bruyoit lors et bruit on encores à présent et que je leur respondis que mes sujets avoient grand tort de vouloir ainsi traverser mon règne d'inquiétudes, veu que je n'avois nul plus grand desir que de leur faire du bien à tous et d'estre aussy aymé de tous, et vous ordonnay d'essayer à me faire ne rencontrent point si heureusement et selon mon gré comme vous faites*'.

seeds refer to the favourites who are protected by the king, who is symbolised by the crown above the fruit.[32] The seeds also allude to the wishes made by the subjects towards the king. This type was created in 1604 to prove that the wish of this monarch was to make peace. This same design was reemployed in 1635, under the reign of Louis XIII for the same reason.

Fig. 2: Copper token of Louis XIII with an open pomegranate on the obverse and a sky filled with stars on the reverse (1635) (Ø 28mm, 6.93g, 12h) (BnF, MMA, JR. 965).

Henry IV rewarded his treasurer for having understood what the monarch wished to see represented on his tokens. This was less the case under Louis XIII since the role of the treasurer in this period was limited to the ordering of royal tokens and their delivery. The prerogative for the design of the tokens was transferred to men of letters or to the intendant of mottos at this time.[33]

Just as the treasurer was rewarded for creating and ordering royal tokens, the *intendant des devises* received a purse of 100 tokens for having created the designs.[34] Dubuisson-Aubenay (*intendant des devises* between 1650 and 1652) probably received a payment similar to this for his work.[35] This gift rewarded the officer for his invention. The engraver of the hallmarks (*tailleur général des monnaies de France*) received two purses of tokens: one purse more than the intendant of mottos.[36] This award demonstrates that the manual labour required for the manufacturing of these items was valued highly, no doubt because of the emphasis on their artistic quality. If engravers received 200 tokens for having created a die matrix, Jean Warin likely received this amount for engraving the dies for the token of 1639, but this was not his only reward. Having had the honour to give tokens to Louis XIV during his reign, Jean Warin was also certainly awarded for this delivery in the same vein as the treasurer of savings.[37]

The will to reward the manufacturers of royal tokens is visible through the remittance of tokens to the workers of the court of moneys. Contrary to the *intendant des devises* and the engraver, these individuals were not rewarded for a particular task but for their daily activity. Above all, tokens maintained a social link between the king and the members of this sovereign court, created in 1552. Officers in the court of money (*cour des monnaies*) had rights, privileges and prerogatives, which are confirmed by documents dating to 1560. In January 1568, the court of money published an edict that allowed the chamber of account (*chambre des comptes*) to write an act concerning these privileges.[38] This act shows the importance of these gifts for the workers of the court of moneys because they constituted an award for the manufacturing of coins and tokens. Beyond this, the gift of tokens to these manufacturers constituted a compensation for the painful and dangerous nature of their work. From the middle of the sixteenth century the use of the mechanical press to strike tokens caused a lot of accidents.[39] For all these reasons, officers enjoyed the right to candles, roses, tokens, feathers, writing cases, paper and money every year. In 1575 this right is restricted to tokens, roses and candles.[40]

[32] De Bie (1636), 289.
[33] Juren (1976), 156–70; Juren (1988), 24–38.
[34] Blanchet (1950), 199.
[35] Juren (1976), 156.
[36] Blanchet (1950), 199.
[37] Jambu (2014), 19: 'les jetons du Conseil de 1671'; 'Jean Warin delivered himself to the king one hundred gold tokens and four thousand silver tokens' ('*Jean Warin remit ensuite lui-même au roi les cent jetons d'or et quatre mille d'argent restant*').
[38] Abot de Bazinghen (1764), 141.
[39] Jambu (2013), 188.
[40] Abot de Bazinghen (1764), 242.

Material, coats of arms and social distinction

Tokens formed a very important award for the court of money that was responsible for permitting the striking of medals or tokens at the mechanical press from 15th May 1628.[41] However, the metal used for the manufacturing of these items was less precious than that reserved for royal tokens. This difference of material is a demonstration of a social hierarchy, as demonstrated in the following mandate of 1631:

> '...humbly begs Pierre Regnier, master, guard, mechanical press worker, following the order of the court, to make and give back one hundred and twenty five tokens in silver weighing three marcs, six gros and a half and two matrix. He was paid for their manufacturing, which one of them was struck with royal coats of arms and the other was made with coats of arms of Monseigneur de Préaux, guard of French seals. Besides, he would have given twelve purses of tokens in brass to the clerk of the court of moneys'.[42]

Tokens struck in silver were delivered to the king and the guard of seals whereas tokens struck in brass were given to the clerk of the court of moneys. The prestige of silver tokens was further highlighted by the inclusion of coats of arms on the obverses. In addition to the value of the metal, the use of coats of arms meant a distinction could be made between royal tokens and those that were delivered to the members of the court of moneys. Given to the chairmen, to the general counsels, and to the officers of this institution in gifts, these items in brass might be deemed a right, along with other gifts.

In addition to the king, officers of royal institutions and some of the populace were allowed to place their coats of arms on the obverse of tokens. The Jesuit author Claude-François Ménestrier wrote in *The real art of the coats of arms* in an address to the king:

> 'To whom else could I address the marks of my gratitude to your eminence in the story of all peoples and in this one of coats of arms of which we owe the origin to the judge of coats of arms?'[43]

This quotation shows that all coats of arms were recorded and new ones were created under the aegis of the monarch and the judge of coats of arms (*juge général des armes de France*), who was mister Hozier. This monopoly on heraldry is visible from 1615, when the *vicomte de Saint-Mauris* became a judge of coats of arms until this citation dated to 1671.[44] Mister Hozier acquired this office in 1641 and was responsible for certifying nobility.[45] His work demonstrates that coats of arms were used to establish a hierarchy between the nobility, the clergy and the common people. Merchants from lower classes bought their own coats of arms. They also succeeded in buying coats of arms that belonged to the clergy and nobility in order to progress from a poorly esteemed job to an honourable one.[46] For merchants, the material of their tokens (normally copper or brass) was less important than the coats of arms they bore, which might be compared to a visiting card.[47]

In the seventeenth century the number of requests for coats of arms grew because merchants gained access to higher positions. This phenomenon was contemporary with the devaluation of money caused by the weakness of monetary production in this period.[48] In this context tokens were considered a 'money sign' and could be exchanged against merchandise even if the metal value of the token was less valuable. Merchants took advantage of this economic crisis by putting their coats of arms on tokens since this gave a value to objects manufactured in debased metal.[49] In addition, the use of coats of arms allowed users

[41] Arch. Nat., Z^{1b} 403: Edict of the Court of moneys dated 15th May 1628 quoted by Mazerolle (1902–1904), 289.

[42] Arch. Nat., Z^{1b} 622: Certificate of the 4th August 1631: '*Supplye humblement Pierre Régnier maître garde et conducteur de la monnoye du Moulin du Roy disant que de l'ordonnance de la Cour il auroit fait et fourny cent vingt-cinq jettons d'argent pesant trois marcs, six gros et demy et deux carrés exprès pour la fabrication d'iceluy l'un aux armes du Roy et l'autre aux armes de Monseigneur de Préaux, garde des sceaux de France et auroit fourny au greffe de lad. Cour douze bourses de jetons de latton*'.

[43] Ménestrier (1671), 6: 'À *qui pourrois-je donc mieux adresser les marques les plus belles de l'honneur qu'à celuy qui les sçait si bien conserver et si l'origine des armoiries demande des juges sçavants dans l'histoire de tous les peuples et dans celle du blason, quel autre pourois-je trouver plus éclairé et mieux instruit de ces Mystères que Votre Éminence qui sait ses estudes diverstissantes et les délassemens de son Esprit de ces connaissances curieuses?*'.

[44] Viton de Saint-Allais (1816), 536.

[45] Palliot (1660), foreword.

[46] Géliot (1660), 5.

[47] Florange (1921), 2.

[48] Foucault (1990), 194–95.

[49] Guéant and Prieur (2007), 8.

to identify the owners of these tokens, as opposed to official currency, which always carried the royal coats of arms or the portrait of the king.[50] These items are akin to tokens of the ancient Agora, which increased the fame of their possessors according to Bill Maurer.[51]

Sometimes, common people or merchants were unable to request their own coats of arms from the judge of coats of arms.[52] In this case, they could acquire a last category of tokens available to all the members of the *Ancien Régime*. These metallic items, which can be compared to money and systematically have the king's coats of arms or portrait on the obverse and simple figures on the reverse, are called commonplace tokens.[53] Their function was pecuniary because these metallic pieces, made of brass and copper, were sold at the price of the metal used for their manufacturing.[54] Contrary to commemorative tokens, these items are devoid of a date in the exergue or other references to an event. This characteristic indicates that this kind of token was destined for the common people and created a last level of distinction. Nevertheless, the coats of arms of France and Navarre on these tokens recalled the supremacy of the royal authority through the use of royal imagery.

A symbolic language dedicated to the aristocracy under the reign of Louis XIV

Having explained how tokens constituted an award for members of the crown and some officers, and served to create social distinction, I shall now explore how Louis XIV and his intendant of mottos invented designs which delivered a political message at the beginning of his reign. From the reign of Louis XIII, tokens contained an aristocratic 'language' that was intentionally difficult to interpret.[55] This language, which only the king, his relatives and his favourites could fully understand, is also found on tokens struck under the reign of Louis XIV. The mottos behaved in a way similar to other areas that served to express French aristocracy, like dress, language and comportment.[56] The theory of Paolo Giovio was followed in creating these designs to make them more mysterious; the reverses often had only two or three figures and a short Latin inscription.[57]

This type of motto represented what Pierre Le Moyne called 'the philosophy of court' because they ensured the circulation of court values.[58] Three tokens dated to the 1650s allude to the monarchical system through differing designs. The first shows a fountain with three washbasins encircled by the inscription '*colligit et spargit*' ('he gathers and scatters', fig. 3).[59] According to Le Moyne the phrase alludes to the idea that the king gives back the subsidies he receives from his subjects (represented by the streams of water), while also highlighting the moderation of these subsidies.[60] The second example (fig. 4) shows a tank from which water spurts out into several little basins. The same legend surrounds this picture, but the 'et' has been replaced by '*ut*': '*colligit ut spargit*'. The third example (fig. 5) shows three columns of steam rising towards the sun. The legend '*exigit ut donet*' means 'he takes for giving'.

Fig. 3: Brass token of Louis XIV, on the reverse a fountain with three washbasins (1652) (Ø 27mm, 6.4g, 12h) (1652) (BnF, MMA, JR. 1335).

All three token designs refer to subsidies that the king asked from his subjects and that he returned to them. These taxes were redistributed to the taxpayers through the delivery of these tokens. These tokens delivered a political message addressed to royal

[50] Roman (1842), 393.
[51] See Maurer's contribution in this volume.
[52] Roman (1842), 393.
[53] Pastoureau (1984), 16.
[54] Rouyer (1887), 421–24; Caron (1897), 447–49.
[55] Boureau (1985), 119.
[56] Sternberg (2014), 11.
[57] Giovio (1561).
[58] Le Moyne (1666), 59–60.
[59] Sarmant and Ploton-Nicollet (2010), no. 3814: Matthew 12, 30: '*Qui mecum non colligit spargit*'.
[60] Le Moyne (1666), 452–53.

Fig. 4: Copper token of Louis XIV, on the reverse a tank from which water spurts out into several little basins (1656) (Ø 27mm, 6.95g, 12h) (BnF, MMA, JR. 1375).

Fig. 5: Brass token of Louis XIV, on the reverse a sun which attracts columns of steam (1657) (Ø 27mm, 7.14g, 12h) (BnF, MMA, JR. 1383).

officers who received these objects as gifts. They paint a picture of a fiscally wise monarch who wished to rebalance the state coffers by lowering the subsidies asked of officers.

On fig. 5 the sun, which attracts columns of steam, represents the king himself who received subsidies from his favourites. This symbolic representation of the monarch in the form of the sun was common from the reign of Charles V le Sage.[61] It reached its apogee under the reign of Louis XIV. This motif appears on the reverse of several tokens intended for an institution called '*Les Fermes*', which collected taxes.[62] Through this kind of token the king wanted to spread his political projects to communities and institutions, and wanted to convince officers of the soundness of his rule.

In the wish to attract the support of the king's subjects, the scholar Louis Douvrier invented a motto to symbolise the supernatural power of Louis XIV in the universe. It represents the image of a shining sun with a human face above the earth. The sun became a monarchical emblem with the famous phrase '*nec pluribus impar*', which literally translates as 'not unequal to many' (fig. 6).[63] The image would illustrate the power of the monarch over his kingdom and other territories. It would mean that the monarch reigned with constancy and firmness over the rest of the universe thanks to his subjects. The sunbeams illustrated the kindness and acts of generosity shown by the king to his subjects for their services.

Fig. 6: Copper token of Louis XIV with two globes on the obverse and a shining sun above the earth on the reverse (1658) (Ø 27mm, 5.86g, 12h) (BnF, MMA, JR. 1390).

Ceremonial tokens

Contrary to reward tokens, which were delivered to the officers associated with the manufacturing of tokens, coronation or wedding tokens were thrown to common people who assisted in the ceremony. This diffusion served to communicate the king's propaganda, among other functions.[64] The distribution of such tokens during the coronation and the wedding of Louis XIII illustrate how these objects served to cement the social link between the king and his people. As the king delivered gold and silver tokens to the people on this occasion, he was accompanied by 12 of his peers and preceded by the heralds of arms, the master of ceremonies and four knights of the Holy Spirit (*saint-esprit*), who carried bread made of gold and silver and a vase filled with wine.[65] The entire procession was a visual demonstration of the king's power.[66] There was also a symbolic or mystical aspect to the

[61] Ziegler (2013), 33.
[62] Sarmant and Ploton-Nicollet (2010), no. 3761.
[63] Ziegler (2013), 30.
[64] Burke (1995), 245 defined the term 'propaganda' as 'the attempt to transmit social and political values'.
[65] Favyn (1612), 1326, quoted by Blanchet (1889), 16.
[66] Chartier (2013).

ceremony. Distributed as a sign of the king's liberality by the heralds of arms, the royal tokens were also imbued with an esoteric power. Thanks to the royal touch (*toucher des écrouelles*), the king was believed to cure people by throwing tokens.[67] The power of the king's touch, passed to the recipient through the token, meant that the monarch became a miracle worker, in full view of all.

Thanks to the ceremonial tokens, the king could get closer to the people and create a bond with them, as with the wedding tokens. An author of the eighteenth century mentions the wedding tokens of Louis XIII and Anne d'Autriche:

> 'After the nuptial benediction, one threw to the people a quantity of gold and silver medals…'[68]

Dazzled by the beauty of the ephemeral decor around the cathedral *Saint-André de Bordeaux*, the crowd received these tokens as if they were medals.[69] The aim of the crown was certainly to give the illusion of getting closer to people. French queens would also distribute tokens to the crowd after nuptial ceremonies in an attempt to establish bonds. When she married Louis XIV in Saint-Jean-de-Luz in 1660, Marie-Thérèse d'Autriche threw silver tokens from the top of the galleries of her house.[70] As well as having material value, these tokens were a mechanism by which one could keep a visual memory of the event.

The iconography of this type of token had to be accessible to everyone. Two kinds of scenes were used for coronation tokens of this kind. One represents the Holy Ampulla held by a hand above the city of Reims (fig. 7). This ampulla held sacred oil used to anoint the king during his coronation; legend held that the vessel held oil of sacred myrrh (called '*Saint-Chrême*' in French) that had been used in the coronation of kings since Clovis.[71] This motif focuses on the nine anointments applied during the coronation from the Holy Ampulla. In the representation of Reims the Palace of Tau is visible, where the kings resided before their coronation in the cathedral.[72] It was a way to recall that Louis XIII was sacred to Reims, contrary to his father, Henry IV. Nicolas Briot, responsible for the engraving of this token, achieved a realistic design, and the hand taking the holy vial alludes to the distribution of these very tokens by the king to the inhabitants of Reims[73].

Fig. 7: Copper token of the coronation of Louis XIII, on the reverse the Holy Ampulla held by a hand above the city of Reims (1610) (Ø 30mm, 2g, 12h) (BnF, MMA, JR.714).

Another picture engraved on coronation tokens represents a fleshless hand that picks up the Holy Ampulla between two fingers (fig. 8). Like the preceding token, the image alludes to the coronation ceremony via the representation of monuments. This motif focuses on a precise moment in time, the nine anointments applied during the coronation from the Holy Ampulla.[74] The image alludes to rituals like offerings, the

Fig. 8: Silver token of the coronation of Louis XIII, on the reverse the Holy Ampulla held by a fleshless hand (Ø 28mm, 8.87g, 12h) (BnF, MMA, JR.716).

[67] Fogel (2000), 46.
[68] Dom Devienne said in 1771 in the *History of the city of Bordeaux*, 195: '*Après que la bénédiction nuptiale eut été donnée, on jeta au peuple une quantité de médailles d'or et d'argent…*', reported in Fayolle (1902), 78.
[69] This ephemeral decor is described in *Le Mercure françois, ou, la Suitte de l'histoire de la paix* (Paris 1615–1617), 25, vol. 4.
[70] Caron (1902), 11.
[71] Bloch (1924), 224–26.
[72] Fogel (2000), 45–46.
[73] Rouyer (1895), 219.
[74] Rouyer (1895), 219; Cosandey (2000), 388–89.

kiss of peace and communion.[75] Just after this ceremony, tokens rained down on the public, thrown by the king and the heralds of arms.

At times, people may not have had the cultural knowledge required to understand this religious imagery. Paul Veyne records a similar phenomenon, noting 'the feeling that a space was occupied by the high power of a complex language which passed the listeners by like a wind high above their heads, a speech of which one can only hear the general meaning.'[76] Nevertheless, this particular cultural and religious reference was well known by all members of society at the time. The preciseness of the design (machine made), as well as the representation of the landscape, and the precious nature of the metal contributed to highlight the 'magnificence' of the piece and to leave an impression on the viewer.[77] Nonetheless these objects memorialised the king's glory and served to close the distance between the king and his people.

Conclusion

Struck in the seventeenth century, French tokens were essentially given in a commemorative way to strengthen the king's power. Delivered each year in purses of 100 tokens, they formed part of a ritual. Manufactured as gifts, they constituted a reward for the king and his officers, who received these objects. They created a link between the monarch and his subjects, based on the act of distribution and also on the act of understanding the motifs the tokens bore. Different social classes may have understood different levels of meaning, but regardless of the level of understanding, these objects served to create a relationship with the monarch. Thrown during royal ceremonies like coronations and weddings, these tokens constituted heavenly manna for the people who collected these items to keep these events in memory.

Bibliography

Abot de Bazinghen 1764: F. Abot de Bazinghen, *Traité des monnoies, et de la juridiction de la Cour des monnoies, en forme de dictionnaire*, 2 vols (Paris, 1764).

Babelon 1982–1983: J.-P. Babelon, 'Architecture et emblématique dans les médailles de Henri IV', *Revue de l'art* 58–59 (1982–1983), 21–40.

Blanchet 1889: J.-A. Blanchet, 'Médailles et jetons du sacre des rois de France', *BSFN* 352 (1889), 1–16.

Blanchet 1950: J.-A. Blanchet, 'Jetons de l'ordinaire des guerres de 1651 à 1653', *RN* 12 (1950), 197–201.

Bloch 1924: M. Bloch, *Les rois thaumaturges: étude sur le caractère surnaturel attribué à la puissance royale particulièrement en France et en Angleterre* (Paris, 1924).

Bourdieu 1979: P. Bourdieu, *La distinction: critique sociale du jugement* (Paris, 1979).

Boureau 1985: A. Boureau, *L'Aigle* (Paris, 1985).

Burke 1995: P. Burke, *The Fabrication of Louis XIV* (French translation *Louis XIV: les stratégies de la gloire*) (Paris, 1995).

Caron 1897: E. Caron, 'Un marché de fabrication de jetons sedanais en 1639', *Gazette Numismatique* (1897), 447–49.

Caron 1902: E. Caron, 'Á propos du jeton du mariage de Louis XIV', *RN* 6 (1902), 11.

Charlet 1996: C. Charlet, 'Les institutions financières de l'Ancien Régime', in Monnaie de Paris (1996), 66–78.

Chartier 2013: R. Chartier, 'Le sens de la représentation', *La Vie des idées* (https://laviedesidees.fr/Le-sens-de-la-representation.html; accessed 26/06/2019).

Cosandey 2000: F. Cosandey, *La reine de France. Symbole et pouvoir* (Paris, 2000).

De Bie 1636: J. de Bie, *La France métallique contenant les actions célèbres tant publiques que privées des rois et des reines remarquées en leurs médailles d'or et d'argent et de bronze* (Paris, 1636).

Elias 1991: N. Elias, *La Société des individus* (Paris, 1991).

Favyn 1612: A. Favyn, *Histoire de Navarre contenant l'origine, les vies et conquestes des rois depuis leur commencement jusqu'à présent* (Paris, 1612).

Fayolle 1902: E. de Fayolle, 'Médailles et jetons municipaux de Bordeaux', *Gazette Numismatique* (1902), 69–80.

[75] Fogel (2000), 46.

[76] Veyne (1988), 3–22 in Sabatier (1991), 418: 'Chacun sentait que l'espace était occupé par une haute puissance au langage débordant, qu'on n'écoutait pas, mais qui passait, comme le vent, très haut au-dessus des têtes, en proférant un discours dont on n'entendait guère que le sens général'.

[77] Burke (1995), 15.

Feuardent 1904: F. Feuardent, *Jetons et méreaux depuis Louis IX jusqu'à la fin du consulat de Bonaparte* (3 vols.) (Paris, 1904).
Florange 1921: J. Florange, *Armorial du jetonophile: guide de l'amateur des jetons armoriés* (Paris, 1921).
Fogel 2000: M. Fogel, *L'Etat dans la France moderne: de la fin du XVème siècle au milieu du XVIIIe siècle* (Paris, 2000).
Foucault 1990: M. Foucault, *Les mots et les choses: une archéologie des sciences humaines* (Paris, 1990).
Furetière 1727: A. Furetière, *Dictionnaire universel, contenant généralement tous les mots françois tant vieux que modernes* (3 vols.) (La Haye, 1727).
Géliot 1660: L. Géliot, *La vraye et parfaite science des armoiries* (Dijon, 1660).
Giovio 1561: P. Giovio, *Dialogo dell'imprese militari e amorose* (Lyon, 1561).
Guéant and Prieur 2007: O. Guéant and M. Prieur, *Bustes des rois et reines de France sur les jetons de l'Ancien Régime* (Paris, 2007).
Jambu 2013: J. Jambu, 'Les jetons des officiers de la Monnaie de Lille', *BSFN* 68 (2013), 182–89.
Jambu 2014: J. Jambu, 'Le jeton des étrennes de Sa Majesté pour l'année 1671', *BSFN* 69 (2014), 16–19.
Juren 1976: V. Juren, 'Les projets de Dubuisson-Aubenay pour les jetons du Conseil d'État', *RN* 18 (1976), 156–70.
Juren 1988: V. Juren, 'Le jeton français et la littérature emblématique', *XVII*[e] *siècle* 158 (janvier–mars 1988), 21–40.
Le Moyne 1666: P. Le Moyne, *De l'art des devises* (Paris, 1666).
Mahudel 1729: N. Mahudel, 'De l'origine et de l'usage des jetons', *Histoire de l'Académie royale des inscriptions et des belles lettres* 5 (1729), 259–64.
Marin 1981: L. Marin, *Le portrait du roi* (Paris, 1981).
Mazerolle 1902–1904: F. Mazerolle, *Les médailleurs français du xv*[e] *au xvII*[e] *siècle* (3 vols.) (Paris, 1902–1904).
Mazerolle 1932: F. Mazerolle, *Jean Warin conducteur de la Monnaie du Moulin, tailleur général des poinçons et effigies de sa vie, sa famille, son œuvre* (2 vols.) (Paris, 1932).
Ménestrier 1671: C.-F. Ménestrier, *Le véritable art du blason et l'origine des armoiries* (Lyon, 1671).
Monnaie de Paris 1996: Monnaie de Paris, *Trésors de la Monnaie: récentes acquisitions du Musée de la Monnaie (1989-1996)* (Paris, 1996).
Mousnier 2005: R. Mousnier, *Les institutions de la France sous la monarchie absolue: 1598-1789* (Paris, 2005).
Palliot 1660: P. Palliot, *La vraye et parfaite science de l'indice armorial du feu maistre Louvan Géliot* (Dijon, 1660).
Pastoureau 1984: M. Pastoureau, *Jetons, méreaux et médailles* (Turnhout, 1984).
Prévôt de Longpérier 1863: A. Prévôt de Longpérier, *Mémoires des sages et royales Oeconomies d'Estat, domestiques, politique et militaires de Henry le Grand l'exemplaire des rois, le prince des vertus, des armes et des lois et le père en effet de ses peuples françois et des servitudes utiles, obéissances convenables et administration loyales* (Paris, 1863).
Roman 1842: J. Roman, 'Jetons banaux du dauphiné', *Bulletin de l'Académie delphinale* 1 (1842), 393–437.
Rouyer 1887: J. Rouyer, 'Une fabrique de jetons d'apparence française à Sedan du temps de Louis XIII, antérieurement à la réunion de cette ville à la France', *RN* (1887), 421–44.
Rouyer 1895: J. Rouyer, *L'œuvre du médailleur Nicolas Briot en ce qui concerne les jetons* (Paris, 1895).
Sabatier 1991: G. Sabatier, 'Les rois de représentation image et pouvoir XVI–XVIIe siècles', *Revue de synthèse*, 112, n°3–4 (1991), 387–422.
Sarmant and Ploton-Nicollet 2010: T. Sarmant and F. Ploton-Nicollet, *Jetons des institutions centrales de l'Ancien Régime* (Paris, 2010).
Sternberg 2014: G. Sternberg, *Status Interaction during the Reign of Louis XIV* (Oxford, 2014).
van Loon 1732: G. van Loon, *Histoire métallique des XVII provinces des Pays-Bas depuis l'abdication de Charles-Quint, jusqu'à la paix de Bade en 1716* (3 vols.) (La Haye, 1732).
Veyne 1988: P. Veyne, 'Conduites sans croyance et œuvres d'art sans spectateurs', *Diogène* 143 (Paris, 1988), 3–22.
Vignal Souleyreau 2013: M.-C. Vignal Souleyreau, *Le trésor pillé du roi, correspondance du cardinal de Richelieu-année 1634* (Paris, 2013).
Viton de Saint-Allais 1816: N. Viton de Saint-Allais, *Dictionnaire encyclopédique de France* (Paris, 1816).
Ziegler 2013: H. Ziegler, *Louis XIV et ses ennemis. Image, propagande et contestation* (translated by A.Virey-Wallon) (Paris, 2013).

FOR CHANGE AND CHARITY: IDENTIFYING THE MOTIVATIONS AND CHARACTERISTICS OF ISSUERS OF TOKENS IN THE BRITISH ISLES IN THE MID-SEVENTEENTH CENTURY

LAURA BURNETT

Introduction

This chapter focuses on the trade tokens issued in the British Isles in the mid-seventeenth century and attempts to address a fundamental question about these tokens that is only partially approached in the existing literature, specifically why certain individuals, and not others, issued tokens. While any 'explanation' is always a difficult prospect, particularly an understanding of the multiple effects that may motivate an individual, I feel it is worth attempting to move beyond the collection of 'facts' about individuals and their tokens to try to recognise broader patterns and study them in a more analytical way. After a brief introduction to this class of tokens for those unfamiliar with them, I will review and expand existing explanations for the issuing of these tokens and try to understand some of the motivations we can look at for any individual. Then, in a more detailed analysis, I shall try to characterise token issuers and attempt to identify evidence for their motivations.

Seventeenth century trade tokens

> '...the *Tokens* which every Tavern and Tippling-house (in the days of the Anarchy among us) presum'd to stamp and utter for immediate Exchange, as they were passable through the Neighbourhood, which tho seldom reaching farther than the next Street, or two, may happily in after times, come to exercise and busie the learned *Critic*, what they should signifie, and fill whole Volumes with their Conjectures; as I am perswaded several as arrant trifles have done, and still do, casually mentioned in antient Authors.'
>
> John Evelyn, *Numismata*, 1697.

Evelyn was correct; there are indeed whole volumes that discuss seventeenth century trade tokens and, like many numismatic items, they have been widely collected. However, much of that work is either popular repetitions of existing work or is focussed primarily on cataloguing. There is still much work to be done and fresh insights to be had, particularly in synthesis and more analytical, comparative work. Some of these insights can hopefully be of use to people thinking about other tokens and non-state coinages, in the past and indeed today.

Seventeenth century trade tokens were issued between 1648 and 1672 (up to 1679 in Ireland) and were denominated as farthings, halfpennies and pennies. They were a very widespread token coinage with over 14,000 types known,[1] issued by both private individuals and town officials across England, Wales and Ireland. They were not legal tender but a money of convenience and designed to work as money. They were explicitly tied into the monetary economy, designed to supplement existing monetary supply rather than replace it, and their period of production and use was tied to the production of state issues. As tokens, therefore, they were an index not of abstract 'value' or 'money' but of specific coins.

Figure 1 gives a typical example of such a trade token. While there are a small minority which show variation in shape, material, and font, there is a uniformity to the series which may come from a unity of production.[2] The example in figure 1 is a farthing token – this smaller denomination is often unlabelled. Such tokens are perfect miniature documents, an archaeologist's dream: an object that tells you how old it is, where it came from, who commissioned it and sometimes what it was used for. This example is of Abraham Crocker of Taunton (Somerset), issued in 1666 for the value of a farthing (1/4 penny). His wife's initial was P and this letter is shown on the reverse along with his

[1] Dickinson (1986), vii. Wetton (1969), 24 suggests over 17,500.
[2] Boon (1973), 26–27; Thompson (1989), 198.

own initials. The token displays the arms of the Weavers' Company on the other side, perhaps indicating he was a weaver.[3] The reverse states the token was issued 'for necessary change'.[4]

Fig. 1: Token issued by Abraham Crocker at Taunton, 1666 (Ø 18.9mm; 0.92g) (Courtesy of Somerset County Council and South West Heritage Trust; museum no: TTNCM: OS. AC.1204).

The monetary context

In England, Wales and Ireland in this period there was – as in many other periods and areas throughout history – a lack of small change, i.e. specie of a value low enough to be used to pay for small items such as single drinks, or food in small quantities, or to be given in change for such purchases.[5] In this period, this lack is primarily due to a lack of production. 'Official' state coinage was only issued in silver, with the value of the coin tied to the value of the metal. This made small issues uneconomical to produce and inconveniently small to use.[6] As they were uneconomical, they often simply were not produced, or otherwise not produced in the numbers they were required for the economy.[7]

This issue, a lack of small change, has been addressed in a variety of ways in different periods. Rennicks in this volume discusses lead tokens; we can also mention the import of foreign money, for example soldini,[8] and the probable use of jettons in this context.[9] There were also attempts to produce an official base metal issue. This could be local, like the Bristol tokens under Elizabeth I (issued between 1577 and the 1580s or 90s),[10] or national, like the Royal copper alloy farthing tokens produced under patent in the reigns of James I and Charles I. Production of patent farthings ended in 1642, again creating a gap in supply. It is notable in Scotland, where billon (base silver) and copper alloy issues had been the norm since the fifteenth century and continue throughout this period, there is almost no private issuing of tokens.[11] Where the phenomenon of seventeenth century trade tokens differs from the above methods of supplementing small change is that the tokens were both specifically manufactured for this purpose and identify the individual issuers unambiguously.[12]

We can also consider the development of privately issued tokens in the light of the development of other privately issued monetary instruments in the seventeenth century. The period between 1620 and 1720 is sometimes referred to as the financial revolution, although the focus of most studies is on higher-level finance, the development of theories of finance and other financial instruments including banknotes, orders, and bills.[13] The extension of

[3] Numerous examples have been identified of token issuers displaying arms of one livery company or stating an occupation on a token but in other documents being identified as carrying out a different employment. The reasons can range from a limited choice of companies to join in small towns, businesses changing over time, businesses being identified by signs (often for a previous or neighbouring business), by-employment (i.e. a secondary employment) and changes in employment over time. See Gaunt and Oddie (2011), 16–17. Keibek (2017), 27, in examining the question of by-employment in general in the seventeenth century, suggests that while by-employments are more common among larger households and wealthier individuals the effects remain small and 'for the purpose of generating reliable male occupational structures, by-employments can safely be ignored'. The issue may however be more important for token issuers, who are usually working in the tertiary sector and are wealthier. As the token is issued at the level of the household, household by-employment is also a factor. That the household was the unit rather than the individual is witnessed by the usual practice of including the wife's initial on a token, suggesting her role and employment are also important.

[4] Boyne and Williamson (1889–1891), 988, no. Somerset 247.

[5] Sargent and Velde (2002) review this issue through time.

[6] Pennies of 1601 weigh at most 8 grains (0.5g) and farthings at a quarter of this weight would be impossible to produce. Indeed, royal farthings do not seem to have been produced for circulation, only as patterns, after 1551. Even without inflation it still took at least four times as much time and effort to produce four farthings as one penny, reducing or eliminating the value of the seigniorage (the profit due to the crown from the difference between the face value of the coins and their value in metal).

[7] Peck (1952), 313–15.

[8] Daubney (2009), 186, 191.

[9] Palmer and Mayhew (1977).

[10] Grinsell (1962). More recent publications suggest the use of these tokens into the 1590s, since the Privy Council permit of 1594 called in only private and unauthorised issues, perhaps providing a spur for the production of authorised issues (Thompson (1988), ix–xii).

[11] Dickinson (1986), 3.

[12] In England the seventeenth century sees the first widespread issues of token halfpennies, farthings and other denominations by corporations and private individuals where they name themselves on the tokens. The practice is subsequently followed on trade tokens of the mid-eighteenth and nineteenth centuries.

[13] Wennerlind (2011).

these instruments into smaller businesses and towns demonstrates the increased acceptance by more people and groups in society of representative money (as opposed to commodity money).

It is also important to place the development of these tokens in the political situation of the time. It is often argued that the death of Charles I was held to have removed the royal prerogative on issuing money.[14] Alternatively the usurpation of this privilege can be seen as part of the general questioning of the prerogative of the state or monarch.[15] It is notable the first examples of trade tokens were issued in 1648, probably after the king's death (on the 30th of January 1648 according to the calendar of the time, January 1649 as it is reckoned now).[16]

Looking at when trade tokens were issued it is clear they respond to contemporary events. Boon, and Gaunt and Oddie, among others, have argued there is a gradual rise over time in the numbers of issuers and their geographical extent, with dips in 1654 and 1660.[17] The dips reflect changes of political regime and accompanying general uncertainty, as well as specific uncertainty regarding the new regime's attitude to token issues and their intention (or not) to issue regal small denominations. There was a rapid decline in production from 1669 when the government started giving orders against token issuing; in 1672 the government issued a strong proclamation against tokens and started issues of copper farthings and halfpennies. As late as 1674 trade tokens were still reported to be in use in some towns but these were clearly unusual with most recalled in 1672.[18] Norwich and Great Yarmouth, for example, redeemed all their tokens and sold off their recalled tokens for scrap in 1672, clearly no longer anticipating any need of them.[19]

There is a gap between the government condemnations of tokens, seen throughout this period but hardening from 1669, the actual cessation of token production and, thereafter, the cessation in active use which ends in recall. I argue this gap demonstrates that, while political uncertainty creates a context in which token issuing is possible, the main motivator is the need for small change and, even when the governmental attitude is clear, only when the need for small change is met (as the new coins come gradually into circulation in 1672–74) do issues cease. This was explicitly recognised at the time, for example in the 1672 order of Charles II.[20]

These broad explanations therefore provide a context in which there exists an issue to be solved (the lack of small change), expanding 'technologies' which can be applied to the problem (e.g. milling),[21] privately issued monetary instruments of various types, and a specific, time bound opportunity caused by the political turmoil of the period. These can be seen to act together to create a situation in which tokens were issued.

However, one of the most interesting features of this series is the large number of issuers, both corporate and private, and therefore, when discussing why these tokens were issued, we must also address the choices of those individuals rather than simply describe a climate in which issuing is both possible and useful.

These tokens have already been described as 'perfect miniature documents', and some indeed helpfully carry short messages explaining why they were issued. Clearly formulaic,

[14] Dickinson (1986), 5.

[15] That issuing tokens was seen as a challenge to this prerogative can be seen in the proclamation of James I authorising a patentee to issue farthing tokens in 1613 and banning lead tokens which were 'some derogation to our Prerogative Royal'. Similarly, in an address by Sir Henry Slingsby (Governor of the Bank of England) to the king in June 1661, recorded in the State Papers (Boyne and Williamson (1889–1891), xl), it is stated 'His Majesty has the undoubted prerogative of coining them [i.e. farthings]'.

[16] Boon (1973), 18.

[17] Boon (1973), 20, Gaunt and Oddie (2011), 32.

[18] Berry (1988), 6–7.

[19] Marsden (2016), 15–16.

[20] 'By the king, a Proclamation for making currant His Majastie's Farthings and Half-pence of Copper, and forbidding all others to be used' as transcribed in Dickinson (1986), 262.

[21] Sargent and Velde (2002), 50–61. While milling had been in use for coin production elsewhere in Europe since the sixteenth century and various trial milled coinages were produced in England (including the state sponsored farthings of the early seventeenth century; Besley (1997), 20), its introduction had been resisted by the mint on cost grounds and perhaps because of tradition. Tokens perhaps provided an opportunity to use this technology in a new market without threatening existing mint workers.

but not ubiquitous, their presence on any particular token can be seen as the choice of the issuers and therefore reflect either individual reasons, or what were held to be publicly expressible reasons, for issuing such tokens. The reasons include (to name just a few): 'For change and charity', 'for the poor' or 'for necessary change'.

We also have corporation records which discuss why tokens were issued. A more detailed national analysis of these discussions is required, but in general these focus on the importance of small change for traders and in particular for the poor, both for spending and receiving alms, particularly the town's own payments through overseers of the poor.[22] Two problems that are mentioned in these records were issuers failing to redeem their tokens, and the phenomenon of tokens travelling so far away they had become useless.[23] Town issues were felt to overcome these problems and while there remained some worry about legality (a worry often balanced by a discussion that this was a temporary measure until such time as the state stepped back in),[24] there was an appetite to issue tokens.

The motivations discussed already are impersonal: to meet a need unfulfilled by the state, who is deemed to have abdicated its role. Another strand, perhaps more difficult to address, is a positive desire to issue tokens because of a perceived benefit to the issuer. Benefits included profit, advertising, encouraging repeat business, a captive market and, perhaps less tangibly, status or fashion – the extent to which issuers were influenced by and wished to emulate others who were also issuing tokens. Valin discusses elsewhere in this volume a situation in which tokens can mark and maintain relationships and statuses with multiple, concurrent, roles in payment, propaganda, and advertising.

The profit to be made by issuing tokens is of four types. Firstly, the users of tokens were in effect providing an interest free loan. Secondly, a percentage of tokens were never redeemed because they were mislaid or travelled too far to be returned. Thirdly, if tokens were only redeemable for particular items in a single shop, then a profit might be made on those items from the captive market. Fourthly, a profit results if the issuer never redeems the tokens, either because the issuer keeps them in circulation until they die, or they refuse to redeem them, perhaps on the excuse they were forgeries.[25] Whether the first two were sufficient for small traders to overcome the high start-up and production costs (see below) is difficult to calculate. It is clear even town issuers did not always consider how they would pay to redeem tokens if they went out of use.[26] Issuers were, in effect, often creating a fiat money backed by the success of their own business.

Having discussed the background reasons for token issue and the theoretical motivations behind an individual's choices to issue them, in the following section I want to try to gain a greater understanding of the individuals involved.

Token issuers in context

A lot of research has been done on token issuers in many counties using a wide range of contemporary sources.[27] What seems not to have been done to any great extent is to analyse this research statistically or use the results to place issuers in the context of their society. What I have therefore done, for the first time, is to look at the issuers within the context of their community. To do this I have used a range of contemporary documents to try to identify whether being a token issuer or not correlates with particular socio-economic characteristics. These are case studies rather than a larger national or regional study, but they provide useful hypotheses that could be tested elsewhere.

[22] Boyne and Williamson (1889–1891), 177 and 452, corporation records at Dorchester, Dorset and Grantham, Lincolnshire for example.
[23] Boyne and Williamson (1889–1891), 273 quoting the proclamation made in Winchester.
[24] Marsden (2016), 14 discussing Kings Lynn. Boyne and Williamson (1889–1891), 184, Council books at Poole, Dorset for example.
[25] Marsden (2016), 13.
[26] Marsden (2016), 15.
[27] As well as the general works combining research on issuers and catalogues of types, already mentioned, specific works focussing mainly on issuers include, for example, Sydenham (1905) and Judson (1987).

Wealth

Wealth is a good place to start, as it is perhaps the easiest attribute to approach. I have used two main sources: hearth taxes and, in a smaller case study, wealth as assessed in probate inventories. Both have issues as sources and as proxies for wealth (see below). It is logical to assume that people issuing tokens had a certain level of wealth, after all the order for one set of dies and a few thousand tokens was about £2.[28] But I wish to go beyond this to try and establish if issuers were the wealthiest in their community (ran the largest inns, had the largest businesses) or if the situation was more varied.

Hearth taxes were levied between 1662 and 1689 at a set fee per hearth. They were levied on the occupier, and people below a certain level of wealth were exempt, although this level varied locally.[29] Where lists survive they provide an important source and are often used to calculate population sizes, especially when exemption certificates also exist, although as a source these lists underestimate the poor who may be exempted, unlisted or live in as tenants or servants. They also list the number of hearths and this can be a useful indication of household size and, while not necessarily a direct mirror of wealth, a high number of hearths are a strong indication of it.[30] For our purposes larger, more active households and businesses (for example, larger inns) were more prominent in their community, although this may not map directly onto a specific level of financial wealth or the capital of the person running them. It is also the case that these lists provide only a snapshot, sometimes of an individual who issued tokens ten years before or five years after the recorded hearth tax and their wealth may have changed over that time.

I have looked at two main case studies, part of Essex and Westmorland.[31] Figures 2 and 3 graph the number of issuers with specific numbers of hearths (black) against the populations in their communities as a whole (grey).

What figures 2 and 3 clearly show is that while the individuals issuing tokens were not the wealthiest in their communities, they were amongst the wealthier sector. The vast majority

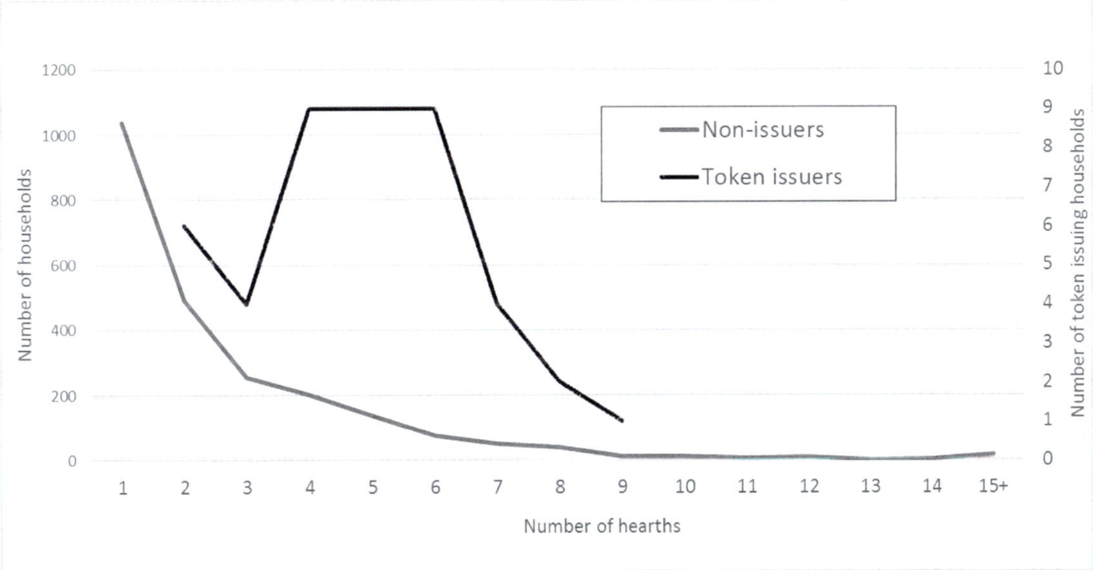

Fig. 2: Number of hearths per household on the 1670 Hearth Tax return for Essex, based on a sample of 15 parishes of various sizes where tokens were issued.

[28] Although as few as 300 could be ordered (at 3s and 6d) (Boon (1973) n. 13) and Boon (1973), 26 argues this may be a typical order for a small tradesman. Gaunt and Oddie (2011), 10 have argued that most are probably ordering 1,000 halfpennies (2,000 farthings) at a cost of around £2 or more as below this the set-up costs (for dies) outweighs any profit made.

[29] Spufford (2000), 213.

[30] Spufford (2000), 204–07.

[31] Figures drawn from the transcriptions of the 1670 returns published by Centre for Hearth Tax Research (www.hearthtax.org.uk; accessed 01/03/2017). The Essex study was based on a sample of 2,346 households across 15 communities of a range of sizes from villages to towns, all of which were communities where tokens were issued. The Westmorland study looks at all communities where tokens were issued.

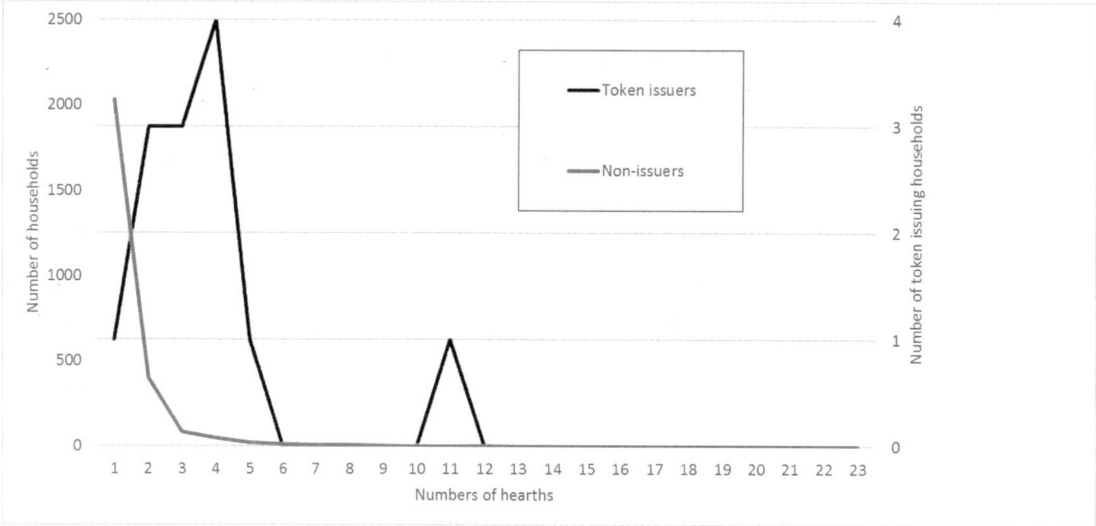

Fig. 3: Number of hearths per household on the 1670 Hearth Tax return for Westmorland in the five parishes where tokens were issued.

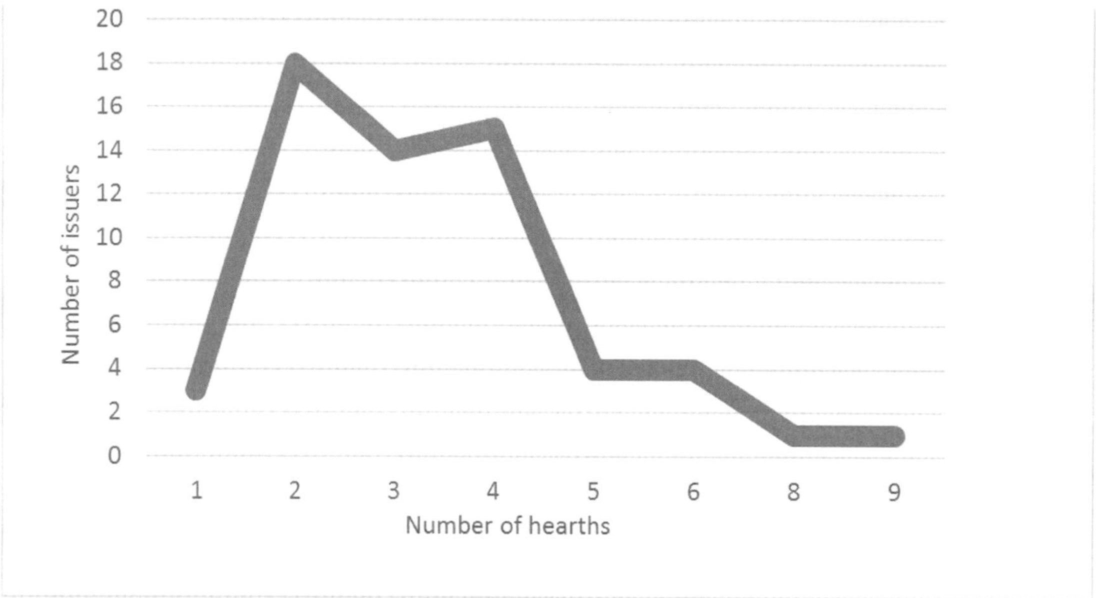

Fig. 4: Number of hearths each token issuer was assessed for on the 1671 Bedfordshire Hearth Tax returns.

of the population, even after the under-recording of those exempted, were assessed for only one or two hearths, whereas most token issuers had more than this: all were above the mean and most above the median. Sixty-five per cent of token issuers in Essex and 61% in Westmorland were in the top 20 percentiles within their communities, but almost none were in the top 5%. Looking at the county samples as a whole, more issuers were in the top 5%, but not in their own communities. This comparison with their own communities is important because there is large variation in wealth and typical numbers of hearths in different regions.[32] Interestingly, unlike the logarithmic decline of the population in general there appears to be, in Essex and possibly Westmorland, a normal distribution around a mid-point of 3–5 hearths. This pattern and the distribution of issues holds true for token issuers

[32] Spufford (2000), 207, 209–18.

Fig. 5: Number of hearths issuer assessed for on the 1671 Bedfordshire Hearth Tax return against the year they issued their token (each dot represents one token issuer).

in Bedfordshire,[33] with perhaps a lower mid-point than normal (fig. 4), Cornwall,[34] and Exeter, which as we will see later (fig. 8), is perhaps more spread. Interestingly looking at the Bedfordshire group, which are generally well dated, there is no obvious change over time (fig. 5).

What we are seeing therefore in the 'typical issuer' is someone who is not running the biggest household in town but is well above the poor, who make up the vast majority of the population. There is a wide range of wealth amongst the issuers that continues over time with a clustering around the size of 3–5 hearths that does not simply reflect a clustering of the population at this level. Whether this may reflect variation in businesses of different sizes, and that larger and wealthier businessmen catered to wholesale rather than retail trade and therefore had less use for tokens, is too large a topic to discuss here. However preliminary indications are that many businessmen involved in wholesale trade were also involved in retail and many of the businesses of token issuers, while involving retail, were not selling items where change of a farthing or halfpenny were often needed (see below).[35]

Secondly, in a smaller case study I looked at probate inventories from Taunton relating to wills proved in the archdeaconry court.[36] Only a small proportion of people had their wills proved in this way, usually those who were wealthier or had a more capital-intensive business. The value of probate cannot be taken as indications of absolute wealth as it varies so much through life – those dying in the midst of an active business career and with a large household obviously leave more physical goods than those dying in old age. The sample (fig. 6) is small and token issuers' estates are scattered over the entire range of values. However, within this dataset token issuers (open circles) were either relatively wealthier than the average, or had more capital wealth than landed wealth, and this difference is statistically significant.[37] What is also of interest is that in no cases, even when inventories were drawn up

[33] Based on data from Gaunt and Oddie (2011).
[34] Mayne and Williams (1985), 20.
[35] See Smith (1999) for the limits of the separation of the wholesale and retail markets in this period, even in London, despite a gradual shift in that direction and the attempts of the merchant companies to separate the two as discussed in Heckscher (1995), 378–80.
[36] As available in the Somerset Record Office.
[37] Using Students t-test there is over a 99% chance of this reflecting a genuine difference, reduced to 87% if the largest and smallest values in each group are omitted.

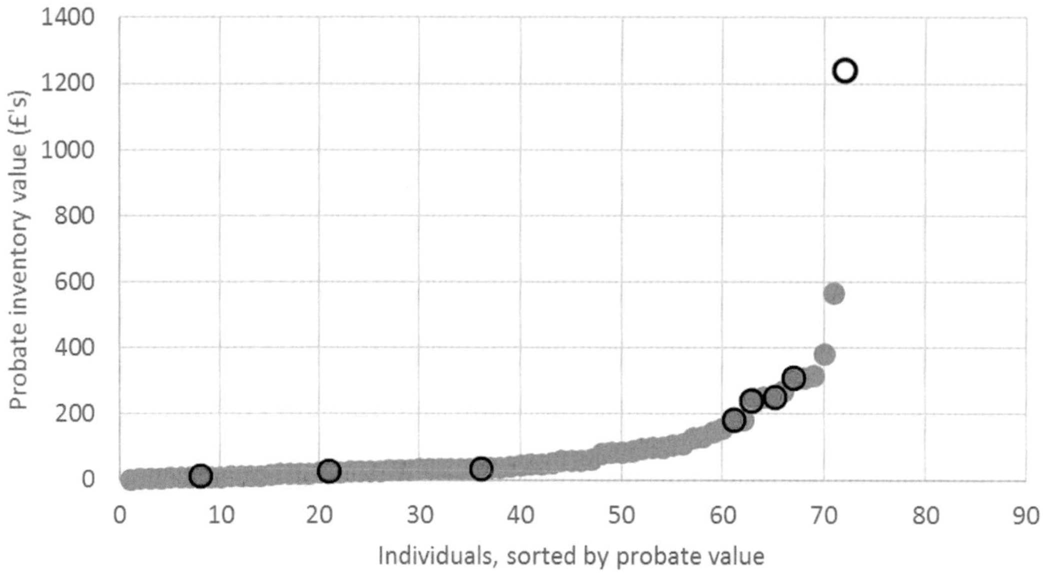

Fig. 6: Probate inventory values of token issuers (black circles) and others (grey dots) in Taunton 1666 to 1685.

during a period of token issuing by the deceased, are tokens or dies mentioned. Whether this was because they were included within the general statement of money on the person or were deliberately excluded as not quite legal is something to explore further in future work.

Occupation

Occupation is often charmingly portrayed on tokens, and many studies, anecdotal and analytical, have looked at the stated occupation on tokens or suggested occupation based on the design.[38] These suggest two trends: 1) a wide range of trades is represented; 2) nationally, inns and taverns are the most common representations, followed by grocers.[39] Assuming the latter to be true, we can ask whether this is the case because these were the most common businesses or is there something about these particular businesses that make their proprietors more likely to issue tokens? Again, we have the problem of finding comparable evidence; this period is unfortunately too early for trade directories or the regular recording of occupations in parish registers. I have so far looked at two areas where we can start to understand the frequency of different occupations in this period: Exeter and some parishes of London.[40]

In London I have drawn upon the hearth tax returns of 1666 which list the occupation of payers and those exempted in 21 parishes.[41] As with other hearth taxes it is likely to greatly underestimate the poor. Identifying token issuers in these returns has proved difficult, more so than in Essex for example. The inconsistency of seventeenth century spelling is an issue in both, but the greater problems in London are possibly due to a more mobile population, the disruption of the plague (this is pre-Fire), or that the street address listed on the token does not reflect that used by the hearth tax enumerators, which can be an issue where a street may run across several parishes.[42]

However, some conclusions can be drawn. Correlating with Evelyn's comment quoted at the start of this chapter, individuals running licensed premises were strongly represented (42% of token issuers rather than 10% in the general population). Contra Evelyn, however,

[38] For example, Whiting (1971), 34–76.
[39] Whiting (1971); Dickinson (1986), 8–9.
[40] Recent work of the Cambridge Group for the History of Population and Social Structure making use of various legal records and probate inventories may provide further opportunities in future to examine more areas (The occupational structure of Britain 1379–1911 research project, outlined in https://www.campop.geog.cam.ac.uk/research/occupations/; accessed 01/12/2018).
[41] As published by the Centre for Hearth Tax Research (http://www.hearthtax.org.uk/).
[42] In the five parishes so far studied (St Gabriel Fenchurch, All Hallows Staining, St Katherine Coleman, St Mary Woolnorth, St Swithin London Stone) 539 occupations were listed and 19 token issuers could be identified.

not every tavern issued tokens (around 20% in this small sample) and amongst this group it tends to be on average larger establishments that issued tokens (an average of ten rather than six hearths). In future it should be possible to build on existing work on London tokens and taverns to expand this analysis.[43]

For a second case study I drew upon the freeman records of the city of Exeter (table 1).[44] Not all traders were freemen: innkeepers and tavern keepers in particular, who could not follow the apprenticeship route to freedom, are known to be under-represented,[45] but many businessmen did take their freedom.[46] There could also be a delay with many clearly trading for many years before they took up their freedom. Sixty-six per cent of male token issuers from Exeter could be firmly identified in the records giving a statement of their occupation. None of those identified were innkeepers or tavern keepers so, including women,[47] and assuming freemen are not innkeepers as a secondary trade, a maximum of 38% of Exeter token issuers could be innkeepers and tavern keepers. This is an interestingly similar proportion to London, although it should be emphasised again this is a maximum and the total is almost certainly lower.

Table 1: Data from the freeman records of the city of Exeter.

Occupations	*Token issuers (56)*	*Freemen (1352)*	*Occupations*	*Token issuers (56)*	*Freemen (1352)*
Manufacturing cloth	12.5%	15.5%	*Merchant*	3.5%	7%
Grocer	12.5%	5%	*Butcher*	3.5%	4%
Tailor	3.5%	3.5%	*Cordwainer*	3.5%	3.5%
Baker	3.5%	3%	*Mercer*	3.5%	2.5%
Apothecary	0	2%	*Hellier*	0	2%
Glover	0	1.5%	*Ironmonger*	5.5%	1.5%
Joiner	0	1.5%	*Goldsmith*	3.5%	1.5%
Haberdasher	3.5%	1.5%	*Cutler*	3.5%	1.5%
Brewer	0	1%	*Cooper*	2%	1%
Chandler	7%	1%	*Other*	1.4%	21%

If we compare the occupations given in the rolls of all the 1,050 men who took their freedom between 1633 (the earliest year a token issuer appears) and 1673 to those of token issuers in the rolls there are clear differences (fig. 7). To pick out just a few trends, cloth manufacturers and merchants (probably importers and exporters, mainly of cloth) are under-represented and, once we take out the unlisted token issuers, grocers and chandlers are significantly over represented. Other trades which theoretically have great need of tokens (bakers and butchers) are not significantly over or under-represented,[48] while a few one would think had no need of tokens (e.g. goldsmiths) are if anything overrepresented.[49] The latter may suggest a secondary trade or other reasons for issuing tokens. These reasons could include advertising, status and notably profit as most goldsmiths were also active in nascent banking.[50]

[43] Berry (1978).

[44] As collated by Rowe and Jackson (1973).

[45] Rowe and Jackson (1973), xii.

[46] Woodward (1970), 90–91 suggests Exeter was particularly restrictive in this period with freemen representing only 5.5% of the population in the 1620s–1640s. Even allowing for the fact that only adult males who met certain criteria of apprenticeship, family relationship, or who could pay large fines could become freemen this is still a small proportion. However, the overlap between token issuers and freemen makes this group useful for our purposes, although not perhaps representative of the population as a whole. Rowe and Jackson (1973), xxiv suggested those involved in retail trade were more likely to take their freedom than those involved in production, which may explain the high overlap with token issuers.

[47] The eight female token issuers were ineligible to be freemen.

[48] Although it is likely they were under-represented amongst freemen (Rowe and Jackson (1973), xiv) and nationally butchers were under-represented as token issuers (Berry (1988), 42).

[49] Boon (1973), 40 similarly suggests, looking at the range of issuers in Wales 'tokens were essentially connected with the trades in prepared and manufactured goods rather than fresh foodstuffs and the like'.

[50] It is hoped in future to expand this work further by looking at licensing agreements to establish if the missing people were running licensed premises or, indeed, they were tavern keepers as a secondary trade.

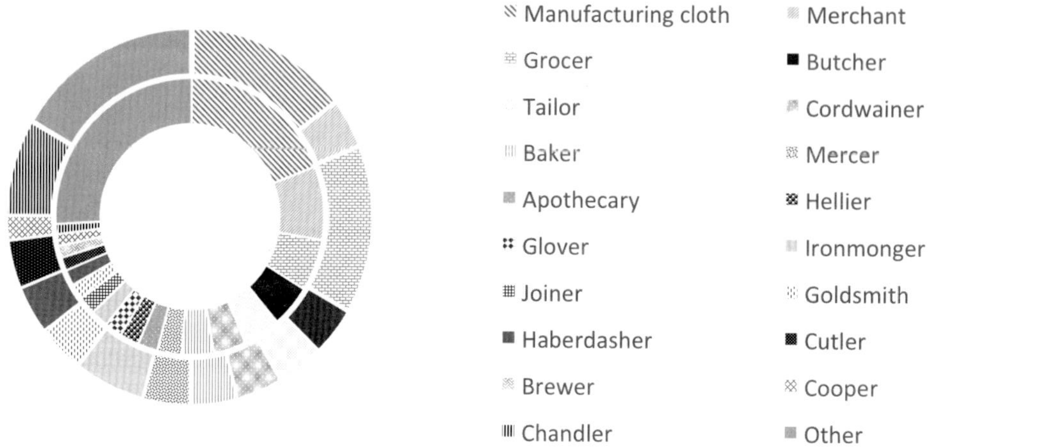

Fig. 7: Occupations as given in the freeman rolls of Exeter, token issuers (outer circle) compared to all freemen (inner circle), 1633 to 1673.

Status

This issue of variation between occupations leads to my third area of analysis, status. This is in many ways the hardest to pin down. We have seen how token issuers in general are amongst the wealthier or larger business holders in the community, but not usually the wealthiest. In Exeter it is also clear they were more likely to be freeman than the rest of the population or others in their profession. While previous research has identified that token issuers are often members of local councils, no one has considered if this is significant.[51] Was issuing tokens to some extent a public good that people felt some obligation to perform and does this correlate with other public services, or is it just chance? Is an important local businessman who is not a non-conformist and around long enough simply likely to take on some official role? To look at status, again in Exeter, we can compare token issuers to the most politically prominent group in the city, the mayors and bailiffs.

Looking at how established they are in the community, issuers had been freemen on average for 10 years before they issued tokens, while mayors and bailiffs had been freeman for an average of 13 years before taking up their positions. As I mentioned above, due to delays in taking up freedom, these figures can only be an underestimation. We can conclude most members of both groups were established businessmen within their community with mayors and bailiffs on average slightly more established.

One counter to this is an interesting peak of people issuing tokens about the same time they took up their freedom. Are they are establishing new businesses or raising their profile in the town? The advertising and status aspect of issuing tokens may be significant here. Gaunt and Oddie have also commented on two examples of a similar coincidence in Bedfordshire although more work needs to be done to establish if this is a statistically valid phenomenon.[52]

Secondly while token issuers do become bailiffs, in general if we compare the number of hearths individuals were assessed for in the 1674 hearth tax (fig. 8),[53] the officials (black line) had more hearths (larger establishments) than the token issuers (dark grey columns). Looking at occupation, mayors and bailiffs are much more likely to be merchants, mercers or apothecaries than token issuers. Compared to the general list of freemen, like the token issuers, they are much less likely to be involved directly in cloth manufacture and more likely to be grocers.

[51] ca. 40% of issuers in Bedfordshire have been identified as having some official role. Of 15 token issuers in Bedford, all but three were members of the council and nine were elected mayor at some point (based on the research on issuers in Gaunt and Oddie (2011)).
[52] Gaunt and Oddie (2011), 15.
[53] Figures drawn from Stoate (1982). Mayors and bailiffs were those elected between 1660 and 1680.

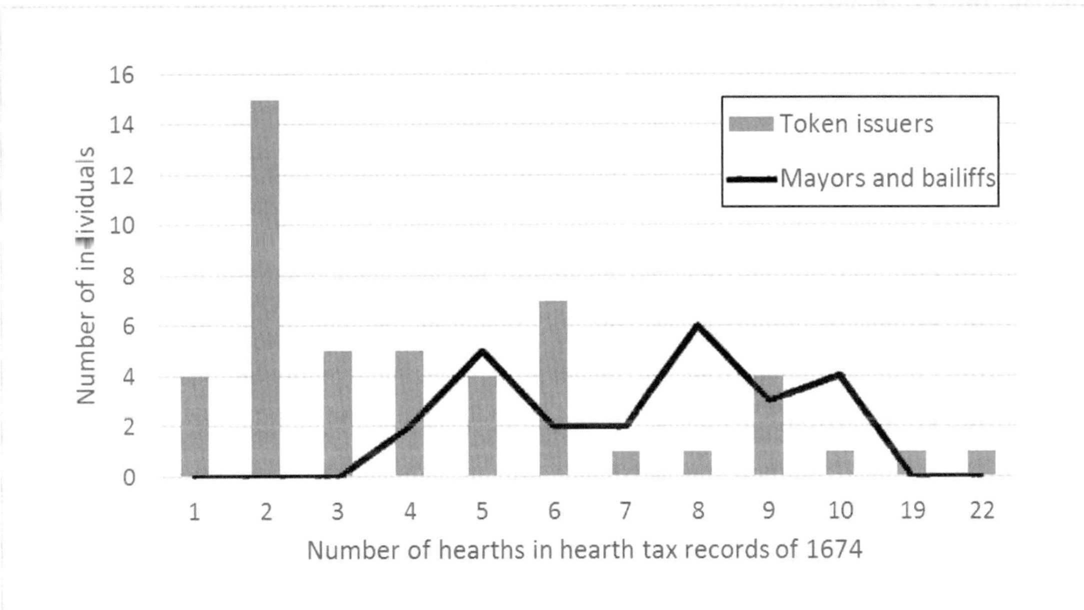

Fig. 8: Number of hearths owned in the Hearth Tax records of 1674 by individuals who were or became Mayor or Bailiff of Exeter compared to people who had been token issuers.

In summary, these case studies point to a position where token issuers are prominent within their communities but are not the most prominent, and this difference between the two groups suggests that having a high responsibility within the community did not necessarily correlate with being the sort of person to issue tokens, at least in a large and commercially diverse city. Obviously, this is just one small case study and we would need to repeat it elsewhere in communities of different sizes to draw any firmer conclusions.

Conclusions

In a monetary economy tokens are often used to supplement or replace cash transactions for various reasons of convenience and are a deliberate creation or embodiment of a restricted (rather than universal) exchange medium. In the case of the trade tokens of the seventeenth century, tokens provided a restricted but necessary supplement by acting as a replacement for low value royal coinage due to the absence of the denominations needed. The varied motives for issuing a token, at a cost to the issuer, have been discussed, as have the historic circumstances which may make such issuing acceptable to the token user and broader society. The focus has been very much on the issuers rather than the users of these tokens; the latter's motivations are only lightly touched on and hopefully can be examined in future work.

While in a general way the patterns of token issue can be clearly linked to historical events, the motivation of any individual can be recognised to be more complex. By placing issuers in the context of their own communities we can start to examine whether token issuing correlated with other notable differences. Three attributes of wealth, occupation and status have been examined here.

Token issuers were clearly a definable group based on their wealth, which in general is higher than the average in their society, but not sufficient to make them the wealthiest in their own communities. The suggestion of a normal distribution, in hearth tax returns at least, would be interesting to explore further, as would the tentative suggestions, from the probate records of Taunton and the hearth tax returns of London, that token issuers were, on average, wealthier than others within their own group, whether that is occupation group or those requiring their wills to be submitted to probate.

Studies of occupation are limited by the difficulties of identifying complete lists of occupations for communities in this period, as well as complicating factors of by-employment and changes in professions for the issuers. However, within these limitations certain groups were clearly more likely to issue tokens. The commonness of innkeepers amongst the London token issuers is revealed, although even there the situation is clearly more complex than tokens being issued by 'every tavern and tippling house'. In Exeter certain groups are clearly over represented, although further work needs to be done to identify if this is repeated in other places and if there is any consistency in the frequency of occupations.

Status is one of the harder attributes to examine but work on Exeter token issuers suggests, as with their wealth, they were not, on average, quite on the same level as the most prominent individuals within this community despite the numerous examples of prominent individuals issuing tokens. Again, further work is needed to compare this to other places.

It is hoped this initial analysis will provide a basis for further work to test the robustness of my identification of token issuers as a definable group. If a tentative conclusion can be reached it is perhaps that token issuers are not the most prominent within their society, certainly not prominent on a county or wider level; but perhaps issuers are locally prominent, with larger or more established businesses than others in the same profession or town. This local prominence would accord well with the very local nature of token issuing in this period, with individuals in many hundreds of communities feeling a desire or need to issue their own tokens rather than using generic items or relying on a few national producers.

Bibliography

Berry 1978: G. Berry, *Taverns and Tokens of Pepys' London* (London, 1978).

Berry 1988: G. Berry, *Seventeenth Century England: Traders and their Tokens* (London, 1988).

Besly 1997: E. Besly, *Loose Change: A Guide to Common Coins and Medals* (Cardiff, 1997).

Boon 1973: G. Boon, *Welsh Tokens of the Seventeenth Century* (Cardiff, 1973).

Boyne and Williamson 1889–1891: W. Boyne and G. C. Williamson, *Trade Tokens issued in the Seventeenth Century in England, Wales and Ireland* (London, 1889–1891).

Daubney 2009: A. Daubney, 'The circulation and prohibition of Venetian soldini in late medieval England', *BNJ* 79 (2009), 186–98.

Dickinson 1986: M. Dickinson, *Seventeenth Century Tokens of the British Isles and their Values* (London, 1986).

Evelyn 1697: J. Evelyn, *Numismata: A Discourse of Medals Ancient and Modern: Together with some Account of Heads and Effigies of Illustrious, and Famous Persons, in Sculps, and Taille-Douce, of Whom we have no Medals extant, and of the Use to be derived from them. To which is added A Digression concerning Physiognomy* (London, 1697).

Gaunt and Oddie 2011: J. Gaunt and G. Oddie, *Bedfordshire Seventeenth Century Tokens* (Llanfyllin, 2011).

Grinsell 1962: L. V. Grinsell, *A Brief Numismatic History of Bristol* (Bristol, 1962).

Heckscher 1995: E. F. Heckscher, *Mercantilism* (Abingdon, 1995).

Judson 1987: E. Judson, *The Lives and Wills of Essex Token Issuers* (Little Bardfield, 1987).

Keibek 2017: S. A. J. Keibek, *By-employments in Early Modern England and their Significance for Estimating Historical Male Occupation Structures* (Cambridge Working Papers in Economic and Social History no. 29) (Cambridge, 2017).

Marsden 2016: A. Marsden, *17th Century Norfolk Tokens in Norwich Castle Museum* (Norwich, 2016).

Mayhew (ed) 1977: Mayhew (ed.) 1977: N.J. Mayhew (ed.), *Edwardian Monetary Affairs (1279-1344)* (Oxford, 1977).

Mayne and Williams 1985: J. A. D. Mayne and J.A. Williams, *Coins and Tokens of Cornwall* (Exeter, 1985).

Palmer and Mayhew 1977: N. J. Palmer and N. J. Mayhew, 'Medieval coins and jettons from Oxford excavations', in Mayhew (ed.) (1977), 81–95.

Peck 1952: C. W. Peck, 'The royal farthing tokens of James I', *BNJ* 27 (1952), 313–33.

Rowe and Jackson 1973: M. M. Rowe and A. M. Jackson, *Exeter Freemen, 1266–1967* (Exeter, 1973).

Sargent and Velde 2002: T. L. Sargent and F. R. Velde, *The Big Problem of Small Change* (Princeton, 2002).

Smith 1999: S. Smith, *The Market Place and the Market's Place in London c. 1660-1840*. PhD thesis, University College London (London, 1999).

Spufford 2000: M. Spufford, 'The scope of local history and the potential of the hearth tax returns', *Local Historian* 30 (2000), 202–21.

Stoate 1982: T. L. Stoate, *Devon Hearth Tax Returns* (Bristol, 1982).

Sydenham 1905: S. Sydenham, *Bath Token Issuers of the Seventeenth Century* (Bath, 1905).

Thompson 1988: R. H. Thompson, *Sylloge of Coins of the British Isles: Norweb Collection: Tokens of the British Isles, 1575-1750. Part 2: Dorset, Durham, Essex and Gloucestershire v. 38: Tokens of the British Isles* (London, 1988).

Thompson 1989: R. H. Thompson, 'Central or local production of seventeenth century tokens', *BNJ* 89 (1989), 198–211.

Wennerlind 2011: C. Wennerlind, *Casualties of Credit: The English Financial Revolution, 1620–1720* (Harvard, 2011).

Wetton 1969: J. L. Wetton, *Seventeenth Century Tradesmen's Tokens* (Newcastle upon Tyne, 1969).

Whiting 1971: J. R. S. Whiting, *Trade Tokens: A Social and Economic History* (New York, 1971).

Woodward 1970: R. Woodward 'Freemen's Rolls', *Local Historian* 9 (1970), 89–95.

‘SUCCESS TO THE SEVENTEEN UNITED BRIGHT STARS’: THE SPITHEAD MUTINY OF 1797 RECORDED ON A SAILOR’S LOVE TOKEN

BRIDGET MILLMORE

Introduction

In the eighteenth century the sailor’s tradition of giving a token of affection to a loved one when going to sea was well established in a range of cultural practices. There were poems and ballads that described the hopes and fears of those separated by the sea often featuring the figure of Jack Tar.[1] These popular rhymes and songs were familiar to a rural and urban audience accustomed to listening to travelling pedlars and ballad singers. They were also highly visible as they were published in broadsheets that were displayed in public spaces, pasted, for instance, to the walls of taverns.[2] The trope of Jack Tar leaving home was also depicted on a range of material culture including paintings and engravings, scrimshaw, pottery such as jugs and cups and domestic utensils such as rolling pins.[3] Even the repertoire of sailors’ tattoos included the familiar figure of the parting couple. One seaman was tattooed on his upper arm with the words ‘Thomas, come home to Ann’.[4]

This paper focuses on a group of love tokens that features the sailor’s farewell. They were made from copper and silver coins.[5] Sailors’ love tokens were decorated with images of ships and anchors as well as idioms of love, separation and return. These sentimental pieces belonged to a practice of marking significant life events such as births, marriages and death on readily available objects that could be re-fashioned into tokens of affection. Seamen offered these as parting gifts for loved ones, gifts made all the more poignant when husbands, sons, fathers and sweethearts did not always return from sea.

The aim of this paper is twofold. Firstly, it explores the values and sentiments expressed on love tokens and on sailors’ pieces in particular. It will do this through a discussion of the inscriptions chosen for love tokens and the use of the familiar trope of the sailor’s farewell. Secondly, it considers how this repertoire of phrases and symbols was adapted to new settings and specifically a naval mutiny. It addresses the question how were tokens used to convey values and beliefs at a time of disobedience and uprising? As Susan Matt remarks in her review essay on the histories of emotion, it is not surprising that events such as revolutions were ‘greatly concerned with affective bonds’ and ‘the revolutionary cause was based on widely shared convictions about passion, sentiment, and sensibility’.[6] This paper examines the material expressions of those ‘affective bonds’ as embodied in tokens. It endeavours to link objects and texts in order to highlight sailors’ values and beliefs in the context of the 1797 Spithead mutiny. It contributes to the field by focusing on how tokens communicated and moreover made manifest a community’s system of beliefs.

Love token production

Love tokens crafted from coins can be organised in a variety of ways depending on the nature and discipline of the investigation. For the purposes of this study that examines these numismatic pieces in the context of a military event, a broad grouping that focuses on family and community interactions is useful. Love tokens can be arranged into three main categories according to the characteristics of the attachment they commemorated.[7] Firstly, there are those that celebrate the family through the marking of key moments such as births, courtships and marriages. Examples that belong in this group include the tokens left by mothers for their babies in the London Foundling Hospital.[8] The second group includes tokens that record a sense of attachment to community and

[1] Land (2009); Begiato (2015), 121–24.
[2] A broadsheet was a sheet of printed paper that carried news and public announcements (http://www.mhs.ox.ac.uk) (accessed 28/04/2019).
[3] Beddoe (2015).
[4] Thursfield (1951), 35.
[5] National Maritime Museum, Greenwich (http://collections.rmg.co.uk/collections) (accessed 28/04/2019); Comfort (2004).
[6] Matt (2011), 120.
[7] Millmore (2015), 55–59.
[8] https://foundlingmuseum.org.uk (accessed 28/04/2019).

place. Included among these are tokens that feature people at work and at home. The third group comprises tokens that were given at times of separation and death. The separations might have been voluntary as well as imposed, for example, imprisonment and transportation. Examples of love tokens belonging to this group are those crafted by convicts awaiting transportation to America and Australia and sailors' farewell tokens given to loved ones at times of separation.[9]

Love tokens were made by effacing the images of the monarch, Britannia or the crowned royal coat of arms from low value copper and silver coins. The smoothed surfaces were then re-engraved with biographical details and affectionate symbols. They are records that the working population chose to make for themselves and were particularly popular gifts during the eighteenth and early nineteenth centuries. Some love tokens record detailed information including names, dates, events, occupations and locations. Others are sparsely engraved with scant personal information, merely a set of initials or a pierced heart or a popular saying. There is little written evidence about the craft of love token making. However, the skills needed for engraving on metal were common to a number of trades in the eighteenth century including those of chaser, copper plate engraver, die sinker, embosser, gun, seal and medal engraver.[10] In addition those practised in the art of forging coins also had the skills to make a love token.[11] A range of artisans and counterfeiters were therefore in a position to apply their engraving and metal working skills in the production of love tokens. Those conscripted or pressed into the navy may have possessed these skills. Moreover, love token making was one of several activities that occupied sailors at sea.[12] Some tokens, given the uneven nature of their inscriptions, were clearly crafted by those unschooled in engraving. A number were copied and adapted from existing examples.

Research has identified a number of sailors' tokens that employed the same design but then adapted it for different individuals, suggesting they were made to order. A token in the Acworth collection and one in Sim Comfort's collection, for example, are engraved with the same design.[13] They both have the words 'Success to the Halsenell' inscribed around the outline of an East Indiaman under full sail (fig. 1). The Acworth token is engraved with the name C. Webster and dated 1784, whereas Comfort's piece shares the same date but the names inscribed are E. Gordon and J. Delap. Both were crafted from Spanish silver dollars or pieces of eight. The ship's name was actually Halsewell, so the incorrect spelling of 'Halsenell' on both tokens strongly suggests that producers were in the habit of crafting multiple tokens using the same design. They were then tailored according to the wishes of individuals.

Fig. 1: Silver love token crafted from a Spanish piece of eight (Ø 38mm). Engraved on one face with 'Success to the Halsenell' and the image of a three masted ship. The name C. Webster and date 1784 appear on the other face (Courtesy of Maidstone Museum).

The Minotaur token

The focus of the discussion is a sailor's love token (henceforth referred to as the Minotaur token) that is re-engraved with the image of a ship and two sets of initials. It is from a

[9] For an example of a love token crafted by a prisoner transported to America see Millmore (2015), 252–59 and for those transported to Australia see Field and Millett (1998).

[10] Campbell (1969).

[11] The counterfeiting of coins was prolific during the eighteenth century. There were a number of contributing factors for this including the insufficient quantity of low value currency produced by the mint and the poor quality of those coins that were in circulation. This was at a time when manufacturers needed halfpennies and pennies to pay an increasingly industrialised and waged work force.

[12] Banks (1974).

[13] Maidstone Museum (https://lovetokens.omeka.net/admin/items/show/167) (accessed 28/04/2019); Comfort (2004), 80–86. The 'Webster' token is also recorded in Milford Haven (1919), 463.

collection of 200 formed by Reverend Acworth and bequeathed to Maidstone Museum in 1951.[14] What makes this token particularly interesting is the fact that, at first glance, it is similar to other sailors' pieces. However, a closer investigation reveals that it takes the tradition of making a love token to remember a person and uses it in a different context, that of remembering a significant maritime event. The token records a naval mutiny.

In 1797 Britain was at war with France and under threat of invasion. The Royal Navy's Channel fleet was anchored at Spithead in Portsmouth harbour on the south coast of Britain. The sailors had grievances concerning their pay and conditions of service. These complaints had been mounting over a long period of time and in February 1797 the sailors petitioned their commander Admiral Richard Howe about them.[15] They asked for increased pay and better treatment in terms of provisions and punishments. Indeed, they had not had a pay rise since the seventeenth century. However, their demands went unacknowledged. The sailors interpreted the lack of a response from Howe as disregard for their petitions. As a result, on Sunday 15th April 1797 the Channel fleet mutinied. The sailors refused the order to sail from Portsmouth, an extraordinary action especially during wartime. Seventeen ships and over 10,000 men were involved.[16] The Spithead mutiny was, in effect, a large-scale act of disobedience in response to an accumulation of grievances experienced by sailors in the Royal Navy.

The Minotaur token is crafted from a silver shilling. It measures 25mm in diameter and is inscribed on one face with the outline of a three-masted warship under sail and the name Minotaur (fig. 2). On the other face are two sets of initials 'R. E.' and 'G. W.' and the words 'Success to the seventeen united bright stars'. HMS *Minotaur* was one of the seventeen ships that mutinied in April 1797. The token has a hole suggesting it was worn around the neck. The phrase 'success to the', followed by the name of a ship, features widely on sailors' love tokens and moreover acts as an identifier for them (fig. 3). Examples include 'Success to the Amacrée', 'Success to the Pacific', 'Success to the Friendship' and 'Success to the Thames'.[17] These words of hope for a victorious battle and a safe return highlight the fears

Fig. 2: Holed love token crafted from a silver shilling (Ø 25mm). Engraved on one face with 'Minotaur' and the other face 'Success to the seventeen united bright stars' (Courtesy of Maidstone Museum).

Fig. 3: Copper alloy love token crafted from a penny trade token (Ø 33mm). On one face there is a three masted sailing ship and 'Success to the Albion' and on the other two pierced hearts with the letters D, H and S (accession number: 1922,0520.1) (Courtesy of The Trustees of the British Museum).

[14] https://museum.maidstone.gov.uk/explore/research-enquiries/ (accessed 28/04/2019). This chapter draws on the detailed analysis of the Acworth tokens that underpins the author's study, *Love Tokens: Engraved Coins, Emotions and the Poor 1700–1856*. The thesis discusses how love tokens offer evidence of material expressions of affection by those traditionally marginalised from historical accounts. See Millmore (2015).

[15] Admiral Richard Howe led the Channel Fleet to victory over the French in 1794 in the battle known as 'The Glorious First of June'. A popular commander with his men, he was brought out of retirement to mediate in the Fleet mutiny in 1797 (https://www.npg.org.uk) (accessed 28/04/2019).

[16] Glasco (2004), 42. Sixteen ships are usually cited in the Spithead mutiny: *Royal George*, *Royal Sovereign*, *London*, *Queen Charlotte*, *Glory*, *Duke*, *Mars*, *Marlborough*, *Ramillies*, *Robust*, *Impétueux*, *Defence*, *Terrible*, *Pompée*, *Minotaur* and *Defiance*. The *Monarch* was initially in Portsmouth harbour, but on 19th April sailed out to the Spithead Anchorage to join the mutiny. Glasco (2001), 330.

[17] National Maritime Museum (http://collections.rmg.co.uk/collections) (accessed 28/04/2019).

families endured and the dangers sailors faced. However, when other contemporary sources and in particular ballads are examined, it becomes clear that the phrase 'Success to the seventeen united bright stars' on the Minotaur token has been adapted for a different purpose. It does not refer to just one ship but to seventeen ships all united in one action: a mutiny. A number of ballads describe the uprising at Spithead in 1797.[18] Two of them use the phrase the 'seventeen united bright stars'.

> Success to the seventeen united bright stars,
> Let their praise echo round every shore,
> And the fifteenth of April will ne'er be forgot
> Till Britannia and freedom's no more.
> from the ballad *The Genius of Britain.*[19]

> Come all you bold Britons to the seas do belong,
> Of the seventeen bright stars I will sing you a song.
> On the 15th of April, at Spithead we lay,
> Lord Bridport he hove out a signal to weigh:
> But we one and all refused to obey.
> from the ballad *The Seventeen Bright Stars.*[20]

The reference to the 'seventeen bright stars' in these two songs confirms the link between the Minotaur token and the Spithead mutiny of 1797. The phrase would have been read and heard; leading, in effect, to the 'seventeen bright stars' being appropriated as a shorthand for the Spithead mutiny and the ships and sailors involved. Interestingly the Minotaur token is crafted from a shilling. This is the amount that the sailors earned per day as a result of the mutiny.

The Spithead Mutiny

The mutiny is well documented. Naval, political and social historians have examined the motivations and actions of the Spithead mutineers using naval records including petitions from the sailors, Admiralty digests, Home Office correspondence, court martial papers, ships' muster books and logbooks as well as newspaper reports. Two perspectives dominate the debates about why the mutiny occurred. The first viewpoint argues that it was about redressing material grievances and sees the conduct of the sailors as well organised, in other words, an orderly mutiny driven by eighteenth century traditions.[21] The second viewpoint argues that the mutiny was part of a larger revolutionary movement of the time, the seamen being roused into action as a result of the addition to the navy of more politicised quota men who were conscripted or pressed into the navy after 1795. To put it another way it was an example of sailors' resistance to capitalist exploitation.[22] Yet within this scholarship, few accounts of the mutiny start from the point of view of the sailors. Isaac Land, in his study of the common seaman, Jack Tar, observes how naval historians frequently present the sailor from the officer's viewpoint.[23]

Indeed, giving shape and characteristics to the eighteenth century seaman is problematic as Ellen Gill comments in her book on naval families, 'whilst contemporary representations of the sailor abounded, and have subsequently been analysed and examined by scholars, many of these are stereotypical, exaggerated portrayals which misrepresent sailors' lived experiences.'[24] Surviving objects that record the mutinies of 1797 reveal a range of responses.[25] The Minotaur token can be seen alongside other mutiny ephemera such as patch-boxes that commemorated the pardon of the mutineers and pamphlets that aimed to restore the damaged reputation of sailors after the event. The crew of the *Mars*, for example, all signed a

[18] Holdstock (2006), 5.
[19] Firth (1907), 279.
[20] Firth (1907), 277.
[21] Coats and MacDougall (2011).
[22] Gill (1913); Thompson (1968), 183–203; Wells (1986), 79–109; Mabee (2007), 133–44.
[23] Land (2009), 3.
[24] Gill (2016), 225–26.
[25] Colville and Davey (2013), 134–51.

letter of apology to their officers in the hope of restoring working relationships. Notwithstanding such evidence, the exploration of sailors' 'lived experiences' in relation to the Minotaur token clearly poses challenges in terms of critical approaches.

More recently historians have begun to address this issue by applying the framework of space and gender to the study of sailor culture in the eighteenth century navy.[26] These studies have drawn attention, among other things, to the experiences of the sailor by examining their material interactions within the temporary community of a ship. Such analyses highlight issues of identity and belonging as the sailor travels between the sea and the shore. The examination of objects such as seamen's chests, for example, reveals how their meanings shifted as they moved between shared and private spaces and functions.[27] In a similar fashion, sailors' love tokens moved between communal and intimate settings acquiring and embedding meanings in the process. As Anne Gerritsen and Giorgio Riello remark in *Writing Material Culture History* 'objects have meanings for the people who produce and own, purchase and gift, use and consume them.'[28] These meanings can operate in the personal and public sphere and it is this fluidity that complicates objects in what Land identifies as the 'grey area between cultures of sea and shore'.[29] Seamen gave love tokens such as the Minotaur token as a demonstration of affection and attachment at times of separation.

However, the customary practice of giving love tokens cannot be seen in isolation for it is embedded in a community's values and beliefs. E. P Thompson, in his article on folklore, anthropology and social history observes that studying the form of a particular ritual aids an understanding of the values it represents.[30] In other words, whatever the details of the ritual and the performances that were part of it, it is the values it enacted that are at the root of a community's system of beliefs.

For this paper, the perspective of customary practice and working families' traditions of commemorating lives and events provides the starting point from which to study the Minotaur token. The investigation considers its use of images and idioms as material expressions of the values and beliefs of a group of sailors. The text concentrates on the language and imagery of love tokens as a means of accessing ideas about belonging and attachment that are embedded in them. The evidence of love tokens, ballads, broadsheets and the Spithead mutineers' petitions provide the contemporary context that will assist in discovering how the verbal and visual language of sailors' love tokens was understood and appropriated to commemorate a mutiny.

Love tokens and the language of attachment

Research into love tokens from a selection of private and public collections in Britain reveals that they share a comparable repertoire of life cycle events and themes.[31] This repertoire can be analysed in a number of ways; for example, according to the nature of the relationship, event, occupation and location they celebrate. However, for the purposes of this chapter that focuses on the actions of a mutiny, attachments to family and to work provide the basis for the discussion of the Minotaur token. Local loyalties were important to family and to occupations. As Roy Porter observes in his book on eighteenth century English society, 'life within the household and the community followed tightly organised, highly regulated, business-like rounds of routine drills, plotted from the cradle to the grave.'[32] It was marks of status rather than ideas about social class that distinguished one group from another. This is reflected, for example, in work-related signs of social standing but also in possessions, such as clothes and small fancy items. These items provided evidence of the differences between people.[33] For groups such as sailors and convicts, these were the clothes they wore,

[26] Glasco (2004), 40–56; Jones (2016).
[27] Jones (2016), 93.
[28] Gerritsen and Riello (2015), 2.
[29] Land (2009), 15.
[30] Thompson (1979), 15.
[31] Millmore (2015), 55–56.
[32] Porter (1982, revised edition 1991), 144.
[33] French and Barry (2004), 22–23.

the tattoos on their bodies, the pipes they smoked and the tins that held their tobacco. It is not surprising then that the engraved outlines on love tokens often depict the style of dress, tools of the trade and the rigging and ordnance of a ship, for it was by these details that people observed and recognised each other and where they belonged (fig. 4).

Fig. 4: Copper alloy love token crafted from a penny trade token depicting a couple on the shore, the man is wearing sailor's striped trousers and ship in distance (Ø 33mm) (accession number: 1952,0904.175) (Courtesy of The Trustees of the British Museum).

Love tokens and family

Many of the tokens that record family relationships do so with details of a birth or a courtship and sometimes both. They are characteristically inscribed with symbols of love including bows, arrows, a winged Cupid, doves, lovers' knots and clasped hands. By far the most widely featured symbol though is that of the heart. There are pierced, flaming and winged hearts. Alongside these symbols are popular idioms such as 'No heart so true as mine to you' and 'Love and Friendship'.[34] These are words and images that come from a familiar vocabulary of affection found in ballads and stories. The heart was employed on tokens to depict romantic and familial love as well as to highlight the importance of constancy between couples and duty between family members.[35] Sailors' tokens are populated with the language of the heart but more predominantly with depictions of family farewells. Wives and sweethearts are shown holding onto an anchor and waving from the shore as ships sail into the distance (fig. 5). The anchor was a familiar symbol of hope among seamen.

Scenes of separation are accompanied by phrases such as 'Farwell tell you return' and 'When this you see think of me when I am far away' highlighting the lengthy separations that families faced.[36] In these images the ship is always present, sometimes in the background, but never out of sight. In effect the sailor is caught between his attachment to home and his attachment to his community at sea. Whilst the evidence of ballads supports the values of family duty and obligation and highlights a dominant narrative of happy family relationships, the story of the sailor is more ambivalent as he wanders between a state of leaving his family, working on board ship and then returning home, albeit temporarily.[37] The sailor portrayed on material culture, dressed in striped trousers with a moll on his arm or with his family beside a cottage, carried a number of associations. These ranged from patriotic fighter, faithful husband to disloyal seaman and promiscuous lover.[38] With regard to sailors' love tokens the values and beliefs attached to them clearly became more fluid depending on the context of their gifting.[39]

Fig. 5: Holed love token crafted from a silver shilling depicting a woman standing next to an anchor and a ship in the background. HMS *Ville de Paris* was launched in 1795 (Ø 26mm) (accession number: J.2072) (Courtesy of The Trustees of the British Museum).

The language of hearts and remembrance conveyed values of loyalty and reciprocity. However, in reality, it was not always possible for seamen to adhere to these beliefs. Convicts, for example, sentenced to exile and dealing with uncertain futures adapted the customary practice of leaving a token with a loved one to reflect their predicaments.[40] They continued

[34] British Museum, J.3294 and 1952,0904.121 (https://www.britishmuseum.org/research/collection_online/search.aspx) (accessed 28/04/2019). The spellings are transcribed as they are found on the coins.
[35] Millmore (2019).
[36] National Maritime Museum, MEC 1651 (http://collections.rmg.co.uk/collections); British Museum, 1952,0904.261 (https://www.britishmuseum.org/research/collection_online/search.aspx) (both accessed 28/04/2019).
[37] Sharpe (1986), 72–73; Begiato (2015), 127.
[38] Gill (2016), 185.
[39] Jones (2016), 318.
[40] Field and Millett (1998).

to employ the rhetoric of separations and reunions on tokens, yet did so in the knowledge that they might never see friends and family again. Whilst in prison awaiting transportation they made love tokens for their female visitors. A prisoner in Newgate, for example, 'had seven penny pieces rubbed down, and [...] verses written on them for seven different girls'.[41] In this instance the love token was part of a commercial exchange with a prostitute as a well as a parting gift. Such an example illustrates the different contexts in which tokens circulated and the problems they pose in terms of accessing the values and beliefs embedded in them.

In the case of the sailor, his loyalties were divided. Ballads tell of unfaithful wives and of sailors with sweethearts in every port, narratives that contribute to ideas about family attachments that were complicated and ambiguous.[42] Whilst references on love tokens to fidelity and duty revealed beliefs in constancy and helping others, they also masked sailors' underlying worries about the future of their relationships and fears for family unity.[43] On shore family duties were foremost. Although prostitutes visited sailors while ships were at anchor, women were mostly not allowed to go to sea.[44] There was a clear division between home and ship. Once the ship sailed, a seaman's allegiances shifted and re-focussed on his shipmates.

Love tokens and work

The outlines of trades and tools feature on love tokens that reflect attachments to work. The words and illustrations engraved on these tokens convey how occupations and identities were inextricably linked. From across the love token collections, there are coins inscribed with the figures of men working, for example as butchers, blacksmiths, coopers, Thames watermen, soldiers, gamekeepers, agricultural labourers as well as sailors.[45] In terms of landscapes and particular locations, there are rural, urban and maritime scenes with places of work such as workshops, shops and harbours. Illustrations of tools provided a form of shorthand for identifying a particular trade. A cooper, for example, was symbolised by a barrel, a shoemaker by a semi-circular knife, a farrier by a horseshoe, a waterman by his oar and boat hook and a gamekeeper by his gun and dog. For sailors, the ship was the symbol of their work; in effect the tools of their trade. The outline of boats, schooners, frigates and warships are depicted on sailors' tokens in great detail showing sails, rigging, decks and gunports. The practice of using tools to indicate a person's occupation was part of a familiar visual culture of work.

It is evident from the images what these men did, and for their contemporaries and communities there was also an unarticulated understanding of, not only their day to day work, but their culture and values. The tools evoked the rhythms of daily life. They were extensions of the workingman's body, part of the identity of an occupation as well as the person carrying out that role. Sailors, whatever their vessel, knew how to 'hand, reef and steer'.[46] They were also familiar with a vocabulary of nautical names, expressions and slang that united them whilst at the same time marking them out from other land based labourers and artisans. The Minotaur token belongs to the customary practices of these working people and in the context of a warship it belongs to the culture of the ordinary seaman.

The sailors on the Minotaur

At the time of the Spithead mutiny there were 640 men on board the *Minotaur* and over 10,000 on the ships that made up the 'seventeen united bright stars'.[47] To survive on board a 74-gun warship such as the *Minotaur*, a sailor needed to deal with the physical challenges of

[41] Reports (1836), 63.
[42] Sharpe (1986), 89.
[43] Millmore (2015), 178.
[44] Colville and Davey (2013), 88–89.
[45] Millmore (2015), 182–222.
[46] Land (2009),19.
[47] Coats and MacDougall (2007), 138.

the sea and the organisational rigours and teamwork required to sail a ship. This meant a division of labour that relied on the trust and solidarity formed within small groups of sailors. Seamen were defined by their rating, their station, their watch and their mess. In a ship numbering over 600 a sailor's close family was his messmates, usually about eight men with whom he ate and drank.[48] The sailor put his trust in his own skill and the seamanship skills of his fellow sailors. As Denver Brunsman remarks in his work on naval impressment, seamen 'shared a common fellowship based on shared skills, language, and knowledge.'[49] They shared a set of beliefs and values that was shaped by a temporary community through the repetition of daily tasks and routines, repeated social and material practices that bound men together. This included when they slept, ate, washed and, in addition, when tasks such as checking sails and guns, washing decks, cleaning clothes and airing bedding were scheduled.[50]

In her article on sailors and their material culture, Beverly Lemire discusses the fellowship of sailors. She compares it to family ties at home. In effect, she writes 'crewmates figured as surrogates for friends and family ashore'.[51] With this in mind, the sailor belonged to two discrete families. In the same way that household members worked together and had to rely on each other in order to navigate the ebb and flow of economic survival on land, sailors had to work and depend on each other to endure the physical dangers of life at sea. Both the household and the ship relied on a collective desire to survive. The bonds between sailors were undoubtedly forged through shared experiences. Indeed no experience was more extreme and therefore more binding than facing death together during, for example, a sea battle or a shipwreck.[52] When the sailors on the *Minotaur* mutinied they were once again brought together to face the possibility of death but this time in the calmer waters of the anchorage at Spithead.[53] In this new setting they needed to rely on each other to remain united during the mutiny and thus avoid failure and punishment. The Minotaur token reflects the importance of unity with the words 'united bright stars'.

Loyalties and the Minotaur token

The engraving of the initials 'R. E.' and 'G. W.' on the Minotaur token, in line with love token practice, indicates that it commemorated a relationship. It was most likely made or 'commissioned' by a member of the crew for a loved one. Unfortunately, the identity of 'R. E.' and 'G. W.' remain elusive.[54] The token clearly belongs to a culture of celebrating ties to family and friends with the engraving of the initials. The mutineers also employed the language of loyalty to family and the need to provide for them in their petitions to the Admiralty. This is the language of family and duty with which seamen were familiar. Sailors were workingmen but also heads of households, fathers, brothers and sons. In this respect they worked in order to support or contribute financially to the families, parents and siblings they left behind. Drawing again on the evidence of convicts' tokens, there are examples of phrases that refer to remorse and regret in respect of failing to perform their family responsibilities.

Prisoners used the language of duty, describing themselves as undutiful for example in the inscription 'A token of love from Harry Adams a undutiful and unfortunate son age 27'.[55] They also asked others to take care of their loved ones on their behalf, for example in the phrase, 'Mother I hope you will think of my wife and child for that is all my thought. Your

[48] Adkins and Adkins (2008), 16–17.
[49] Brunsman (2013), 166.
[50] Lavery (1989), 203.
[51] Lemire (2015), 291.
[52] Land (2009), 38.
[53] Coats and MacDougall (2007), 40.
[54] An examination of HMS *Minotaur*'s muster book for April 1797 reveals that there were two seamen with the initials 'R. E.' and also two with the initials 'G. W.' Royal Navy Ships' Musters, ADM 36/12830, National Archives, Kew (http://www.nationalarchives.gov.uk) (accessed 28/04/2019).
[55] See online auction, 14 May 2016 (https://www.the-saleroom.com) (accessed 04/11/2018).

undutiful son G. Johnson'.[56] Sailors in the same way as convicts used the language of duty in asking for help with family responsibilities. When negotiating for increased pay, the mutineers explained that they needed higher wages to support their wives and families. They stressed how the pay that sailors sent home was barely enough to save families from 'being burdensome to the parish'.[57] At the same time they expressed their loyalty to their sovereign and reminded the Admiralty of their courage in the face of the enemy. As Brunsman explains, the seamen 'presented themselves to the British public as patriots and family men'.[58] They clearly believed that the navy and moreover the public would value the language of family dependency.[59]

By focusing on their needs as family providers the sailors were viewed sympathetically, as dutiful men rather than revolutionaries. Their emphasis on loyalty to kin also acted as an expression of loyalty to the nation. Once the negotiations were resolved and the mutiny successful, the sailors were keen to voice their allegiance to Britain, saying they wanted 'to meet the Enemies of our Country and show the nation at large that we have not the least principle of Jacobinism'.[60] They wanted to be seen as patriotic seamen defending their country rather than radicals caught up in the ideology and fervour of revolution and liberty at the end of the eighteenth century.

Conclusion

The Spithead mutiny was resolved peacefully with concessions to the sailors. These included dismissal of the most brutal officers from the Spithead fleet, provision of better quality food, increase in pay and a royal pardon for the mutineers.[61] As previously noted the Minotaur token was crafted from a shilling.[62] This was the revised amount that sailors were paid per day as a result of the mutiny. In this way the Minotaur token embodied not only the sentiments and aspirations associated with the act of mutiny, but it also represented the success of the mutiny. It is not surprising then that the token was holed and very likely worn around the neck.

The Minotaur token can be considered from a number of perspectives; for example, as an expression of the outrage ordinary seamen felt at the behaviour of their officers, the navy and the government in treating them badly and ignoring their petitions, or as a demonstration of a growing awareness of revolution among seamen. Yet the use of the language of family and duty in the petitions clearly prioritises the needs of sailors as husbands, fathers, sons, brothers and friends united by bonds of obligation. This paper has shown how the Minotaur token was a development of a sailors' farewell love token, illustrating the process of adapting a customary practice to commemorate a significant maritime event. The vocabulary and imagery employed on love tokens was already charged with sentiments of family duty as well as loyalty to a brotherhood of sailors. The seaman was obligated to two networks of people: his family and friends on shore and his surrogate family of messmates and crew on board ship. The discussion has revealed how loyalty to family and to crew were continually put under stress by the very nature of the work of the sailor, work that involved irregular periods separated from one of his 'families'.

Studying the Minotaur token within the context of love token production and circulation has shown how it employed a language of affection and family duty and reciprocity. Tokens were material expressions of these values. Sailors were known at times for their inconstancy and dissoluteness, but when involved in a mutiny, the risks they took for the sake of others exposed the strength of attachment they had for both their 'families', those they worked

[56] British Museum, J.3308 (https://www.britishmuseum.org/research/collection_online/search.aspx) (accessed 28/04/2019).
[57] Quoted in Manwaring and Dobree (1935), 23.
[58] Brunsman (2013), 198.
[59] Gill (2016), 221.
[60] Quoted in Gill (2016), 219.
[61] Steel (2013), 4.
[62] Although a concession on pay was made, matters were far from resolved after the Spithead mutiny and the following month in May 1797 sailors from the North Sea Fleet on the ship the *Nore* led by Richard Parker continued to press for reforms to Navy conditions. Following the *Nore* mutiny 29 men were hung and more were transported.

alongside and those they worked to provide for. The Minotaur token communicated the expectations of sailors shaped not only by their behaviour at work and at home, but also their behaviour at times of disruption and uncertainty such as a mutiny. It acted, in effect, as a badge of allegiance and solidarity. The token expressed a sailor's desire to say, 'I was at Spithead', and to display his sense of belonging to a community of sailors in a state of uprising. But it also illustrated the risks sailors were prepared to take in asking for a pay rise in order to improve the conditions of their families and relatives. It made manifest sailors' desires to provide for those at home whilst supporting their fellow mutineers. In the case of the Minotaur token two loyalties became united as one.

Bibliography

Adkins and Adkins 2008: R. Adkins and L. Adkins, *Jack Tar. The Extraordinary Lives of Ordinary Seamen in Nelson's Navy* (London, 2008).

Banks 1974: S. Banks, *The Handicrafts of the Sailor* (Newton Abbott, 1974).

Barclay and Reddan (eds.) 2019: K. Barclay and B. Reddan (eds.), *The Feeling Heart* (Kalamazoo, 2019) (forthcoming).

Beddoe 2015: S. Beddoe, *A Potted History: Henry Willett's Ceramic Chronicle of Britain* (Woodbridge, 2015).

Begiato 2015: J. Begiato, 'Tears and the manly sailor in Britain', *Journal for Maritime Research* 17 (2015), no. 2, 117–33.

Brunsman 2013: D. Brunsman, *The Evil Necessity: British Naval Impressment in the Eighteenth-century Atlantic World* (Charlottesville, VA, 2013).

Campbell 1969: R. Campbell, *The London Tradesman 1747* (Newton Abbott, 1969).

Coats and MacDougall (eds.) 2007: A. V. Coats and P. MacDougall (eds.), *The Naval Mutinies of 1797. Unity and Perseverance* (Woodbridge, 2007).

Colville and Davey (eds.) 2013: Q. Colville and J. Davey (eds.) *Nelson Navy & Nation* (London, 2013).

Comfort 2004: S. Comfort, *Forget Me Not, A Study of Naval and Maritime Engraved Coins and Plate (1745–1918)* (London, 2004).

Field and Millett (eds.) 1998: M. Field and T. Millett (eds.), *Convict Love Tokens: The Leaden Hearts the Convicts Left Behind* (Kent Town, 1998).

Firth 1907: C. Firth, *Naval Songs and Ballads* (London, 1907).

French and Barry (eds.) 2004: H. French and J. Barry (eds.), *Identity and Agency in England, 1500-1800* (London, 2004).

Gerritsen and Riello (eds.) 2015: A. Gerritsen and G. Riello (eds.), *Writing Material Culture History* (London, 2015).

Gill 1913: C. Gill, *The Naval Mutinies of 1797* (Manchester, 1913).

Gill 2016: E. Gill, *Naval Families, War and Duty in Britain 1740-1820* (London, 2016).

Glasco 2001: J. D. Glasco, *«We are a neglected set». Masculinity, Mutiny and Revolution in the Royal Navy of 1797*. PhD thesis, University of Arizona (Tucson, AZ, 2001).

Glasco 2004: J. D. Glasco, 'The seaman feels him-self a man', *International Labor and Working-Class History* 66 (2004), 40–56.

Holdstock 2006: R. Holdstock, 'Ballads of the Great Mutiny of 1797', *Article MT* 183 (2006) (http://www.mustrad.org.uk/articles/mutiny.htm) (accessed 28/04/2019).

Jones 2016: E. Jones, *Masculinity, Materiality and Space on Board the Royal Navy Ship, 1756-1815*. PhD thesis, Queen Mary, University of London (London, 2016).

Land 2009: I. Land, *War, Nationalism and the British Sailor, 1750-1850* (London, 2009).

Lavery 1989: B. Lavery, *Nelson's Navy: The Ships, Men and Organisation 1793-1815* (London, 1989).

Lemire 2015: B. Lemire, 'Men of the World: British mariners, consumer practice and material culture in an era of global trade', *Journal of British Studies* 54 (2015), 288–319.

Mabee 2007: F. Mabee, 'The Spithead mutiny and urban radicalism in the 1790s', *Romanticism* 13 (2007), no 2, 133–44.

Manwaring and Dobree 1935: G. E. Manwaring and B. Dobree, *The Floating Republic: An Account of the Mutinies at Spithead and the Nore in 1797* (London, 1935).

Matt 2011: S. Matt, 'Current emotion research in history: or, doing history from the inside out', *Emotion Review* 3 (2011), no. 1, 117–24.

Milford Haven 1919: L. Milford Haven, *British Naval Medals…by Admiral the Marquess of Milford Haven* (London, 1919).

Millmore 2015: B. Millmore, *Love Tokens: Engraved Coins, Emotions and the Poor 1700-1856*. PhD thesis, University of Brighton (Brighton, 2015).

Millmore 2019: B. Millmore, '«An heart that can feel for another»: love tokens and attachment to family in eighteenth and nineteenth-century England', in Barclay and Reddan (eds.) (2019).

Porter 1991: R. Porter, *English Society in the Eighteenth Century* (London, 1991).

Reports 1836: 'Reports of the Inspectors appointed under the provisions of the act 5 & 6 Will. IV. c. 38, to visit the different prisons of Great Britain', *House of Commons Papers. Reports of Commissioners* 117 (1836), no. 1, 1–78.

Sharpe 1986: J. A. Sharpe, 'Plebeian marriage in Stuart England: some evidence from popular literature', *Transactions of the Royal Historical Society* 36 (1986), 69–90.

Steel 2013: P. Steel, 'The Spithead and Nore mutinies of 1797', *SERTUC* (2013), 1–8.

Thompson 1968: E. P. Thompson, *The Making of the English Working Class* (Harmondsworth, 1968).

Thompson 1979: E. P. Thompson, *Folklore, Anthropology and Social History* (Studies in Labour History Pamphlet) (Brighton, 1979).

Thursfield 1951: H. G. Thursfield, *Five Naval Journals 1789-1817* (London, 1951).

Wells 1986: R. Wells, *Insurrection. The British Experience, 1795-1803* (Gloucester, 1986).

THE POLITICS OF TOKEN ECONOMICS, THEN AND NOW[1]

BILL MAURER

Introduction: token economics, today

'We're having a Cambrian explosion in crypto', announced an invitation to a conference call held on 6 November 2017. Using an expression my colleagues and I have deployed to describe the proliferation since 2008 of new and diversely engineered electronic platforms for transferring value,[2] the invitation explained that something called 'token economics' would determine the fate of the latest of these innovations, cryptocurrencies and blockchain technology. Blockchain refers to a system of digital ledgers replicated across a network of computer servers acting collaboratively, based on consensus, to verify changes to the ledger and maintain it. Cryptocurrencies are the digital alternative currencies that inhabit such ledgers. The invitation promised that the conference call would cover the 'dense' and 'complicated' field of token economics, an area 'in it's [sic] infancy', and that it would also include discussion of 'oracles' and 'how to design the best token economy'.[3]

On 8 March 2018, an online publication devoted to cryptocurrencies and blockchain, CoinDesk, reported that the West African country of Sierra Leone had used the services of Agora, The Swiss Lab and Foundation for Digital Democracy (a private foundation), to oversee the nation's presidential election. Agora, the article explained, had provided an auditable and transparent digital voting solution: paper ballots were registered electronically on a blockchain in order to verify election results in real time without relying on a central vote tallying agent who might alter the count.[4] Eleven days later, however, the country's National Electoral Commission denied the report that it had used Agora to verify or audit the results. It used the microblogging social media platform, Twitter, to convey the news (fig. 1). Apparently, Agora had entered votes from the paper ballots into its blockchain itself, using its capacity as an officially registered election observer to obtain access to the ballots, and had done so only for one district.[5] Publicity stunt? Or an earnest attempt to demonstrate what it saw as the revolutionary potential of its technology to support direct democracy?

In its own report on the Sierra Leone story, Agora wrote:

> 'Agora is committed to spreading transparent elections around the world, which in our view has the potential to offer great value for global human rights. We passionately believe that a true democracy should reflect the voice of its people, with honest elections being a foundational element'.[6]

In a whitepaper documenting the technical aspects of its system, Agora explained that its system uses both its own custom blockchain, and, for certain aspects of its operations, the Bitcoin blockchain – that is, the replicated database underlying the Bitcoin digital currency, discussed below. Agora's system consists of a network of 'witness servers' that receive encrypted ballots from voters (presumably via other computational machines). One witness server is randomly selected to serve as an 'oracle server'. The oracle server receives votes from the witnesses and proposes them to the whole network. This provides a check against double voting. The network's consensus serves as the final arbiter of the vote's authenticity. The oracle then writes confirmed blocks of votes to the Bitcoin blockchain, where they are stored in Bitcoin's own distributed, separately verified ledger.[7] Although

[1] I am extremely grateful to Clare Rowan for the invitation to participate in the Warwick conference on tokens, as well as to the other participants for their welcoming collegiality toward this interloping anthropologist. Clare pointed me toward references and helped me see how the understanding of ancient tokens can inform the analysis of modern ones. I also thank two anonymous reviewers for their insights and suggestions. I owe special thanks to Vagias (Vaios) Karavas: his fortuitous visit to UC Irvine while I was working on this chapter and his critical reading of the first version were indispensable. I thank Taylor Nelms and Farah Qureshi for important suggestions as well as for research assistance. I continue to learn from long-term interlocutors involved in blockchain technology and the payments industry, whom I cannot thank by name but who will see their insights represented. Lana Swartz, Quinn DuPont and Rachel O'Dwyer prove to me the value of long term, interdisciplinary conversations on cryptocurrencies and blockchain. Thanks, too, to the US National Science Foundation Law and Social Sciences Program (grant SES 0960423 and SES 1455859). Any opinions, findings, and conclusions or recommendations expressed in this material are those of the author and do not necessarily reflect the views of the National Science Foundation.

[2] Deville (2014); Future of Money Research Collaborative (2018).

[3] Kerner (2017).

[4] Del Castillo (2018).

[5] Biggs (2018).

[6] Agora (2018).

[7] Agora (n.d.), 20–21.

Fig. 1: Sierra Leone's response on Twitter to the Agora controversy.

it relies in part on the Bitcoin system, Agora is powered by its version of token economics (which it calls 'tokenomics') based on its own digital currency, VOTE:

> 'VOTE is the native token on the Agora network, which is used to incentivise and reward permissionless auditor nodes that validate cryptographic proofs, as well as permissioned witness nodes that process transactions for elections on the network'.[8]

In a related domain, meanwhile – the mundane early twenty-first century practice of using a plastic credit or debit card with an embedded chip to make a monetary payment – 'tokenisation' is also avidly discussed. So-called tokenised credit and debit card transactions are meant to protect identifiable consumer data while facilitating electronic payment. Chip cards have already replaced so-called magstripe cards – bearing a stripe of magnetic tape – in much of the world. The magnetic tape on such cards bears magnetised metal ions that form patterns of bars representing ones and zeros and directly encoding, in binary form, the cardholder's account data. An archaeologist of the future could relatively easily reveal these patterns simply by scattering iron filings over the stripe (fig. 2). Decoding the patterns of bars and gaps would require some kind of Rosetta stone to translate between binary code and account information rendered alphanumerically, and then between those alphanumeric codes and the accounts they represented, but it would be possible. Chip cards, however, operate in a very different fashion. The chip generates a numeric token in dynamic interaction with the entire payment network, and a different token each time, sequentially numbered. Our archaeologist would require most of the technological system behind this form of electronic payment in order to regenerate the tokens, and would then be left with a

[8] Agora (n.d.), 37.

Fig. 2: Experimental archaeology with payment technology. Detail of the reverse of the author's credit card. Full object 8.56 × 5.39cm (Photo by the author)

series of sequentially numbered and ordered identifiers – of what, he or she would only be able to wonder. Each token is unique.

The Agora, oracles, tokens: there is an element of the contemporary community of blockchain enthusiasts and developers explicitly invoking the token voting systems of ancient Athens. Although they likely misunderstand the actual functioning and purpose of those systems, I argue in this chapter that the design and implementation of their technologies may approximate what actually happened more than they realise. And, although it is a very different kind of technology and operating at an enormous scale compared to blockchain-based systems that are at present (2018) only really toys (albeit expensive toys), I argue that tokenised card transactions are enmeshed in a similar set of political relations as the token economies of blockchain promoters. With an eye back to the tokens of the actual Agora, this chapter sketches those relations.

To anticipate the argument: today's tokens elide and equate political operations with economic valuation. This does not result, however, in the kind of homogenisation or deracination of specificity associated with modern money. It is not an extension of pure, neoliberal market logic. Rather, it is a distinctive variant that makes of all things a unique value – lending to entities as diverse as votes or commodities the character of liberal possessive individualism or an inherent uniqueness or singularity.[9] This singularity, I will argue, paradoxically reintroduces hierarchy or rank. This matters because it complicates contemporary understandings of market societies as *market* societies, or as societies in which all values are subsumed by the market or its ideologies. The specific form of hierarchy I will outline takes things out of the pure market logic of supply, demand, and price, and introduces rank, honour, and regard. I will further argue that contemporary tokens, put forward as ideals of direct democracy, as in Agora and related blockchain projects, in this respect actually do reverberate with the ancient ones. The story of fifth-century Athenian tokens and voting by allotment is a story of aristocrats competing over the *demos* and the long hold of a politics of honour in the process of transforming into a politics of civic virtue. Blockchain projects, by misrecognising their own nature and reading into themselves their own libertarian version of the Agora, miss the relationships of hierarchy subtending them. They thus also displace the possibility of virtue onto a flattened out idea of direct democracy which was never obtained in Athens in the way they imagine. For the voting citizen holding a token was not representing his own voice but embodying, part for whole, the community or deme.[10]

At the same time, therefore, given this part-whole relationship, the ancient story does hold out a hope for the present and maybe even a remaking of blockchain and other token

[9] On possessive individualism, see Macpherson (1962). Euro-American biogenetic understandings of kinship proceed from the idea that individual people are self-evident and unique, and that relationships need to be surfaced in order to be seen. This understanding depends on the person being conceptualised as possessive of a 'natural singularity' (see Strathern (1992), 53) despite its having been the effect of the recombination of genetic elements from its parents. Genetic relatedness might suggest that every person is a combination of or resurfacing of old ones (and old relations), not that 'babies [are] new people' (55).

[10] I use the masculine pronoun when referring to the persons involved in these Athenian practices.

economies. If contemporary tokens suggest hierarchies of singularities and an elision of the political and the economic, Athenian tokens open into a world where honour and virtue required inquiry into the regard of others: an ethics, in other words – or, one might say, the anthropological stance.

From the Cambrian explosion to Cryptoeconomics

When my colleagues and I had used the term, 'Cambrian explosion', we referred to the huge expansion of technologies and communications channels used to carry information about payment. Beginning in 2007-08 when the telecommunication provider, Safaricom, deployed the mobile phone money transfer service M-Pesa in Kenya, and continuing with the launch of the iPhone and its ecology of applications, paying for things had begun to take on new forms. During the Cambrian explosion of life on planet Earth, evolution provided a variety of body templates, many quite alien to extant phyla today. The payments industry – the industry encompassing the credit and debit card networks, wire services, the checking system, as well as cash – had been relatively settled and staid until the coming of the mobile phone, and the smart phone in particular. New payment industry start-ups exploited different technological pieces and different data sources and streams of the mobile phone's toolkit. Developers were creating ways to pay using the phone's earphone jacks, Bluetooth low-frequency transmission, the camera (acting as an optical scanner), the screen (acting as a visual data generator), Near Field Communication and Radio Frequency ID technology, to say nothing of the mobile and wireless networks themselves.[11] New gizmos and attachments entered the realm of payment, no longer limited to plastic cards or point-of-sale devices specific to them, but artefacts like the company Square's dongle (fig. 3),[12] used to input magnetic stripe data off a card into the phone through the earphone jack, or LevelUp's specialised device (fig. 4), used to read a code off a mobile phone screen. A Cambrian explosion, indeed.

Included in the profusion of new ways to pay was Bitcoin, the first of the so-called cryptocurrencies. Based on a digital ledger maintained across a network of participating nodes (computers or, more often, servers and banks of servers running high-speed processors), Bitcoin served as a kind of proof of concept for a digital currency that would resist unauthorised duplication because the veracity of transactions was guaranteed by the collaborative work of participants in the system. Instead of a central records keeper or source of authorisation, Bitcoin used a consensus algorithm according to which transactions were authorised based on their verification by fifty per cent plus one of the participating nodes. Such authority was thereby distributed through the network, which simultaneously maintained the record, in a decentralised manner, of all transactions by reduplicating the ledger on the notes of the network. The books, so to speak, lived on every computer in the system, and every computer worked to verify new entries in the books.[13]

Fig. 3: Square dongle. Main unit: 2.44 x 2.44cm (width and length), 1.35cm height; dongle attachment: 1.35cm (height), 0.33cm (dongle width), 1.70cm (dongle attachment length); 4.14cm combined length (Courtesy of Institute for Money, Technology and Financial Inclusion, UC Irvine; used with permission).

[11] See Maurer (2015).

[12] On the history of the dongle, see Mainwaring (2017).

[13] This is a gross simplification of the operations of Bitcoin and blockchain. For more in-depth discussion, see Narayanan, Miller, Felten, Bonneau and Goldfeder (2016). For more discussion of the political, social and linguistic entailments of cryptocurrencies, see Lustig and Nardi (2015); Maurer, Nelms and Swartz (2013); Dallyn (2017) and DuPont (2018). I use the past tense deliberately to indicate the unpredictability of the future duration of the Bitcoin blockchain as it currently operates.

Fig. 4: LevelUp Chase Pay point-of-sale device. Base: 6.05 x 6.05cm (width and length), 2.95cm height, 0.63cm base height; camera unit: 7.24cm width x 7.37cm length, 6.91cm height; camera lens: 2.90cm width and length; 10.75cm combined length (Courtesy of Institute for Money, Technology and Financial Inclusion, UC Irvine; used with permission).

At the time of my writing (April 2018), there are over 1,500 such cryptocurrencies, including Agora's VOTE, all operating under essentially the same principles as Bitcoin: a replicated ledger, stored on a decentralised network of computers, which perform transaction verification in a distributed manner via a consensus algorithm. In many cases, as with Bitcoin, the nodes doing the work of transaction verification receive a reward, generally in the form of the cryptocurrency, or digital token native to the system in question. These are conceived of as monetary awards. Some systems use a complex game of chance to structure the rewarding of tokens: there are built-in odds of winning, and increasing the computational power devoted to the game increases one's chances of winning. Other systems provide a reward based on some other initial or evolving stake in the system.

Ethereum, a blockchain platform launched in 2015, inaugurated a new model for the use of such replicated ledgers beyond serving as a way to record an alternative digital currency or an alternative digital asset class. Ethereum provided a native computer programming language and interface which permitted the creation of executable code on top of its blockchain – commands that would execute when certain external conditions were met, and the execution of which, and validation of said execution, were similarly distributed across the network. Ethereum's developers termed these 'smart contracts'. Developers used the word contracts because they associated contracts with their binding force, not with their breach or negotiation.[14] Smart contracts are similarly binding, or, rather, bound by the preconditions programmed into them which, when met, instruct the network to execute the code. A simple example is a smart contract that instructs a payment to be made from one party to another when electronic sensors detect that a shipping container has arrived in port and still weighs what it did when it left its origin point. A simple digital switch could perform the same operation. A blockchain-based smart contract has the advantage – at least, in theory

[14] DuPont and Maurer (2015); Levy (2017).

– of permitting anonymity among transacting parties with a trusted system for authenticating the state of the shipping container and the transacting parties, and validating the funds transfer, without the need for any intermediaries to carry out these functions, possibly eliminating additional costs and time. A blockchain-based system also has the virtue of being decentralised and thus more resistant to hacking or unauthorised transaction modification without requiring a central monitor or auditor. It would also (again, in theory) carry out its instructions automatically, as soon as the pre-set conditions were met.

With Bitcoin, the token and the decentralised database are of a piece and inseparable. One cannot take a bitcoin out of the digital ledger and have it remain a bitcoin. It would need to be converted into something else, a state-issued currency, for example, via a separate, external exchange. Bitcoins only exist within the network. The network is, in a sense, its own digital world. Points of entry and exit are the interfaces through which users initiate commands to transact or exchanges through which users convert value into another form like the US dollar.

Smart contracts, however, rely on indicators from the physical world. These could come from humans, entering changes to physical or digital world entities or environments through a user interface into the network. But doing so would undermine one of the core virtues of smart contracts: their automaticity and independence from any intermediaries. This is where the oracles come in. 'Oracle' in a smart contract context is the term given to the system that detects the condition of the pre-determined variable of interest in the outside world, and feeds it into the network. Just as an ancient oracle would serve as a bridge between the gods and mortals, an oracle in a blockchain context is a portal between one world – the rest of the online world beyond the blockchain, or the physical world – and the blockchain itself. In some smart contract applications, the oracle even becomes a signatory to the contract.[15] The usage by Agora is a variation on the theme: its oracle server is still a portal between worlds, but instead of bringing data into the system from the outside, the Agora oracle server brings data from its witness servers out of the Agora system and into the Bitcoin blockchain.

The chief vulnerability in platforms that use oracles lies in what a long-term interlocutor of mine calls the periphery of the network, or the edges where data enters. Take sensor networks detecting things like temperature or weight. Sensors can provide fuzzy or shifting results. As the temperature hovers around 40 degrees Celsius, for example, what should the sensor report, and when, if the executable 'contract' specifies environmental conditions must reach 40 degrees before an operation is to be conducted? In addition, the agents at those edges – which provide the transit points between the physical world or non-blockchain online world and the blockchain – must themselves be trusted and verified. The oracle itself requires an authorising agent: who is the god of the oracle providing that source of authority?

Ethereum and smart contracts also changed the nature of the token economics inherent to these systems, and, in fact, helped differentiate 'coins' from 'tokens' without, however, delineating a clear boundary between the two. Recall how the process of transaction verification for Bitcoin works: independent validators compete in a game of chance for a reward that is given for the work of transaction verification. The system provides an incentive to conduct this work in the form of the token native to the system – in this case, Bitcoin – and is built so that the odds of winning increase with increasing effort or computational power. This is one type of token economics, a straightforward incentive for effort. The model derives from human applied behavioural analysis often used to channel the behaviour of non-neurotypical humans – people on the autism spectrum, for example, or with communication disorders – to behave more normatively. Providing a token to reward a preferred behaviour assists in reinforcing those 'target' behaviours and extinguishing others.

Behavioural analysis sometimes uses money as the reinforcing token, but often stickers, buttons, or other markers are used. In other words, there is no reason that the token has to be imagined as economically valuable. Similarly, there is no reason why the token in a blockchain token economy powering smart contracts has to be considered a currency. Regulatory discussions underway at the time of my writing hinge on the distinction between whether a

[15] See https://blockchainhub.net/blockchain-oracles/.

token is considered a currency – a coin, with value, which is issued as a tradable asset and thus, like a security – or merely a token, an internal part of a system for allocating resources (computational or bandwidth resources, or, say, the ability to issue or execute commands) to achieve some other goal. Regulators and developers are currently arguing over the boundary between equity tokens which function like a stock, providing the holder with an equity stake in a company issuing the tokens, and utility tokens, functioning more like a promise of access to the future functionality of a company's system, or a coupon for a future service.[16]

Decentralised autonomous governance by token, and the rediscovery of demarchy

In one storied experiment using the Ethereum blockchain, another group formed in Switzerland set up a new digital token, the DAO token, for use in a distributed governance project called 'The DAO', which specifically aimed at providing an alternative to venture funding for start-up enterprises. The holders of DAO tokens could use them to 'vote' on projects they thought worthy and would receive a return in proportion to their share of the vote, should the project be funded. Rather than being paid in DAO tokens, however, they were to be paid in Ethereum's native cryptocurrency. The DAO took its name from the acronym for distributed autonomous organisation. The idea behind this concept was that a new form of organisation – business, governmental, non-profit – was made possible by a collection of blockchain based smart contracts operating in tandem which would automate organisational functions based on physical-world or digital-world inputs (via oracles) and eliminate the need for human intervention or decision-making. Wrote Ethereum founder, Vitalik Buterin, a corporation is 'nothing more than people and contracts all the way down. However, here a very interesting question arises: do we really need the people?'[17]

There are, of course, other ways of imagining the corporation. Social scientists have long pointed out that corporate relations and contracts themselves are bound together by non-contractual forms of communication and commitment.[18] But blockchain proponents like Buterin tend to reduce the corporation to the contractual structures animating it, and to understand the contract, again, in terms of its binding force, its determinism over future contingencies.

In its initial formulation, The DAO was to have been a 'decentralised, crowdfunded, direct-management (or direct-democracy) organization and investment platform'.[19] Voting for a proposal put forward on the DAO platform, DuPont argues, was 'conceptually the same as funding it' but would also give DAO token holders some degree of control over the enterprise by 'voting for (e.g. funding) specific decisions. For example, voting members could decide – directly – if a new employee was hired or not by using their votes to approve or deny the decision'.[20] Voting in this sense is akin to shareholding.

The DAO was launched on 28 May 2016. It was hacked on 17 June 2016, and drained of the equivalent of around US $60–70 million.[21] In the end, good, old-fashioned human governance stepped in to make decisions about staunching the haemorrhage and creating an alternative blockchain to the original Ethererum chain on which the exploit had taken place.

Nevertheless, The DAO brought to life the potential of blockchain based token economics to be used for voting, and to be constitutive of new kinds of organisational actors. In addition to Agora, the Swiss foundation involved in the Sierra Leone vote, there are at

[16] Such a coupon could be valued in monetary terms, too, and so a utility token might also in some cases function like an equity. The law in the United States here is guided by a US Supreme Court decision, SEC vs W. J. Howey Co., a 1946 case that established the so-called Howey Test to determine whether a contract qualifies as a security and thus comes under the regulatory purview of the Securities and Exchange Commission. See BitTrust (2017).
[17] Buterin (2013).
[18] Macaulay (1963).
[19] DuPont (2017), 3. Pagination is from DuPont's archived version available at http://iqdupont.com/wp-content/uploads/2018/06/DuPont-Experiments_in_Algorithmic_Governance-2017.pdf (accessed 05/12/2018).
[20] DuPont (2017), 3.
[21] DuPont (2017), 6.

present two other companies or foundations that use some variant of the word agora as their name or the name of their software platform.[22] Agoric.co describes its concept thus:

> 'Decentralized Autonomous Communities are springing into existence, stigmergic swarms of people expressing value to each other, collaborating, and socializing, and in general interacting in many different forms. Now, today, communities are creating brand new business models and unlocking agoric opportunities for people to earn their keep in this world. People are opting out of the traditional economy and joining a new one – the digital economy'.[23]

The concept has older roots in the technology world than blockchain. Agoric systems were first described by a computer scientist, Mark Miller (now at Google), and an engineer, K. Eric Drexler (now at Oxford), in 1988. Miller and Drexler proposed a way to solve problems of processor time and storage in complex computational systems based on a market-model with incentives.[24] As I type these words, different programs running at the same time on my computer demand different processing capabilities and different degrees of access to storage space in my system's memory. One way to allocate for these competing demands would be to centralise control by empowering one program to check in with all the others to see what its needs are, moment to moment. That, however, might slow things down to an unacceptable level. Another way, proposed by Miller and Drexler, would be to use a market mechanism to determine the allocation. In effect, providing a means for different programs to 'pay' for computational time and storage would permit resources to go to the highest bidder. Right now, Microsoft Word needs my computer's processing time and space the most. It would therefore 'pay' more for it. Miller and Drexler wrote:

> 'Like all systems involving goals, resources, and actions, computation can be viewed in economic terms. Computer science has moved from centralised toward increasingly decentralised models of control and action; use of market mechanisms would be a natural extension of this development. The ability of trade and price mechanisms to combine local decisions by diverse parties into globally effective behaviour suggests their value for organizing computation in large systems'.[25]

The inspiration was the Greek Agora, 'a meeting and market place' as they state in the introduction to one of their foundational papers.[26] (Such a narrow understanding of the Agora!) In incentivising access to computing resources using something like an auction and something like a payment mechanism, agoric systems efficiently allocate those resources without having to rely on a central controller. This is very much like the incentivisation of transaction verification in blockchain systems.

There is another origin point for contemporary agoric economics. Samuel Edward Konkin was a Canadian libertarian and anarchist who authored *The New Libertarian Manifesto* (first published in 1980), in which he outlined principles of what he called agorism, based on the Greek Agora, he wrote, the 'open marketplace'.[27] Agorism is based on free market principles, a philosophy without a party or organisational apparatus: in Konkin's view, the co-optation of libertarianism by moneyed interests or political parties flies in the face of the kind of voluntary, non-coercive action he views as part and parcel of the open market, a 'counter-market', he called it, in which all human conduct is mediated by exchange. One can detect – implicitly, or sometimes explicitly – Konkin's influence among the contemporary 'cryptoanarchists' involved in cryptocurrency experiments. One can also trace from Konkin and Austrian School economic theory the far-right elements of a faction of some cryptocurrency adherents.[28] Experiments like The DAO promise emergent organisation and order without the state's violence, but instead an in-built incentive structure in line with free market libertarian ideology.

[22] At the time of my writing, there are at least two besides Agora: agoric.co; and the Economic Space Agency's programming language, Agoric (see https://medium.com/economic-spacing/our-strategy-344bbd2b4d98). Both are efforts like The DAO's in decentralised governance.
[23] https://agoric.co/about, archived version in author's possession.
[24] Miller and Drexler (1988a).
[25] Miller and Drexler (1988b), 133.
[26] Miller and Drexler (1988b), 135.
[27] Konkin (1983).
[28] See Golumbia (2016); but see also Dallyn (2017), 469 on the political heterogeneity of the Bitcoin community.

Contemporary blockchain enthusiasts' use of the words agora, oracle and token reference their specific understanding of ancient Athens. Their vision is of a decentralised collectivity of independent agents in a direct democracy who meet in a market place, as Miller and Drexler had it. This permits also the elision of voting with a market transaction or stake holding as shareholding. It is the libertarian vision of ancient Greek democracy. Even further, it is a vision of a collectivity of individuals – not really a 'society' – governed by algorithmic systems and technologies of voting that ensure individual representation without intermediation, the 'true democracy' or 'voice' of the people extolled by Agora, as noted above.

The term 'demarchy' has been taken up in libertarian philosophy to refer to government by allotment, drawing on the ancient deme or minimal unit of political organisation in sixth- and fifth-century BC Athens. As Aristotle discussed in both the *Constitution of the Athenians* and *Politics*, the deme as a territorial unit would erode and replace connections to tribe:

> 'the private rites of families should be restricted and converted into public ones; in short, every contrivance should be adopted which will mingle the citizens with one another and get rid of old connections'.[29]

Allotment of public offices by chance based on membership in a deme broke up the power of the tribes and was a check on oligarchy. Allotment of oracle server status in the Agora network by chance serves as a check against malicious or accidental voting interference by any of the witness servers, decentralising the authority to write the votes to the Bitcoin blockchain. Friedrich von Hayek, the Austrian school economist and intellectual touchstone for many cryptocurrency advocates, advocated for demarchy as opposed to modern institutions of democracy which he saw as concentrating privilege among the 'coalitions and organised interests' who were able to use power and position to maintain their authority.[30] Demarchy would return rule to the 'ideal of an equal law for all'. Demarchy has also been picked up by organisations like the P2P Foundation, devoted to decentralised 'peer to peer dynamics' (see https://p2pfoundation.net/). Such dynamics are built into most blockchain systems.

Tokens, then: sortition, vote buying, and hierarchy

The literature on those fifth century tokens presents a much more nuanced and complex picture. As scholars of ancient tokens know, they likely played a principle role in the allotment of offices. Mabel Lang aligned textual sources on allotment with archaeological evidence to deduce the use of tokens in the allotment procedure. Allotment using black and white beans was subject to vote buying and concentration, potentially reinstituting the power of tribal leaders. '[N]othing prevented a few of the larger demes from 'buying' the smaller demes' representation [...] since no individual identification was provided for'.[31] So-called puzzle tokens – tokens painted with tribal names and cut in half 'in jig-saw fashion across the tribal name'[32] – seem to have been introduced to improve upon the bean system and prevent vote buying. They also created a system of identity verification and fraud prevention: they replaced the fungibility of beans with tokens that became singularly unique when cut in two, like unique puzzle-pieces. And once drawn and used in allotment, these tokens had no further use – their use was, in short, also singular. They would then become a souvenir, or simply be discarded.

What strikes me as an anthropologist reading this numismatic and archaeological literature is just how messy the apparent transition from oligarchic leadership and vote buying to sortition and democracy seems to have been. Aristotle wrote in the 300s BC that offices allotted in the *Theseion* were allotted for the whole tribe instead of by deme, in order to

[29] Aristotle, *Athenaion Politeia*, 6.4.
[30] Hayek (1981), 40.
[31] Lang (1959), 85.
[32] Lang (1959), 85.

dilute demotic power.[33] Lang dates this change to around 403 BC, which would suggest that the tokens she considered were from the period before the change, meaning that they may have been used during the period when the offices allotted in the *Theseion* were selected from the demes and subject to manipulation.[34] Tokens would have been both the object of manipulation by deme leaders, and the solution to that manipulation.

Raaflaub argues that the period between Solon in the early sixth century and Pericles in the 400s was one of both 'incremental change' and 'sudden rupture'.[35] This is a period of continuing 'aristocratic competition for the *demos*' leadership', right up through the 400s.[36] '[T]he evolution toward democracy', he writes, 'was not linear and even'.[37] Our tokens are from this period of nonlinear, uneven change. The stage was set by Solon:

> 'I gave to the *demos* as much esteem/power as is sufficient, not detracting from their honour or giving out more. To those who had power and were admired for their wealth, I also declared that they should have nothing unseemly'.[38]

If aristocrats during this period were continually jockeying with one another and re-establishing hierarchies among themselves and between themselves with respect to the demes,[39] allotment may have helped mix up – if not straightforwardly dilute – aristocratic power, while permitting new interests to arise. Still, giving to the *demos* 'sufficient' power and nothing more is not the same as the vision of token voting imagined by blockchain enthusiasts or the political theory of possessive individualism in which each citizen votes his 'own' voice.

Furthermore, the evidence suggests that honour, esteem and rank ebbed and flowed in the social and political relations throughout this period. In turn, this meant that community expectations of aristocrats would have constrained their actions: people would have assumed that men of rank would act with honour. Wallace writes: 'The community always had higher expectations of wealthier members, recompensed by greater honor'.[40]

And yet, incremental change and sudden rupture implies that these elites were probably constantly trying to game the system. Hence the invention of the elaborate allotment processes in the first place, as well as the complicated technological systems that developed to enforce them – or at least to make fraud more challenging. In the classic paper on allotment, Sterling Dow argues that even the invention of the *kleroteria* (fig. 5) – that fantastic device for randomly selecting jurors or assembly members – required a lot of time and coordination in actual use.[41] This would have been overseen by an archon, one of the chief magistrates, and in turn would have depended on people's trust in the archon. In effect, then, the practice of allotment reinstated hierarchy through the use of the very technology meant to mitigate it.

Cynthia Farrar nicely summarises the problem of reading contemporary liberal concerns back into the practices of Athenian democracy. We can extend her observation beyond 'reading' and into 'coding' for blockchain developers. Moderns expect others to act in their own self-interest.[42] We know from Hirschman that *la doux commerce* was intended to reduce the passions associated with honour and regard – which could lead to violence – with the deliberative calculations of trade.[43] Self-interest thereby became framed in market terms, and everyone's interests were presumed thereby to be of the same kind: market interests. But the Athenians had a different practice of assessing the interests of others. Rather than assuming each acts in his own interest and that those interests were of the same kind – what we moderns would call 'economic' – the Athenian assembly member knew he would be

[33] Aristotle, *Athenaion Politeia*, 62.1.
[34] Lang (1959), 83.
[35] Raaflaub (2007), 16.
[36] Raaflaub (2007), 17.
[37] Raaflaub (2007), 18.
[38] Aristotle, *Athenaion Politeia*, 12.1 (translation adapted from Wallace (2007), 69).
[39] Eder (1998).
[40] Ober (1989); Wallace (2007), 62.
[41] Dow (1939).
[42] Farrar (2007), 176.
[43] Hirschman (1977).

Fig. 5: Reconstructed *kleroteria* in the Ure Museum (Photo by Philafrenzy, made available under the Creative Commons CC0 1.0 Universal Public Domain Dedication).

replaced by another, who will someday make 'decisions that affect him, and that they will also be scrutinizing his performance after the fact'.[44] Officeholders therefore had to always place themselves in the position of the other, 'broaden[ing] the citizen's perspective beyond his own particular interests, to consideration of how those interests related to the concerns of the *polis* as a whole'.[45] This is a much more expansive notion of interest than that presumed in the idea of the Agora as merely a 'marketplace'.

The token of the ancient Agora was therefore a political device, even a virtue machine, not an economic one, and a political device designed specifically to thwart the political use of exchange to buy and sell votes. The remedy provided by tokens to possible vote buying suggests that democracy was under constant threat. (One whole chapter out of the five in Staveley's account of Greek voting is devoted to fraud).[46] Nevertheless, given the analysis

[44] Farrar (2007), 183.
[45] Farrar (2007), 182.
[46] Staveley notes that though aristocratic clubs were banned at the end of the fifth century they continued to operate 'underground' (1972), 106. He also argues that 'Attempts to tamper with the operation of the lot in Athenian public life must have

provided by historians of the period, and informed by the anthropological record of societies in which people use idioms of rank and honour to settle disputes,[47] such buying and selling of votes cannot be seen in a strictly economic idiom. High-ranking men would presumably have sought votes as a means to enforce and secure their own political status, not their wealth *per se*. Or, put another way, their wealth accrued in people indexed by their fame, esteem, and ability to get things done by assembling the talents and labour of others.[48] Other scholars of ancient tokens are at pains to differentiate them from money.[49] Even when coins and tokens appear to have been circulating alongside one another, the latter were associated more with status than economic value, as higher-ranking men disbursed favours and sought loyalty in what was later transmuted into expressions of charity.[50]

Conclusion: A singular politics, not direct democracy

If, as I am suggesting, ancient tokens were political devices associated with, even as they were designed to thwart, high-ranking men's fame, they can therefore also be seen as distinctively singular. Like fame itself, they are non-fungible, non-market devices for facilitating a specific politics: a politics where people and things are of singular regard in ranked hierarchies maintained by non-economic exchanges.[51] The political logic of singularity at play here is not in contradiction to the ideals of democracy, but operating at a different level of scale. The high ranking man in a deme seeking a reassertion of tribal authority is a higher-order version of the individual citizen whose vote represents the larger whole of which he is a part and through which he has to take into consideration the regard of others, now, and in the future. This is not, *nota bene*, the 'direct' democracy imagined by blockchain voting systems. The debate, as it were, is between those who would hold that the man of rank encompasses the whole, and those who would permit the citizen that same ability, albeit on a rotating basis. Allotment randomises rank among the citizens, 'rank' here taken to be not just status but the ability to encompass that larger whole.

I invoke the notion of singularity here loosely referencing the economic sociologist Lucien Karpik,[52] whose *Valuing the Unique: The Economics of Singularities* provocatively outlines the non-market mechanisms in the contemporary period determining the assessment of the value of what he calls singularities, those unique and non-commensurable commodities valued not by the law of supply and demand but by very specific forms of judgment (his examples include markets in luxury goods and fine wine). There is a sense in which token economies, ancient and modern, are economies of singularities, whether of rank and status or simply singular uniqueness. It is a hypothesis only, but my suggestion is that contemporary token economies, whether in blockchain or tokenised card transactions, do not represent an evacuation of the politics of rank, but their (re-)instantiation at the level of individual agent or transaction or object.

In the ancient context, token mechanisms provided a safety valve to release the pressure of the tribe or high status leader on the political order by elevating the randomly selected individual citizen. Yet that citizen did not vote his voice, so to speak. He tried to anticipate the voices of other free men in the deme, standing part for whole. His singularity was not that of his own incommensurable distinctiveness but that of the deme itself. Athenian token mechanisms at the same time also may have permitted the assemblage of wealth in people by high-ranking leaders figuring out ways to game the system or secure clients, bolstering their own fame, that is, their own singularity vis-à-vis the deme or tribe.

In the contemporary context, token mechanisms ensure the identity and veracity of transactions, transacting parties, and transacted physical or digital objects or data.

---

been common, and that they were initially successful appears to be suggested by the increasingly sophisticated methods which the Athenians felt themselves obliged to adopt' (115).

47 Collier (1988).

48 Guyer and Belinga (1995).

49 Crosby (1964); Kroll (2015).

50 Bubelis (2011).

51 On the concept of market devices, see Callon, Millo and Muniesa (2007).

52 Karpik (2010).

Tokenisation in credit and debit card transactions provides a unique identifier to every transaction to prevent fraud. Token economies in blockchain contexts provide the incentive to verify identity and whatever 'truths' are to be maintained indefinitely in replicated ledgers held by individual nodes in a decentralised network.

Blockchain tokens' operations belie the rhetoric of their own 'trustless' nature: as the possible problems with oracles make evident, there are always boundary-control issues and the need for new intermediaries to assist in the 'unmediated' flow of transactions. The situation is not unlike that of the *kleroteria*, which required trust in the archon despite being a device for obviating that trust. Agoric systems today are thus after all not so unlike ancient token systems – they need wealth in other computational agents, intermediaries like oracles or exchanges, in order to elevate their own singular status.

An archaeologist from the future considering the technological remnants of blockchain – whatever they might be – would be puzzled by the apparent fascination with the idea that everything and everyone could and should be given a unique identifier and registered in a digital database or ledger, its transactions tracked from beginning to end, and maintained forever, an eternal record of singularities in singular transactions with one another, one after the other, chronicled, verified by others, time-stamped as if each unit of time itself has its own discrete and unique status. This archaeologist would see the (messy and contingent) transition from the magstripe card to the chip-enabled card and similarly identify a system that attempted to record every transaction's singular specificity, and sequential identity. Assuming our archaeologist also had at their disposal the record from the ancient Agora, and the textual evidence and analysis regarding tokens as contained in the volume you are reading, would their conclusion be that the fifth century BC and twenty-first century AD posed a study in contrasts, or had more in common than meets the eye? In the fifth century, tokens broke up the authority of rank and honour while providing opportunities for new ways to capture esteem and elevate rank. They also provided the technology for assuming a civics of regard, elevating the individual citizen to a perspective encompassed by others' perspectives – a new form of honour, a civic virtue. In the twenty-first century, tokens both derived from a modern, libertarian reading of those ancient systems, and seemingly undergirded a fiercely individualistic, monetary and market conception of the corporation, human nature, and all transactions. Yet at the same time they are animated by an underlying commitment to singularity and uniqueness, incommensurability, or radical distinctiveness. If money does not equilibrate these incommensurable values, then how else to understand them than in terms of another politics of rank? And if they could have been reinserted into another politics of rank, our archaeologist might wonder, would they also have had the potential to surface another form of virtue?

Bibliography

Agora 2018: Agora, 'Agora official statement regarding Sierra Leone election', *Medium* (March 19, 2018) (https://medium.com/agorablockchain/agora-official-statement-regarding-sierra-leone-election-7730d2d9de4e) (accessed 06/05/2018).

Agora. n.d.: Agora, 'Bringing our voting systems into the 21st cntury', *Agora Whitepaper, version 0.1* (https://agora.vote/Agora_Whitepaper_v0.1.pdf) (accessed 06/05/2018) (copy in author's possession).

Biggs 2018: J. Biggs, 'Sierra Leone government denies the role of blockchain in its recent elections', *TechCrunch* (19 March 2018) (https://techcrunch.com/2018/03/19/sierra-leone-government-denies-the-role-of-blockchain-in-its-recent-election/) (accessed 06/05/2018).

BitTrust 2017: BitTrust, 'Passing the Howey test: how to regulate blockchain tokens', *Medium* (4 March 2017) (https://medium.com/bittrust/passing-the-howey-test-how-to-regulate-blockchain-tokens-d218da93a8b6) (accessed 06/05/2018).

Bubelis 2011: W. Bubelis, 'Tokens and imitation in ancient Athens', *Marburger Beiträge zur antiken Handels-, Wirtschafts- und Sozialgeschichte* 28 (2011), 171–95.

Buterin 2013: V. Buterin, 'Bootstrapping a decentralized autonomous corporation: part I', *Bitcoin Magazine* (19 September 2013) (https://bitcoinmagazine.com/articles/bootstrapping-a-decentralized-autonomous-corporation-part-i-1379644274/) (accessed 06/05/2018).

Callon, Millo and Muniesa 2007: F. Muniesa, Y. Millo and M. Callon, 'An introduction to market devices', *The Sociological Review* 55 (2007), n. 2, 1–12.

Campbell-Verduyn (ed.) 2018: M. Campbell-Verduyn (ed.), *Bitcoin and Beyond: Cryptocurrencies, Blockchains, and Global Governance* (London, 2018).

Collier 1988: J. Collier, *Marriage and Inequality in Classless Society* (Stanford, 1988).

Crosby 1964: M. Crosby, 'Lead and clay tokens. Part II', in Lang and Crosby (1964), 69–146.

Dallyn 2017: S. Dallyn, 'Cryptocurrencies as market singularities: the strange case of Bitcoin', *Journal of Cultural Economy* 10 (2017), n. 5, 462–73.

del Castillo 2018: M. del Castillo, 'Sierra Leone secretly holds first blockchain-audited presidential vote', *CoinDesk* (8 March 2018) (https://www.coindesk.com/sierra-leone-secretly-holds-first-blockchain-powered-presidential-vote/) (accessed 06/05/2018).

Deville 2014: J. Deville, 'Infrastructures of money', *Transactions: A Payments Blog* (http://transactions.socialcomputing.uci.edu/post/100503617345/infrastructures-of-money-joe-deville-centre-for) (accessed 06/05/2018).

Dow 1939: S. Dow, 'Aristotle, the *kleroteria*, and the courts', *Harv. Stud.* 50 (1939), 1–34.

DuPont 2017: Q. DuPont, 'Experiments in algorithmic governance: a history and ethnography of "The DAO," a failed decentralized autonomous organization', in Campbell-Verduyn (ed.) (2018), no pagination, also available on line: http://iqdupont.com/wp-content/uploads/2018/06/DuPont-Experiments_in_Algorithmic_Governance-2017.pdf.

DuPont 2018: Q. DuPont, *Cryptocurrencies and Blockchains* (Cambridge, 2018).

DuPont and Maurer 2015: Q. DuPont and B. Maurer, 'Ledgers and law in the blockchain', *King's Review* (23 June 2015) (http://kingsreview.co.uk/magazine/blog/2015/06/23/ledgers-and-law-in-the-blockchain/) (accessed 06/05/2018).

Eder 1998: W. Eder, 'Aristocracts and the coming of Athenian democracy', in Morris and Raaflaub (eds.) (1998), 105–40.

Farrar 2007: C. Farrar, 'Power to the people,' in Raaflaub, Ober and Wallace (eds.) (2007), 170–95.

Future of Money Research Collaborative 2018: Future of Money Research Collaborative, 'Social payments: innovation, trust, bitcoin, and the sharing economy', *Theory, Culture and Society* 35 (2018), n. 3, 13–33.

Golumbia 2016: D. Golumbia, *The Politics of Bitcoin: Software as Right-Wing Extremism* (Minneapolis, MN, 2016).

Guyer and Belinga 1995: J. I. Guyer and S. M. E. Belinga, 'Wealth in people as wealth in knowledge: accumulation and composition in Equatorial Africa', *The Journal of African History* 36 (1995), n. 1, 91–120.

Hayek 1981: F. von Hayek, *Law, Legislation, and Liberty. Volume 3: The Political Order of a Free People* (Chicago, IL, 1981).

Hirschman 1977. A. O. Hirschman, *The Passions and the Interests: Political Arguments for Capitalism Before Its Triumph* (Princeton, NJ, 1977).

Huberman (ed.) 1988: B. Huberman (ed.), *The Ecology of Computation* (North-Holland, 1988).

Karpik 2010: L. Karpik, *Valuing the Unique: The Economics of Singularities* (Princeton, 2010).

Kerner 2017: L. Kerner, 'The emerging science of token economics – conference call on Nov. 6, 2pm-3pm est [sic]'. October 29, 2017 (https://hackernoon.com/the-emerging-science-of-token-economics-conference-call-on-nov-6-2pm-3pm-est-c9ab3946ed6b) (accessed 06/05/2018).

Konkin 1983: S. Konkin, *New Libertarian Manifesto* (Durham, NC, 1983).

Kroll 2015: J. H. Kroll, 'Small bronze tokens from the Athenian agora: *symbola* or *kollyboi*?', in Wartenberg and Amandry (eds.) (2015), 107–16.

Lang 1959: M. Lang, 'Allotment by tokens', *Historia: Zeitschrift für Alte Geschichte* 8 (1959), n. 1, 80–89.

Lang and Crosby 1964: M. Lang and M. Crosby, *The Athenian Agora X: Weights, Measures and Tokens* (Princeton, 1964).

Levy 2017: K. Levy, 'Book-smart, not street-smart: blockchain-based smart contracts and the social workings of law', *Engaging Science, Technology, and Society* 3 (2017), 1–15.

Lustig and Nardi 2015: C. Lustig and B. Nardi, 'Algorithmic authority: the case of Bitcoin', *IEEE Computer Society, presented at the 48th Hawaii International Conference on System Sciences* (2015) (DOI 10.1109/HICSS.2015.95).

Macaulay 1963: S. Macaulay, 'Non-contractual relations in business: a preliminary study', *American Sociological Review* 28 (1963), 55–67.

Macpherson 1962: C. B. Macpherson, *The Political Theory of Possessive Individualism: Hobbes to Locke* (Oxford, 1962).

Mainwaring 2017: S. Mainwaring, 'Dongles', in Maurer and Swartz (eds.) (2017), 1–9.

Maurer 2015: B. Maurer, *How Would You Like To Pay? How Technology is Changing the Future of Money* (Durham, NC, 2015).

Maurer and Swartz (eds.) 2017: B. Maurer and L. Swartz (eds.), *Paid: Tales of Dongles, Checks, and Other Money Stuff* (Cambridge, MA, 2017).

Maurer, Nelms and Swartz 2013: B. Maurer, T. C. Nelms and L. Swartz, '«When perhaps the real problem is money itself»! The practical materiality of Bitcoin', *Social Semiotics* 23 (2013), n. 2, 261–77.

Miller and Drexler 1988a: M. S. Miller and K. E. Drexler, 'Incentive engineering for computational resource management', in Huberman (ed.) (1988), 231–66.

Miller and Drexler 1988b: M. S. Miller and K. E. Drexler, 'Markets and computation: agoric open systems', in Huberman (ed.) (1988), 133–76.

Morris and Raaflaub 1998: I. Morris and K. A. Raaflaub (eds.), *Democracy 2500? Questions and Challenges* (Dubuque, IA, 1998).

Narayanan, Miller, Felten, Bonneau and Goldfeder 2016: A. Narayanan, A. Miller, E. Felten, J. Bonneau and S. Goldfeder, *Bitcoin and Cryptocurrency Technologies: A Comprehensive Introduction* (Princeton, NJ, 2016).

Ober 1989: J. Ober, *Mass and Elite in Democratic Athens: Rhetoric, Ideology, and the Power of the People* (Princeton, NJ, 1989).

Raaflaub 2007: K. A. Raaflaub, 'Introduction', in Raaflaub, Ober, and Wallace (eds.) (2007), 1–21.

Raaflaub, Ober, and Wallace (eds.) 2007: K. A. Raaflaub, J. Ober, and R. W. Wallace (eds.), *Origins of Democracy in Ancient Greece* (Berkeley, CA, 2007).

Staveley 1972: E. S. Staveley, *Greek and Roman Voting and Elections* (Ithaca, NY, 1972).

Strathern 1992: M. Strathern, *After Nature: English Kinship in the Late Twentieth Century* (Cambridge, 1992).

Wallace 2007: R. W. Wallace, 'Revolutions and a new order in Solonian Athens and archaic Greece', in Raaflaub, Ober, and Wallace (eds.) (2007), 49–82.

Wartenberg and Amandry (eds.) 2015: U. Wartenberg and M. Amandry (eds.), *ΚΑΙΡΟΣ. Contributions to Numismatics in Honor of Basil Demetriadi* (New York, 2015).

INDEX